Maine Mountain Guide

10th Edition

**AMC's Comprehensive Guide to Hiking Trails
of Maine, featuring Baxter State Park
and Acadia National Park**

Compiled and edited by
Carey Michael Kish

Appalachian Mountain Club Books
Boston, Massachusetts

AMC is a nonprofit organization, and sales of AMC Books fund our mission of protecting the Northeast outdoors. If you appreciate our efforts and would like to become a member or make a donation to AMC, visit outdoors.org, call 800-372-1758, or contact us at Appalachian Mountain Club, 5 Joy Street, Boston, MA 02108.

outdoors.org/publications/books

Distributed by The Globe Pequot Press, Guilford, Connecticut.

Front cover photograph © Eliot Cohen
Back cover photograph © aaronpriest / Fotolia.com
Cartography by Larry Garland, © Appalachian Mountain Club
Cover design by Matthew Simmons, myselfIncluded.com
Interior design by Jennie Sparrow

ISBN 978-1-934028-30-8

ISSN 1544-3604

The paper used in this publication meets the minimum requirements of the American National Standard for Information Sciences-Permanence of Paper for Printed Library Materials, ANSI Z39.48-1984.

Outdoor recreation activities by their very nature are potentially hazardous. This book is not a substitute for good personal judgment and training in outdoor skills. Due to changes in conditions, use of the information in this book is at the sole risk of the user. The author and the Appalachian Mountain Club assume no liability for accidents happening to, or injuries sustained by, readers who engage in the activities described in this book.

Interior pages contain 30% post-consumer recycled fiber.
Cover contains 10% post-consumer recycled fiber.
Printed in the United States of America, using vegetable-based inks.

10 9 8 7 6 5 4 3 2   14 15 16 17 18

MIX
Paper from
responsible sources
FSC® C005010

Editions of the Maine Mountain Guide

First Edition	1961	Sixth Edition	1988
Second Edition	1968	Seventh Edition	1993
Third Edition	1971	Eighth Edition	1999
Fourth Edition	1976	Ninth Edition	2005
Fifth Edition	1985	Tenth Edition	2012

KEY TO LOCATOR MAPS

The numbers within the boxes on the locator map presented at the beginning of each section indicate which AMC maps show trails discussed in that section. The page numbers listed at the beginning of each section indicate the start of trail descriptions covering a given area.

Map 1: Baxter State Park–Katahdin
Map 2: 100-Mile Wilderness
Map 3: Bigelow Range
Map 4: Camden Hills
Map 5: Eastern Mt. Desert Island
Map 6: Mahoosuc Range
Map 7: Evans Notch

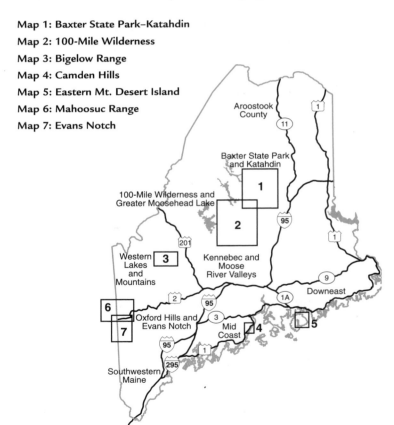

CONTENTS

Key to Locator Maps   *iv*

Legend   *vi*

Foreword   *vii*

Acknowledgments   *viii*

How to Use This Book   *x*

Introduction   *xvi*

Abbreviations and Acronyms   *xlii*

SECTION ONE: Baxter State Park and Katahdin   1

SECTION TWO: 100-Mile Wilderness and Greater Moosehead Lake   62

SECTION THREE: Western Lakes and Mountains   106

SECTION FOUR: Evans Notch and Oxford Hills   167

SECTION FIVE: Kennebec and Moose River Valleys   213

SECTION SIX: Southwestern Maine   231

SECTION SEVEN: Midcoast   256

SECTION EIGHT: Downeast   278

SECTION NINE: Acadia   307

SECTION TEN: Aroostook County   364

APPENDIX A: *Helpful Information and Contacts*   380

APPENDIX B: *New England Four–Thousand Footers*   387

APPENDIX C: *New England Hundred Highest*   391

Index   393

LEGEND

The following icons are used in this guide's in-text maps.

▢	Federal or State Conservation Land
🛉	Entrance Station
⬟	Campground
⬟	Tentsite
🛈	Observation Tower
🛆	Lighthouse
═══	Federal or State Highway
═══	Improved Road
====	Unimproved Road
────	Trail

FOREWORD

This hiker has been tramping the woods and mountains of Maine for four decades, since moving to the state in 1971 at the age of twelve. As a kid, I always had a curiosity for any patch of woods, whether behind a neighbor's house or out back beyond the ball field fence. Blazing trails into those dark and mysterious woods always meant great adventure, and my friends and I would emerge hours later dirty from head to toe with cuts and scratches and insect bites, and smiles a mile wide. Living in Maine, where big woods were seemingly everywhere, certainly changed the scale of these childhood explorations. When the forests and trails around Bangor had been thoroughly covered and mentally mapped as far as our feet and bikes could take us, my adventurous group of pals moved on to hitchhiking to the hills east of town, then south to the mountains of Acadia. And when my dad finally took me up to Baxter State Park and I climbed Katahdin, I might as well have been standing atop Mt. Everest, such was the elation. I was irrevocably hooked on hiking. I bought my first *Maine Mountain Guide* in 1976 and with that, realized the amazing wealth of mountains and trails across the state and knew that I had to hike them all. I was so inspired I decided to hike the entire Appalachian Trail from Springer Mtn. in Georgia to Katahdin, a life-changing trek I completed in 1977. Ever since then I've been seeking out the forested trails and craggy summits of our beautiful state of Maine, still striving to hike all the trails in the guide. That task has just gotten a lot tougher with the publication of the 10th edition, which includes a host of new trails and summits for your hiking pleasure. Open it wide, thumb through the pages, scribble some notes, pore over the maps, dream a little, then plan your next adventure or two. So many wild and scenic natural places in Maine await your footsteps, your eyes and ears, and the company of family and friends. Start your own journey here with this guide, then go enjoy and savor time well-spent in the Maine woods.

Carey M. Kish
Bowdoin, Maine
October 1, 2011

ACKNOWLEDGMENTS

This guide is the product of the hard work and dedication of many people, including those who contributed to the nine previous editions of the book since its inception in 1961.

Sincere thanks are due the staff at AMC Books, particularly Editor Kimberly Duncan-Mooney, who provided advice, guidance, and support throughout the writing and editing process; Publisher Heather Stephenson, who got me started on this great guidebook adventure; and Production Manager Athena Lakri, who shepherded the book through the production process. Much appreciation goes to Larry Garland, AMC cartographer, and to Steve Smith, editor of AMC's *White Mountain Guide*. Many thanks for your sage advice and support. Thanks also to Jerry and Marcy Monkman for their work on *Discover Acadia National Park*, 3rd edition as Section Four: Acadia was adapted from the guide.

A plethora of thanks goes out to many people across Maine: those dedicated and caring individuals from state and federal agencies and public and private organizations, who provided much-needed assistance in the reshaping of this guide, from reviewing trail descriptions, to identifying many new trails for inclusion, to hitting the trail in earnest and gathering firsthand information in the field. This guide could not have achieved its present form without your help and encouragement.

From the state of Maine: Rex Turner, who worked closely with me throughout the project and provided a wealth of information on Maine's public lands; Jeanne Curran and Matt LaRoche, Maine Dept. of Conservation, Bureau of Parks and Lands; Jensen Bissell, director of Baxter State Park, provided a comprehensive review of the Baxter trails; Scott Thompson, Aroostook State Park; Bill Elliot and Jim Tatgenhorst, Camden Hills State Park; David Hinton, Maine Forest Service. From the U.S. Dept. of the Interior, National Park Service: Charlie Jacobi and Gary Stellpflug of Acadia National Park provided a detailed review of the Acadia trail system. From the U.S. Dept. of Agriculture, U.S. Forest Service: Bryan Johnston, White Mountain National Forest.

From conservation organizations: Jim Logan and William Geller hiked large parts of the Aroostook County, 100-Mile Wilderness and

Greater Moosehead Lake, and Kennebec and Moose River Valleys sections and provided detailed trail review and updated descriptions; Mike and Barbara Zimmerman field-checked a host of new and existing trails Downeast; Bill Cobb provided a cover-to-cover review of the existing 9th edition; Carrie Walia, Laura Flight, Peter Roderick, Doug Ofiara, Keith Chapman, Jeff Aceto, Larry Dyer, Jeff Libby, and Mike LaRoss of Maine Chapter, Appalachian Mountain Club; Lindsay Bourgoine (who hiked and described most of the Maine Woods Initiative trails), Bryan Wentzell, Rob Burbank, Gary Dethlefsen, Casey Mealey, and Shannon LeRoy, of the Appalachian Mountain Club; Heather Sable, Downeast Coastal Conservancy; Jeff Romano of the Maine Coast Heritage Trust did a comprehensive review of the 9th edition; Peter Kallin, Belgrade Region Conservation Alliance; Theresa Kerchner, Kennebec Land Trust; Landon Fake, Blaine Mills, Saranne Taylor, and Wende Gray of Mahoosuc Land Trust; Boz Savage, Maine Audubon; Nancy Sferra, Maine Chapter, The Nature Conservancy; Scott Bennett, Great Pond Mountain Conservation Trust; Tom Henderson, Greater Lovell Land Trust; Robin Kerr, Mt. Agamenticus Conservation Region; Buck O'Herin, Sheepscot Wellspring Land Alliance.

Lester Kenway, Ron Dobra, Dick Fecteau, Tom Gorrill, Ray Ronan, Rick Ste. Croix, and Julian Wiggins of Maine Appalachian Trail Club; Dick Anderson and Herb Hartman, International Appalachian Trail; Michael Zlogar, George Brown, and Marvin Swartz of Chatham Trails Association; Eric Savage, AMC Four Thousand Footer Club.

Thanks also to Ethan Austin, Sugarloaf; Mark Shea, Big Rock Ski Area; John Banks and Sparky Clark, Penobscot Indian Nation; Dave Herring, Maine Huts & Trails.

A number of other individuals from the trails community also lent their valuable assistance, including Dan Hester, Chris Keene, Tedd Davis, Cloe Chunn, Dana Thurston, Phil Poirier, Scott Olsen, Jim Melcher, Jillian Sanders, Elwood Doran, Betty Jamison, Jim Radmore, Jeremiah Crockett, Gary Dick, and Bill Hancock.

Finally, thanks to my wife and favorite trail companion, Fran Leyman, for accompanying me on many of the hikes and putting up with my incessant note and picture taking, for hiking many trails and collecting notes on her own while I was at home hunkered down in front of my laptop, and, finally, for looking the other way from the enormous mess I made of the house during the research and writing of this book.

HOW TO USE THIS BOOK

This book aims to provide comprehensive coverage of hiking trails located in Maine's mountains, which are found scattered across a large and geographically diverse area ranging from the coast to the inland hills to the remote mountains of the northern interior. More than 200 summits are described, from Mt. Agamenticus in the southwestern corner of the state to Deboullie and Black mountains in northern Aroostook County, and from Aziscohos Mtn. in northwestern Maine near the New Hampshire border to Magurrewock Mtn. near the St. Croix River, which forms the boundary between Maine and New Brunswick, Canada.

The trails are segmented into ten geographic regions. The Southwestern Maine, Midcoast, Downeast, and Acadia sections describe the mountains in proximity to the coast, including Acadia National Park (ANP), as well as some of the inland hills. The Oxford Hills stretch westward from the Androscoggin River to meet the mountains of the Evans Notch region in the White Mountain National Forest (WMNF) near the New Hampshire border. To the north are the high mountain summits of the Longfellow Range and the Appalachian Trail (AT) corridor, which are described in the Western Lakes and Mountains and 100-Mile Wilderness and Greater Moosehead Lake sections. This mountainous chain culminates with Katahdin and a jumble of wilderness summits within the boundaries of Baxter State Park (BSP). North and east of the park are the vast forestlands and scattered mountains of Aroostook County. The mountain character of the Kennebec and Moose River valleys ranges from scattered low hills in the south to remote high peaks near the Canadian border in the north.

For this edition we have revised, updated, and expanded many existing trail descriptions, and added 75 new mountains and more than 200 trails, thereby increasing the already wide variety of hiking possibilities available for every level of interest and ability. In all, more than 450 trails are described, totaling more than 1,000 mi., ranging from easy woodland walks to moderate hill climbs to strenuous mountain traverses. Complementing the hike descriptions is a series of detailed topographic sheet maps highlighting seven popular hiking destinations, and five topographic, in-text maps. It is our hope that the user of this book will find it to be a helpful companion that leads to many days of outdoor pleasure and healthful exercise on the trails through the scenic woods and mountains of Maine.

TRAIL DESCRIPTIONS

Each trail in this book is described individually and usually in the ascending direction. In some cases where a hike uses a combination of trails, several descriptions may need to be consulted. A typical trail description first provides an overview of the trail, including its origin and destination and, if notable, its general character (gradient, roughness, etc.), and perhaps the view to be seen from the summit. Driving directions to the trailhead are then given, where appropriate. This is followed by concise directions for following the trail. The description notes important features such as trail junctions, stream crossings, viewpoints, summits, and any significant difficulties. The acronym in parentheses next to the trail name and above the description, where noted, refers to the organization responsible for maintaining that trail.

SUGGESTED HIKES

At the end of each section of this guide is a list of suggested hikes, selected to provide a number of options for easy, moderate, and strenuous hikes within a region. Criteria can vary from trail to trail, but in general, an easy hike may have little to no elevation gain, covers a relatively short distance, and can be completed in several hours or less. A moderate hike can take as long as half a day and cover a longer distance with more elevation gain. A strenuous hike will require a full day of six to eight hours, with significant mileage or elevation gain. The abbreviations "rt," "ow," and "lp" denote "round-trip," "one-way" and "loop," respectively. The numbers indicate distance, elevation gain, and time required. When choosing a trail, hikers should consider mileage, elevation gain, time required, available daylight, and difficulty of the terrain as well as the experience, physical fitness, ambition, and size of the group.

DISTANCES, TIMES, AND ELEVATIONS

The summary table below the trail description lists the trail name followed in parentheses by the map or maps that cover the trail route. For trails covered by the AMC maps included with this guide, the appropriate map number is referenced. Where applicable, a Maine Appalachian Trail Club (MATC) map may also be referenced. For trails in ANP, the National Park Service (NPS) rating for that particular trail will also be indicated (e.g., NPS rating: easy).

For all other trails, the U.S. Geological Survey (USGS) quad map or maps that cover the trail are indicated, and again where applicable, an MATC map. A DeLorme map reference is also included to aid with driving to the trailhead. Below this is a summary of distances and times between points on the trail route. These figures are cumulative from the starting point of the trail. The map number and grid reference(s) and the elevations at particular points en route are also noted.

The following examples demonstrate how to read the information in the summary tables:

Burnt Mtn. Trail (AMC map 1: B2)

Distance from Burnt Mtn. Day Use Site (1,050 ft. **[elevation]**) to
  • Burnt Mtn. summit (1,793 ft. **[elevation]**): 1.3 mi. **[distance]**, 50 min. **[time]**

For Burnt Mtn. Trail, refer to AMC Map 1 included with the guide. To locate the trail, use the grid references on the left (letters) and top (numbers) edges of the map. The trail is found at the intersection of B and 2. The starting point is Burnt Mtn. Day Use Site at an elevation of 1,050 ft. The distance covered to the summit is 1.3 mi., which will take an estimated time of 50 min. Returning to the trailhead, the total distance and estimated time are calculated to be double those figures: 2.6 mi. and 1 hr. 40 min.

Where no AMC map reference is noted in the table, it means that the trail is not listed on any of the maps provided with the guide. In such cases, please refer to the trail summary for the name of the appropriate USGS topographic map (and in some cases, the applicable MATC map) and the DeLorme map reference. See the following example:

Osgood Trail (USGS Blue Hill quad, DeLorme map 15)
Distance from Mountain Rd. (350 ft.) to
  • Blue Hill summit (934 ft.): 0.9 mi., 45 min.

Elevations of places, where they are precisely known, are indicated. Otherwise, elevations are estimated to the nearest 50-ft. contour. Because trail distances have been measured by a variety of means, from the use of global positioning system (GPS) technology to a surveyor's wheel to estimation and rounding, there may be minor inconsistencies. Distances may also differ from posted trail signs.

No reliable method exists for predicting how much time a particular hiker or group of hikers will take to complete a hike on a specific day. However, to give hikers a rough basis for planning, estimated times have been calculated for this book by using the formula of 30 minutes for each mile of distance or 1,000 ft. of elevation gain, often referred to as "book time." The time allowances are estimates and do not include time for snack or lunch stops, scenery appreciation, or rest breaks. Some parties may require more time, and others may need less. Special factors, such as stream crossings, steep slopes, and rough footing, can affect trail times. For example, a 6-mi. hike on easy terrain will require less effort, though perhaps more time, than a 3-mi. hike over rough trail with 1,500 ft. of elevation gain. No attempt has been made to adjust the given times for the difficulties of specific trails, so hikers should plan accordingly, always leaving a good margin for safety.

MAPS AND NAVIGATION

This guide features two folded map sheets that contain seven full-color maps covering many of Maine's popular hiking areas, including Baxter State Park–Katahdin (Map 1), 100-Mile Wilderness (Map 2), Bigelow Range (Map 3), Camden Hills (Map 4), Eastern Mt. Desert Island (Map 5), Mahoosuc Range (Map 6), and Evans Notch (Map 7). These high-quality, GPS-rendered maps indicate a range of data useful to the hiker, including trails, trail segment mileage, tentsites, shelters and campsites, campgrounds, public land ownership, parking areas, visitor centers and ranger stations, fire towers, ecological zones, boat launches, and picnic areas. Each map uses a contour interval of 100 ft. The scales vary from map to map, as does the magnetic declination, which in Maine ranges from 15 to 20 degrees west of true north. Latitude and longitude coordinates and Universal Transverse Mercator (UTM) grid coordinates are included on the maps and allow their use with a handheld GPS unit. Contact information pertinent to the map is also included. A waterproof Tyvek version of the Baxter State Park–Katahdin and 100-Mile Wilderness map may be purchased from AMC online at outdoors.org, at most AMC lodges and visitor centers, and at many bookstores and outdoor retailers.

A number of maps are also provided in the text of this guide. Please refer to the Legend on p. vi near the start of this book.

Given the geographic distribution of mountains and hiking trails in Maine, not every trail described in the guide appears on the maps provided. For the areas not covered, please refer to the USGS 7.5-minute quadrangle map listed in the trail summary. Although the topographic quality of these maps is excellent, be aware that some trails may not be accurately depicted or may not appear at all. Quad maps are available from local retailers and outdoor shops or directly from the USGS by visiting store.usgs.gov or by calling 888-ASK-USGS. USGS maps may also be viewed online and purchased from USGS Business Partner Program (BP) and Cooperative Research and Development Agreement (CRADA) partner sites. For a list, go to nationalmap.gov/gio/viewonline.

Many of the mountain peaks along the AT in Maine are described in this guide, and the reader may find the *Appalachian Trail Guide to Maine* (15th edition, 2010) to be a helpful companion guide. Published by the MATC, the guide contains seven topographic and profile maps that cover the 281-mi. trail route from Katahdin to the New Hampshire state line, plus numerous side trails. The guidebook and maps are available at outdoor retailers and many bookstores or by contacting MATC at matc.org or P.O. Box 283, Augusta, ME 04332-0283.

References to the appropriate DeLorme *Maine Atlas & Gazetteer* map are included with each trail description, except for those trails covered by the maps included in the guide. The atlas is a useful tool for trip planning and road navigation to the trailhead, indicating back roads, dirt roads, trails and trailheads, elevation contours, lakes and streams, contours, public lands, land use cover, and boat ramps. DeLorme also publishes the

Maine Map and Guide, a detailed road map complete with travel information. Both are available at bookstores and from DeLorme at delorme.com or 800-561-5105.

Other useful AMC maps for Maine hikers include the *Mahoosuc Map and Guide*, the *Acadia National Park Discovery Map*, and the *Southern Piscataquis Regional Recreation Map and Guide*, available at outdoors.org and a variety of other retail locations. National Geographic also publishes two Trails Illustrated maps: *Baxter State Park/Mount Katahdin/Katahdin Iron Works* and *Acadia National Park.*

Many state parks, land trusts, and other conservation and recreation organizations provide useful trail maps. Refer to Appendix A: Helpful Information and Contacts for more information.

Hikers should always carry a map and compass, carefully keeping track of their approximate location on the map. Carrying this guide, or a photocopied section of the intended hike, for reference to the trail description is also a good idea. A protractor compass—a circular, liquid-filled compass that turns on a rectangular base made of clear plastic—is well-suited for hiking use. Such a compass is easily set to the desired bearing, and then it is a simple matter of keeping the compass needle aligned to north and following the arrow on the base. There is deviation—known as *declination*—of between 17 degrees and 20 degrees between true north and magnetic north in Maine. This means true north will be anywhere from 17 degrees to 20 degrees to the right (clockwise from) the north needle of the compass. (Each USGS quad map will indicate the particular declination for that map on its legend.) When taking a bearing from a map, you therefore will need to add between 17 degrees and 20 degrees to the bearing when the compass is set. On the maps included with this guide, the black lines running from top to bottom are aligned with true north.

GPS units are popular with many hikers. When used in conjunction with a map and compass, a GPS unit can be a very useful tool in the woods, but it is not a substitute for a map and compass. GPS reception can be poor in deep valleys and under heavy foliage, and units are subject to damage or battery failure. Extra batteries are a must. Hikers should be certain to practice with the GPS unit and become familiar with its operation and features before starting out on a trip.

INTRODUCTION

MAINE'S PUBLIC AND PRIVATE LANDS

The forestlands of Maine cover 17.7 million acres, or 90 percent, of the state, making it the most heavily forested state in the United States. Large tracts of undeveloped forestland, much of it commercial timberland, are found in northern and eastern Maine. In other parts of the United States, particularly in the west, such large blocks of land are usually publicly owned and managed by the federal government (primarily the Forest Servivce (USFS) or Bureau of Land Management). In Maine, however, just 6 percent of forestland in the state, or about 1 million acres, is owned by the public, and the remaining 94 percent, or 16.7 million acres, is privately owned.

The state of Maine owns more than 800,000 acres of land. This includes 36 state parks totaling 67,000 acres, 34 public reserve lands totaling 466,000 acres, and 15 historic sites totaling 276 acres. These state lands are managed by the Maine Dept. of Conservation, Bureau of Parks and Lands. The 210,000-acre Baxter State Park (BSP) is administered as a separate entity by the Baxter State Park Authority, which consists of the attorney general, the director of the Maine Forest Service (MFS), and the Commissioner of Inland Fisheries and Wildlife.

The federal government owns about 200,000 acres of land. This includes the 45,000-acre section of the White Mountain National Forest (WMNF) in and around Evans Notch in western Maine, 45,000 acres in Acadia National Park (ANP) on Mt. Desert Island, Schoodic Point, and Isle au Haut; ten National Wildlife Refuges, including Moosehorn, the largest in the state; and the Appalachian Trail (AT) corridor administered by the Appalachian Trail Conservancy (ATC) under the guidance of the National Park Service (NPS).

Maine has a robust network of 96 land trusts and conservation organizations, including the Appalachian Mountain Club (AMC), that together own more than 300,000 acres, or 2 percent of the land. The Maine Chapter of The Nature Conservancy (TNC) owns the largest parcel, about

180,000 acres along the St. John River in Aroostook County in northwestern Maine. Land trusts and conservation organizations have helped protect nearly 300,000 additional acres through conservation easements, which ensure public access while keeping land in private ownership.

Industrial forest landowners who run paper mills, sawmills, and other wood processing facilities own nearly 5 million acres, or 28 percent, of the forestland, including large tracts in northern and eastern Maine. Large nonindustrial landowners—individuals, families, and public and private companies that own more than 100,000 acres—account for 14 percent, or 2.5 million acres. Investment companies such as banks, insurance companies, mutual and pension funds, and university endowment funds own more than 2.6 million acres, or about 15 percent. American Indian tribal landowners own about 184,000 acres, or 1 percent.

North Maine Woods (NMW) is a nonprofit corporation comprising a variety of public and private landowners that manages recreational access to 3.5 million acres of forestland in northern Maine, roughly from the Canadian border east to BSP and north through Aroostook County, including all of Allagash Wilderness Waterway and the upper reaches of the St. John River. NMW also manages access to the KI-Jo Mary Multiple Use Forest west of the ME 11 and Brownville Junction. Hikers entering NMW-managed lands must pass through a checkpoint and pay a fee for day use and camping. These fees help maintain hundreds of miles of roads and more than 500 campsites.

TRAIL COURTESY

The many hundreds of miles of trails on Maine's public and private lands exist because of the generosity of landowners and the stewardship of many organizations and individuals. On all public lands and some private lands, agreements—some formal and some not—exist to allow for foot trails and their public use. Some trails cross private land with no formal permission from the landowner. In such cases, these trails exist by virtue of a long tradition of public use.

Regardless of whether a trail is located on public or private land, hikers must exercise care to observe all regulations that have been designed to protect the land itself and the rights of the landowners. Despite a history of public use and enjoyment, trails—especially those on private land—are subject to closure at the will of the landowner. Therefore, it is imperative that hikers treat all trails and property with great respect, as if the land were your own. This might require cleaning up after others less mindful.

Hikers should be aware that they will sometimes be sharing designated trails with other users, such as ATV riders, mountain bikers, and horseback riders. There is room for enjoyment for all in the Maine outdoors, so please be courteous.

Dog owners should have their pets under control at all times, whether by leash or voice control. Dogs are not allowed in BSP and on some land trust properties.

APPALACHIAN TRAIL

With the passage of the National Trails System Act (NTSA) by Congress in 1968, the AT became the first federally protected footpath in the United States and was officially designated the Appalachian National Scenic Trail. In 1978, amendments to the NTSA authorized funds and directed the NPS and USFS to acquire lands to protect the AT corridor. In 1984, the Department of the Interior delegated the bulk of the responsibilities for managing the trail to the Appalachian Trail Conference, which changed its name to the Appalachian Trail Conservancy in 2005 to better reflect its role. Today the ATC works to maintain and protect the AT in conjunction with a host of organizations—including the Maine Appalachian Trail Club (MATC)—in the 14 states through which the trail passes.

The 2,180-mi. route of the AT enters Maine at the Maine–New Hampshire border in the Mahoosuc Range, negotiates the difficult milelong stretch of Mahoosuc Notch, and proceeds to climb over a long series of high peaks—many exceed 4,000 ft.—that make up the Longfellow Mountains. After traversing the Bigelow Range, the AT crosses the wide and swift Kennebec River at Caratunk on its way to Monson, the last outpost of civilization before the 100-Mile Wilderness. Rugged mountains, lakes, ponds, waterfalls, and deep forests characterize this final leg of the trail to BSP. The northern terminus of the AT, and its 281-mi. route through Maine, is atop the lofty alpine summit of Katahdin, the highest mountain in the state. The majority of the mountains along the AT in Maine are described in this guide.

INTERNATIONAL APPALACHIAN TRAIL

The brainchild of Dick Anderson of Freeport, the International Appalachian Trail (IAT) was first proposed to the public in 1994. Anderson "visualized a trail that would connect two countries and cultures, link a state and two provinces and traverse two major watersheds—the Gulf of Maine and the Gulf of St. Lawrence." Today, the IAT extends from just east of Katahdin and BSP across northern Maine, through New Brunswick and Quebec, to Crow Head on the northernmost tip of Newfoundland, also the northernmost point of the Appalachian Mountains in the Western Hemisphere, a distance of more than 1,900 mi. Parts of the IAT route have now been extended to Prince Edward Island and Nova Scotia.

In Maine, the IAT leaves from its starting point at the BSP boundary and soon reaches the summits of Deasey and Lunksoos mountains. Just west of the Canadian border, the IAT climbs Mars Hill for a final view across Aroostook County before entering New Brunswick. Each of these three peaks traversed by the IAT is described in this guide.

GEOGRAPHY

Maine, the easternmost state in the United States, is bordered by New Hampshire, the Canadian provinces of Quebec and New Brunswick, and the Atlantic Ocean. At more than 33,000 square mi., Maine is nearly as large as the other five New England states combined. It is 39th in size among all states. The state is roughly 390 mi. long from south to north and 190 mi. wide from west to east. Its latitude ranges from 43° 4' north to 47° 28' north, and its longitude ranges from 66° 57' west to 71° 7' west. The geographic center of Maine is located in Piscataquis County, 18 mi. north of Dover Foxcroft.

To the south, Maine is bounded by the Atlantic Ocean from the Piscataqua River at Kittery to Passamaquoddy Bay at Eastport. The eastern boundary is a meridian line between Canada to the east and the United States to the west and extends from Hamlin to Pole Hill east of North

Amity. The international boundary then follows Mountain Brook to North Lake, Grand Lake, and on to Spednik Lake. From Vanceboro to Passamaquoddy Bay, the St. Croix River forms the state boundary. To the west, a meridian line separates Maine and New Hampshire from the jct. of the Maine, New Hampshire, and Quebec borders west of Bowman Hill south to Grand East Lake in Acton. From that point to Portsmouth Harbor and the Atlantic Ocean, the Salmon Falls River and then the Piscataqua River is the boundary. The northern boundary is the most complex. From Bowman Hill in Bowmantown Township, the boundary follows the mountainous height-of-land separating the St. Lawrence River watershed from the Kennebec and Penobscot river watersheds. From Little St. John Lake, the Southwest Branch of the St. John River is the border as far as a point just west of Hardwood Mtn. in T9 R18 WELS. From there, a straight line runs to Lac Frontiere, then another angles northwest to the Crown Monument at Estcourt. From here, the St. Francis River flows east to empty into the St. John River near the village of St. Francis. The St. John River is the border as far as Hamlin just west of Grand Falls, Canada.

Maine can be divided into four distinct physical regions: the coastal lowlands, the hilly interior belt, the western mountains, and the dissected uplands.

The coastal lowlands include the sandy beaches from York to Casco Bay. Between Casco Bay and Penobscot Bay is the peninsula coast, characterized by long arms of land extending out into the ocean. Farther north between Rockland and Schoodic Point is an area of large bays, wide peninsulas, and large islands, and includes Penobscot, Blue Hill, and Frenchman bays. The area between Frenchman and Passamaquoddy bays is known as Downeast, where the wide bays are more exposed to the ocean and the peninsulas are broader, with fewer and smaller islands. The coastal lowlands are interrupted by a stretch of interior hills that reach from Montville to the Camden Hills on the coast. The mountains of Mt. Desert Island and ANP are also part of the hilly interior that reaches south to the ocean. This region includes some of the mountains of the Southwestern Maine, Midcoast, and Downeast sections, and all of the Acadia section.

Inland from the coast is the hilly interior belt, a region of rolling hills; woods and farmlands; and lakes, ponds, and rivers that extends across the state from the New Hampshire border to Bangor and on to the New Brunswick border. These hills are mostly scattered and range from a few hundred feet to about 2,000 ft. in elevation. Included are the mountains of the Evans Notch and Oxford Hills sections; many of the trails of the Southwestern Maine, Midcoast, and Downeast sections; and some of the trails of the Kennebec and Moose River Valleys section.

The western mountains extend from the White Mountains along the New Hampshire border east and north across the state to Katahdin and the cluster of mountains nearby. This heavily forested region is characterized by the chain of high peaks known as the Longfellow Range and a series of large lakes, from Umbagog to Flagstaff to Moosehead to Grand Lake Matagamon. The western mountains encompass the entire Maine section of the AT, BSP, and a variety of large conservation lands, including AMC's Maine Woods property. The mountains and trails of the Western Lakes and Mountains, Greater Moosehead Lake and 100-Mile Wilderness, and Baxter State Park sections, and the northernmost mountains of the Kennebec and Moose River Valleys section are included.

The dissected uplands comprise the majority of Aroostook County in northern Maine. Forestlands and farmlands, scattered low mountains ranging as high as 2,000 ft. in elevation, the Allagash Wilderness Waterway, and the valley of the St. John River characterize this region, which includes all of the mountains in the Aroostook County section.

GEOLOGY

The bedrock geology of Maine is the result of a series of complex natural forces, primarily sedimentation, and volcanic and mountain building activities ranging from as early as the Late Proterozoic era of about 650 million years ago to the Mesozoic era of about 66 million years ago. The continental rift between the combined European and African plates and the North American plate of the Late Mesozoic era led to continued uplift, erosion, faulting, and fracturing of the bedrock of the Appalachian Mountains of western Maine during the Tertiary period of the Cenozoic era about 1.6 million years ago.

Much of the natural landscape we see today in Maine was shaped by the glaciation events of the Pleistocene period. Starting about 35,000 years ago, the Laurentide Ice Sheet spread across southern Quebec and New England. The ice sheet was as much as 10,000 ft. thick and covered the highest mountains in the state, including Katahdin. The sheer mass of the ice sheet depressed the land many hundreds of feet. The movement of the glacial ice scoured the mountains and valleys, eroding the rock and carving enormous basins out of the mountainsides, and moving great quantities of sand and gravel southward.

Because of climatic warming, the glaciers began to retreat about 21,000 years ago. The melting waters flooded as far as 75 mi. inland, creating the long peninsulas and islands that exist today. The retreating ice sheet dramatically changed the coastline, changed the mountain landscape, left behind more than 6,000 lakes and ponds, and changed the courses of the major rivers. The glaciers disappeared altogether about 11,000 years ago.

CLIMATE AND VEGETATION

Given Maine's geographic location on the eastern edge of the North American continent, its climate is influenced primarily by continental air masses flowing across the land on the westerly winds. This can be the cold, dry air from Canada or the warm, moist air from the Gulf of Mexico. The climate is influenced to a lesser degree by cool, moist air from the Atlantic Ocean, which moderates the temperatures along the coast. Maine's northern location between the latitudes 43 degrees and 47½ degrees north reduces the sun's influence, making for generally mild, but not hot, summers and cold winters. The higher elevations in the mountains are generally cooler in the summer and much colder in winter. The mean January temperature ranges from 20 degrees along the coast to 15 degrees inland to 10 degrees in the far north. The mean July temperature ranges from 65 degrees along the coast and in the far north to 67 degrees inland. Annual rainfall ranges from around 50 inches along the coast to 36 inches in northern Maine, although the western mountains receive significant precipitation due to the influence of the cooler air at higher elevations. Snowfall totals range from as much as 80 inches along the coast to 81 to 100 inches inland to more than 110 inches in the western mountains and northern interior.

Maine occupies a transition zone between the predominantly deciduous forests to the south and the predominantly coniferous forests to the north. Within this zone, the broad mix of forest cover types is influenced to some degree by latitude, although soil variation and local climate also play a role. Along the coast from Casco Bay east to Passamaquoddy Bay, in the western mountains and into the dissected uplands, the dominant tree species are spruce, fir, cedar, and larch. In southwestern Maine, and the western section of the hilly interior belt, the dominant species are oak, white pine, and hemlock. The northern hardwood mix of beech, maple, and birch dominates in a band stretching from the western mountains east to Washington County in the hilly interior, and north in a band east of BSP to Canada and down along the St. John Valley of eastern Aroostook County.

TRIP PLANNING, WEATHER, AND SAFETY

The traditional hiking season extends from Memorial Day to Columbus Day, although many hikers have come to know the joy of empty trails in the shoulder months of early spring and late fall. Trail conditions in Maine vary by geography, as coastal trails and those just inland will be snow-free much earlier than those farther north along the mountains of the AT corridor and will remain so longer, into fall and possibly even early winter. In some years, ice or snowdrifts can linger at higher elevations into late May or early June and possibly later than that in some of the major ravines, on north-facing slopes, and in other sheltered areas such as Mahoosuc Notch. Such conditions vary greatly from year to year and place to place. When snow or ice are present, trails may be more difficult to follow and more hazardous to hike on. If icy trail conditions are expected, it is prudent to bring some type of traction footgear.

Even if it feels like summertime in the lower elevations, it can be like winter on the high ridges and summits of the mountaintops. In fact, winter conditions can occur in the higher mountains in any month of the year. Keep in mind that air temperatures will drop from 3 to 5 degrees with each 1,000 feet of elevation gain, without factoring in the impact of windchill. As a result, even on sunny days in midsummer, hikers venturing to the alpine summits should always be prepared for cold weather with a minimum of a synthetic fleece jacket or wool sweater, hat, gloves, and a wind parka, all of which will provide comfort and protection against sudden storms.

Plan your trip schedule with safety in mind. Consider the strength of your party and the strenuousness of the trip: the overall distance, the amount of climbing, and the roughness of the terrain. Get a weather report, but be aware that a forecast may not apply to the mountain regions. The National Weather Service in Gray, Maine, issues a daily forecast that covers the northern New England region and broadcasts the forecast on its shortwave radio station. A recorded forecast may be obtained by calling 207-688-3210. Frequent weather updates are also available on weather.com.

Plan to finish your hike with daylight to spare (remember that days grow shorter rapidly in late summer and fall). Hiking after dark, even with flashlights or headlamps (which frequently fail), makes finding trails more difficult and crossing streams hazardous. Let someone else know where you will be hiking, and don't allow people to become separated from the group, especially those who are inexperienced.

Many unpaved roads may not be passable until Memorial Day or after, and extra precautions should be taken to ensure that your vehicle has a full gas tank and a usable spare tire, and that you have extra food, water, and clothing before driving into the remote regions of Maine's north woods.

Consider bringing your own children or those of friends on appropriate hikes, as introducing young people to the outdoors has many benefits. Kids who are exposed to frequent, unstructured outdoor play are healthier, do better in school, have higher self-esteem, feel more connected to nature, and are more likely to be tomorrow's conservation leaders. AMC is committed to helping kids build strong connections to the outdoor world, including its protection. Bringing children into the outdoors teaches them the need to take care of the world around them. See outdoors.org/kidtips.

hikeSafe HIKER RESPONSIBILITY CODE

You are responsible for yourself, so be prepared:

1. With knowledge and gear. Become self-reliant by learning about the terrain, conditions, local weather, and your equipment before you start.

2. To leave your plans. Tell someone where you are going, the trails you are hiking, when you will return, and your emergency plans.

3. To stay together. When you start as a group, hike as a group, end as a group. Pace your hike to the slowest person.

4. To turn back. Weather changes quickly in the mountains. Fatigue and unexpected conditions can also affect your hike. Know your limitations and when to postpone your hike. The mountains will be there another day.

5. For emergencies. Even if you are headed out for just an hour, an injury, severe weather, or a wrong turn could become life threatening. Don't assume you will be rescued; know how to rescue yourself.

6. To share the hiker code with others.

hikeSafe: It's Your Responsibility.

The Hiker Responsibility Code was developed and is endorsed by the WMNF and New Hampshire Fish and Game, and is supported by Baxter State Park. For more information, visit hikesafe.com.

FOLLOWING TRAILS

In general, trails are maintained to provide a clear pathway while protecting the environment by minimizing erosion and other damage. Some may offer rough and difficult passage. Many hiking trails are marked with paint blazes on trees or rocks, with signs marking the trailhead and intermediate points en route. The route of the AT in Maine is marked with white 2 x 6–in., vertical paint blazes. Side trails off the AT are usually marked with blue paint blazes. Other trails may be marked in a variety of paint colors, and some will exhibit colored flagging (plastic tape) along the way. Some trails lack any signs or trail markers whatsoever. Above treeline, on open ridges and ledge areas, cairns (piles of rocks) usually mark the trails.

Below treeline, the treadway is usually visible except when it is covered by snow or fallen leaves. In winter, signs at trailheads and intersections and blazes also are often covered by snow. Trails following or crossing woods roads require you to take special care at intersections to distinguish the trail from diverging roads, particularly because blazing may be sporadic or nonexistent while the trail follows the road. Around shelters or campsites, beaten paths may lead in all directions, so look for signs and paint blazes.

Hikers should be aware that some trails in this book (as noted in descriptions) are less easy to follow than others. The presence of signs and blazes varies, and some trails are too new to have a well-defined footway; others have received very little use and are overgrown and becoming obscure. Trails may not be cleared of fallen trees and brush until summer, and not all trails are cleared every year. Inexperienced hikers should avoid trails described as being difficult to follow, and all trail users should observe and follow trail markings carefully.

Although trails vary greatly in the amount of use they receive and the ease with which they can usually be followed, almost any trail might be closed unexpectedly or suddenly become obscure or hazardous under certain conditions. Trails can be rerouted or abandoned or closed by landowners. Signs are stolen or fall from their posts. Storms may cause blowdowns or landslides, which can obliterate a trail for an entire hiking season or longer. Logging operations can cover trails with slash and add a bewildering network of new roads. Development and road construction can obliterate trails.

Momentary inattention to trail markers, particularly arrows at sharp turns or signs at junctions, or misinterpretation of signs or guidebook descriptions, can cause hikers to become separated from all but the most heavily traveled paths—or at least lead them into what may be a much longer or more difficult route. So please remember that this book is an aid to planning, not a substitute for observation and judgment. All the trail-maintaining organizations, including AMC, reserve the right to discontinue any trail without notice and expressly disclaim any legal responsibility for the condition of any trail.

IF YOU'RE LOST

Keeping track of where you are at all times and how long ago you observed the last trail marker is the best way to avoid becoming lost. In the event you find that you've wandered off the trail and you are no longer sure where you are, stop and briefly assess the situation. Often just by looking side to side, you can find the trail. If not, try backtracking a short distance to the last known trail marker.

If you are hiking with companions, yell or blow a whistle. They or others are likely nearby. If the trail still cannot be found and no one answers your calls, try to remain calm. Many situations where a person has become lost for any length of time involve panic and aimless wandering, so it is important to stop now and take a break, make an inventory of useful information, decide on a course of action, and stick to it. (The caution against allowing inexperienced persons to become separated from a group should be emphasized here because they are most likely to panic and wander aimlessly. Make sure also that all party members are familiar with the route of the trip and the names of the trails to be used, so that if they do become separated they will have some prospect of rejoining the group.)

Even when the trail cannot be immediately found, the situation is concerning but not necessarily serious. If you have carefully kept track of your location on the map, some careful forays from your current position should help you relocate the trail. Should this effort fail, you can usually find a nearby stream, trail, or road to which a compass course may be followed. In many areas, distances are short enough (except in the North Maine Woods in Aroostook County, the northern reaches of Somerset and Piscataquis counties, and along the Canadian border) that it is possible, in the absence of alternatives, to reach a road in half a day, or at most in a whole day, simply by hiking downhill until you come upon a river or brook. Follow it downstream, and it should lead to civilization.

WHAT TO CARRY AND WEAR

Adequate equipment for a hike in the mountains of Maine varies greatly according to the time of year, the geographic location, the length of the trip, the potential terrain hazards to be encountered, and the difficulty of getting to the nearest trailhead if a problem arises.

Good things to have in your pack for an ordinary day hike in spring, summer, and fall in the Maine mountains include the following:

- guidebook and maps
- minimum of 2 quarts of water
- compass
- pocket knife
- rain/wind gear
- synthetic or wool jacket/sweater(s)
- long pants
- sunglasses
- warm hat
- gloves
- extra shirt(s)
- watch
- lunch and high-energy snacks
- bandanna or handkerchief
- personal medications
- first aid/repair kit
- nylon cord
- trash bag
- toilet paper
- sunscreen
- insect repellent
- cell phone
- whistle
- space blanket or bivouac sack
- headlamp or flashlight
- extra batteries and spare bulb
- lighter or waterproof matches
- notebook and pen/pencil

Wear comfortable, broken-in hiking boots. Light-to-medium-weight boots provide the needed ankle support on rough and rocky trails. Two pairs of socks are recommended—a lightweight inner pair and a heavier outer pair that is at least partly wool. Adjustable trekking poles offer many advantages to hikers, especially on descents, traverses, and stream crossings.

Jeans, sweatshirts, and other cotton clothing are not recommended because once they become wet, they dry very slowly. In adverse weather conditions, they can quickly drain a cold and tired hiker's heat reserves; thus, the hiker's maxim "cotton kills." Synthetics and wool are superior materials for hiking apparel, especially for those intending to travel in adverse conditions, to remote places, or above treeline. Synthetics and wool retain much of their insulating value even when wet and are indispensable for hikers wanting to explore remote places from which return to the trailhead might require substantial time and effort if conditions turn bad. Hats, gloves, and other such gear provide an extra margin of safety in adverse conditions, and they allow one to enjoy the summits in comfort on those crisp, clear days when the views are particularly fine. A camera, binoculars, nature identification guides, altimeter, book, and global positioning system (GPS) are nice extras to consider.

CAMPING

Trailside camping is available on a first-come, first-served basis at established lean-tos and tentsites along the AT corridor, from Carlo Col Shelter in the Mahoosuc Range just north of the New Hampshire border to Abol Pines Campsite on the Penobscot River at Abol Bridge just south of BSP. Where caretakers are in place, a fee may be charged. Backcountry campsites are also available at a number of Maine's Public Reserved Land (PRL) units, including Deboullie, Little Moose, Donnell Pond, Mahoosucs, Wassataquoik, and others. The Maine Bureau of Parks and Lands (MBPL) allows dispersed camping on most PRLs, provided backpackers practice Leave No Trace principles. Lean-tos and tentsites in the remote areas of BSP are available with advanced reservations only. Three lean-tos along the IAT, two just east of BSP, and one on Mars Hill west of the Canadian border are available to hikers. Overnight camping is permitted in nearly all of the WMNF backcountry, although campers should check with the USFS on the latest Forest Protection Area rules, if any, for the areas they wish to visit.

Roadside camping is available at a variety of public campgrounds, including Blackwoods and Seawall campgrounds in ANP, eight drive-in campgrounds in BSP, and five WMNF campgrounds in the Evans Notch area, including Cold River, Basin, Wild River, Hastings, and Crocker Pond campgrounds. Nine state parks from Aroostook to Sebago Lake feature vehicle-accessible camping. Hundreds of privately operated campgrounds located throughout Maine offer a wide variety of facilities and amenities.

More than 500 primitive campsites are available within the boundaries of North Maine Woods, and another 71 campsites are within the KI-Jo Mary Multiple Use Forest.

See Appendix A: Helpful Information and Contacts for information on campsite reservations.

FIRE REGULATIONS

Campfire permits are required for some remote campsites in the unorganized townships. Permits are site-specific and valid only for a short time frame. In organized towns, landowner permission must be obtained and a permit issued by the town forest fire warden. Most Maine maps, including the DeLorme *Maine Atlas & Gazetteer*, distinguish between campsites that require a permit (permit sites) and those that do not (authorized sites). If unsure, contact the nearest MFS office (see Appendix A: Helpful Information and Contacts). Campfire permits are not required when the ground is snow-covered. Permits are free.

In BSP, ANP, and Maine PRL units and state parks, fires are allowed only at designated sites. Along the AT, fires are allowed only at designated shelter and tentsites. Use of backpacker stoves is strongly encouraged, on the AT and elsewhere to help minimize environmental impact and campsite degradation. Fires are allowed in the backcountry of the WMNF, except where prohibited by the specific rules of Forest Protection Areas.

In 2009, the Maine legislature implemented a ban on all firewood brought from outside the state to help control the spread of potentially devastating insect pests, such as the emerald ash borer and Asian longhorned beetle. If firewood is transported, it must be completely burned within 24 hours. Campers are urged to leave all firewood at home and buy it locally where it will be used.

WINTER CONSIDERATIONS

This book describes trails in the snowless season, which can vary considerably from year to year. Higher elevations have much shorter snowless seasons. However, because snowshoeing and winter hiking in the woods and mountains of Maine are popular, a few general considerations are provided here. As more hikers have discovered the beauty of the woods in winter, advances in clothing and equipment have made it possible for experienced winter travelers to enjoy greater levels of comfort and safety.

Though travel on lower-elevation trails in average conditions can be relatively safe, much more experience is required to foresee and avoid dangerous situations in winter than in summer. Summer hiking boots are inadequate, regular headlamp batteries fail quickly, and drinking water freezes unless carried in an insulated container. The winter hiker must be in good physical condition and must dress carefully to avoid overheating and excessive perspiration, which soaks clothing and soon leads to chilling. Cotton clothes should be avoided in winter; only synthetic fabrics and wool retain their insulating values when wet. Fluid intake must increase, as dehydration can be a serious problem in the cold and dry winter air. Larger packs are needed to carry the extra clothing and gear required in winter.

Snow, ice, and weather conditions are constantly changing, and a relatively trivial error in judgment may have serious, even lethal, consequences. Conditions can vary greatly from day to day, and from trail to trail. Days are very short, particularly in early winter when darkness falls shortly after 4 P.M. Trails are frequently difficult or impossible to follow in deep snow, and navigation skills may be hard to apply in adverse weather conditions. (Thus, out-and-back hikes—where one retraces one's tracks—are often preferable to loop hikes, where unknown conditions ahead could make completion of the trip much more difficult than anticipated.) Brook crossings can be difficult and potentially dangerous if they are not well frozen.

Deep snow requires snowshoes or skis and the skill to use them efficiently (although some popular trails may be packed out through most of the winter). Breaking trail on snowshoes through new snow can be strenuous and exhausting work. Trail courtesy suggests that winter hikers wear snowshoes when trails are not solidly packed out. Post-holing in soft snow is unnecessarily tiring and creates unpleasant and potentially hazardous trail conditions for those who follow.

When ice is present on trails, as it often is in late fall, early spring, and after winter freeze-thaw cycles, mountains with steep, open slopes or ledges are particularly dangerous. If icy trail conditions are expected, hikers should bring traction footgear such as crampons (full or instep) or ice cleats. In spring, deep snowdrifts may remain on northern slopes and wooded ridgelines, even at lower elevations, after all snow has melted on southern exposures.

It is important to note that some trails, such as those on Katahdin, pass through areas that may pose a danger of avalanches. Basin walls, ravines, and open slopes are especially prone to avalanches, though avalanches can also occur below treeline. These areas should be regarded as technical terrain and strictly avoided unless group leaders have been trained in avalanche safety.

Above timberline, conditions often require specialized equipment and skills and experience of a different magnitude. The conditions on Katahdin, the Bigelows, Saddleback, and other high and exposed alpine summits can be severe and should be attempted by only the most experienced and well-equipped climbers. Severe storms can develop suddenly and unexpectedly, but perhaps the most dangerous aspect of winter in the higher elevations of the Maine mountains is the variability of the weather. It is not unusual for a cold, penetrating, wind-driven rain to be followed within a few hours by a cold front that brings below-zero temperatures and high winds.

No book can begin to impart all the knowledge necessary to cope safely with the potential for such serious conditions, but those interested in learning more about winter hiking should consult the *AMC Guide to Winter Hiking and Camping*, by Yemaya Maurer and Lucas St. Clair (AMC Books, 2009). Hikers who are interested in extending their activities into the winter season, especially at higher elevations, are strongly advised to seek out organized parties with leaders who have extensive winter experience. AMC's Maine Chapter sponsors numerous evening and weekend workshops, in addition to introductory winter hikes and regular winter schedules through which participants can gain experience. Information on these activities can be found at amcmaine.org or outdoors.org.

No attempt is made to cover any kind of skiing in this guide, although a number of the hiking trails described are well-suited to cross-country and backcountry skiing.

BACKCOUNTRY HAZARDS

Safe hiking means knowing how to avoid potentially dangerous situations as well as being prepared to deal with problems when they do occur. Courses that teach the principles of backcountry safety, wilderness first aid, and incident management are offered by AMC and many other outdoor organizations. Dozens of helpful books are available on these subjects. Some of the common hazards encountered in the Maine outdoors and how to approach them are outlined here.

Falls and Injuries

Injuries on the trail are a serious matter anytime, but more so with increasing distance from the trailhead. Be alert for places where the footing may be poor, especially in rainy weather and on steep, rough, or wet sections of trail. In autumn, wet leaves and hidden ice are particular hazards. Remember that carrying a heavy pack can affect your balance. Another potential cause of injury in mountainous areas is rockfall from ledges that rise above the trail.

In case of serious injury, apply first aid and keep the injured party warm and comfortable. Then take a minute to assess the situation before going or calling for help. Backcountry evacuation can take many hours, so don't rush. Write down your location, the condition of the injured person, and any other pertinent facts. If cell phone service is not available, at least one person should stay with the injured hiker while two others go for help. (Hence the maxim that it is safest to hike in the backcountry in groups of four or more.)

Hypothermia

Hypothermia, the most serious danger to hikers in the Maine woods and mountains, is the loss of ability to preserve body heat and may be caused by injury, exhaustion, lack of sufficient food, and inadequate or wet clothing. This often occurs on wet, windy days at between 32 and 50 degrees Fahrenheit.

Symptoms of moderate hypothermia include uncontrolled shivering, impaired speech and movement, lowered body temperature, and drowsiness. Be on the lookout for what current hypothermia education programs refer to as the *umbles*—stumbles, mumbles, and bumbles—which amount to a loss of agility, an inability to speak clearly, difficulty with knots and zippers, and similar issues that indicate loss of normal muscular and mental functions. A victim should be given dry clothing and placed in a sleeping bag, if available, then given quick-energy food to eat and something warm (not hot) to drink.

In cases of severe hypothermia, which occurs when a body's temperature has reached a point below 90 degrees Fahrenheit, shivering ceases, but a victim becomes afflicted by an obvious lack of coordination to the point that walking becomes impossible. Sure indicators are slurred speech, mental confusion, irrational behavior, disorientation, and unconsciousness. Only prompt evacuation to a hospital offers reasonable hope for recovery. Extreme care must be used in attempting to transport such a person to a trailhead because even a slight jar can bring on heart failure. The victim should be protected from further heat loss as much as possible and handled with extreme gentleness, and trained rescue personnel should be called for assistance.

Successful rescue of a profoundly hypothermic person from the backcountry is difficult, so the need for prevention or early detection is essential. The advent of hypothermia is usually fairly slow, and in cold or wet weather all members of a hiking group must be aware of the signs of developing hypothermia and pay constant attention to the first appearance of such signs—which may be fairly subtle—in all fellow party members.

Heat Exhaustion

Excessive heat can also be a serious problem in the mountains, particularly in midsummer on hot, humid days. Heat exhaustion, usually in a mild form, is quite common. The hiker feels tired, perhaps light-headed or nauseous, and may have cramps in large muscles. The principal cause is dehydration and loss of electrolytes (mostly salt) through perspiration, often combined with overexertion. On a hot day, a hiker can often be well on the way to serious dehydration before any thirst is felt. To prevent heat exhaustion, hikers should carry plenty of water (and the means to treat or filter it), and drink copiously before thirst is evident. Wearing a hat to block sun is another preventive measure.

The treatment is to provide adequate water and possibly salt (salt without adequate water will make the situation worse), help the victim cool down (especially the head and torso) by moving them into the shade, and minimize further physical exertion. Heat exhaustion must be taken seriously because it can progress to life-threatening cardiac problems or to heat stroke, a medical emergency in which irreversible damage to the brain and other vital organs can quickly occur. This condition requires immediate cooling of the victim.

Lightning

Lightning is another serious potential hazard on any open ridge or summit. Avoid these dangerous places when thunderstorms are likely. Look for shelter in thick woods as quickly as possible if an unexpected "thumper" is detected. Most thunderstorms occur when a cold front passes, or on very warm days. Storms produced by cold fronts are typically more sudden and violent. Weather forecasts that mention cold fronts or predict temperatures much above 80 degrees Fahrenheit in the lowlands and valleys should arouse concern.

Wildlife

In recent years, there have been hundreds of collisions between automobiles and moose, most occurring in spring and early summer, though the hazard exists year round. Motorists need to be aware of the seriousness of the problem, particularly at night when these large, dark-colored animals are both active and very difficult to see. Instinct often causes them to face an auto rather than run from it, and they are apt to cross the road unpredictably as a car approaches. Be aware that where one moose crosses, there may well be another coming right behind it. Moose normally constitute little threat to hikers on foot, though it would be wise to give a wide berth to a cow with young, or to a bull during the fall mating season.

Bears are common but tend to keep well out of sight. The black bear is a large and unpredictable animal that must be treated with respect. Deliberate feeding of bears or allowing harassment by a dog may unnecessarily provoke an attack. No animal in the wild should be approached, startled, or fed. Bears are omnivorous opportunists, especially fond of nuts and berries, and sometimes hiker's food bags. They have become a nuisance and even a hazard at some popular campsites, as any bear that has lost its natural fear of humans and gotten used to living off us is potentially very dangerous. Hikers confronted by a bear should attempt to appear neither threatened nor frightened, and should back off slowly, but never run. Food should not be abandoned unless the bear appears overly aggressive. A loud noise, such as that made by a whistle or by banging metal pots, is often useful.

Careful protection of food and scented items such as toothpaste at campsites is essential. Food bags should never be kept overnight in a tent, but rather hung between trees well off the ground—at least 10 ft. high and 4 ft. away from the tree trunk. This helps keep other curious critters out of your larder as well.

There are no known poisonous snakes in Maine.

Insect Pests

Mosquitoes and blackflies are the woodland residents most frequently encountered by hikers in Maine. Mosquitoes are worst throughout the summer in low, wet areas, and blackflies are most bloodthirsty in late May, June, and early July. Head nets of fine nylon mesh can be useful. The most effective repellents for mosquitoes and blackflies, as well as gnats, no-see-ums and chiggers, are based on the active chemical ingredient N,N-Diethyl-meta-toluamide, generally known as DEET. It is available in a variety of forms, from aerosols and pump sprays to lotions and wipes. There are also different concentrations, from 100 percent DEET to lesser mixtures with more inert ingredients. There are some questions about the safety of using DEET, and hikers should probably apply such repellents to clothing rather than directly on the skin where possible, and avoid using them on small children. Alternatives to DEET include picaridin, which is odor-free and not oily like DEET, and repellents made using natural ingredients such as citronella and eucalyptus.

Ticks are most common along the coast and in the woods and fields of southern and central Maine. More than a dozen species of ticks reside in the woods of the state, but the deer tick *Ixodes scapularis* is the most troublesome. This tick can transmit the bacterium that causes Lyme disease. In the early stages, flu-like symptoms may appear, as well as an expanding or "bull's-eye" rash around the site of the tick bite. Detected early, Lyme disease can be treated with antibiotics. Left untreated, this serious disease can spread to joints, the heart, and the nervous system and lead to chronic health issues.

Countermeasures against ticks include using insect repellent on shoes, socks, and pant legs, wearing light-colored long pants tucked into your socks, and making frequent visual checks of clothing and skin. Ticks wander for several hours before settling on a spot to bite, so they can be removed easily if found promptly. Once a tick is embedded, care must be taken to remove it in its entirety, as the head detaches easily and may remain in the skin, possibly producing infection.

Bee stings may be painful, and for some individuals with allergies, they can cause potentially deadly anaphylactic reactions. Hikers with known allergies should carry Benadryl tablets and a prescription epinephrine pen.

Poison Ivy

Two types of poisonous plants are common in Maine: poison ivy and poison sumac. Poison ivy is found throughout the state, but poison sumac is much less common, being found mostly in the southern part. Poison ivy generally has three very shiny, dark green leaves that shine in the sun but are dull in the shade.

Direct contact with the oil (*urushiol*, an allergen) from the leaves, roots, stems, flowers, or fruit of these plants, or indirect contact from an object that has been in contact with the plant, may result in an allergic skin rash. Symptoms include itchy skin and a red area or red streaks where the plant touched the skin, small bumps or larger raised areas, and blisters with fluid that may leak out and cause the rash to spread. The rash usually appears from 8 to 48 hours after contact. Early treatment involves thoroughly washing the contact area with soap and water. The next step is the use of a topical cortisone cream. In severe cases, antibiotics may be necessary.

Stream Crossings

Streams, brooks, and rivers are often crossed without bridges, and you can usually step from rock to rock. Trekking poles, a hiking staff, or a stout stick can be a great aid to balance in these cases. Use caution, however, as serious injuries or worse can result from a fall on slippery rocks, especially in the middle of a stream. If you need to wade across a stream, it is recommended that you wear your boots (but not necessarily socks). If you know in advance that wading may be required, a good option is to carry lightweight sandals with straps or other water footwear. Unbuckle backpack straps so you can shrug out of the pack if necessary in a fall.

Many water crossings that may be only a nuisance in summer can be a serious obstacle in cold weather when feet and boots must be kept dry. Another type of hazard can occur in late fall, when cold nights may cause exposed rocks to be coated with a treacherous thin layer of ice. Higher waters can turn innocuous brooks into raging torrents, come spring as snow melts, or after heavy rainstorms, particularly in fall when trees drop their leaves and take up less water. Avoid trails with potentially dangerous stream crossings during these high-water periods. If you are cut off from roads by swollen streams, it is better to make a long detour, even if you need to wait and spend a night in the woods. Rushing currents can make wading extremely hazardous and not worth the risk. Floodwaters may subside within a few hours, especially in small brooks. It is particularly important not to camp on the far side of a brook from your exit point if the crossing is difficult and heavy rain is predicted.

Hunting Seasons

Deer hunting season (with firearms) in Maine generally starts on the Monday of the first week of November and lasts through the Saturday after Thanksgiving. A youth deer-hunting day is usually held the third Saturday in October, and a Maine resident day is held the fourth Saturday in October. Archery season is generally from late September through late October, and muzzleloader season is usually late November through early to mid-December. The start and duration of moose hunting season varies by region, generally from late September to late November. The start and duration of wild turkey hunting in spring varies be region, usually from late April to early June; in fall, the season is generally from early to late October.

Most hunters stay fairly close to roads, and, in general, the harder it would be to haul a deer out of a given area, the lower the probability that a hiker will encounter hunters there. In any case, avoid wearing brown or anything that might give a hunter the impression of the white flash of a white-tailed deer running away. Wearing at least two pieces of bright orange clothing, the same as required of hunters, is strongly recommended.

For the specific dates of Maine hunting seasons, visit maine.gov/ifw or call 207-287-8000. Hunting is not allowed on Sundays in Maine.

Drinking Water

The presence of microscopic cysts of the intestinal parasite *Giardia lamblia* in water sources in the Maine is thought to be common, though difficult to prove. *Cryptosporidium* is another similar parasite of concern. It is impossible to be sure whether a given source is safe, no matter how clear the water seems or how remote the location. The safest course is for hikers to carry their own water from home. For those who use sources in the woods, it is prudent to purify the water before drinking it.

Water purification methods include boiling, chemical treatment (tablets or drops), ultraviolet treatment, and water filters. When boiling water, bring it to a rolling boil and boil for at least five minutes. The downside to boiling is the increased consumption of fuel. Water can be treated with an iodine-based disinfectant. Allow extra contact time, and use twice as many tablets, if the water is very cold. Chlorine-based products are ineffective in water that contains organic impurities, and all water-purification chemicals tend to deteriorate quickly. Sterilizer pens using ultraviolet (UV) light are relatively new and apparently very effective. Inserting the pen into the water for a few minutes kills viruses, bacteria, and protozoa. The water must be filtered before sterilizing, and extra batteries should be carried. Various types of pump filters purify the water and remove impurities, often making the water look and taste better, so that sources that are unappealing in the untreated state can be made to produce drinkable water. Several new gravity filters eliminate hand pumping and allow for water storage.

The symptoms of giardiasis and cryptosporidiosis are similar and include severe intestinal distress and diarrhea. But such discomforts can have many other causes, making the diseases difficult to diagnose accurately. The principal cause of the spread of these noxious ailments in the woods is probably careless disposal of human waste (see Sanitation).

Sanitation

When dealing with human waste, keep it at least 200 ft. away from water sources. If no toilets are nearby, dig a hole 6 to 8 in. deep (but not below the organic layer of the soil) for a latrine and cover the hole completely after use. The bacteria in the organic layer of the soil will then decompose the waste naturally. It is advisable to be scrupulous about washing hands or using a hand sanitizer after answering calls of nature. Put used toilet tissue in a plastic bag and pack it out to minimize impact.

Break-ins

Cars parked at trailheads are frequently targets of break-ins, so valuables or expensive equipment should never be left inside your vehicle while you are off hiking, particularly overnight.

Search and Rescue

In emergencies, call 911 or any of the Maine State Police regional communications centers (toll-free):
- Gray: 800-228-0857
- Augusta: 800-452-4664
- Orono: 800-432-7381
- Houlton: 800-924-2261

Hikers should be aware that cell phone coverage in the backcountry can be very unreliable, particularly in deep valleys but also on some summits, and you have absolutely no assurance that a cell phone call will get through to authorities in an emergency. Both phones and their batteries can fail, often at inconvenient times.

By state law, the Maine Warden Service of the Maine Dept. of Inland Fisheries and Wildlife is responsible for search and rescue operations in the Maine outdoors. Whenever the commissioner receives notification that any person has gone into the woodlands or onto the inland waters of the state and has become lost or stranded, the commissioner will take reasonable steps to ensure the safe and timely recovery of that person. The commissioner reseves the right to end a search-and-rescue operation by members of the department when all reasonable efforts have been exhausted. The person for whom the search and rescue was conducted may be responsible for all directly related costs.

Search-and-rescue operations are serious matters. A fair amount of time is required to organize rescue parties, which normally require a minimum of 18 people for litter carries. In addition, an unnecessary rescue mission may leave no resources if a real emergency occurs. Please make sure that there really is an emergency before you call or go for help.

STEWARDSHIP AND CONSERVATION

Trail Maintenance

Trails don't just happen. The trails that we use and enjoy are the product of the dedication and hard work of local, state, and federal agencies, many public and private nonprofit organizations, and a host of volunteers. A significant number of trails in Maine are on private property and are open for public use through the generosity of the various landowners. Many trails, particularly on private property, are cared for by one dedicated person or a small group. Funds for trail work are scarce, and unless hikers contribute both time and money to the maintenance of trails, the diversity of trails available to the public may be threatened. Every hiker can make some contribution to the improvement of the trails, if nothing more than pushing a blowdown off the trail rather than walking around it. But a more formal commitment, even if it is just one day or one weekend each year, is welcomed. Many hands do make light work, and working together for the betterment of our trails is a fun and satisfying way to give something back.

Volunteer trail maintenance opportunities abound in Maine, through public agencies such as BSP, MBPL, ANP, and WMNF. The primary mission of the MATC is to oversee the 281-mi. AT corridor, its many shelters and campsites, and miles of side trails. AMC's Maine Chapter is very active in building and maintaining trails throughout the state. And dozens of local and regional land trusts, conservation commissions, and recreation departments can all use your assistance. Many of these organizations are listed in Appendix A: Helpful Information and Contacts.

Leave No Trace

AMC is a national educational partner of Leave No Trace, a nonprofit organization dedicated to promoting and inspiring responsible outdoor recreation through education, research, and partnerships. The Leave No Trace Program seeks to develop wild land ethics—ways in which people think and act in the outdoors to minimize their impact on the areas they visit and to protect our natural resources for future enjoyment. Leave No Trace unites four federal land management agencies—the USFS, NPS, Bureau of Land Management, and U.S. Fish and Wildlife Service—with manufacturers, outdoor retailers, user groups, educators, organizations such as AMC, and individuals. The Leave No Trace ethic is guided by these seven principles:

- Plan ahead and prepare.
- Travel and camp on durable surfaces.
- Dispose of waste properly.
- Leave what you find.
- Minimize campfire impacts.
- Respect wildlife.
- Be considerate of other visitors.

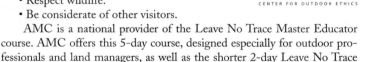

AMC is a national provider of the Leave No Trace Master Educator course. AMC offers this 5-day course, designed especially for outdoor professionals and land managers, as well as the shorter 2-day Leave No Trace Trainer course at locations throughout the Northeast.

For Leave No Trace information and materials, contact the Leave No Trace Center for Outdoor Ethics, P.O. Box 997, Boulder, CO 80306, 800-332-4100 or 302-442-8222, or lnt.org. For a schedule of AMC Leave No Trace courses, see outdoors.org/education/lnt.

ABBREVIATIONS AND ACRONYMS

The following abbreviations and acronyms are used in this book.

est.	estimate
ft.	foot, feet
hr.	hour(s)
jct.	junction
ln.	lane
lp	loop
mi.	mile(s)
MPH	miles per hour
Mt.	Mount
Mtn.	Mountain
ow	one way
rt	round trip
yd.	yard(s)

AMC	Appalachian Mountain Club
ANP	Acadia National Park
AT	Appalachian Trail
ATC	Appalachian Trail Conservancy
BHHT	Blue Hill Heritage Trust
BKP	Bingham's Kennebec Purchase
BPP	Bingham's Penobscot Purchase
BRCA	Belgrade Region Conservation Alliance
BSP	Baxter State Park
CMLT	Coastal Mountains Land Trust
CTA	Chatham Trails Association
DCC	Downeast Coastal Conservancy
ED	Eastern Division
FBC	Frenchman Bay Conservancy
FMWMA	Frye Mountain Wildlife Management Area
FR	Forest Route
FSHT	Frances Small Heritage Trust
GHP	Georges Highland Path
GPMCT	Great Pond Mountain Conservation Trust
GRLT	Georges River Land Trust

GWRLT	Great Works Regional Land Trust
IAT	International Appalachian Trail
KIW	Katahdin Iron Works
KLT	Kennebec Land Trust
LELT	Loon Echo Land Trust
MA	Maine Audubon
MACC	Mt. Agamenticus Conservation Committee
MATC	Maine Appalachian Trail Club
MBPL	Maine Bureau of Parks and Lands
MD	Middle Division
ME	Maine
MFS	Maine Forest Service
MHT	Maine Huts & Trails
MLT	Mahoosuc Land Trust
MNWR	Moosehorn National Wildlife Refuge
ND	Northern Division
NH	New Hampshire
NPS	National Park Service
PRL	Public Reserved Land
R	Range
SD	Southern Division
SFMA	Scientific Forest Management Area
SIA	Sentier International des Appalaches
SWLA	Sheepscot Wellspring Land Alliance
T	Township
TNC	The Nature Conservancy
US	United States
USFS	United States Forest Service
USGS	United States Geological Survey
WMNF	White Mountain National Forest
WELS	West of the Easterly Line of the State

SECTION ONE
BAXTER STATE PARK AND KATAHDIN

Katahdin 7

The Owl 25

Mt. OJI . . . . : . 25

North Brother and South
Brother 26

Mt. Coe 27

Daicey Pond 28

Sentinel Mtn. 29

Kidney Pond 32

Doubletop Mtn. 33

Burnt Mtn. 35

South Branch Ponds 35

South Branch Mtn. and
Black Cat Mtn. 38

North Traveler Mtn., The Traveler,
and Center Ridge. 39

Scientific Forest
Management Area 42

Fowler Ponds 44

Trout Brook Mtn. 46

Horse Mtn. 47

South Turner Mtn. 48

Katahdin Lake 48

Abol and Togue Ponds 51

International Appalachian Trail . . 53

Deasey Mtn. and Lunksoos
Mtn. 54

Owl's Head 56

Mt. Chase 56

Sugarloaf Mtn. 57

Norway Bluff 58

Suggested Hikes 59

**AMC map 1: Baxter State Park–
Katahdin**

Katahdin is Maine's highest mountain at 5,268 ft. It is located in Piscataquis and Penobscot counties about 80 mi. north of Bangor, between the East and West branches of the Penobscot River, at the northern edge of Piscataquis County. Katahdin is as wild and alluring as any mountain in the East. Katahdin is the predominant natural feature of

Baxter State Park (BSP), which was created by a gift of former Governor Percival P. Baxter in 1931. By the time of his death in 1969, Governor Baxter had extended the grant to more than 200,000 acres. A condition of his gift—there are variant wordings and differing interpretations by Governor Baxter and others—is that the area "shall forever be left in its natural wild state, forever be kept as a sanctuary for wild beasts and birds, and forever be used for public forest, public park, and public recreational purposes." The Baxter State Park Authority has continued to expand the park in recent years, adding more than 8,000 acres through purchase or gift, including 4,100 acres around iconic Katahdin Lake in 2006. The current park size is now 209,501 deeded acres.

This section provides comprehensive coverage of BSP and features trails to the high mountain peaks, as well as a wide variety of hikes along streams and rivers and to remote ponds. This includes the six major summits of the Katahdin massif, from Pamola, Chimney, South, and Baxter peaks to Hamlin and Howe peaks. To the west are The Owl, Mt. OJI, Mt. Coe, North and South Brother, and Doubletop Mtn. In the southwest corner of the park is Sentinel Mtn. East of Katahdin lies South Turner Mtn. In the northern part of the park are the mountains surrounding the South Branch ponds. East of the ponds are North Traveler Mtn., The Traveler, and Center Ridge. To the west are South Branch and Black Cat mountains. Burnt Mtn. is farther west. West of Matagamon Gate are Horse and Trout Brook mountains. Wadleigh Mtn. is the northernmost summit in the park. East of Katahdin Lake and the park boundary, along the International Appalachian Trail, are Deasey and Lunksoos mountains. North and east of Matagamon Gate are Sugarloaf Mtn., Mt. Chase, Owl's Head, and Norway Bluff. In all, this section describes 24 summits and 72 trails.

Park Access

The south entrance of Baxter State Park at Togue Pond Gate is reached by traveling on I-95 to Exit 244 at Medway. From there, travel east on ME 157 through East Millinocket and Millinocket to reach the park. It is 18 mi. from Millinocket to the gate.

The north entrance of the park at Matagamon Gate is reached by traveling on I-95 to Exit 264 at Sherman. From there, go north on ME 11 to Patten, then northeast on ME 159 to Shin Pond. Beyond, take Grand Lake Rd. west to the park. It is 24 mi. from Patten to the gate.

All park visitors must stop at the entrance gate to register and get a park pass. Rangers can also assist with directions and information about hiking trails and camping. Hikers entering the park via the AT must register at the trail kiosk at the park boundary south of Daicey Pond.

Most visitors enter the park at Togue Pond Gate. An entrance fee is charged for non-Maine-licensed vehicles. Just beyond the gate, the road forks. The right fork is Roaring Brook Rd., which leads 8.1 mi. to Roaring Brook Campground. To the left is Park Tote Rd., leading 41.1 mi. to the north entrance at Matagamon Gate.

In accordance with the terms of former Governor Baxter's deeds of trust, park roads are unpaved and relatively unimproved. Park Tote Rd. and Roaring Brook Rd. are very narrow and winding dirt and gravel roads. Dense foliage along the roads restricts views to the immediate corridor for much of the way, but there are occasional viewpoints.

From Togue Pond Gate, Park Tote Rd. first leads northwest and then generally north. It skirts the southern and western flanks of Katahdin. During the first 5 mi. of the drive, the mountain is briefly visible a few times. After passing Abol and Katahdin Stream campgrounds, the road reaches Foster Field, where you can see Doubletop Mtn., Mt. OJI, and other mountains in the range west of Katahdin. After that, the views are very restricted much of the way to the Matagamon Gatehouse. Most of Park Tote Rd. follows the routes of old logging roads.

Park Tote Rd. from Togue Pond Gate to
- Roaring Brook Rd.: 100 ft.
- Abol Campground: 5.7 mi.
- Katahdin Stream Campground: 7.7 mi.
- Foster Field: 10.3 mi.
- Daicey Pond via access road from Foster Field: 11.8 mi.
- Kidney Pond via access road from Foster Field: 11.8 mi.
- Nesowadnehunk Field Campground: 16.8 mi.
- Trout Brook Crossing: 33.8 mi.
- South Branch Pond Campground via access road from Trout Brook Crossing: 36.1 mi.
- Trout Brook Campground: 38.5 mi.
- Matagamon Gate: 41.1 mi.

Roaring Brook Rd. diverges right from Park Tote Rd. 100 ft. beyond Togue Pond Gate. Katahdin is immediately visible on the left across Helon Taylor and Rum ponds. Roaring Brook Rd. then proceeds through the woods, following along the base of the mountain to the east, passing Rum Brook Day Use Site, Bear Brook Group Site, and Avalanche Field before its terminus at Roaring Brook Campground.

Roaring Brook Rd. from Togue Pond Gate to
- Rum Brook Day Use Site: 1.3 mi.
- Bear Brook Group Site: 5.2 mi.
- Avalanche Field: 6.6 mi.
- Roaring Brook Campground: 8.1 mi.

Day-use visitors, especially those desiring to climb Katahdin, are strongly urged to use the Day Use Parking Reservation (DUPR) system. This service is available for hikers wanting to climb Katahdin from Roaring Brook, Abol, or Katahdin Stream campgrounds. DUPRs can be made by phone at 207-723-3877 or online at baxterstateparkauthority.com.

The park is open to the public twelve months a year, although access is often limited during the spring thaw in April to mid-May. Roads are not maintained for winter vehicle travel (except snowmobiles).

Note: Baxter State Park is not part of the state park system. The park is operated through user fees, income from trust funds provided by Governor Baxter and revenue from timber sales.

Camping

The park offers a wide variety of camping opportunities at ten campgrounds, from drive-in campsites and walk-in tentsites to cabins and bunkhouses to remote backcountry lean-tos and tentsites. Seven campgrounds are located along Park Tote Rd. These include Abol, Katahdin Stream, Nesowadnehunk Field, Kidney Pond, Daicey Pond, South Branch Pond, and Trout Brook. Group camping sites are also available at Foster Field, Nesowadnehunk Field, and Trout Brook. Located on Roaring Brook Rd. are Roaring Brook Campground and Bear Brook Group Site.

Backcountry campgrounds, accessible only on foot, are located at Chimney Pond and Russell Pond. Gain access to Chimney Pond by trail from Roaring Brook Campground. Russell Pond may be reached by trails from Roaring Brook, Nesowadnehunk Field, and South Branch Pond campgrounds.

All campgrounds have lean-tos (except Daicey Pond and Kidney Pond) and tentsites (except Chimney Pond, Daicey Pond, and Kidney Pond). Daicey Pond and Kidney Pond have cabins only. Bunkhouses are located at Roaring Brook, Nesowadnehunk, South Branch Pond, Russell Pond, and Chimney Pond. All of these sites offer only the most basic facilities. No hot showers, grocery stores, or gas stations are available. Water is available but is untreated throughout the park, so some method for purifying water is essential. Campers and visitors must supply their own camping gear, food, and cooking utensils. Fires are permitted only at designated sites.

Backcountry campsites (may be lean-tos or tentsites, please inquire) are available at Davis Pond, Katahdin Lake, Martin Ponds, Wassataquoik Stream, Wassataquoik Lake, Little Wassataquoik Lake, Center Mtn., Pogy Pond, Upper South Branch Pond, Lower and Middle Fowler ponds, Long Pond, Billfish Pond, Littlefield Pond, Frost Pond, Hudson Pond, Webster Lake, Webster Stream, and Second Matagamon Lake. A number of water-access-only campsites are available.

Canoes, paddles, and personal flotation devices are available for rent at many campgrounds and backcountry sites. Check with a ranger for more information.

Reservations

Camping reservations are mandatory and can be made via a rolling reservation system. A reservation may be made by mail (check) or in person (cash or check) at park headquarters in Millinocket as early as four months in advance of the desired trip date. Reservations are limited to seven days at any one site and 14 days total for any one visit to the park. Last-minute reservations may be made by phone 14 days or less before the desired arrival date. Reservations made by phone must be paid by credit card. To get a printable camping reservation form, view campsite availability, or make a camping reservation for as many as seven days at a single campsite, go to baxterstateparkauthority.com or call the reservation office at 207-723-5140.

Regulations

Persons planning to camp, hike, and use the facilities in the park should be familiar with the rules and regulations, which are revised periodically. A complete list can be found at baxterstateparkauthority.com. The salient points for hikers and campers are summarized as follows:

- Camping is permitted by reservation only and only at authorized campgrounds and campsites between May 15 and October 15, and from December 1 through March 31.
- All persons entering the park by road or trail must register at the first opportunity at a staffed gatehouse or self-registration station. Prior registration is required for groups of 12 or more.
- Hiking or mountain climbing may be restricted at the discretion of the park director.
- Hunting or trapping are prohibited, except in specifically designated areas. Maine fishing laws apply within the park.
- Pets and other domestic animals are not allowed in the park. Do not bait, feed, or disturb any animal in the park.
- Fires and cooking or heating devices are permitted only at designated campsites or picnic areas.
- Anything carried into the park must be carried out, for example, trash and gear.
- No person may use electronic devices in any way that impairs the enjoyment of the park by others.
- No person may disturb or remove natural objects, plants, or animals.
- Single vehicles over 9 ft. high, 7 ft. wide, or 22 ft. long, or 44 ft. long for combined units are prohibited. Motorcycles, ATVs, and motorized trail bikes are prohibited. Bicycles are allowed only on park roads.
- All groups of five or more persons under the age of 16 must be accompanied by an adult.

Caution: Severe injuries and deaths have occurred in the park over the years. Visitors must be responsible for their own safety and that of their group. The upper summits are very rugged and exposed above the timberline. Weather and trail conditions can change quickly, even in summer. The weather on Katahdin is similar to that of Mt. Washington, but longer access routes can make conditions even more dangerous in many cases.

Hikers planning to go to higher elevations should take plenty of food, water, and warm clothing. The trails on many of the routes are among the steepest and most difficult in New England. Hikers should be in good physical condition if they plan to climb the higher and more distant summits. Others may want to limit their activities accordingly. Do not leave the trails, particularly on Katahdin or during severe weather or limited visibility.

The alpine environment above treeline on Katahdin is home to many rare and unusual plants and animals. Please help care for their fragile environment by staying on marked trails. All wildlife should be observed from a safe distance.

All of the more than 200 mi. of park trails are maintained by the staff of Baxter State Park Authority and volunteers. All trails are blazed with blue paint; the only exception is the white-blazed AT.

Katahdin (5,268 ft.)

Katahdin is a great, irregular-shaped mountain mass that rises abruptly from comparatively flat terrain to a gently sloping plateau above the treeline. The massif culminates on its southeastern margin in a series of low summits, of which the southern two are the highest. These peaks are 0.3 mi. apart, and Baxter Peak (5,268 ft.) to the northwest is the higher of the two. From the southeastern South Peak (5,240 ft.), a long, serrated ridge of vertically fractured granite, known as Knife Edge, curves away to the east and northeast. About 0.7 mi. from South Peak, this ridge ends in a rock spire called Chimney Peak. Immediately beyond Chimney Peak, and separated from it by a sharp cleft, is the broader peak of Pamola Peak (4,919 ft.), named for the spirit that inhabited the mountain according to American Indian mythology. To the east is the tableland, a broad open plateau of alpine terrain ranging from Baxter Peak to Thoreau Spring and The Gateway north to The Saddle. North of The Saddle, the wide mass of Hamlin Peak (4,756 ft.) rises above the tableland, which ends at Howe Peak (4,750 ft.) and the Northwest Plateau.

The first recorded ascent of Katahdin was in 1804 by a party of eleven, including Charles Turner Jr., who wrote an account of the trip. There may have been unrecorded ascents during the next fifteen years, but it is known the mountain was climbed again in 1819 and 1820. After this date, ascents became more regular.

The tableland is nearly 4 mi. long and drops away abruptly by 1,000 to 2,000 ft. on all sides. After that, the slope becomes gentler. Great ridges extend out and around to encompass a series of glacial cirques, or basins. Great Basin and its branch, South Basin, are the best known. In the floor of the latter, at an elevation of 2,914 ft., Chimney Pond lies flanked by impressive cliffs and bordered by dense spruce and fir forest. It is about 8 acres in size and is a base for many and varied mountain climbs. North of Great Basin, but still on the eastern side of the mountain, is North Basin at an elevation of 3,100 ft., where high mountain walls surround a barren, boulder-strewn floor. Nearby Little North Basin is trailless and sees few visitors. On the western side of the tableland, remote Northwest Basin lies at about 2,800 ft., and farther south is a broad valley known as the Klondike. Klondike Pond rests in a small glacial arm of this valley, just below the plateau, at 3,435 ft. The pond is 0.3 mi. long, deep, narrow, and remarkably beautiful.

From the peaks at its northern and southern ends, the tableland slopes gradually toward the center, known as The Saddle. From the eastern escarpment of The Saddle, the land falls off gently toward the dense scrub that carpets the northwestern edge. Many avalanches have scored the walls of the tableland, but only two of these scorings are now trails—Saddle Slide at the western end of Great Basin and the Abol Slide on the southwestern flank of the mountain.

The isolated location of Katahdin allows for exceptional views that take in dozens of lakes and ponds, including Moosehead Lake, the many windings of the Penobscot River, and, to the south, the peaks of Mt. Desert Island and the Camden Hills on the coast. To the west are the mountains along the AT corridor; Whitecap, the Bigelows, and Mt. Abraham are among the peaks visible. Katahdin is the northern terminus of the 2,180-mi. AT, which follows Hunt Trail on Katahdin itself. West of Katahdin, across the Klondike, are found The Owl, Barren Mtn., Mt. OJI, Mt. Coe,

South Brother, North Brother, and Fort Mtn. On the west side of Neso-wadnehunk Stream is the twin-peaked Doubletop Mtn.; Sentinel Mtn. Mullen Mtn. and Wasstaquoik Mtn. lie in the remote area between Fort Mtn. and Wassataquoik Lake. Sprawling Traveler Mtn. is the principal mountain in the northern section of the park. South Branch ponds and campground lie at its western base. Turner Mtn. is to the northeast of Ka-tahdin and offers fantastic views. The magnificent Katahdin Lake lies at the base of Katahdin massif just to the east.

Katahdin Stream Campground

This campground is situated on Katahdin Stream at the base of Katahdin on its southwestern flank, 7.7 mi. from Togue Pond Gate. Facilities include twelve lean-tos and ten tentsites. Nearby Foster Field Group Area (2.6 mi. north) has a capacity of 50 people. The AT enters Katahdin Stream Camp-ground and merges with Hunt Trail on its way to the summit of Katah-din. A variety of other day hikes are possible from this location: to Katah-din Stream Falls; The Owl; Tracy, Elbow, Daicey, and Grassy ponds; and Blueberry Ledges.

Hunt Trail

The white-blazed Hunt Trail is the route of the AT up Katahdin and climbs the mountain from the southwest. The trail was first cut in 1900 by Irving O. Hunt, who operated a sporting camp on Nesowadnehunk Stream. The trail leaves from Katahdin Stream Campground. From the treeline to the tableland, this trail is long, steep, and rough.

The trail follows the northern side of Katahdin Stream. At 1.1 mi. from the campground, Hunt Trail passes the trail to The Owl on the left, then crosses Katahdin Stream. Soon after, a short spur trail departs left to Katahdin Stream Falls. Hunt Trail steepens through the spruce and fir for-est and, at 2.7 mi., reaches two large rocks that form a cave. A spring (un-dependable in dry periods) is 50 yd. up the trail from this feature.

The trail passes through a growth of small spruce and fir and, in 0.2 mi., emerges on Hunt Spur, a bare, steep crest on the southwestern shoulder of the mountain. Here, cairns mark the trail, which proceeds to wind among huge boulders. Iron rungs and ladders aid the ascent in places. The trail then traverses a broad shelf and climbs steeply 0.5 mi. over broken rock to the open tableland at 3.7 mi., where two slabs of rock mark the "Gateway."

The trail continues east, following a worn path and paint blazes, until it reaches Thoreau Spring at 4.5 mi., an unreliable water source. At the spring, Baxter Peak Cutoff trail goes off to the left and reaches Saddle Trail in 0.9 mi. To the right, Abol Trail descends 3.2 mi. to Abol Campground. From the spring, Hunt Trail climbs moderately northeast for 1.0 mi. to the summit of Baxter Peak, with its commanding panoramas and outstanding views of South Basin, Chimney Pond, and Knife Edge.

Note: A traverse of Katahdin from Katahdin Stream Campground to Chimney Pond and Roaring Brook campgrounds is a long, arduous route and should be attempted only by experienced hikers in excellent physical condition. Such a hike would require spotting a vehicle at Roaring Brook because no shuttle service is available. Backpacking with overnight gear from one side of Katahdin to the other is not recommended by park staff. Bivouacking on the mountain is not allowed, and visitors are responsible for their own group safety as well as rescue costs if found hiking in violation of park regulations.

Hunt Trail (AMC map 1: E2–E3)

Distances from Katahdin Stream Campground (1,099 ft.) to
- Owl Trail jct. (1,500 ft.): 1.1 mi., 45 min.
- Thoreau Spring and jct. Abol Trail and Baxter Peak Cutoff (4,650 ft.): 4.5 mi., 4 hr. 15 min.
- Baxter Peak (5,268 ft.): 5.5 mi., 5 hr.

Abol Campground

This campground is situated on Abol Stream at the foot of Abol Slide on the southwest side of Katahdin, 5.7 mi. from Togue Pond Gate. Facilities include twelve lean-tos and nine tentsites.

Abol Trail leaves from the campground and climbs the 1816 slide, which offers the shortest and most direct—albeit difficult—route to the tableland below the summit of Katahdin. A side trail to Little Abol Falls offers a pleasant short walk.

Abol Trail

Abol Trail is believed to be the oldest route up Katahdin, and evidence exists that the first recorded ascent took place near this trail. It follows a great slide up the southwestern side of the mountain. (*Note:* This route is steep and entails hiking over a large amount of loose rock and gravel in the slide. Please climb and descend with great care.)

The trail leaves Park Tote Rd. at Abol Campground. The trail passes through the campground and, at 0.2 mi., enters an old tote road to reach the southern bank of a tributary of Abol Stream. Abol Trail continues along the stream for 0.6 mi., before the trail bears sharply right (northeast) away from the brook. The trail reaches a gravel wash of old Abol Slide (1.3 mi.) and climbs to reach a second slide at 1.9 mi. Beyond this point, the route is steeper and is almost entirely bare rock and loose gravel. Large boulders and increasing steepness mark the latter part of this climb. Upon reaching the tableland, the trail leads 0.1 mi. to Thoreau Spring (unreliable water source) and the jct. with Hunt Trail at 3.2 mi. Turn right on Hunt Trail and continue northeast up gentler slopes to the summit at Baxter Peak, which is reached in an additional 1.0 mi.

Note: It is possible to make a long but rewarding circuit using Hunt and Abol trails. This would require either leaving cars at both the Abol and Katahdin Stream campgrounds or walking the 2.0 mi. between them on Park Tote Rd. Ascent via Abol Trail is recommended.

Abol Trail (AMC map 1: E3)

Distances from Abol Campground (1,300 ft.) to
- Thoreau Spring and Hunt Trail jct. (4,650 ft.): 3.2 mi., 3 hr. 20 min.
- Baxter Peak (5,268 ft.) (via Hunt Trail): 4.2 mi., 4 hr. 5 min.
- Katahdin Stream Campground (1,099 ft.) (via Hunt Trail): 9.7 mi., 9 hr. 30 min.

Little Abol Falls Trail

This short, scenic trail leads easily from Abol Campground to a series of falls on Abol Stream. Views of Katahdin are possible en route.

Little Abol Falls Trail (AMC map 1: E3)

Distance from Abol Campground (1,300 ft.) to
- Little Abol Falls (1,550 ft.): 0.8 mi., 30 min.

Roaring Brook Campground

This campground is situated on the southern bank of Roaring Brook at the terminus of Roaring Brook Rd., 8.1 mi. from Togue Pond Gate. Facilities include nine lean-tos, ten tentsites, several walk-in sites, and a 10-person bunkhouse. Nearby Bear Brook Group Site has three campsites with a capacity of 42 persons. The campground is the base for ascending Katahdin from the east and for backpacking into the southern interior of the park. Trails to Chimney Pond and Russell Pond start here. Closer by are Sandy Stream Pond, where hikers can often see moose and other wildlife, and South Turner Mtn.

Helon Taylor Trail

This trail offers a direct route from Roaring Brook Campground to Pamola Peak and follows the exposed Keep Ridge. The trail provides the most sustained views of any trail on Katahdin. Hikers on this route are exposed to the elements for most of the climb. Consider avoiding this trail in bad weather, particularly if hiking plans include Baxter Peak via Knife Edge.

The trail leaves left (south) from Chimney Pond Trail at a point 0.1 mi. west of Roaring Brook Campground. Helon Taylor Trail climbs 0.5 mi. through mixed growth to a ridge crest, then levels off for a short period, passing through scrub and a boulder field. After that, the trail climbs steeply through small birch, enters an old flat burn, and drops to the small Bear Brook, one of the branches of Avalanche Brook, and the only water on the trail.

Beyond, the trail ascends steeply through scrub, a fine stand of conifers, and a boulder field with wide views in all directions. The trail then climbs over and between boulders to Keep Ridge and then along the open ridge with spectacular views ahead to Knife Edge, north to Basin Ponds and South Turner Mtn., and east to Katahdin Lake. The trail reaches the summit of Pamola at 3.6 mi. and excellent views of Baxter Peak, Great Basin, Chimney Pond, and the high peaks of the Katahdin massif.

Helon Taylor Trail (AMC map 1: D4–E4)

Distances from Roaring Brook Campground (1,489 ft.) to
- start (1,550 ft.) (via Chimney Pond Trail): 0.1 mi., 5 min.
- Pamola Peak summit (4,919 ft.) and Dudley and Knife Edge jct.: 3.6 mi., 3 hr. 30 min.
- Baxter Peak (5,268 ft.) via Knife Edge: 4.7 mi., 5 hr. 15 min.
- Chimney Pond Campground (2,914 ft.) (via Knife Edge and Cathedral Trail): 6.2 mi., 7 hr. 15 min.

Chimney Pond Trail

This trail begins at the ranger cabin at Roaring Brook Campground. Just ahead, Russell Pond Trail leaves right (leads 6.6 mi. to Russell Pond), and at 0.1 mi., Helon Taylor Trail leaves left (leads 3.6 mi. to Pamola Peak). Continuing on, Chimney Pond Trail climbs west along the south bank of Roaring Brook. After 0.6 mi., the trail bears gradually away from the brook and climbs more steeply. A brook, the outlet of Pamola Pond, is crossed at 1.0 mi.

Lower Basin Pond is reached at 1.9 mi., and a short side trail to the right leads to the pond. At 2.0 mi., the trail goes left uphill into the woods. At 2.1 mi., North Basin Cutoff leaves to the right. Ahead, pass a depression known as Dry Pond, which holds water in spring and after heavy rains. At 2.8 mi., North Basin Trail to Hamlin Ridge and North Basin leaves to the right. At 3.0 mi., enter a small clearing. Beyond, the trail proceeds gently downhill through Chimney Pond Campground to the ranger cabin at Chimney Pond.

Chimney Pond Trail (AMC map 1: D4, E4)

Distances from Roaring Brook Campground (1,489 ft.) to
- Brook crossing (1,900 ft.): 1.0 mi., 35 min.
- North Basin Cutoff jct. (2,500 ft.): 2.1 mi., 1 hr. 30 min.

- North Basin Trail jct. (2,850 ft.): 2.8 mi., 2 hr. 20 min.
- Chimney Pond Campground (2,914 ft.): 3.0 mi., 2 hr. 30 min.

Chimney Pond Campground

This campground, the oldest in the park, is situated in a spectacular setting on the shore of Chimney Pond in Katahdin's South Basin, where the walls of the mountain rise more than 2,000 ft. to the high summits of Baxter and Pamola peaks. The campground is accessible only via a 3.2-mi. hike from Roaring Brook Campground. Facilities include nine lean-tos and a ten-person bunkhouse. Open fires are not allowed at Chimney Pond, so campers must use a portable backpacking stove. Saddle, Cathedral, and Dudley trails leave from Chimney Pond and ascend to the high summits and ridges of Katahdin: Baxter Peak, Knife Edge, and Pamola Peak. Nearby Hamlin Ridge Trail leads to Hamlin Peak, and North Basin Trail leads to the basin and Blueberry Knoll.

Dudley Trail

This trail ascends from Chimney Pond to Pamola Peak via its north ridge. The trail starts from the ranger cabin and heads east to cross the outlet of the pond, then bears right, climbs over huge boulders, and reenters the woods. At 0.3 mi. from the pond, a side trail leads left 0.4 mi. to Pamola Caves, where visitors must wiggle through small, winding passages to reach three remarkably straight, spacious corridors.

Dudley Trail continues east from the jct. to reach a major cleft in the cliffs. Beyond, the trail climbs steeply to emerge into the open at treeline and onto a well-worn path that traverses patches of heath and krummholz. The trail bears slightly right (southwest) nearly to the edge of South Basin, then heads south again up the long north slope of Pamola Peak, where huge boulders rival those on Hunt Trail. Beyond the boulders, the going gets easier. Pass to the right of Index Rock, a prominent fingerlike boulder, at 1.0 mi. Ahead, continue at a more gradual angle to reach the summit of Pamola at 1.4 mi. and the jct. with Helon Taylor and Knife Edge trails.

Dudley Trail (AMC map 1: E4)

Distances from Chimney Pond Campground (2,910 ft.) to
- side trail to Pamola Caves (3,050 ft.): 0.3 mi., 15 min.
- Pamola Caves (via side trail) (3,200 ft.): 0.7 mi., 1 hr.
- Pamola Peak summit (4,919 ft.) and Helon Taylor and Knife Edge jct.: 1.4 mi., 2 hr.
- Baxter Peak (5,268 ft.) via Knife Edge: 2.5 mi., 3 hr. 45 min.
- Chimney Pond Campground (via Saddle Trail): 4.5 mi., 5 hr. 45 min.
- Chimney Pond Campground (via Cathedral Trail): 4.5 mi., 5 hr. 45 min.

Knife Edge

This long, narrow, serrated ridge tops the southern wall of South Basin and connects South Peak with Pamola Peak. Steep cliffs plummet more than 2,000 ft. into South Basin to the north, and in places, the ridge narrows to only 2 or 3 ft. The narrow ridge, the dizzying height, and the sheer cliffs create a hike with extreme exposure and combine to make this is one of the most spectacular mountain trails in the East.

From the summit of Pamola, follow cairns leading southwest before dropping abruptly into the sharp cleft at the top of The Chimney. The trail then climbs the equally steep rock tower of Chimney Peak (4,900 ft.), using several iron bars as an aid. Beyond, the trail takes an undulating route over a series of rocky knobs before descending to the low point of the ridge. The trail then climbs steeply to South Peak (5,240 ft.) and from there continues along the spine of the summit ridge to Baxter Peak.

Note: Knife Edge is completely exposed and can be hazardous in bad weather. Under no circumstances should hikers leave the trail, as there are no safe alternate routes. Over the years, a number of attempts at shortcuts down to Chimney Pond have had tragic results. Knife Edge is not recommended for persons with a fear of heights.

Knife Edge (AMC map 1: E3–E4)

Distance from Pamola Peak summit (4,919 ft.) and Helon Taylor and Dudley jct. to
- Baxter Peak (5,268 ft.): 1.1 mi., 1 hr. 45 min.

Cathedral Trail

This trail provides the shortest route to Baxter Peak from Chimney Pond, climbing past the three immense, columnar Cathedral Rocks on its route to the summit. From the ranger cabin at Chimney Pond, the trail climbs through thick forest to reach Cleftrock Pool on the right at 0.3 mi. At 0.4 mi., by a large cairn, the trail turns right toward the Cathedrals, crosses a bridge of rock covered with low growth, climbs steeply through boulders to a highpoint, and from there, continues upward through low trees.

Blazes mark the way around to the right, then up the steep side of the first Cathedral (0.8 mi.). The climb of the second Cathedral is interesting and offers spectacular views of The Chimney and Knife Edge. The route continues to the top of the third Cathedral. Ahead, at 1.5 mi., the trail forks. The right (west) fork is Cathedral Cutoff (leads 0.2 mi. to Saddle Trail). Cathedral Trail bears left (south) 0.3 mi. over large boulders to join Saddle Trail at 1.8 mi. Baxter Peak is reached at 2.0 mi.

Cathedral Trail (AMC map 1: E3–E4)

Distances from Chimney Pond Campground (2,914 ft.) to
- Cathedral Cutoff jct. (4,700 ft.): 1.5 mi., 2 hr. 20 min.
- Saddle Trail jct. (5,150 ft.): 1.8 mi., 2 hr. 35 min.
- Baxter Peak (5,268 ft.) (via Saddle Trail): 2.0 mi., 2 hr. 45 min.
- Chimney Pond Campground (via Saddle Trail): 4.5 mi., 4 hr. 45 min.
- Chimney Pond Campground (via Knife Edge and Dudley Trail): 4.5 mi., 5 hr. 15 min.
- Roaring Brook Campground (1,489 ft.) (via Knife Edge and Helon Taylor Trail): 6.7 mi., 6 hr.

Saddle Trail

Climbers have taken this general route out of South Basin since Saddle Slide occurred in 1899. Saddle Trail offers a moderate route up Katahdin from Chimney Pond. From the ranger cabin, the worn trail climbs a rocky path through dense softwoods. Beyond, the trail swings to the right (north) and becomes easier underfoot and more gradual. It crosses Saddle Brook at 0.8 mi., and then climbs steeply over large boulders. At 0.9 mi., the trail bears left up Saddle Slide and passes through stunted birches. At

1.0 mi., the trail emerges into the open and climbs for 0.2 mi. up the loose rocks and gravel of the slide.

At 1.4 mi., the trail reaches the top of the slide and gains the level, open tableland of The Saddle between Baxter and Hamlin peaks and a trail jct. To the right (north), Northwest Basin Trail leads to Hamlin Ridge Trail, North Peaks Trail, Northwest Basin, and eventually to Russell Pond. To the left (south), Saddle Trail continues south over moderate slopes, and cairns mark the well-worn path. At 1.9 mi., the trail passes a large boulder and a jct. To the left (east), Cathedral Cutoff connects after 0.3 mi. to Cathedral Trail. To the right (west), Baxter Peak Cutoff contours southwest along the base of the summit cone for 0.9 mi. to connect with Abol and Hunt trails at Thoreau Spring. Continuing on, Cathedral Trail from Chimney Pond enters on the left at 2.3 mi. Ahead, Saddle Trail climbs to Baxter Peak at 2.5 mi.

Saddle Trail (AMC map 1: E3–E4)

Distances from Chimney Pond Campground (2,914 ft.) to

- Saddle and Northwest Basin Trail jct. (4,250 ft.): 1.4 mi., 1 hr. 25 min.
- Cathedral Cutoff and Baxter Peak Cutoff jct. (4,700 ft.): 1.9 mi., 1 hr. 55 min.
- Baxter Peak (5,268 ft.): 2.5 mi., 2 hr. 30 min.
- Chimney Pond Campground (via Cathedral Trail): 4.5 mi., 4 hr. 30 min.
- Chimney Pond Campground (via Knife Edge and Dudley Trail): 5.0 mi., 5 hr.
- Roaring Brook Campground (1,489 ft.) (via Knife Edge and Helon Taylor Trail): 7.2 mi., 6 hr. 15 min.

Baxter Peak Cutoff

This trail leaves Saddle Trail 1.7 mi. from Chimney Pond and leads southwest over the open tableland along the base of Baxter Peak, ending at Thoreau Spring and the jct. of Hunt and Abol trails, making it possible to hike a loop over Baxter Peak. In addition, the cutoff provides an alternative path to a safer descent trail if you are caught on the mountain in bad weather.

Baxter Peak Cutoff (AMC map 1: E3)

Distances from Chimney Pond Campground (2,914 ft.) to

- start of cutoff (4,700 ft.) (via Saddle Trail): 1.9 mi., 1 hr. 55 min.
- Thoreau Spring (Hunt Trail and Abol Trail jct.) (4,650 ft.): 2.8 mi., 2 hr. 25 min.

North Basin Trail

From Chimney Pond, follow Chimney Pond Trail northeast toward Basin Ponds. At 0.2 mi., North Basin Trail starts on the left (north) and runs through spruce-fir forest to a jct. with Hamlin Ridge Trail on the left (west) at 0.6 mi. It then passes across the foot of Hamlin Ridge to a jct. (signs, large cairn) with North Basin Cutoff Trail at 0.8 mi. Ahead, North Basin Trail continues to the lip of North Basin and then reaches Blueberry Knoll at 1.0 mi., where there is a sweeping view of both the North and South basins as well as the landscape to the east.

North Basin Trail (AMC map 1: D4)

Distances from Chimney Pond Campground (2,914 ft.) to
- start of trail (2,850 ft.) (via Chimney Pond Trail): 0.2 mi., 10 min.
- North Basin Cutoff jct. (3,000 ft.): 0.8 mi., 30 min.
- Blueberry Knoll (3,050 ft.): 1.0 mi., 45 min.
- Roaring Brook Campground (1,489 ft.) (via North Basin Cutoff and Chimney Pond trails): 3.6 mi., 2 hr. 45 min.

North Basin Cutoff

This trail from Basin Ponds to Hamlin Ridge and North Basin forks right (sign) at a point 2.1 mi. from the Roaring Brook Campground on Chimney Pond Trail. The cutoff traverses an area of second-growth softwoods, goes past several active beaver ponds, and then climbs steeply through old growth to a jct. with North Basin Trail at 0.7 mi. To reach Hamlin Ridge, turn left (southwest). To reach Blueberry Knoll and North Basin, turn right (northeast).

North Basin Cutoff (AMC map 1: D4)

Distances from Roaring Brook Campground (1,489 ft.) to
- start of trail (via Chimney Pond Trail) (2,500 ft.): 2.1 mi., 1 hr. 30 min.
- North Basin Trail jct. (3,000 ft.): 2.8 mi., 2 hr. 25 min.
- Blueberry Knoll (3,050 ft.) (via North Basin Trail): 3.0 mi., 2 hr. 35 min.
- Hamlin Ridge Trail (3,000 ft.) (via North Basin Trail): 3.2 mi., 2 hr. 25 min.
- Chimney Pond Campground (2,914 ft.) (via North Basin and Chimney Pond trails): 3.8 mi., 2 hr. 55 min.

Hamlin Ridge Trail

The trail climbs largely in the open up Hamlin Ridge, which separates North and South basins. The views are superb. From Chimney Pond Campground, follow Chimney Pond Trail 0.2 mi. to North Basin Trail. Follow this for 0.4 mi. to the start of Hamlin Ridge Trail.

Hamlin Ridge Trail reaches treeline after about 20 min. of climbing. After a short stretch of boulder-strewn slope, the trail rises to the ridge proper, then ascends moderately, following the open ridge to Hamlin Peak (4,756 ft.) and a jct. at 2.1 mi. From here, North Peaks Trail leads right (north) for 1.2 mi. to the 4,750-ft. summit of Howe Peak.

Beyond Hamlin Peak, Hamlin Ridge Trail leads 0.2 mi. west across the open tableland and through a boulder field to Caribou Spring (unreliable) and another trail jct. at 2.3 mi. To the right, Hamlin Peak Cutoff leads along the headwall of North Basin and reaches the 4,750 ft. summit of Howe Peak in about 1.0 mi. To the left (south), Northwest Basin Trail leads 0.9 mi. to meet Saddle Trail.

Hamlin Ridge Trail (AMC map 1: D3–D4)

Distances from Chimney Pond Campground (2,914 ft.) to
- start of trail (2,850 ft.) (via Chimney Pond and North Basin trails): 0.6 mi., 20 min.
- Hamlin Peak (4,756 ft.): 2.1 mi., 2 hr. 30 min.
- Caribou Spring (4,650 ft.): 2.3 mi., 2 hr. 40 min.

Hamlin Peak Cutoff

Following a good path along the contour, this trail connects North Peaks Trail with Northwest Basin Trail at Caribou Spring. It is 0.2 mi. in length.

Northwest Basin Trail

This route climbs from near Russell Pond to The Saddle through the wild and secluded Northwest Basin, with its old-growth trees, glacial sheepback rocks, five ponds, waterfalls, and interesting central ridge.

The trail diverges right (west) from Russell Pond Trail at a point 0.1 mi. from Russell Pond Campground, and soon crosses a dam at the foot of Turner Deadwater. From there, Northwest Basin Trail proceeds through the woods to join the route of the old Wassataquoik Tote Rd. With Wassataquoik Stream on the left, the trail stays on the tote road and climbs gradually, crossing Annis Brook. Beyond, the trail crosses a small brook draining the eastern slope of Fort Mtn. and continues through thick woods to cross Wassataquoik Stream. (*Note:* Use caution at high water.)

The trail climbs steadily, soon approaching Northwest Basin Brook and following along it for a short distance. Above the jct. of the outlets from Lake Cowles and Davis Pond, the trail climbs steeply to the north shore of Lake Cowles. The trail then turns left and crosses the outlet of Lake Cowles. Ahead, the trail climbs to a heath-covered glacial sheepback rock, where there are enjoyable views of the entire basin. The trail continues down to the Davis Pond Lean-to, situated on the north side of Davis Pond, at 5.2 mi.

From Davis Pond Lean-to, the trail first goes southwest and then south as it climbs through a steep and rough area up the basin wall. The trail emerges from the scrub and reaches a large cairn that marks a small peak (4,410 ft.) near the west end of Northwest Plateau, a level extension of the northern tableland separating the basin from Klondike Pond Ravine and reaching far out into the Klondike. Beyond, the trail climbs gradually across the plateau, passing through a belt of scrub growth. The trail then continues more to the south across open tableland to Caribou Spring, which is reached at 7.6 mi. Here, Hamlin Peak Cutoff leads sharply left (north) to Howe Peak via North Peaks Trail, and Hamlin Ridge Trail climbs left (east) to Hamlin Peak in 0.2 mi. Beyond the spring, the trail descends to the south and, at 8.5 mi., merges with Saddle Trail in The Saddle.

Northwest Basin Trail (AMC map 1: D3–D4, E3)
Distances from Russell Pond Campground (1,333 ft.) to
- Davis Pond Lean-to (2,950 ft.): 5.2 mi., 3 hr. 15 min.
- Hamlin Ridge Trail and Hamlin Peak Cutoff at Caribou Spring (4,650 ft.): 7.6 mi., 5 hr. 35 min.
- Saddle Trail jct. at The Saddle (4,250 ft.): 8.5 mi., 6 hr.

Russell Pond Trail

This trail extends from Roaring Brook Campground northward to Russell Pond Campground through the valley of Wassataquoik Stream between

Katahdin and Turner Mtn. The trail is the principal approach to the Russell Pond area.

Soon after leaving Roaring Brook Campground, the trail crosses a bridge over Roaring Brook. At 0.1 mi., the trail turns left (northwest). To the right, Sandy Stream Trail leads to Sandy Stream Pond and on to South Turner Mtn. via South Turner Trail. In the next 0.5 mi., Russell Pond Trail crosses several brooks while gradually climbing to the low height-of-land between Sandy Stream Pond and Whidden Pond. The trail then descends and passes east (right) of the latter, where an extensive view of the basins and peaks on the east side of Katahdin can be seen. At 1.1 mi., Sandy Stream Pond Trail joins from the right. Ahead, an open area yields good views. Beyond, Russell Pond Trail moves into denser forest and crosses several brooks, and at 3.1 mi., the trail reaches a jct. on the right with Wassataquoik Stream Trail (leads 2.3 mi. to Wassataquoik Stream Campsite and rejoins Russell Pond Trail in 3.6 mi.).

Ahead, Russell Pond Trail crosses the South Branch of Wassataquoik and soon crosses another brook. (*Note:* No bridges are available here. The crossing is knee-deep in dry weather, and in wet weather, the high-water crossing can be hazardous.)

The trail, now on the west side of the valley, passes under an overhanging rock. Moving away from Wassataquoik Stream, the trail passes several brooks and springs and climbs gently for about 2 mi. It then descends gradually to cross the main branch of Wassataquoik Stream at 6.3 mi. At 6.5 mi., Russell Pond Trail crosses the old Wassataquoik Tote Rd. and passes a clearing on the right. At a jct., Wassataquoik Stream Trail leads right (east) 1.3 mi. to Wassataquoik Stream Campsite. Immediately beyond the tote road, Russell Pond Trail crosses Turner Brook. At 6.7 mi., Northwest Basin Trail to The Saddle leaves to the left (west). Soon after, Russell Pond Trail reaches Russell Pond.

Russell Pond Trail (AMC map 1: D4)

Distances from Roaring Brook Campground (1,489 ft.) to
- Sandy Stream Pond Trail jct. (1,550 ft.): 1.1 mi., 30 min.
- Wassataquoik Stream Trail jct. (1,500 ft.): 3.1 mi., 1 hr. 40 min.
- Wassataquoik Tote Rd. jct. (1,350 ft.): 6.3 mi., 3 hr. 10 min.
- Northwest Basin Trail jct. (1,350 ft.): 6.7 mi., 3 hr. 40 min.
- Russell Pond Campground (1,333 ft.): 6.8 mi., 3 hr. 45 min.

Wassataquoik Stream Trail

Formerly known as Tracy Horse Trail or Wassataquoik South Branch Trail, this trail runs from Russell Pond Trail along the South Branch of Wassataquoik Stream to the main branch of Wassataquoik Stream. Wassataquoik Stream Trail leaves on the right (east) side of Russell Pond Trail 3.1 mi. north of Roaring Brook Campground, just before that trail crosses the South Branch (*Caution:* Hazardous during high water). Wassataquoik Stream Trail then leads 2.3 mi. to the jct. with the main stream and continues along its southern bank for about 100 yd. Wassataquoik Stream Campsite is located here at the site of the old Hersey Dam (some remains of the dam are still visible).

Continuing to Russell Pond, cross to the north side of Wassataquoik Stream upstream from the lean-tos (no bridge) and merge with the old Wassataquoik Tote Rd. and the jct. with Grand Falls Trail (leads 1.6 mi. to Inscription Rock, 2.0 mi. to Grand Falls, and 3.8 mi. to the north side of Russell Pond). Beyond this jct., Wassataquoik Stream Trail reaches a jct. with Russell Pond Trail at 3.6 mi., just south of the Turner Brook crossing. Turn right on Russell Pond Trail to reach the campground at 4.1 mi.

Wassataquoik Stream Trail (AMC map 1: D4)
Distances from Roaring Brook Campground (1,500 ft.) to
- start of trail (1,500 ft.) (via Russell Pond Trail): 3.1 mi., 1 hr. 40 min.
- Wassataquoik Stream Campsite (1,250 ft.): 5.4 mi., 3 hr.
- Russell Pond Campground (1,333 ft.) (via Russell Pond Trail): 7.2 mi., 3 hr. 45 min.

Russell Pond Campground

Located on the southwestern shore of Russell Pond (1,333 ft.) in the heart of the wilderness north of Katahdin, this campground makes a convenient hiking base for exploring the interior of the park. The wildlife in this remote area is especially intriguing. Facilities include three tentsites, five lean-tos, and an eight-person bunkhouse. Little Wassataquoik and Island Campsite on Wassataquoik Lake, and Wassataquoik Stream and Pogy Pond backcountry campsites are easily reached from Russell Pond. Short trails lead to Caverly Lookout, Grand Falls, Six Ponds, and Wassataquoik Lake.

Wassataquoik Lake Trail

This trail connects Russell Pond Campground with the Wassataquoik Lake area and continues on to the west to Park Tote Rd. at Nesowadnehunk Field Day Use Site just east of Nesowadnehunk Field Campground.

The trail diverges northwest from Pogy Notch Trail at a point 0.2 mi. from Russell Pond. At 0.5 mi., take the left fork (the right fork leads to Deep Pond). At 1.5 mi., the trail crosses a dam between two of the Six Ponds. Beyond, it crosses a brook, and at 2.2 mi., a side trail leads right (north) 300 ft. to a canoe landing for Island Campsite on Wassataquoik Lake.

Ahead, the trail follows the south shore of the lake. About halfway along, a trail leads left (south) uphill to beautiful Green Falls. Near the north end of Wassataquoik Lake, the trail joins an old road. After crossing the outlet stream from Little Wassataquoik Lake several times, the trail reaches the lake itself and follows the west shore. Shortly after leaving the lake, the trail passes Little Wassataquoik Lake Campsite at 4.8 mi.

Beyond, the trail rises to a height-of-land and then descends into the Trout Brook drainage area, following an old tote road for about 1.5 mi. before leaving the road and turning left. Wet in places, the trail crosses a brook several times and, at 7.7 mi., passes Center Mtn. Campsite and crosses the South Branch of Trout Brook. The trail then skirts a series of small hills to reach Center Pond, with fine views of the Brothers. Several miles beyond the pond, the trail reaches and follows Little Nesowadnehunk Stream to a ford. Cross and follow the south bank to Park Tote Rd. at 13.5 mi.

Wassataquoik Lake Trail (AMC map 1: C2–C4, D2, D4)

Distances from Russell Pond Campground (1,333 ft.) to
- start (via Pogy Notch Trail) (1,350 ft.): 0.2 mi., 5 min.
- Deep Pond side trail jct. (1,350 ft.): 0.5 mi., 20 min.
- side trail to Wassataquoik Lake (1,350 ft.): 2.2 mi., 1 hr. 10 min.
- Green Falls (1,450 ft.) (via side trail): 3.1 mi., 1 hr. 45 min.
- Little Wassataquoik Lake Campsite (1,600 ft.): 4.8 mi., 3 hr. 10 min.
- Center Mtn. Campsite (1,600 ft.): 7.7 mi., 4 hr. 20 min.
- Park Tote Rd. at Nesowadnehunk Field Campground (1,300 ft.): 13.5 mi., 6 hr. 15 min.

Grand Falls Trail

This trail leads from Russell Pond Campground to several interesting locations in Wassataquoik Valley. From the campground, follow Pogy Notch Trail around the west shore of the pond. Wassataquoik Lake Trail leaves to the left soon after the start of the route. Just ahead, at a jct. at 0.2 mi., Pogy Notch Trail continues north (left), and Grand Falls Trail heads right, passes the ranger station, and continues to the next jct. at 0.4 mi. Here, Caverly Lookout Trail leaves to the left (north) and leads 0.9 mi. to a viewpoint.

To the right, Grand Falls Trail continues ahead through woods and over relatively level ground, passing Bell Pond. At a jct. close to Wassataquoik Stream at 2.0 mi., a side trail leaves to the left (north) and follows the north side of the stream 0.4 mi. to Grand Falls, which drops steeply between high granite walls. The ruins of a logging dam lie just upstream. From the same jct., another side trail to the right leads 50 ft. to the bank of the stream and Inscription Rock, a huge boulder inscribed with a historical 1883 notice about logging in the area.

Beyond, Grand Falls Trail follows the west bank of Wassataquoik Stream, passing Ledge Falls and a side trail to Wassataquoik Stream Campsite, to meet Wassataquoik Stream Trail at the South Branch of Wassataquoik Stream at 3.6 mi.

Grand Falls Trail (AMC map 1: C4, D4)

Distances from Russell Pond Campground (1,333 ft.) to

- Caverly Lookout Trail jct. (via Pogy Notch Trail) (1,350 ft.): 0.4 mi., 10 min.
- Inscription Rock (1,150 ft.) (via side trail): 2.0 mi., 1 hr. 20 min.
- Grand Falls (via side trail) (1,100 ft.): 2.4 mi., 1 hr. 30 min.
- South Branch of Wassataquoik Stream (1,250 ft.): 3.6 mi., 2 hr.

Caverly Lookout Trail

This high outlook (1,730 ft.) offers views ranging from Traveler Mtn. to Katahdin and is easy to reach from Russell Pond Campground. Follow Pogy Notch and Grand Falls trails for 0.4 mi. and turn left at a jct. Caverly Lookout Trail climbs moderately and steadily for 0.9 mi. to the ledges.

Caverly Lookout Trail (AMC map 1: C4, D4)
Distances from Russell Pond Campground (1,333 ft.) to
  • start of trail (via Pogy Notch and Grand Falls trails) (1,350 ft.): 0.4 mi.,
    10 min.
  • Caverly Lookout ledges (1,730 ft.): 1.3 mi., 50 min.

The Owl (3,670 ft.)

This mountain is the first summit in the long, high range that runs west
and north from Katahdin around The Klondike. The distinctive cliffs on its
southern face overlooking the valley of Katahdin Stream are especially steep.

The Owl Trail

From Katahdin Stream Campground, follow Hunt Trail for 1.1 mi. to a
jct. Here, The Owl Trail leads left at a point just before the crossing of
Katahdin Stream. The trail then follows the north bank of a tributary before turning sharply right (southeast) and crossing the tributary at 1.6 mi.
(last source of water). The trail climbs gradually through dense spruce and
fir and follows the western spur toward the summit. At 2.9 mi., the trail
rises steeply through a ravine and then across the upper part of The Owl's
prominent cliffs. At 3.4 mi., the trail reaches the first outlook. After a more
gradual climb, it reaches the summit at 3.5 mi. Views in all directions are
outstanding, especially those into the Klondike and Witherle Ravine.

The Owl Trail (AMC map 1: E3)
Distances from Katahdin Stream Campground (1,099 ft.) to
  • start of trail (1,500 ft.) (via Hunt Trail): 1.1 mi., 45 min.
  • The Owl summit (3,670 ft.): 3.5 mi. (5.3 km.), 2 hr. 40 min.

Mt. OJI (3,434 ft.)

Mt. OJI got its name from three slides on its southwestern slope that at
one point formed the shape of the three letters. After a major storm in
1932, however, the slides began to enlarge, and the letter shapes have become distorted. A fourth large slide came down in 1954.

Mt. OJI Trail

This trail leaves Park Tote Rd. at Foster Field, directly opposite the access road to Kidney Pond. The trail immediately crosses a brook, and then follows an old road. At 1.8 mi., the trail continues as a narrow trail. As the gravel wash from the slide becomes noticeable on the forest floor, the trail bears right and soon reaches the open wash at 2.0 mi. Climb to the head of the slide and through brush and scrub to the summit ridge and a jct. with OJI Link Trail at 2.9 mi. (leads 0.5 mi. to Mt. Coe Trail at a point 0.5 from Mt. Coe summit). Continue northwest on Mt. OJI Trail to reach the summit at 3.1 mi. From here, a trail leads left an additional 0.3 mi. to Old Jay Eye Rock, a fine observation point.

Another approach to OJI is by climbing the Mt. Coe slide via Marston and Mt. Coe trails to OJI Link Trail, which leads 0.5 mi. from the Mt. Coe slide across the col to a jct. with Mt. OJI Trail 0.2 mi. from the summit.

Mt. OJI Trail (AMC map 1: D2, E2)

Distances from Park Tote Rd. at Foster Field (1,050 ft.) to
- Mt. OJI summit (3,434 ft.): 3.1 mi., 3 hr.
- Old Jay Eye Rock (3,000 ft.): 3.4 mi. 3 hr. 15 min.

North Brother (4,151 ft.) and South Brother (3,970 ft.)

North and South Brother mountains are open peaks that offer splendid views in all directions, especially of the Katahdin massif. (*Caution:* Early in the hiking season, sometimes through mid-June, hikers should expect to find deep snow at the higher elevations in this area, often starting at about 1.5 mi. from the trailhead.)

Marston Trail

This trail is the best approach for exploring the Brothers area. Trailhead parking is found on the east side of Park Tote Rd. at Slide Dam Day Use Site, about 7 mi. north of Katahdin Stream Campground, and about 4 mi. south of Nesowadnehunk Field Campground.

At 0.2 mi., the trail crosses a brook, then bears left and climbs over a slight rise into the drainage area of a second brook. Climbing steadily, the trail follows this brook closely. At 0.8 mi., the trail crosses the brook. Several more crossings appear in the next 0.4 mi. before the trail reaches a jct. with Mt. Coe Trail at 1.3 mi.

Marston Trail leads to the left and climbs gradually through extensive blowdowns. Teardrop Pond is reached at about 2 mi. Beyond the pond's outlet, climb steeply, passing several viewpoints. After leveling off, the trail reaches the upper jct. with Mt. Coe Trail at 3.6 mi. To the right, Mt. Coe Trail leads 0.9 mi. to South Brother via a side trail. To the left, it is 0.9 mi. to North Brother via Marston Trail.

Continuing on Marston Trail, after crossing a fairly level area, the trail passes a spring and then climbs steeply. Ahead, the trail leaves the scrub and continues among open boulders, reaching the summit of North Brother at 4.5 mi. Here are fine views of the western slopes of Katahdin and, in the opposite direction, of the Nesowadnehunk Lake area and Little Nesowadnehunk Stream.

Marston Trail (AMC map 1: D2–D3)

Distances from Park Tote Rd. at Slide Dam (1,150 ft.) to
- Mt. Coe Trail, lower jct. (2,150 ft.): 1.3 mi., 50 min.
- Mt. Coe Trail, upper jct. (3,450 ft.): 3.6 mi., 3 hr. 20 min.
- North Brother summit (4,151 ft.): 4.5 mi., 3 hr. 45 min.

Mt. Coe (3,795 ft.)

This peak, just north of Mt. OJI, has excellent views into the Klondike and is well worth the challenge of the climb. Mt. Coe's high summit ridge provides access to Mt. OJI and South Brother.

Mt. Coe Trail

Follow Marston Trail to the sign 1.3 mi. from Park Tote Rd. Turn right to reach the bottom of the Mt. Coe slide (it follows a stream) at 1.5 mi. Beyond, the climb is steady, moderate at first, then steep. At about 2.6 mi., the trail bears left and climbs the left center of a wide slide area to a jct. at 2.7

mi. with OJI Link Trail (leads right 0.5 mi. to Mt. OJI Trail and 0.2 mi. farther to the summit of OJI).

At about 3 mi., Mt. Coe Trail enters scrub growth. The summit is reached at 3.2 mi. Continuing on, the trail descends the eastern ridge of Coe and proceeds toward South Brother. At 4.2 mi., pass two clearings with fine views of Mt. Coe. At 4.4 mi., a side trail leads right 0.3 mi. to the summit of South Brother. At 5.0 mi., reach the jct. with Marston Trail. Ahead, it is 0.9 mi. to the summit of North Brother. To the left, it is 3.6 mi. to Park Tote Rd. at Slide Dam via Marston Trail.

Mt. Coe Trail (AMC map 1: D2–D3)

Distances from Park Tote Rd. at Slide Dam (1,150 ft.) to

- start of Mt. Coe Trail (via Marston Trail) (2,150 ft.): 1.3 mi., 50 min.
- Mt. Coe summit (3,795 ft.): 3.2 mi., 3 hr. 20 min.
- side trail to South Brother summit (3,600 ft.): 4.4 mi., 4 hr.
- South Brother summit (3,970 ft.) (via side trail): 4.7 mi., 4 hr. 10 min.
- Marston Trail jct. (3,450 ft.): 5.0 mi., 4 hr. 30 min.

Daicey Pond
Daicey Pond Campground

Established as a sporting camp in the early 1900s and operated as York's Twin Pine Camps until 1971, this scenic campground offers outstanding views of the west side of Katahdin, and from a canoe on the pond, fine views may be had of Doubletop Mtn. The campground features ten self-service cabins, a library, canoe and kayak rentals, and trailhead parking.

The AT passes within a short distance of the campground and follows the north shore of the pond for a short distance. South of the pond, the AT passes an old dam on Nesowadnehunk Stream and Little and Big Niagara falls. All are worth seeing and are within an easy walk of the campground. Daicey Pond was once a good starting point for access to Sentinel Mtn. and Kidney Pond; now, only trails to the south and east provide access to other outlying ponds, including Tracey, Elbow, and Grassy.

Sentinel Mtn. (1,842 ft.)

This low mountain rises above the northern bank of the West Branch of the Penobscot River and offers fine views of the west side of Katahdin. Access to the mountain is via Kidney Pond Campground; access from Daicey Pond has been closed.

Sentinel Mtn. Trail

[*Note:* As of this 2014 printing, the portion of Sentinel Mtn. Trail from Daicey Pond is closed as the bridge over Nesowadnehunk Stream is gone and will not be replaced. From Kidney Pond, Sentinel Mtn. Trail now follows the path of former Sentinel Link Trail (see below) on its route to the summit. Access is still available to Lily Pad Pond Trail via Sentinel Landing.]

From Kidney Pond Campground, skirt the west side of Kidney Pond for 0.5 mi. to reach Sentinel Landing. From the landing, the trail leads right (southwest). At 0.8 mi. (sign), the trail bears right onto a section that was relocated to avoid a beaver flow. At 1.2 mi., cross Beaver Brook on stepping stones. The trail climbs the northeast side of the mountain along a brook, which crosses the trail at 1.6 mi. The trail reaches the summit ledges at 2.0 mi. Follow the ledges to the right (north) to reach the true summit at 2.1 mi.

A short 0.5-mi. loop trail on the summit ridge leads to several viewpoints overlooking the West Branch of the Penobscot River.

Access to Lily Pad Pond Trail from Sentinel Landing is still open. From the landing, continue to the left (east) and soon reach Lily Pad Pond Trail at 0.9 mi on the south side of Kidney Pond.

Sentinel Mtn. Trail (AMC map 1: E2)

Distances from Kidney Pond Campground (1,051 ft.) to
- Sentinel Landing (1,087 ft.): 0.5 mi., 15 min.
- Lily Pad Pond Trail via Sentinel Landing: 0.9 mi., 25 min.
- Sentinel Mtn. summit (1,842 ft.): 2.6 mi., 1 hr. 40 min.

Sentinel Link Trail

[*Note:* As of this 2014 printing, Sentinel Link Trail is now the permanent route of Sentinel Mtn. Trail due to the loss of access from Daicey Pond.]

Appalachian Trail to the South

From Daicey Pond at a point just west of the campground on the access road, follow the AT south. At 0.1 mi., Nature Trail leaves left to circumnavigate Daicey Pond in 1.1 mi. Ahead on the AT, reach a side trail to Toll Dam on Nesowadnehunk Stream at 0.9 mi. Just ahead (about 100 yd.), another side trail leads to Little Niagara Falls. At 1.2 mi., reach a side trail leading 200 ft. to Big Niagara Falls. Continuing south, the AT reaches the West Branch of the Penobscot River at Abol Bridge at 7.5 mi.

Appalachian Trail to the South (AMC map 1: E2–E3, F1–F3, MATC map 1)

Distances from Daicey Pond (1,087 ft.) to
- Big Niagara Falls: 1.2 mi., 40 min.
- Abol Bridge (650 ft.): 7.5 mi., 3 hr. 45 min.

Appalachian Trail to the North

From Daicey Pond at a point just west of the campground on the access road, follow the AT north. Climb over a knoll, then descend to the shore of Daicey Pond and follow the AT to a jct. Here, Tracy and Elbow Ponds Trail leaves left, leading 1.0 mi. to Park Tote Rd. Continuing on the AT, the trail follows the pond to a jct. with Nature Trail at 0.6 mi. (leads 0.7 mi. along the south shore of the pond to the campground). Ahead, the AT makes its way through a pleasant mix of forest to a jct. with Grassy Pond Trail at 1.1 mi. (connects with Tracy and Elbow Ponds Trail in 0.8 mi.). Beyond, the AT skirts the south end of Grassy Pond, crosses the outlet, and ends at Park Tote Rd. at the entrance road to Katahdin Stream Campground at 2.1 mi.

Appalachian Trail to the North (AMC map 1: E2–E3, MATC map 1)

Distance from Daicey Pond (1,087 ft.) to
- Park Tote Rd. at Katahdin Stream Campground (1,099 ft.): 2.1 mi., 1 hr. 5 min.

Tracy and Elbow Ponds Trail

This trail departs left (north) from the AT 0.4 mi. from Daicey Pond. The trail climbs over a low ridge before descending to follow along the southeast shore of Elbow Pond. At 0.6 mi., Grassy Pond Trail enters from the right. Ahead, Tracy and Elbow Ponds Trail crosses the outlet of Elbow Pond on a bridge, climbs a knoll, then descends to cross the outlet of Tracy Pond on a bridge. Beyond, the trail follows an esker to meet Park Loop Rd. at 1.0 mi.

Grassy Pond Trail

This short 0.8-mi. trail connects Tracy and Elbow Ponds Trail and the AT and makes a good loop hike from Daicey Pond.

Lost Pond Trail

This trail leaves from Nature Trail on the south shore of Daicey Pond, 0.5 mi. from Daicey Pond Campground, and heads southeast over easy terrain to reach Lost Pond and the jct. with Foss and Knowlton Pond Trail at 1.4 mi.

Nature Trail

This trail leaves Daicey Pond Campground and follows the south shore of the pond. At 0.5 mi., Lost Pond Trail leaves to the right (south). Ahead, Nature Trail ends at its jct. with the AT at 0.7 mi. Turn left (west) here and follow the AT for 0.6 mi. around the north shore of the pond to return to Daicey Pond Campground.

Foss and Knowlton Pond Trail

This trail heads south from Lost Pond at a point 1.4 mi. south of Daicey Pond via Nature and Lost Pond trails. Foss and Knowlton Pond Trail heads south to join the AT near the West Branch of the Penobscot River 1.9 mi. from Abol Bridge. Foss and Knowlton Pond Trail uses fire roads built to fight the Baxter fire of 1977, and traverses the burned area that is now being reclaimed by the forest.

Foss and Knowlton Pond Trail (AMC map 1: E2–E3)
Distances from Daicey Pond trailhead parking (1,087 ft.) to
- Foss and Knowlton Pond Trail jct. (via Nature and Lost Pond trails): 1.4 mi., 40 min.
- AT jct. (650 ft.): 5.4 mi., 2 hr. 30 min.

Kidney Pond
Kidney Pond Campground
The cabins at Kidney Pond were established as a sporting camp in 1899 and operated as a private camp until 1988. Kidney Pond Campground now serves as a center point for hiking, fishing, and canoeing on Kidney Pond and the surrounding ponds, including Rocky, Celia, Jackson, and Lily Pad ponds. The campground features twelve self-service cabins, a library, canoe and kayak rentals, and trailhead parking. Kidney Pond is a good base for hikes to Sentinel and Doubletop mountains, and many of the pretty outlying ponds.

Rocky Pond Trail
This trail leads 0.6 mi. from Kidney Pond Campground to Rocky Pond. Beyond, the trail reaches Little Rocky Pond at 1.2 mi.

Celia and Jackson Ponds Trail
From Kidney Pond Campground, follow Sentinel Mtn. Trail south around the pond to the jct. with Celia and Jackson Ponds Trail at 0.3 mi. Turn right (west) on Celia and Jackson Ponds Trail to reach the north shore of Celia Pond at 1.4 mi. Jackson Pond is 0.2 mi. farther west.

Kidney Pond Outlet Trail

[*Note:* This trail has been abandoned by BSP and access to Daicey Pond and Sentinel Mtn. Trail via this route is no longer possible. See Sentinel Mtn. Trail for access to Lily Pond Trail and Sentinel Mtn. Refer to outdoors.org/bookupdates for more information.]

Lily Pad Pond Trail

This trail leaves from Sentinel Mtn. Trail at a point 0.9 mi. east of Kidney Pond Campground. Lily Pad Pond Trail heads south to reach Beaver Brook in 0.4 mi.

Doubletop Mtn. (South Peak, 3,455 ft.; North Peak, 3,489 ft.)

The steep, slide-scarred eastern slopes of Doubletop Mtn. make it easy to identify from many points in the Katahdin region. The views of Katahdin, South Brother, Mt. Coe, Mt. OJI, and Barren Mtn. from Doubletop's two peaks are impressive. Doubletop can be climbed from Kidney Pond in the south or, alternatively, from Nesowadnehunk Field Campground in the north.

Doubletop Mtn. Trail

Doubletop Mtn. Trail starts at Kidney Pond. At 0.3 mi., the trail reaches a side trail leading 0.1 mi. to Draper Pond. Ahead, cross Slaughter Brook and skirt the south shore of Deer Pond. At 1.3 mi., bear left and follow an old woods road (the old Slaughter Pond Tote Rd.) to reach a jct. at 1.9 mi. Doubletop Mtn. Trail forks right (north) here, leaving the old Camp 3 clearing near its northwest corner. Straight ahead (west), Slaughter Pond Trail continues 1.0 mi. to Slaughter Pond. (Watch carefully: This jct. can be easy to miss.)

Doubletop Mtn. Trail follows an old woods road northwest up a valley, crossing a stream four times. The stream and trail run together for a while, which makes the route wet and muddy. The trail passes close under the cliffs on Moose's Bosom, the peak west of Doubletop Mtn. Just after crossing a small stream, the trail reaches a thick stand of spruce and fir woods and passes a spring. Turning north again, the trail climbs to a saddle west of Doubletop. Beyond, the trail angles up a steep, timbered slope on the west side of the mountain to reach the open summit of the south peak of Doubletop at 4.6 mi. The trail continues on to reach the north peak of Doubletop at 4.8 mi. From this peak, the trail descends steadily (steeply at times) to the north, eventually reaching a brook at about 6.5 mi. Beyond the brook, the descent becomes more gradual. The last mile follows a fairly level course, reaching Nesowadnehunk Field Campground at 7.9 mi.

Doubletop Mtn. Trail (AMC map 1: D2, E2)

Distances from Kidney Pond (1,051 ft.) to
- Slaughter Pond Trail jct.(1,150 ft.): 1.9 mi., 45 min.
- Doubletop Mtn., south peak (3,455 ft.): 4.6 mi., 3 hr. 20 min.
- Doubletop Mtn., north peak (3,489 ft.): 4.8 mi., 3 hr. 30 min.
- Nesowadnehunk Field Campground (1,300 ft.): 7.9 mi., 6 hr. 30 min.

Distances from Nesowadnehunk Field Campground (1,300 ft.) to
- stream crossing: 1.4 mi., 45 min., 2 hr. 35 min.
- Doubletop Mtn., north peak (3,489 ft.): 3.1 mi., 3 hr. 30 min.
- Doubletop Mtn., south peak (3,455 ft.): 3.3 mi., 3 hr. 40 min.
- Kidney Pond Campground (1,051 ft.): 7.9 mi., 6 hr. 30 min.

Nesowadnehunk Field Campground

This beautiful campground located on Nesowadnehunk Stream is the base for the approach to Doubletop from the north and for trails to Center Pond, Wassataquoik Lake, and Russell Pond to the northeast. The campground features ten tentsites, eleven lean-tos, several walk-in sites, and a four-person bunkhouse. Two group areas accommodate as many as 48 people.

Dwelley Pond Trail

This easy trail starts from Park Tote Rd. at a point 5.7 mi. north of Nesow-adnehunk Field Campground and follows the route of a former park road for its 3.2-mi. length. Reach Dwelley Pond and Dwelley Pond Day Use Site at 1.6 mi. Beyond, the trail swings east then north around the base of McCarty Mtn. Ahead, the trail follows the South Branch of Trout Brook before finally crossing it. The trail then bears northwest around Burnt Mtn. to end at Park Loop Rd. at 5.4 mi.

Dwelley Pond Trail (AMC map 1: B2, C2)

Distances from Park Tote Rd. (1,500 ft.) north of Nesowadnehunk Field Campground to

- Dwelley Pond: 1.6 mi., 45 min.
- Park Tote Rd. south of Burnt Mtn. Day Use Site (1,350 ft.): 5.4 mi., 2 hr. 45 min.

Burnt Mtn. (1,810 ft.)

Burnt Mtn. Trail begins at Burnt Mtn. Day Use Site on Park Tote Rd., about 14 mi. west of Matagamon Gate. The trail climbs to the summit in 1.3 mi. Trees are gradually blocking what were once excellent views from the top of Burnt Mtn., but a good view can be gained from the ledges 0.1 mi. to the southeast of the former fire tower footings.

Burnt Mtn. Trail (AMC map 1: B2)

Distance from Burnt Mtn. Day Use Site (1,050 ft.) to

- Burnt Mtn. summit (1,810 ft.): 1.3 mi., 50 min.

South Branch Ponds
South Branch Pond Campground

The South Branch ponds have one of the most spectacular surroundings of any in Maine, situated in a deep valley between Traveler Mtn. to the east and South Branch and Black Cat mountains to the west. The campground, located at the north end of Lower South Branch Pond, is a base for hiking the peaks of the Traveler Mtn. From the pond visitors are rewarded with choice views of the peaks and ridges of Traveler Mtn. rising south and east of the pond, and of the bulk of South Branch Mtn. rising to the south and west. The campground features 21 tentsites, 12 lean-tos, an eight-person bunkhouse, two walk-in/canoe-in sites on Lower South Branch Pond, one walk-in/canoe-in site on Upper South Branch Pond, a picnic area, canoe and kayak rentals, and trailhead parking.

Ledges Trail

From South Branch Pond Campground, walk north on the access road for 0.1 mi. Turn right onto Middle Fowler Trail and climb a series of ledges to reach a jct. at 0.3 mi. Ledges Trail begins here and heads left (north) across open ledges with good views south across the steep-walled valley that contains Lower and Upper South Branch ponds. Beyond, the trail descends to end at the access road. At 0.7 mi., turn left and hike 0.5 mi. back to the campground.

Ledges Trail (AMC map 1: B4)

Distances from South Branch Pond Campground (981 ft.) to

- start of trail (via access road and Middle Fowler Trail): 0.3 mi., 10 min.
- complete loop (via Ledges Trail and access road): 1.2 mi., 35 min.

Pogy Notch Trail

This trail connects South Branch Pond Campground with the trails to Traveler Mtn., to Pogy Pond, and finally to Russell Pond Campground.

From South Branch Pond Campground, enter woods on the trail toward the eastern shore of the pond. North Traveler Trail diverges left at 0.1 mi. At 0.9 mi., the trail reaches Howe Brook and Howe Brook Trail, which leaves to the left (east). Ahead, Pogy Notch Trail climbs over the end of the cliff between Lower and Upper South Branch ponds. Center Ridge Trail diverges left at 1.4 mi. Pogy Notch Trail descends, follows the east shore of Upper South Branch Pond, and reaches a jct. with South Branch Mtn. Trail at 2.0 mi. Upper South Branch Pond Campsite is a short distance west on this trail.

Pogy Notch Trail continues south, passing through an alder swamp and beaver works at 2.8 mi. The trail crosses several brooks and rises and falls moderately in the next 0.5 mi. At 3.3 mi., the trail forks. Turn right here, and climb gradually to pass through Pogy Notch. Bear left at 3.9 mi. into a sparsely grown old burn. The trail then crosses a beaver canal and descends into the Pogy Pond watershed. The trail crosses a brook several times while passing out of the notch area, then crosses several other brooks, and reaches the head of Pogy Pond, where there are good views of Traveler and Turner mountains, as well as Katahdin from the shore of the pond.

Ahead, the trail bears right, uphill, and at 5.7 mi., a side trail to the left leads 0.2 mi. to Pogy Pond Campsite. The main trail descends nearly to the pond, then bears right, away from the pond. The trail rises gradually, then descends through an old burn, traverses a series of shallow rises, and bears right. Beyond, the trail drops into the gully of the western tributary of Pogy Brook, crosses it, and climbs the opposite slope. Then the trail runs through a swampy hollow, climbs a rocky rise, and descends gradually to cross another brook. Immediately after this second brook, the trail bears right and climbs gradually through sparse mixed growth. The trail crosses a beaver meadow, reaches a rough boulder field, and descends through it and toward Russell Pond. Just before the pond, the trail to Grand Falls and Caverly Lookout leaves to the left, and a short distance ahead, Wassataquoik Lake Trail leaves to the right. Russell Pond Campground is reached at 9.1 mi.

Pogy Notch Trail (AMC map 1: B4, C4, D4)

Distances from South Branch Pond Campground (981 ft.) to
- North Traveler Trail jct. (1,000 ft.): 0.2 mi., 5 min.
- Howe Brook Trail jct. (1,050 ft.): 0.9 mi., 30 min.
- Center Ridge Trail jct. (1,050 ft.): 1.4 mi., 45 min.
- South Branch Mtn. Trail jct. (950 ft.): 2.0 mi., 1 hr.
- Pogy Pond (1,150 ft.): 5.7 mi., 3 hr.
- Russell Pond (1,333 ft.): 8.9 mi., 4 hr. 30 min.
- Russell Pond Campground (1,333 ft.): 9.1 mi., 4 hr. 40 min.

South Branch Mtn. (2,630 ft.) and Black Cat Mtn. (2,611 ft.)

South Branch and Black Cat mountains rise above the western shore of Lower and Upper South Branch ponds and offer commanding views of the peaks of the Traveler Mtn. massif.

South Branch Mtn. Trail

This trail runs from South Branch Pond Campground over both summits and down to Pogy Notch Trail, which South Branch Mtn. Trail joins at the southern end of Upper South Branch Pond.

South Branch Mtn. Trail starts at the northwest corner of Lower South Branch Pond, across the outlet brook from the campground. The trail parallels the brook for a distance, then follows a ridge to lookouts with vistas of the ponds and the peaks of Traveler Mtn. After contouring for a short while, the trail turns abruptly to the right and climbs more steeply to the summit of South Branch Mtn., which is reached at 2.0 mi.

Ahead, the summit of Black Cat Mtn. is reached at 2.5 mi., after an easy hike along the high saddle connecting the two summits. Beyond, the trail descends through meadows and rock fields to open ledges on the southern side of the mountain, then swings eastward and descends through mixed forests. After a brief climb, the trail continues toward Upper South Branch Pond. The trail soon passes a side trail on the left leading to Upper South Branch Campsite, then crosses a brook with beaver works before joining Pogy Notch Trail at 4.7 mi. Turn left (north) here to head to South Branch Pond Campground or right (south) for Pogy Notch and Russell Pond Campground.

South Branch Mtn. Trail (AMC map 1: B4, C3–C4)

Distances from South Branch Pond Campground (981 ft.) to

- South Branch Mtn. summit (2,630 ft.): 2.0 mi., 2 hr.
- Black Cat Mtn. summit (2,611 ft.): 2.5 mi., 2 hr. 15 min.
- Pogy Notch Trail jct. (950 ft.): 4.7 mi., 4 hr.
- South Branch Pond Campground (via Pogy Notch Trail) (981 ft.): 6.7 mi., 5 hr.

North Traveler Mtn. (3,152 ft.), The Traveler (3,550 ft.), and Center Ridge (3,254 ft.)

This great, starfish-shaped mountain mass has four high ridges that sprawl out to the south, west, northwest, and north, with four shorter spurs between them. Fires have ravaged the mountain, the last one in 1902, so that although its lower parts support trees of some size, its upper slopes are mostly bare. This is the highest volcanic mountain in New England, and possibly the highest on the East Coast.

An excellent, if long and strenuous, loop hike may be had by combining Pogy Notch, Center Ridge, Traveler Mtn., and North Traveler trails. (*Note:* It is recommended that hikers attempting this loop make the ascent via Center Ridge Trail and descend by way of North Traveler Trail.)

North Traveler Trail

From South Branch Pond Campground, follow Pogy Notch Trail for 0.1 mi. to North Traveler Trail, which diverges left. The trail climbs through open woods to the crest of the north ridge, which it follows over bare ledges in places. The view improves until the trail enters birch woods. After that, the trail passes through pretty alpine meadows and fine old woods that alternate with steep ledges. At about 1.7 mi., in one of the wooded sections, a side trail leaves left to a spring. After emerging from the last section of woods, North Traveler Trail continues in the open up the ridge to the summit of North Traveler at 2.9 mi. and the jct. with Traveler Mtn. Trail.

North Traveler Trail (AMC map 1: B4)

Distances from South Branch Pond Campground (981 ft.) to
- start (via Pogy Notch Trail) (1,000 ft.): 0.1 mi., 5 min.
- North Traveler Mtn. summit (3,152 ft.) and Traveler Mtn. Trail jct.: 2.9 mi., 2 hr. 30 min.

Howe Brook Trail

Howe Brook Trail begins at the southeastern corner of Lower South Branch Pond, where the rocky, fanlike delta of Howe Brook merges with the pond. This inlet is 0.9 mi. south along the Pogy Notch Trail from the campground. Leaving left (east), Howe Brook Trail follows the route of the brook to the first chutes and potholes. Howe Brook is noted for its many pools, potholes, slides, and chutes, which continue for quite a distance up the valley. The trail crosses the brook a number of times before ending at a beautiful waterfall.

Howe Brook Trail (AMC map 1: B4)
Distances from South Branch Pond Campground (981 ft.) to
- start (via Pogy Notch Trail) (1,050 ft.): 0.9 mi., 30 min.
- waterfall (est. 1,500 ft.): 2.9 mi., 1 hr. 45 min.

Center Ridge Trail

This route starts at the foot of Center Ridge at the northeastern corner of Upper South Branch Pond, at a point 1.4 mi. south on Pogy Notch Trail from South Branch Pond Campground. Diverging left (east) from Pogy Notch Trail, Center Ridge Trail climbs steadily through woods before breaking out into the open. Excellent views of Howe Brook Valley and North Traveler can be seen en route. Follow the open ridge over ledges and slabs, boulders and scree, and numerous false summits to reach the summit of Center Ridge at 3.7 mi., and a jct. with Traveler Mtn. Trail. From this vantage point, the summit of The Traveler looms ahead in the distance.

Center Ridge Trail (AMC map 1: B4, C4)
Distances from South Branch Pond Campground (981 ft.) to
- start (via Pogy Notch Trail) (1,050 ft.): 1.4 mi., 45 min.
- Center Ridge (3,254 ft.): 3.7 mi., 2 hr. 50 min.

Traveler Mtn. Trail

The Traveler Mtn. Trail starts from the summit of Center Ridge (reached via Center Ridge and Pogy Notch trails) and traverses across and down "Little Knife Edge," a vertical spine of columnar rhyolite rock. At the base of this rock formation, cross a small alpine meadow and begin to climb through stunted coniferous forest and several small scree walls of stone to reach a huge talus field. Cairns lead diagonally up the mass of loose rock to the summit cone of The Traveler, which is reached at 1.5 mi. from Center Ridge.

Beyond, the trail traverses long stretches of open terrain. (*Caution:* In bad weather, particular care should be exercised here; watch carefully for blaze and cairn route markers.) At a highpoint known as Traveler Ridge, the trail drops sharply through dwarf birch, mountain ash, and balsam fir to a col before climbing to the peak of North Traveler at 4.5 mi. and a jct. with North Traveler Trail, which leads an additional 2.9 mi. to South Branch Pond Campground.

Traveler Mtn. Trail (AMC map 1: B4, C4)

Distances from South Branch Pond Campground (981 ft.) to
- Center Ridge Trail (via Pogy Notch Trail) (1,050 ft.): 1.4 mi., 45 min.
- Center Ridge (3,254 ft.) and start of Traveler Mtn. Trail: 3.7 mi., 2 hr. 50 min.
- The Traveler summit (3,550 ft.) (via Traveler Mtn. Trail): 5.2 mi., 4 hr.
- North Traveler Mtn. summit (3,152 ft.) (via Traveler Mtn. Trail): 8.2 mi., 5 hr. 30 min.
- South Branch Pond Campground (via North Traveler and Pogy Notch trails): 11.1 mi., 7 hr. 30 min.

Trout Brook Campground

Trout Brook Campground is on the site of a farm dating to 1837 that once supported logging operations. The campground is located on the north side of Park Tote Rd., about 27 mi. west of Patten and 2.6 mi. west of Matagamon Gate. The campground is 4.7 mi. east of the Trout Brook Crossing Day Use Site, where the road to South Branch Pond Campground leads south.

The campground features twelve tentsites, three walk-in sites along Trout Brook, a group camping area for as many as 50 people, canoe rentals, and trailhead parking. The campground is a good starting point for many trips in this area of the park, including hikes on Freezeout Trail to the north and the network of trails in the Fowler Ponds area to the south. The trail to Trout Brook Mtn. leaves just across the road from the campground. Trout Brook Campground is also a good base for canoe trips on the brook and nearby Grand Lake Matagamon.

Scientific Forest Management Area

This 29,587-acre area comprises the northern tier of the park, from Matagamon Lake in the east and Webster Lake in the west, and generally north of Park Tote Rd. This is the only area in the park where timber harvesting is allowed, per the desires of Percival Baxter, who believed having such an area set aside was in the interest of good forestry science. The SFMA, established in the mid-1950s, was mandated to serve as "a show place for those interested in forestry, a place where a continuing timber crop can be cultivated, harvested, and sold—an example and inspiration to others," wrote Baxter in 1955. Hikers may pass through areas of active or recent timber harvesting and at times may hear harvesting equipment, but most often will experience a true sense of the remoteness of this wild northern part of the park. Hunting is also allowed in this area. Freezeout, Wadleigh Brook, and Frost Pond trails pass through the SFMA.

Freezeout Trail

This trail starts from Trout Brook Campground, at the end of the campground road that leads to Trout Brook. Immediately cross Trout Brook on a footbridge, and soon pass several campsites to the left. Beyond, continue on the wide trail, formerly a woods road. Cross two branches of Boody Brook and then pass over several low ridges. Cross Frost Pond Brook and ahead, at about 3.5 mi., reach a large sawdust pile (the remains of an old mill site) on the right on the shore of Matagamon Lake. At 4.0 mi., Frost Pond Trail diverges left (south).

Ahead, cross Hinckley Brook and continue to parallel the lake. Pass by Northwest Cove Campsite at 5.0 mi., and soon reach a sharp left turn in Freezeout Trail at 5.4 mi. A short walk straight ahead is Little East Campsite (lean-to), at the confluence of the East Branch of the Penobscot River and Webster Stream.

From this point west to Webster Lake, the trail follows the south bank of Webster Stream. At 5.8 mi., a side trail leads 0.2 mi. to Grand Pitch, a thundering falls on Webster Stream. This trail loops to rejoin Freezeout Trail in 0.3 mi. Pass Webster Stream Campsite (lean-to) on the left at 9.7 mi. Continuing easily on, pass over Pine Knoll and reach a jct. with Wadleigh Brook Trail, which enters from the left at 11.7 mi. Ahead, follow sections of old corduroy road and cross Ice Wagon Field. With Webster Lake in sight, reach a privy on the left and a side trail on the right leading to Webster Lake Campsite (lean-to) on the east end of the lake at 14.1 mi.

Freezeout Trail (AMC map 1: A2–A4, B2)

Distances from Trout Brook Campground (680 ft.) to
- Frost Pond Trail jct.: 4.0 mi., 2 hr.
- Northwest Cove Campsite: 5.0 mi., 2 hr. 30 min.
- Little East Campsite: 5.4 mi., 2 hr. 45 min.
- side trail to Grand Pitch: 5.8 mi., 3 hr.
- Webster Stream Campsite: 9.7 mi., 4 hr. 50 min.
- Wadleigh Brook Trail jct.: 11.7 mi., 6 hr. 50 min.
- Webster Lake Campsite (900 ft.): 14.1 mi., 8 hr. 45 min.

Frost Pond Trail

This trail leaves left (west) from Freezeout Trail at a point 4.0 mi. from Trout Brook Campground. Frost Pond Trail ascends gradually southwest for 1.5 mi. to reach Frost Pond Campsite (lean-to) at 5.5 mi. Beyond, the trail continues west, climbing to the long ridge of Wadleigh Mtn. (1,259 ft.), where there are good views to the peaks of Traveler Mtn. and South Branch Mtn. in the south. At about 6 mi., the trail crosses a gravel road. At 6.3 mi., the trail ends at a jct. with Wadleigh Brook Trail, at a point 1.4 mi. north of Park Tote Rd.

Frost Pond Trail (AMC map 1: A3–A4, B3–B4)

Distances from Trout Brook Campground (680 ft.) to
- start of trail (via Freezeout Trail): 4.0 mi., 2 hr.
- Frost Pond Campsite: 5.5 mi., 2 hr. 45 min.
- Wadleigh Brook Trail jct. (850 ft.): 10.3 mi., 5 hr. 30 min.

Wadleigh Brook Trail

The trail leaves Park Tote Rd. about 1 mi. west of the bridge over Trout Brook at Trout Brook Crossing Day Use Site. The trail follows Wadleigh Brook west for a short distance, then turns north. At 1.4 mi., Frost Pond Trail enters from the right. At about 4.3 mi., Wadleigh Brook Trail follows around the upper side of Wadleigh Bog, then crosses a brook draining Blunder Pond. At 6.8 mi., Wadleigh Brook Trail crosses a gravel road at Blunder Pond Day Use Site. Ahead, the trail crosses the inlet of Hudson Pond and soon reaches the pond proper at 7.8 mi. Here, a short side trail leads uphill to Hudson Pond Campsite (lean-to). Beyond, the trail follows the north shore of the pond before turning to the northeast to reach Hudson Brook and, soon after, a jct. with Freezeout Trail at 9.8 mi. To the left, it is 2.4 mi. to Webster Lake and its campsite. To the right, it is 11.7 mi. to Trout Brook Campground, passing three campsites en route.

Wadleigh Brook Trail (AMC map 1: A2–A3, B2–B3)

Distances from Park Tote Rd. (800 ft.) to
- Frost Pond Trail jct. (850 ft.): 1.4 mi., 40 min.
- Blunder Pond Day Use Site (1,000 ft.): 6.8 mi., 3 hr. 25 min.
- Hudson Pond Campsite (900 ft.): 7.8 mi., 4 hr.
- Freezeout Trail jct. (850 ft.): 9.8 mi., 5 hr.

Fowler Ponds

A series of scenic ponds are located west of Horse Mtn., south of Trout Pond Mtn., and northeast of South Branch Pond Campground in the northeast corner of the park. From west to east, these include Lower and Middle Fowler ponds, High and Long ponds, Round and Billfish ponds, and Littlefield Pond. A system of trails connects the ponds and eight backcountry campsites and provides fine day- and overnight hiking opportunities. Access to trails may be gained from the Park Tote Rd. at several points, and from South Branch Campground.

Fowler Brook Trail

Fowler Brook Trail leads south from Park Tote Rd. about 2 mi. west of Trout Brook Campground. The trail generally follows Fowler Brook and leads to the north end of Lower Fowler Pond, Lower Fowler Outlet Campsite, and the jct. with Lower Fowler Pond Trail at 1.2 mi.

Fowler Brook Trail (AMC map 1: B4)
Distance from Park Tote Rd. (650 ft.) to
  • Lower Fowler Pond (850 ft.): 1.2 mi., 40 min.

Lower Fowler Pond Trail

This short 0.7-mi. trail connects Five Ponds Trail with Lower Fowler
Pond, Middle Fowler Pond, and Fowler Brook trails. Lower Fowler Pond
Trail diverges south from Five Ponds Trail at a point 2.0 mi. from Park
Tote Rd. at Trout Brook Campground. At 2.4 mi., the trail reaches a jct.
with Middle Fowler Pond Trail. Continuing on, Lower Fowler Pond Trail
reaches Lower Fowler Pond Campsite at about 0.5 mi. and, just ahead,
ends at Lower Fowler Outlet Campsite at 0.7 mi. From here, it is 1.2 mi. to
Park Tote Rd. via Fowler Brook Trail.

Middle Fowler Pond Trail

From the north end of South Branch Pond Campground, follow Ledges
Trail for 0.3 mi. to a jct. Here, Middle Fowler Pond Trail continues ahead,
and Ledges Trail diverges left. Beyond the jct., Middle Fowler Pond Trail
climbs gradually, following a small brook to open ledges. From there, the
trail proceeds through the gap between Big Peaked and Little Peaked
mountains. The trail then traverses the north slope of Traveler Mtn., providing occasional views. At 2.8 mi., a side trail leads left (north) 0.3 mi.
to the open summit of Barrell Ridge, where there are fine views of Traveler Mtn. From this point, the trail descends, and reaches Middle Fowler
Pond and a jct. at 3.7 mi. (sign). To the right (south), it is 0.2 mi. to Middle Fowler South Campsite. Continuing to the left (north), the trail follows the west shore of the pond to reach Middle Fowler North Campsite
at 4.3 mi. Beyond, the trail crosses the pond outlet and proceeds to a jct.
with Lower Fowler Pond Trail at 5.2 mi. From here, it is 1.1 mi. to Long
Pond or 2.0 mi. to Park Tote Rd. via Five Ponds and Lower Fowler Pond
trails via the right fork. To the left, it is 1.5 mi. to Park Tote Rd. via Lower
Fowler Pond and Fowler Brook trails.

Middle Fowler Pond Trail (AMC map 1: B4)
Distances from South Branch Pond Campground (981 ft.) to
- side trail to Barrell Ridge (1,800 ft.): 2.8 mi., 1 hr. 45 min.
- Middle Fowler Pond (950 ft.): 3.7 mi., 2 hr. 15 min.
- Lower Fowler Ponds Trail jct. (1,000 ft.): 5.2 mi., 3 hr.
- Park Tote Rd. (via Middle Fowler Pond and Fowler Brook trails) (650 ft.):
  6.7 mi., 3 hr. 45 min.

Five Ponds Trail

This trail makes a loop around the base of Trout Brook Mtn. and passes five scenic ponds en route. The trail is described in a counterclockwise direction. From Park Tote Rd., the trail immediately forks. Follow the right fork and climb over the west shoulder of Trout Brook Mtn. to reach a jct. with Lower Fowler Pond Trail at 2.0 mi. (leads 0.4 mi. to Middle Fowler Pond Trail and 0.7 mi. to Lower Fowler Pond). Five Ponds Trail continues to the left, reaching a side trail to Long Pond Outlet Campsite at 2.7 mi. Ahead, the trail runs between High and Long ponds, passing a side trail to Long Pond Pines Campsite at the east end of Long Pond. The trail continues past Round Pond to Billfish Pond and Billfish Pond Campsite at 3.5 mi. Just ahead, Horse Mtn. Trail merges from the right. At 4.2 mi., Five Ponds Trail passes Littlefield Pond Campsite, and at 5.0 mi., Trout Brook Mtn. Trail enters from the left. Close the loop at Park Tote Rd. at 6.0 mi. at Trout Brook Campground.

Five Ponds Trail (AMC map 1: B4–B5)
Distance from Park Tote Rd. (700 ft.) to
- complete Five Ponds Loop Trail: 6.0 mi., 3 hr. 30 min.

Trout Brook Mtn. (1,767 ft.)

This low mountain rises to south of Trout Brook Campground and offers fine views of the Traveler Mtn. massif and surrounding ponds from its summit.

Trout Brook Mtn. Trail

The trail starts from Trout Brook Campground and climbs through mixed growth and hardwoods to the open summit ledges at 1.4 mi., where there are excellent views. Beyond the summit, the trail descends to a valley between Trout Brook and Horse mountains. Here, the trail merges with Five Ponds Trail at 2.5 mi. To the left (north), it is 1.0 mi. to the trailhead and the close of the loop via Five Ponds Trail.

Trout Brook Mtn. Trail (AMC map 1: B4)

Distances from Park Tote Rd. (700 ft.) to
- Trout Brook Mtn. summit (1,767 ft.): 1.4 mi., 1 hr. 20 min.
- complete loop via Five Ponds Trail: 3.5 mi., 3 hr.

Horse Mtn. (1,589 ft.)

This mountain rises above the west shore of Grand Lake Matagamon in the northwest corner of the park and features sheer cliffs on its east face.

Horse Mtn. Trail

The trail leaves the south side of Park Tote Rd. 2.5 mi. west of the bridge over the East Branch of the Penobscot and just west of Matagamon Gate. The trail rises gradually to the jct. with a side trail leading left (east) 0.4 mi. to a viewpoint. Just ahead on the main trail, a side trail leaves right and goes 0.2 mi. to the true summit of Horse Mtn. Ahead, Horse Mtn. Trail descends to the shore of Billfish Pond, which the trail follows to merge with Five Ponds Trail at 3.0 mi. Via Five Ponds Trail, to the right, it is 2.5 mi. to Park Tote Rd.; to the left, it is 3.5 mi. to Park Tote Rd.

Horse Mtn. Trail (AMC map 1: B5)

Distances from Park Tote Rd. (750 ft.) to
- side trail to viewpoint (1,450 ft.): 1.2 mi., 1 hr. 5 min.
- Billfish Pond outlet (950 ft.): 2.2 mi., 2 hr.
- Five Ponds Trail jct. (950 ft.): 3.0 mi., 2 hr. 30 min.

South Turner Mtn. (3,110 ft.)

This mountain northeast of Katahdin offers magnificent views of the Katahdin massif and its sheer-walled basins. The approach to South Turner is from Roaring Brook Campground and involves a moderate climb up its southwestern slide.

South Turner Mtn. Trail

This trail leaves from Sandy Stream Pond Trail at a point 0.7 mi. from Roaring Brook Campground. From the campground, follow Chimney Pond Trail past the ranger station and quickly arrive at a jct. with Russell Pond Trail. Take this trail across the bridge over Roaring Brook. At 0.1 mi., where Russell Pond Trail diverges left, continue straight ahead on Sandy Stream Pond Trail. Follow this around the south shore of the pond. Excellent views of the Katahdin massif appear. At 0.7 mi., reach a jct. with South Turner Mtn. Trail, which leaves to the right. Sandy Stream Pond Trail continues to the left toward Whidden Ponds.

Continue easily ahead on South Turner Mtn. Trail, then climb moderately up the south slope of the mountain. Ahead, the trail enters a small boulder field and follows cairns and paint blazes on the rocks. Beyond, the trail turns left, rises steeply, and soon passes a side trail right to a spring. Eventually, the trail leaves the scrub and climbs over open ledges, reaching the alpine summit at 1.8 mi.

South Turner Mtn. Trail (AMC map 1: D4)

Distances from Roaring Brook Campground (1,489 ft.) to
- start of trail (via Russell Pond and Sandy Stream trails): 0.7 mi., 20 min.
- South Turner Mtn. summit (3,110 ft.): 1.8 mi., 1 hr. 55 min.

Katahdin Lake

In 2006, 4,119 acres to the east of Katahdin were gifted to Baxter State Park. The predominant feature of this parcel of land is the iconic 640-acre Katahdin Lake, which offers outstanding views of Katahdin, including Baxter Peak, Knife Edge, Pamola Peak, Hamlin Peak, and Howe Peaks. In 2009, a system of trails was opened for hikers, and three backcountry campsites are now available for overnight camping. The private Katahdin Lake Wilderness Camps, a traditional sporting camp on the south shore of the lake, operates under a lease agreement with the park. Trailhead access to Katahdin Lake is from Avalanche Field on Roaring Brook Rd., 1.5 mi. south of Roaring Brook Campground.

Katahdin Lake Trail

This trail leaves Roaring Brook Rd. at Avalanche Field (parking, toilet, register box) and heads east on an old woods road, which the trail follows for much of its route to Katahdin Lake. The trail crosses a small stream at 0.1 mi., and Sandy Stream at 0.5 mi. The trail ascends gently to crest a low ridge before descending to cross the old park boundary. At 1.7 mi., Martin Ponds Trail diverges to the left (northwest). It leads 0.6 mi. to the Martin Ponds and Martin Ponds Campsite.

Continuing on, Katahdin Lake Trail trends mostly downhill to a jct. at 3.0 mi. To the left, it is 100 yd. to South Katahdin Lake Campsite, 0.1 mi. to the Day Use Picnic Site, and 0.2 mi. to Katahdin Lake and the store of rental canoes. To the right, it is 0.3 mi. to Katahdin Lake Wilderness Camps, and 2.1 mi. to the park boundary. (*Note:* The lower jct. of Martin Ponds Trail can be found by walking past Katahdin Lake Campsite [lean-to] to the shore of the pond and turning left along the beach. Cross the outlet and pick up the trail on the far shore.)

Katahdin Lake Trail (AMC map 1: E4–E5)

Distances from Avalanche Field at Roaring Brook Rd. (1,250 ft.) to
- Martin Ponds Trail upper jct.: 1.7 mi., 55 min.
- Katahdin Lake Campsite at jct.: 3.0 mi., 1 hr. 40 min.
- Katahdin Lake Wilderness Camps (650 ft.): 3.3 mi. 1 hr. 50 min.

Martin Ponds Trail

This trail diverges left (northwest) from Katahdin Lake Trail at a point 1.7 mi. from Avalanche Field. Martin Ponds Trail traverses a low ridge before skirting a beaver flowage and crossing the outlet of South Martin Pond. At 2.3 mi., reach a jct. with a short side trail to Martin Ponds Campsite, where there is an excellent view of Katahdin. Ahead, the trail passes to the west and north of North Martin Pond before descending to an outlook to the Turner mountains. The jct. with North Katahdin Lake Trail is reached at 2.6 mi. Beyond, Martin Ponds Trail descends gradually to reach Katahdin Lake, making several streams crossings en route. From here, the trail follows the east shore to an inlet and an old beaver dam. Cross this and bear left along the sandy beach of the lake to reach South Katahdin Lake Campsite and just ahead, a jct. with Katahdin Lake Trail at 4.4 mi.

Martin Ponds Trail (AMC map 1: D5, E5)

Distances from Avalanche Field at Roaring Brook Rd. (1,250 ft.) to
  - start of trail via Katahdin Lake Trail: 1.7 mi., 55 min.
  - Martin Ponds Campsite (1,250 ft.): 2.3 mi., 1 hr. 10 min.
  - South Katahdin Lake Campsite and Katahdin Lake Trail jct. (640 ft.): 4.4 mi., 2 hr. 15 min.

North Katahdin Lake Trail

This trail leaves from Martin Ponds Trail at a point 0.9 mi. from Katahdin Lake Trail and 2.6 mi. from Avalanche Field. North Katahdin Lake Trail crosses a ridge to the north before descending toward Katahdin Lake, crossing several streams en route. The trail reaches North Katahdin Lake Campsite at 1.8 mi. From the lakeshore, there are good views of the Katahdin massif. From the lake and campsite, the trail continues north around the base of North Turner Mtn. before climbing its eastern slope. After crossing Twin Pond Brook the trail ends at Twin Ponds, a small lower pond and a larger upper pond, at the base of a cirque below the steep walls of North Turner Mtn. at 3.9 mi. from Katahdin Lake.

North Katahdin Lake Trail (AMC map 1: D4–D5)

Distances from Avalanche Field at Roaring Brook Rd. (1,250 ft.) to
  - start of North Katahdin Lake Trail via Katahdin Lake and Martin Ponds trails: 2.6 mi., 1 hr. 20 min.
  - North Katahdin Lake Campsite (640 ft.): 4.4 mi., 2 hr. 15 min.
  - Twin Ponds (1,850 ft.): 8.2 mi., 4 hr. 50 min.

Abol and Togue Ponds

A variety of easy trails weave through the interesting terrain in the southern end of the park in the area of Abol and Togue ponds and the Togue Pond Gate, passing by numerous ponds that offer nice views and a good chance for wildlife watching.

Cranberry Pond Trail

This trail departs from Togue Pond Day Use Site, just beyond the Visitor Information Center and just south of Togue Pond Gate. The trail ambles southwest of the road past Togue, Cranberry, and Rocky ponds. The trail ends at Park Tote Rd. at 1.4 mi., just across from the Kettle Pond trailhead.

Cranberry Pond Trail (AMC map 1: E4, F4)
Distance from Togue Pond Day Use Site (650 ft.) to
  • Park Tote Rd., upper jct.: 1.4 mi., 45 min.

Kettle Pond Trail

This short but scenic trail intersects Park Tote Rd. at both ends. The southern trailhead is on the right (north) side of the road, 1.0 mi. from Togue Pond Gate. At 0.1 mi., the trail forks. To the right, Rum Pond Trail leads 2.0 mi. past Rum Pond to Park Tote Rd. south of Rum Brook Day Use Site. Follow the left fork past several small ponds to the intersection with Park Tote Rd. at 1.4 mi.

Kettle Pond Trail (AMC map 1: E3–E4)
Distances from Park Tote Rd. (650 ft.) to
  • Park Tote Rd., north jct.: 1.4 mi., 40 min.

Rum Pond Trail

Rum Pond Trail forks right from Kettle Pond Trail, 0.1 mi. from its southern trailhead. This trail winds east past Caverly and Rum ponds to meet

Roaring Brook Rd. at 2.0 mi., at a point about 0.1 mi. south of Rum Brook Day Use Site. Togue Pond Gate is 1.0 mi. from either end of this trail.

Rum Pond Trail (AMC map 1: E4)

Distances from Park Tote Rd. (650 ft.) to
- jct. Kettle and Rum Pond trails: 0.1 mi., 5 min.
- Roaring Brook Rd. (650 ft.): 2.0 mi., 1 hr.

Abol Pond Trail

This trail diverges right (north) from the AT at a point 0.9 mi. from Abol Bridge. At 0.2 mi. from the AT jct., Blueberry Ledges Trail leaves left. Continuing to the right, Abol Pond Trail proceeds over easy terrain to reach the access road to Abol Beach Day Use Site at 1.7 mi. From the road, the trail continues to its end at Park Tote Rd. at 2.0 mi.

Abol Pond Trail (AMC map 1: E3)

Distance from AT jct. (650 ft.) to
- Abol Beach Day Use Site access road (600 ft.): 1.7 mi., 50 min.
- Park Tote Rd. (650 ft.): 2.0 mi. 1 hr.

Abol Stream Trail

This trail connects the AT with Abol Beach Day Use Site. The trail leaves right (east) from the AT at a point 0.7 mi. from Abol Bridge and leads 1.2 mi. to Abol Pond.

Abol Stream Trail (AMC map 1: E3)

Distance from AT jct. (550 ft.) to
- Abol Beach Day Use Site (600 ft.): 1.2 mi., 35 min.

Blueberry Ledges Trail

From Katahdin Stream Campground, this trail travels 4.2 mi. through a variety of forest types and offers many interesting landscapes before meeting up with the AT near the West Branch of the Penobscot River. Much of the trail goes through the area burned in the Baxter fire of 1977. The trail's namesake ledges are located about midway through the route, along the tumbling waters of Katahdin Stream. The area features large expanses of exposed bedrock with views of Katahdin and other geologic features. The Birches AT hiker shelter and tent platforms are located at the northern trailhead of Blueberry Ledges Trail.

Blueberry Ledges Trail (AMC map 1: E3)
Distances from Katahdin Stream Campground (1,099 ft.) to
- Abol Pond Trail jct. (650 ft.): 4.1 mi., 2 hr. 5 min.
- jct. with AT (650 ft.): 4.2 mi., 2 hr. 10 min.

International Appalachian Trail

The International Appalachian Trail (IAT) officially begins at the eastern boundary of Baxter State Park, 5.4 mi. by foot trail east of Avalanche Field on Roaring Brook Rd. at a point 1.5 mi. south of Roaring Brook Campground. The 1,900-mi. trail extends across the northern Maine woods to reach the Canadian border just east of Mars Hill. From there, the IAT makes its way across New Brunswick and Québec, to its terminus at Crow Head in Newfoundland.

Just east of Katahdin Lake and Baxter State Park, the IAT crosses two scenic mountains, Deasey and Lunksoos. Outstanding views of Katahdin may be had from the open summits of these peaks. From the eastern boundary of the park, 5.4 mi. from Avalanche Field, it is an additional 11.3 mi. to Deasey Mtn. and 12.3 mi. to Lunksoos Mtn. A roundtrip from Avalanche Field therefore totals about 36 mi., so a hike to these mountains via the IAT will require at least one overnight stay and perhaps more. Lean-tos at are available at Wassataquoik Stream at 5.5 mi. (10.9 mi. from Avalanche Field) and on the north side of Lunksoos Mtn. at 13.0 mi. (18.4 mi. from Avalanche Field). (*Note:* The IAT publishes a map called East Branch of the Penobscot River Section that is helpful for navigating this trail.)

Deasey Mtn. (1,964 ft.) and Lunksoos Mtn. (1,811 ft.)
Via the IAT

From Avalanche Field, proceed east on the blue-blazed Katahdin Lake Trail for 3.3 mi. to Katahdin Lake and Katahdin Lake Wilderness Camps. (See description for Katahdin Lake Trail, p. 49). From the camps, follow the unmarked section of Katahdin Lake Trail via an old woods road and then a gravel road to the park boundary at 5.4 mi. (IAT register).

From this point, continue on the IAT on a gravel road to a jct. with Gardner Rd. at 5.8 mi. Turn left (north) and follow this road. Cross a washed-out bridge (passable for hikers but not vehicles) over Katahdin Brook and climb a long grade to a jct. with a logging road at 8.2 mi. Turn right (east) on this road and follow the IAT around the north side of Bernard Mtn. to a jct. with the old Wassataquoik Tote Rd. at 10.4 mi. Follow this to the right (south) to reach Wassataquoik Lean-to at 10.9 mi.

Beyond the campsite, continue on the tote road, cross Katahdin Brook, and follow an esker south. At 11.4 mi., the trail leads left (east) down to Wassataquoik Stream. Cross the stream (*Caution:* May be dangerous in high water) and follow the east bank. At 12.4 mi., the trail turns right (east), and crosses a gravelly area and a small tributary stream before joining the old Keep Path (the original AT to the summit of Katahdin). Continue to follow the stream, cross another small tributary, and then turn northeast away from the stream. At 12.9 mi., the IAT bears left from the old Keep Path and begins to climb to a col on the south side of Deasey Mtn. Pass the house-sized boulder dubbed Earl's Erratic. At 15.9 mi., the IAT joins the old fire warden's trail and climbs gradually to the abandoned warden's cabin at 16.3 mi. From here, the trail climbs steeply toward the peak of Deasey Mtn. At 16.7 mi., a short side trail leads to the summit and the fire lookout, where there are panoramic views.

Beyond, the IAT descends northeast to a col before climbing to the summit ledges of Lunksoos Mtn., which the trail reaches at 17.7 mi., and where there are views of Chase and Sugarloaf mountains and the East Branch of the Penobscot River. Ahead, the IAT descends to reach an overgrown tote road, which it follows to Lunksoos Campsite at 18.4 mi. from Avalanche Field.

Deasey Mtn. and Lunksoos Mtn. via IAT (AMC map 1: C6, D5–D6, E5)
Distances from Avalanche Field (1,250 ft.) to
- start of IAT at eastern boundary of Baxter State Park (via Katahdin Lake Trail): 5.4 mi., 4 hr.
- Wassataquoik Lean-to: 10.9 mi., 5 hr.
- Deasey Mtn. summit (1,964 ft.): 16.7 mi., 9 hr.
- Lunksoos Mtn. summit (1,811 ft.): 17.7 mi., 9 hr. 45 min.
- Lunksoos Lean-to: 18.4 mi., 10 hr. 30 min.
- round trip: 36.8 mi., 2–3 days

From Sandbank Stream

Deasey and Lunksoos mountains can also be reached via a short day hike from the south at Sandbank Stream. From ME 11 in Stacyville, where the highway makes a 90-degree turn, turn onto Swift Brook Rd. (labeled Old Matagamon Rd. on DeLorme map 51) and drive west. At 5.2 mi., the road bears sharply to the left (southwest), and at 7.1 mi. from ME 11, reaches Whetstone Falls on the East Branch of the Penobscot River. Cross the bridge and, just ahead, take the first right turn. Follow this road north for 1.1 mi. to its end at Sandbank Stream.

The trail heads north on an old road through mature forest, roughly paralleling the course of the East Branch of the Penobscot River, but at a fair distance. After crossing a shallow stream, the road soon enters Wassataquoik Public Reserve Land (sign). After crossing Wassataquoik Stream on a bridge, the trail swings to the east and follows the north bank of the stream for about 0.5 mi. The trail then turns north, eventually crossing Owen Brook soon after passing the north boundary of Wassataquoik PRL. Beyond, the trail leaves the old tote road to the left (marked by a cairn and flagging) just before a dry streambed.

The trail is the route of old fire warden's trail, which continues westerly, paralleling a stream. The trail merges with the IAT at the abandoned warden's cabin. From here, the trail climbs steeply toward the peak of Deasey Mtn. and its summit fire tower. To reach Lunksoos Mtn., continue north on the IAT, descending to a sag before climbing to its summit ledges.

Deasey Mtn. and Lunksoos Mtn. from Sandbank Stream
(USGS Deasey Mtn. quad, DeLorme Map 51)
Distances from parking at Sandbank Stream (350 ft.) to

- Wassataquoik Stream (400 ft.): 2.0 mi., 1 hr.
- jct. with old fire warden's trail (left turn off old road) (400 ft.): 3.3 mi., 1 hr. 45 min.
- Deasey Mtn. summit (1,964 ft.) via IAT: 5.3 mi., 2 hr. 45 min.
- Lunksoos Mtn. summit (1,811 ft.) via IAT: 6.3 mi., 3 hr. 15 min.

Owl's Head (870 ft.)

Scraggly Lake Public Reserved Land, an 836-acre preserve just northwest of Baxter State Park, features a climb to Owl's Head, a rocky knob overlooking Scraggly Lake and the forestlands north of the park.

From the jct. of ME 11 and ME 159 in Patten, travel west on ME 159 for 17.0 mi. to Shin Pond. The paved ME 159 ends at 18.9 mi. Here, the road becomes the graveled Grand Lake Rd. Follow this road and cross the Seboeis River at 24.9 mi. At 25.6 mi., turn right onto Scraggly Lake Rd., and follow this to the outlet of Scraggly Lake at its southeast corner at 35.1 mi. from Patten, where there is trailhead parking.

Owl's Head Trail (MBPL)

The trail meanders easily along the lakeshore to reach a peninsula at the east end of Scraggly Lake. From here, the trail begins a short climb to a fork, and a 0.5-mi. loop around the summit area.

Owl's Head (USGS Hay Lake quad, DeLorme map 57)

Distances from Scraggly Lake outlet (750 ft.) to
- Owl's Head summit (870 ft.): 1.1 mi., 35 min.
- complete loop: 2.8 mi., 1 hr. 30 min.

Mt. Chase (2,440 ft.)

This mountain in the town of Mt. Chase in Penobscot County is the highest of a cluster of peaks extending in a northeast-southwest line, a few miles north of Patten and just west of the Aroostook County line.

Mt. Chase is reached by traveling north on ME 11 for 6.4 mi. from the northernmost jct. of ME 11 and ME 159 in Patten. Turn left (west) on Mountain Rd. and follow this for 2.1 mi. to a large clearing and a branch road that turns left (south). Parking is just beyond the branch road on the right.

The trail (an old, woods road) begins 100 ft. up the road on the right, on the far side of an intermittent stream. There is a large red arrow on a tree where the trail leaves the road 50 ft. left of the parking area, and another red arrow on a rock on the right as the trail leaves the road. The start of the trail is also marked with a black and white sign that reads "Mount Chase Hiking Trail."

The trail climbs the hillside for 200 yd. before bearing left (west). At about 0.4 mi., the trail crosses a logging road headed directly up the mountain. The trail begins to work its way back to the north, passing Rolling Rock (signed) and ending in a clearing where the collapsing warden's cabin is situated. The marked trail begins here and quickly crosses a brook. The footway is clear and the route is flagged. The trail rises steeply to a sag in the southwest ridge. Here, a short side trail leads to the bald summit of Eagle Peak.

Beyond, the trail continues up the ridge to the summit, an open rock ledge with good views (though somewhat restricted to the east), and a small communications tower. Katahdin and Traveler Mtn. are to the west, Rocky Brook Range to the north-northeast, Peaked Mtn. to the north, Haystack Mtn. to the northeast, and Mars Hill to the east.

Mt. Chase (USGS Mt. Chase quad, DeLorme map 52)
Distances from Mountain Rd. parking (1,000 ft.) to
- old fire warden's cabin: 0.8 mi., 45 min.
- Mt. Chase summit (2,440 ft.): 1.5 mi., 1 hr. 30 min.

Sugarloaf Mtn. (1868 ft.)

The mountain in T5 R7 WELS is west of Shin Pond and east of Seboeis River. Panoramic views are possible from its bare summit ledges.

From the jct. of ME 159 and ME 11 in Patten, drive northwest on ME 159 for 5.7 mi. Turn left (west) on Grondin Rd. Begin new mileage. At 5.9 mi. from ME 159, bear left at the fork, and at 6.6 mi., pass straight through a four-way intersection. At the next four-way intersection at 7.2 mi., turn left and go 150 yd. to a parking area on the right (sign).

The well-marked and maintained trail leaves the back of the parking lot and ascends the west side of the ridge. At 0.3 mi., the trail gains the ridge proper and follows it the rest of the way to the top of the mountain. After passing through an old-growth spruce forest, the trail crosses open ledges to reach the summit. The 360-degree views from the summit include Katahdin and the peaks of Baxter State Park, White Cap Mtn. and the Barren-Chairback Range, Norway Bluff and Round Mt., and Haystack Mtn. and Mars Hill. Grand Pitch on the Seboeis River is visible immediately below the peak to the west.

Sugarloaf Mtn. (USGS Shin Pond quad, DeLorme map 51)
Distance from parking area (950 ft.) to
• Sugarloaf Mtn. summit (1,868 ft.): 1.1 mi., 1 hr.

Norway Bluff (2,285 ft.)

Norway Bluff rises above Munsungan Lake north of Baxter State Park and west of ME 11 in T9 R10 WELS. A fire tower and communications tower are located on this remote summit, which provides panoramic views ranging south to Katahdin, east to Mt. Chase, north to Priestly, Horseshoe, and Round mountains, and west to the lakes of the Allagash Wilderness Waterway.

From ME 11 in Ashland, travel west on American Realty Rd. to the Six Mile Checkpoint. Norway Bluff is within the boundaries of the North Maine Woods, a large block of forestland, most of which is privately owned and cooperatively managed to provide recreational opportunities to the public. Visitors must register at the checkpoint and pay a day-use and camping fee to enter the area.

Just beyond the checkpoint, bear left on Pinkham Rd. and follow it to mile post 31, just west of Mooseleuk Stream and where Pell & Pell Rd. enters from the right (northwest). Turn right on Pell & Pell Rd. and follow it northwest for 8.7 mi. to a side road. Turn left onto this side road and drive another 4.1 mi. to a small gravel pit and park.

The trail is an old roadway used by ATVs to service the communications tower. Facing the ridgeline of Norway Bluff, look for a cairn on the left side of the gravel pit. Just beyond, you will see trees marked with colored flagging tape at the edge of the woods. This is the start of the trail. The trail route has been logged to either side, but the pathway itself is clearly discerned, well-marked, and runs through a corridor of large trees. The trail rises directly up the side of a ridge with two long switchbacks near its top. The ATV track ends at a communications tower on the middle of the ridge, where there are good views. Continue along the ridge to the summit fire tower at 1.0 mi.

Norway Bluff (USGS Mooseleuk quad, DeLorme maps 56, 57)
Distance from the gravel pit parking area to
 • Norway Bluff summit (2,285 ft.): 1.0 mi., 1 hr.

SUGGESTED HIKES

Easy Hikes

Ledges Trail [lp: 1.2 mi., 35 min.]. A short loop hike to open ledges with good views south across the steep-walled valley that contains Lower and Upper South Branch ponds.

Daicey Pond Loop [lp: 1.7 mi., 50 min.]. A beautiful walk around a scenic pond via Nature and Appalachian trails with outstanding views of Katahdin and a good chance to see wildlife.

Little Abol Falls Trail [rt: 1.6 mi., 55 min.]. This short, scenic trail leads easily from Abol Campground to a series of falls on Abol Stream. Views of Katahdin are possible en route.

Big and Little Niagara Falls [rt: 2.4 mi., 1 hr. 10 min.]. An easy jaunt from Daicey Pond to three thundering waterfalls: Toll Dam and Little and Big Niagara falls.

Katahdin Stream Falls [rt: 2.4 mi., 1 hr. 15 min.]. A scenic walk on the AT next to Katahdin Stream that culminates at the impressive cascades of Katahdin Stream Falls.

Abol Pond Loop [lp: 2.9 mi., 1 hr. 25 min.]. A pleasant hike from Abol Pond to the AT, returning along Abol Stream. A refreshing swim at the beach at Abol Pond makes for a nice finish.

Owl's Head [rt: 2.8 mi., 1 hr. 30 min.]. A nice walk along the east shore of Scraggly Lake is followed by a short climb to ledges and broad views of the northern forestlands.

Burnt Mtn. Trail [rt: 2.6 mi., 1 hr. 30 min.]. An easy hike to ledges and views of the northwest corner of the park.

Caverly Lookout [rt: 2.6 mi., 1 hr. 40 min.]. A short hike from Russell Pond via Pogy Notch, Grand Falls, and Caverly Lookout trails to a panoramic view of the interior of the park.

Moderate Hikes

Trout Brook Mtn. Trail [lp: 3.5 mi., 3 hr.]. A fun loop hike to fine views of the Traveler Mtn. massif and surrounding ponds.

South Turner Mtn. [rt: 4.4 mi., 3 hr. 15 min.]. This hike via Sandy Stream Pond and South Turner Mtn. trails takes you past Sandy Stream Pond, which is frequented by moose, and ends on the summit of South Turner Mtn., where there are exceptional views of the park.

Sentinel Mtn. [rt: 5.2 mi., 3 hr.]. A fine hike from Kidney Pond via Sentinel Mtn. Trail to viewpoints overlooking the West Branch of the Penobscot River.

Howe Brook Trail [rt: 6.0 mi., 3 hr.]. A beautiful walk with little elevation change along a mountain brook, with chutes and potholes, ending at a small waterfall.

Five Ponds Trail [lp: 6.0 mi., 3 hr. 30 min.]. A loop around the base of Trout Brook Mtn. passes five scenic ponds en route: Long, High, Round, Billfish, and Littlefield.

Katahdin Lake [lp: 7.9 mi., 4 hr.]. A fine walk from Avalanche Field into the scenic environs of Katahdin Lake via Katahdin Lake Trail. Return via Martin Ponds Trail, with more outstanding views of Katahdin.

North Traveler Mtn. [rt: 5.8 mi., 4 hr. 30 min.]. An interesting hike via Pogy Notch and North Traveler Mtn. trails that traverses alpine meadows, old woods, and ledges to an impressive view from the summit of North Traveler Mtn.

Strenuous Hikes

Hamlin Peak Loop [lp: 4.6 mi., 4 hr. 45 min.]. Leaving from Chimney Pond, this route climbs the barren Hamlin Ridge to the alpine summit of Hamlin Peak before swinging south to The Saddle and descending Saddle Slide back to the pond.

Knife Edge—Baxter Peak Traverse [lp: 4.5 mi., 5 hr. 45 min.]. This exciting alpine hike starts from Chimney Pond and climbs Dudley Trail to Pamola Peak, then goes across the airy crest of Knife Edge to Baxter Peak before descending Cathedral Trail back to the pond.

Doubletop Traverse [ow: 7.9 mi., 6 hr. 30 min.]. An outstanding hike to a craggy alpine summit with impressive views of Katahdin, South Brother, Mt. Coe, Mt. OJI, and Barren Mtn.

Mt. Coe—South Brother Loop [lp: 8.0 mi., 7 hr.]. This hike via Marston and Mt. Coe trails gains access to the high peaks of Mt. Coe and South Brother, whose summits provide excellent views of the surrounding terrain.

Abol Trail to Baxter Peak via Hunt Trail [rt: 8.4 mi., 7 hr. 30 min.]. This is believed to be the oldest route up Katahdin. The trail climbs steeply up the rocks and scree of the Abol Slide, then follows Hunt Trail (AT) to Baxter Peak and the northern terminus of the AT.

Traveler Mtn. Loop [lp: 11.1 mi., 7 hr. 30 min.]. A demanding loop hike over Center Ridge, The Traveler, and North Traveler mountains via Pogy Notch, Center Ridge, Traveler Mtn., and North Traveler Mtn. trails. Outstanding views are possible from the high ridges and summits.

SECTION TWO
100-MILE WILDERNESS AND GREATER MOOSEHEAD LAKE

Nahmakanta Public Reserved
  Land 66

Nesuntabunt Mtn. 70

White Cap Mtn. 70

Gulf Hagas. 73

AMC Maine Woods Trails 76

Indian Mtn. 81

Chairback Mtn. 85

Third Mtn. 86

Barren Mtn. 87

Borestone Mtn. 89

Little Wilson Falls. 90

Little Moose Public Reserved
  Land 91

Little Moose Mtn. 91

Big Moose Mtn. 93

Eagle Rock 95

Elephant Mtn. 96

Number Four Mtn. 96

Mt. Kineo. 97

Little Kineo Mtn. 99

Big Spencer Mtn. 100

AMC map 2: 100-Mile Wilderness

**AMC Little Moose Mtn. and Big
  Moose Mtn. map (p. 94)**

Little Spencer Mtn. 100

Green Mtn. 101

Little Russell Mtn. 102

Suggested Hikes 103

The 100-Mile Wilderness and Greater Moosehead Lake section includes a portion of Somerset County north and west of Moosehead Lake and the area between Monson and Katahdin known as the 100-Mile Wilderness in south–central Piscataquis County. To the northeast, the region is bordered by BSP and the West Branch of the Penobscot River. The watersheds of the St. John and Allagash rivers form a rough boundary in the northwest. ME 15/6 is the southern boundary, and the headwaters of the Kennebec River form the western border.

Moosehead Lake, at 35 mi. long and with an area of 120 sq. mi., is the largest lake in Maine and the predominant natural feature in this section. The Moose River feeds into Moosehead Lake from the west, and the Roach River empties into the lake from the east. The Kennebec River flows from two outlets on the west side of the lake, emptying into the Atlantic Ocean 170 mi. downriver at Popham Beach.

This section describes 18 mountains and 43 trails. The approach to most of the mountains in this section is via Brownville Junction and ME 11 in the east, or by way of Greenville, a convenient and bustling gateway community on ME 15/6 at the southern end of Moosehead Lake. Other mountains require considerable travel over gravel logging roads.

Big Moose and Little Moose mountains rise above the southwest corner of Moosehead Lake. North of Seboomook Lake are Green and Little mountains. In the area between the main road that connects Greenville to the area south of BSP (named Lily Bay Rd. in its southern section, then Sias Hill Rd., and finally Golden Rd. as it approaches the Penobscot River) and Moosehead Lake are the peaks of Big Spencer, Little Spencer, and Little Kineo mountains. The iconic Mt. Kineo rises precipitously above Moosehead Lake just north of Rockwood. East of the road between Greenville and the Penobscot River in the area south of Kokadjo and First Roach Pond are Number Four and Elephant mountains.

The AT traverses this section from Monson to the West Branch of the Penobscot River, a distance of 100 mi. Known as the 100-Mile Wilderness because it is the longest stretch of the trail that does not cross a paved road, this part of the AT is considered by many in the hiking community to be one of the wildest and most remote stretches of the entire 2,180-mi. trail from Georgia to Maine. Several rugged mountain areas—including the five peaks of the Barren–Chairback Range and four peaks of the White Cap Range—must be crossed before you reach the somewhat gentler lake country to the north. Borestone Mtn. rises above Lake Onawa just south of the AT.

More than 500,000 acres of contiguous conservation lands exist today between the area in and around BSP south through the 100-Mile Wilderness and on to Moosehead Lake, thanks to the determined efforts of a host of public agencies and private conservation groups in recent years. From the 46,000-acre Debsconeag Lakes Wilderness Area owned by TNC to the 43,000-acre Nahmakanta PRL unit of the MBPL to the 66,500 acres owned by AMC, a significant portion of the 100-Mile Wilderness is now permanently protected.

Several of the mountains in this section lie within the boundaries of North Maine Woods and the KI–Jo Mary Multiple Use Forest, two large blocks of forestland. Most of this forestland is privately owned and cooperatively managed for renewable resources while providing outdoor recreational opportunities for the public. Visitors must register at a checkpoint and pay camping and day-use fees to enter these areas. See p. xvii for information about access to the lands managed by North Maine Woods.

Camping

Trailside camping is available along the AT corridor at 20 lean-tos and campsites.

In Nahmakanta PRL, numerous primitive campsites located throughout the preserve allow for extended visits. Vehicle accessible campsites are found at Pollywog West, Wadleigh North End, Wadleigh South End, Nahmakanta South End, Musquash Stream, Musquash Field, and Leavitt Pond. East Side, West Side, and East Beach on Nahmakanta Lake can be reached by canoe or boat. And access to Leavitt Pond North, Tumbledown Dick Pond, and Pollywog Southeast is by foot trail only. Check with MBPL about other dispersed camping opportunities in the Nahmakanta backcountry. Primitive campsites are available for backpackers at four ponds in Little Moose PRL, including Big and Little Moose ponds and Big and Little Notch ponds. Lily Bay State Park on Moosehead Lake just north of Greenville offers 90 drive-in campsites, hot showers, restrooms, and other amenities. Numerous primitive roadside campsites are found within the boundaries of North Maine Woods, and 60 drive-in campsites are available within the KI–Jo Mary Multiple Use Forest. Numerous privately operated campgrounds throughout this section offer a variety of camping and lodging choices and amenities. AMC's Maine Woods property features three wilderness lodges with private cabins and shared bunkhouses, and a number of drive-in, paddle-in, and walk-in campsites.

AMC's Maine Woods Initiative Land

The Maine Woods Initiative is AMC's strategy for land conservation in the 100-Mile Wilderness region. The initiative is an innovative approach to conservation that combines outdoor recreation, resource protection, sustainable forestry, and community partnerships. The strategy represents the most significant investment in conservation and recreation in AMC's history. The initiative seeks to address the ecological and economic needs of the Maine Woods region by supporting local forest-products jobs and traditional recreation, creating new multiday recreational experiences for visitors, and attracting new nature-based tourism to the region.

With the purchase of the 29,500-acre Roach Ponds Tract in 2009, and the 37,000-acre Katahdin Iron Works tract in 2003, AMC has permanently protected more than 66,500 acres of land in the region, creating a 63-mile-long corridor of conservation land stretching from AMC's property near Greenville north to BSP. This land is open to the public for recreational uses including hiking, paddling, camping, skiing, and snowshoeing. Fishing and hunting are also permitted in accordance with state law.

AMC is supporting regional, nature-based tourism efforts by creating an interconnected network of overnight accommodations and trails and offering guided outdoor recreation programs. AMC's Maine Wilderness Lodges—Gorman Chairback on Long Pond, Little Lyford at Little Lyford ponds, and Medawisla on Second Roach Pond—offer private cabins and bunkhouses and home-cooked meals, with many opportunities for hiking, paddling, fly fishing, snowshoeing, and cross-country skiing nearby. The lodges also offer a variety of guided programs. Reservations are required. Visit outdoors.org/mainelodges or call 603-466-2727 for more information.

In addition to the lodges, AMC maintains five campsites and a backcountry shelter on its property, all open to the public. These include drive-up sites near Horseshoe Pond, at Pearl Ponds, and at Long Pond; walk-in sites at Horseshoe Pond and Baker Pond; Phoenix Shelter at Trout Pond for backpackers; and the paddle-in Coyote Rock Campsite on Long Pond. A fee is charged. Campsite reservations can be made through the KI–Jo Mary Multiple Use Forest by calling 207-965-8135. AMC will open new paddle-in campsites on the Roach Ponds in 2012.

Nahmakanta Public Reserved Land

This remote 43,000-acre preserve, the largest in Maine's public lands system managed by MBPL, is located in the unincorporated townships of T1 R12 WELS, T1 R11 WELS, and Rainbow Township, southwest of Katahdin and BSP and north of Katahdin Iron Works.

Pristine Nahmakanta Lake is the predominant natural feature among the 24 lakes and ponds of more than 10 acres in size, and a series of mountain peaks and ridges range as high as 2,524 ft. in elevation, offering fine views of the forested terrain. Nearly one-quarter of the preserve, or 11,802 acres, has been designated as an ecological reserve to ensure that environmentally sensitive plant life will remain in its natural condition and be periodically monitored. This includes the 9,200-acre roadless area known as the Debsconeag Backcountry.

Twenty-eight miles of hiking trails are in Nahmakanta, including Turtle Ridge Loop, Tumbledown Dick, and Debsconeag Backcountry trails. A 9-mi. stretch of the AT traverses the preserve, entering in the east at Nahmakanta Stream and exiting in the north at Rainbow Stream.

Turtle Ridge Loop Trail (MBPL)

This scenic figure-eight loop hike on the southern boundary of the unit traverses Turtle Ridge and passes by a series of remote mountain ponds. Excellent views of the surrounding countryside of this wild region southwest of Katahdin may be had from various outlooks.

From ME 11 in T4 R9 NWP just south of the Piscataquis–Penobscot County line and about halfway between Brownville Junction and Millinocket, turn north on Jo-Mary Rd. and quickly reach the North Maine Woods checkpoint. A fee is charged to pass through the gate. Travel 16.0 mi., passing through the automated Henderson Checkpoint, to reach the east trailhead. The west trailhead is reached by continuing north and west on Jo-Mary Rd. for 3.8 mi. to a jct. Turn left (west) on Nahmakanta Rd. and proceed 1.2 mi. to Long Pond Rd. Turn left (south) and drive 1.0 mi. to the trailhead on the left. The Turtle Ridge area can also be reached from Greenville via Lily Bay, Sias Hill, Smithtown, and Nahmakanta roads.

The loop is described from the west trailhead. Walk easily 1.1 mi. east to a jct. near the southwest corner of Sing Sing Pond. Turn left (north) and cross the outlet of the pond on a footbridge. The cliffs of Turtle Ridge are visible from this spot. After a short climb, the trail emerges at the west end of the cliffs and proceeds through semi-open spruce forest and across ledges to a cliff-top viewpoint overlooking the pond. The trail then descends to a jct. at the northeast corner of Hedgehog Pond. The trail to the right connects to the loop on the opposite side of the pond. Continuing straight ahead, reach a jct. with the eastern half of the loop. Turn left and soon reach Rabbit Pond and the pretty granite slabs at its outlet. Past the pond, the trail trends downhill to the next jct. Here, it is 0.2 mi. to the east trailhead on Jo-Mary Rd.

Continuing to the right, the trail climbs the spine of a ridge to reach a series of cliffs with views to Katahdin and the many lakes to the north and east. Ahead, the loop follows the ridgeline to a side trail leading to a lookout over Henderson and Long ponds. Beyond, the loop descends to the north shore of Henderson Pond before turning west and rising easily through semi-open forest to a height-of-land. The loop then drops down through mature forest to return to the loop jct. Turn left (west) to reach Hedgehog Pond, then continue along the south shore of Sing Sing Pond and farther on to the west trailhead and the completion of the loop.

Turtle Ridge Loop Trail (AMC map 2: C5)

Distance from west trailhead (1,250 ft.) to
- Sing Sing Pond outlet (1,250 ft.): 1.1 mi., 30 min.
- Hedgehog Pond jct. (via Turtle Ridge) (1,350 ft.): 3.3 mi., 1 hr. 50 min.
- Hedgehog Pond jct. (via south shore of Sing Sing Pond) (1,350 ft.): 2.3 mi., 1 hr. 10 min.
- East trailhead (via Turtle Ridge and Rabbit Pond) (1,100 ft.): 4.7 mi., 2 hr. 45 min.
- East trailhead (via Sing Sing Pond and Henderson Pond) (1,100 ft.): 5.0 mi., 2 hr. 30 min.
- Entire figure-eight loop: 9.3 mi., 5 hr. 30 min.

Tumbledown Dick Trail (MBPL)

This connector trail links Turtle Ridge Loop to the AT and Debsconeag Backcountry Trail and makes possible a number of overnight backpacking possibilities. The trail leaves Jo-Mary Rd. at a point 150 yd. north of the Turtle Ridge Loop east trailhead on Jo-Mary Road.

Traveling easterly, Leavitt Pond is soon visible through the trees, and a side trail leads to a viewpoint on its northwest shore. Ahead, the trail follows the edge of the pond before bearing away to reach a jct. Here, a side trail leads right 175 yd. to a campsite and another viewpoint across the pond. Continuing on through mostly cutover forest, the trail arrives at Tumbledown Dick Pond and a campsite set in the pines. The trail follows the west shore, and, after crossing the pond's outlet, contours above Tumbledown Dick Stream. At a new logging road, the trail goes left and crosses the stream on a bridge and soon reaches Tumbledown Dick Falls. From an open spot immediately northeast of the falls is a view of Katahdin. The falls is a wonderful narrow drop worthy of exploration. Just ahead, a side trail right leads to a pool at the base of the falls. Beyond is a gentle downhill walk to a jct. with the AT. To the left (west), it is 0.6 mi. to a campsite, boat launch, and beach on the south shore of Nahmakanta Lake.

Tumbledown Dick Trail (AMC map 2: C5–C6)

Jo-Mary Rd. trailhead (1,100 ft.) to
- AT jct. (700 ft.): 4.4 mi., 2 hr.
- Nahmakanta Lake, south end (via AT) (650 ft.): 5.0 mi., 2 hr. 15 min.

Debsconeag Backcountry Trail (MBPL)

From ME 11 in T4 R9 NWP just south of the Piscataquis–Penobscot county line and about halfway between Brownville Junction and Millinocket, turn north on Jo-Mary Rd. and quickly reach the North Maine Woods checkpoint. A fee is charged to pass through the gate. Travel 21.0 mi., passing through Henderson Checkpoint, to reach Nahmakanta Stream Rd. To reach the south trailhead, turn right (east) here and drive 6.0 mi. to trailhead parking on the left, crossing the AT at a bridge over Nahmakanta Stream en route. To reach the north trailhead, continue north on the Wadleigh Pond Rd. for 6.0 mi. to a small parking area just north of Nahmakanta Lake Camps near the north end of the lake.

From the south trailhead, the trail heads north through mixed woods and occasional sandy-soiled openings to a jct. just south of Fifth Debsconeag Pond at 0.9 mi. To the right, it is 0.5 mi. along a stream to a woods road on Fourth Debsconeag Pond, and 1.0 mi. back to the south trailhead, an alternate start if desired. To the left, it is 2.0 mi. to the west side of Sixth Debsconeag Pond. Continue straight ahead to begin the loop.

Cross the outlet stream and continue along the east shore of Fifth Debsconeag Lake. Bear away from the lake, cross a stream, and climb alongside it to reach Stink Pond. Bear west and climb to the ledges above the pond before dropping into a shallow valley. Beyond, the trail climbs to the open ledges above Seventh Debsconeag Pond, where you will have views of Nesuntabunt and White Cap mountains, Fifth Debsconeag Lake, and Pemadumcook Lake. On the descent of the ledges, come to a jct. at 4.4 mi. To the left, a section of the loop trail leads 1.0 mi. past Sixth Debsconeag Pond to the east shore of Nahmakanta Lake. Ahead, the trail crosses a stream and passes south of a pond on ledges, soon reaching Eighth Debsconeag Pond. After the pond, the trail swings west and descends moderately to reach Gould Brook and a jct. at 6.9 mi. To the right, a spur trail leads 0.9 mi. to the north trailhead.

Following Gould Brook downhill, the trail reaches a small sand beach at the north end of Nahmakanta Lake. Nahmakanta Lake Camps can be seen a short distance west along the lake. The trail then parallels the shore for nearly half the length of the lake, until finally bearing east away from the water, and rising through a small ravine. At 9.6 mi., the trail reaches a jct. at Sixth Debsconeag Pond. Straight ahead, the trail connects in 1.0 mi. to the loop above Seventh Debsconeag Lake. To the right, the trail contours along the south side of Sixth Debsconeag Pond and then Fifth Debsconeag Pond before arriving at the original trail jct. at 11.6 mi. Straight ahead, it is a direct 0.9 mi. back to the trailhead parking area. To the left leads to Fourth Debsconeag Pond and then on to the same trailhead.

Debsconeag Backcountry Trail (AMC map 2: B5)

Distances from trailhead parking area (650 ft.) to
- Loop jct. at Fifth Debsconeag Pond (800 ft.): 0.9 mi., 35 min.
- jct. connector trail to Sixth Debsconeag Pond (1,150 ft.): 4.4 mi., 2 hr. 10 min.
- jct. spur trail to north trailhead (850 ft.): 6.9 mi., 3 hr. 25 min.
- Sixth Debsconeag Pond (via loop) (950 ft.): 9.6 mi., 4 hr. 45 min.
- Loop jct. at Fifth Debsconeag Pond (800 ft.): 11.6 mi., 5 hr. 45 min.
- Complete loop: 12.5 mi., 6 hr. 15 min.

Nesuntabunt Mtn. (1,550 ft.)

This mountain rises to the west of Nahmakanta Lake in T1 R11. Its summit offers excellent views of Katahdin from the south as well as views over the wilderness region around Nahmakanta Lake. The Wadleigh Stream Lean-to on the AT is about 2.0 mi. south of the summit.

To reach the trailhead, take ME 11 about 16 mi. northeast of Brownville Junction, and turn left (north) onto Jo-Mary Rd. immediately after crossing Bear Brook. A checkpoint with a fee is just off ME 11 on Jo-Mary Rd. Follow this road for about 25 mi., passing through the automated Henderson Checkpoint, toward the northwestern end of Nahmakanta Lake. Park where the AT crosses the road. Follow the AT south to the northern summit. A 250-ft. side trail leads to splendid views.

Nesuntabunt Mtn. (AMC map 2: B4–B5, MATC map 1, DeLorme map 42)
Distance from AT crossing (1,050 ft.) to
  • Nesuntabunt Mtn. summit (1,550 ft.): 1.2 mi., 45 min.

White Cap Mtn. (3,654 ft.)

White Cap Mtn. in Bowdoin College Grant East Township is the highest point on the AT between Katahdin and Bigelow and the highest peak in the east–west range of mountains that includes Hay Mtn., West Peak, and Gulf Hagas Mtn. Rising north of the West Branch of the Pleasant River in the heart of the 100-Mile Wilderness, White Cap Mtn. offers outstanding views from its high ridges and alpine summit. There are three approaches to White Cap Mtn.: from the south via White Brook Trail and the AT; from the south and west via the AT across the White Cap Range; and from the north via the AT and Logan Brook.

White Brook Trail (MATC)

To reach White Brook Trail—the former route of the AT, and still maintained by the MATC—turn left (northwest) off ME 11 5.5 mi. north of Brownville Junction. The sign for Katahdin Iron Works at the turnoff marks the start of a 6.8-mi. drive on the K-I Rd. from ME 11 to a gate at Katahdin Iron Works, an interesting state historical site with a blast furnace and a beehive charcoal burner. Register at the gate and pay a fee to pass into the KI–Jo Mary Multiple Use Forest, a 175,000-acre block of privately owned commercial forestland located between Millinocket, Greenville, and Brownville.

Bear right after driving through the gate and cross the West Branch of the Pleasant River. At the 3.0-mi. mark, take the right fork. At about 5.8 mi. from Katahdin Iron Works, the road crosses the "High Bridge," a high, narrow bridge over White Brook. At the next jct., continue straight ahead up the west side of White Brook. (The left fork leads to Hay Brook and Gulf Hagas.) Follow the major gravel road for another 3.8 mi., taking the main branch at each fork, and park to the side of the road just south of where it crosses two brooks (the culverts have been removed, and this is likely as far as you can comfortably drive).

The trail follows the old logging road uphill for 1.0 mi. to a large wood yard. The White Cap–Hay Mtn. sag is clearly visible from this yard. A blue-blazed trail leaves the left side of the yard at the end of the road and climbs the southern slope toward the sag through a heavily logged area. At 1.4 mi., the trail crosses White Brook near the ruins of the old fire warden's cabin. Just beyond is a jct.

To the left, White Brook Trail climbs more steeply and reaches a jct. with the AT in another 0.5 mi. From this, it is a 1.1 mi. hike along a high ridge to the open summit of White Cap Mtn. To the right, the very steep and eroded Fire Warden's Trail (not recommended) climbs 0.8 mi. to join the AT just 0.3 mi. west of the summit.

Panoramic views from the summit include the long ridge of Saddleback to the east, Little Spruce and Big Spruce mountains just to the southeast, Baker Mtn. and the peaks of the White Cap Range to the west, Big Moose to the southwest, and Big Spencer Mtn. to the northwest, as well as the vast lake country to the north, rising all the way to the Katahdin massif. The view is arguably one of the finest in the state.

White Brook Trail (AMC map 2: F3, E3–E4, MATC map 2, DeLorme map 42)

Distances from end of drivable logging road (1,950 ft.) to

- White Brook crossing (2,600 ft.): 1.4 mi., 1 hr.
- AT jct. (2,950 ft.): 1.9 mi., 1 hr. 30 min.
- White Cap Mtn. summit (3,654 ft.) (via AT): 3.0 mi., 2 hr. 25 min.

Via the AT from the south (MATC)

The summit of White Cap Mtn. can be reached from the K-I Rd. (at a point 15.5 mi. west of ME 11) in the south by way of an 11.3-mi. hike along the AT and a short 0.2-mi. spur trail. Such a trek involves a significant amount of ascent and descent over the high peaks of Gulf Hagas Mtn., West Peak, and Hay Mtn. before reaching the top of White Cap Mtn. It is therefore suited to a multiday backpack trip rather than a day hike. Three campsites—Carl A Newhall Lean-to, Sidney Tappan Campsite, and Logan Brook Lean-to—are available for overnight stays. Please refer to the MATC Guide to the Appalachian Trail in Maine for complete details on this extended hike. Refer to the driving directions for Gulf Hagas to reach the trailhead parking for this trip.

White Cap Mtn. via AT from south (AMC map 2: F3, E3–E4, MATC map 2, DeLorme map 42)

Distances from K-I Rd. trailhead parking area (650 ft.) to

- Gulf Hagas Mtn. summit (2,690 ft.): 6.6 mi., 4 hr. 20 min.
- West Peak summit (3,178 ft.): 8.2 mi., 5 hr. 25 min.
- Hay Mtn. summit (3,250 ft.): 9.8 mi., 6 hr. 15 min.
- White Cap Mtn. summit (3,654 ft.): 11.5 mi., 7 hr. 20 min.

Via the AT from the north (MATC)

From the blinking traffic light in the center of Greenville on ME 15/6, follow Lily Bay Rd. north for 18 mi. to Frenchtown Rd., a wide dirt road on the right marked by both a street sign and a long row of mailboxes. Turn right onto Frenchtown Rd. and follow this along the south shore of First Roach Pond and beyond. Reach a jct. at 10.9 mi. from Lily Bay Rd. and bear left. Pass West Branch Pond Camps, and soon after, drive between First and Second West Branch ponds. At 11.6 mi. from Lily Bay Rd., bear left and drive another 1 mi. (a rough stretch of road that may be impassable by most passenger cars). At 12.6 mi., bear right and proceed to a gate at 13.7 mi. Parking is available off the road to either side.

Walk east along the road for 0.5 mi. to its intersection with the AT (sign). Turn right here and start to climb the east slope of White Cap Mtn., moderately at first, then more steeply along the south bank of Logan Brook. At 1.9 mi., the trail reaches Logan Brook Lean-to. Beyond, the trail rises steadily via a long series of rock steps to emerge into the open at the summit ridge. Follow the rocky trail to the open summit of White Cap Mtn. at 2.8 mi.

White Cap Mtn. via AT from north (AMC map 2: E4, MATC map 2, DeLorme map 42)

Distances from parking and gate on logging road (1,650 ft.) to
- AT jct. (1,700): 0.5 mi., 15 min.
- Logan Brook Lean-to (2,450 ft.): 1.9 mi., 1 hr. 20 min.
- White Cap Mtn. summit (3,654 ft.): 2.8 mi., 2 hr. 25 min.

Gulf Hagas

Popularly known as the "Grand Canyon of Maine," Gulf Hagas is located just west of the AT and the White Cap Mtn. Range. This unique scenic area consists of a deep, narrow, slate canyon on the West Branch of the Pleasant River. The river drops about 400 ft. in about 4 mi., and in many places, the vertical walls of the canyon force the river into very narrow channels that form a series of waterfalls, rapids, chutes, and pools. The falls are particularly spectacular in late spring during peak runoff. In winter, ice builds up on the walls and, because the sun rarely reaches certain faces, often lasts into late June.

Gulf Hagas was designated a registered natural landmark in 1968, and 500 acres, including the entire canyon, were set aside for public enjoyment. In 1986, the National Park Service obtained nearly 2,000 acres, including the Gulf and the corridor along Gulf Hagas Brook, to permanently protect the unique natural beauty of this area.

Much of the Gulf Hagas trail system runs near the rim of the canyon, with frequent side trails to viewpoints and falls. And by using the old Pleasant River Rd. on the return trip, a loop hike is possible.

To reach the main Gulf Hagas trailhead, drive north on ME 11 from Brownville Junction for 5.5 mi. Turn left (west) on Katahdin Iron Works Rd. and drive 6.8 mi. to the KI–Jo Mary Forest Checkpoint. A fee is charged to pass through the gate. Beyond the gate, take the right fork. At 3.4 mi. from the gatehouse, the road reaches a second fork. Stay left here, crossing the West Branch of the Pleasant River on a bridge. The

K-I Rd. reaches the trailhead parking area on the right at 6.7 mi. from the gatehouse.

From the parking area, follow the spur trail downhill to a jct. with the AT at 0.2 mi. Turn right, and quickly reach the south bank of the West Branch of the Pleasant River. Ford the river (knee-deep in normal water conditions) to reach a jct. with Pleasant River Tote Rd. at 0.4 mi. Turn left (west) here and walk through the Hermitage, a 35-acre preserve of old white pines that is a National Natural Landmark. At 1.5 mi., the AT bears sharply right (north). To enter Gulf Hagas, proceed straight ahead, and ford Gulf Hagas Brook (no bridge; use caution in high water).

Rim Trail (MATC)

Immediately after the crossing, reach a jct. Pleasant River Tote Rd. continues straight ahead for 2.2 mi. to the Head of the Gulf. Most hikers use this trail for the return trip.

Rim Trail leaves left and descends steeply along Gulf Hagas Brook past Screw Auger Falls and on to the rim of the canyon. The trail then continues west, and at 0.7 mi., a side trail leads left to Hammond Street Pitch, a point high above the canyon that offers a fine view of the gorge. Return to the rim trail and turn left (at 0.9 mi., a short connector trail leads back to Pleasant River Rd.).

Continuing along the Rim Trail, at 1.2 mi. from Pleasant River Rd., is a series of side paths leading to views of the Jaws, where the river squeezes around a slate spur and narrows in many places. Back on the Rim Trail, at 1.8 mi., Gulf Hagas Cutoff diverges right, crosses Pleasant River Tote Rd. in 0.2 mi., and meets the AT in 1.2 mi. To the left, a spur trail leads to a viewpoint below Buttermilk Falls.

Beyond, the canyon gradually becomes shallower, and at times, the trail approaches the banks of the West Branch. At 2.5 mi. from Pleasant River Rd., the trail passes Billings Falls. At 2.6 mi., the trail reaches the ledge above Stair Falls, where the narrow river drops into a large pool. In another 0.1 mi., the trail bears sharply away from the river. (At this point, a short side trail leads left to the edge of the river near a rocky island called Head of the Gulf, where you can see some interesting logging artifacts.)

The trail reaches a jct. at 2.8 mi. To the right (east), the Pleasant River Tote Rd. proceeds on a contour high above Gulf Hagas back to the jct. with the AT in 2.4 mi. Although it is often very marshy and wet, the road offers a quicker return than the Rim Trail. To the left, Head of the Gulf Trail leads 1.2 mi. to a bridge over the West Branch of the Pleasant River (an alternative route to Gulf Hagas during high-water conditions).

Gulf Hagas Loop (AMC map 2: F2–F3, MATC map 2 or 3)

Distances from K-1 Rd. trailhead parking area (650 ft.) to
- AT jct. and West Branch of Pleasant River: 0.2 mi., 5 min.
- Rim Trail/Pleasant River Tote Rd. jct. via AT: 1.5 mi., 45 min.
- Gulf Hagas Cutoff (via Rim Trail): 3.2 mi., 1 hr. 40 min.
- Head of the Gulf/Pleasant River Tote Rd. jct. (via Rim Trail): 4.3 mi., 2 hr. 10 min.
- AT jct. (via Pleasant River Tote Rd.): 6.5 mi., 3 hr. 15 min.
- Complete Gulf Hagas Loop via AT and spur trail from parking area: 8.0 mi., 4 hr.

Head of the Gulf Trail (AMC)

This trail provides access to the Gulf Hagas area with the advantage of not requiring you to ford the West Branch of the Pleasant River. So, in high-water conditions or with small children or otherwise, this trail is a good choice. The trail leaves the east side of Upper Valley Rd. at an information kiosk. Trailhead parking is 50 ft. past the trailhead to the left (north).

The trail starts out wide and flat. In 200 ft., bear left at a jct. At 0.2 mi., the trail crosses a bridge over a small brook, and in another 0.2 mi., the trail crosses a grassy floodplain on bog bridges. At 0.5 mi., the trail joins a gravel road and turns right to cross the West Branch of the Pleasant River on a bridge. The trail leaves the road to the right at 0.6 mi., and continues as a wide path. An unmarked angler's trail leaves left to Lloyd Pond at 0.9 mi., and just ahead, the trail crosses the rocky outlet of that pond. After a stretch of rocky footing, the trail enters a balsam fir stand at 1.4 mi. After the trail crosses a brook and ascends briefly, a short spur trail to the right leads to views of the West Branch of the Pleasant River. After a short descent, Head of the Gulf Trail makes a sharp right turn and enters NPS land (yellow sign). Beyond, the trail narrows and crosses a brook on a split-log bridge. At 1.7 mi., the trail reaches a jct. To the right, Rim Trail leads along the canyon rim of Gulf Hagas canyon for 2.8 mi. to a jct. with the AT near Screw Auger Falls. Straight ahead, Pleasant River Tote Rd. follows an easier route high above the river canyon, reaching a jct. with the AT at 2.2 mi.

Head of the Gulf Trail (AMC map 2: E2–E3, F3)

Distances from Upper Valley Rd. trailhead (1,150 ft.) to
- bridge over West Branch Pleasant River (1,150 ft.): 0.5 mi., 15 min.
- jct., Rim Trail and Pleasant River Tote Rd. (1,150 ft.): 1.7 mi., 50 min.
- complete Gulf Hagas loop: 8.4 mi., 4 hr. 15 min.

AMC Maine Woods Trails

AMC maintains more than 80 mi. of public hiking, showshoeing, and ski trails on its Maine Woods conservation and recreation property. Hikers can connect with the AT by taking the Third Mountain Trail from near Gorman Chairback Lodge and Cabins, or the Pleasant River Trail from near Little Lyford Lodge and Cabins. Connector trails also lead from near both lodges to the Rim Trail along Gulf Hagas. A variety of shorter trails in and around the lodges offers miles of pleasant hiking.

A KI–Jo Mary Multiple Use Forest gate fee is charged from May through October for vehicle access to the southern half of AMC's Maine Woods property. Information on local trail conditions is available from AMC's Greenville office by calling 207-695-3085.

AMC's Maine Woods property is located in the heart of the 100-Mile Wilderness east of Greenville and west of ME 11 outside of Brownville Junction. Please note that the access roads are not paved and are subject to washouts and potholes. Roads may not be passable by cars with low clearance. Please limit speed to 25 MPH, and yield to logging trucks. No fuel is available after you leave the state highways. Call AMC in advance for road conditions during spring, fall, or when storms are expected.

From the west via Greenville: At the blinking traffic light in the center of Greenville on ME 15/6, proceed north one block and turn right onto Pleasant St. After 2.0 mi., the road becomes gravel. At 11.0 mi. from Greenville, stop and register at the KI–Jo Mary Hedgehog checkpoint (gate fee charged).

To Little Lyford: Proceed 1.8 mi. farther, and turn left on Upper Valley Rd. Go another 1.1 mi., and bear left again, then go 1.0 mi. to the Little Lyford Lodge and Cabins entrance on the right. Follow the blue squares with reflective arrows to the guest parking area a short distance from the lodge area.

To Gorman Chairback: Proceed 1.8 mi. farther, and turn right at the T intersection onto K-I Rd. Continue 3.5 mi., and turn right onto Chairback Mtn. Rd. Continue for 1.3 mi., and turn right onto the Gorman Chairback Lodge and Cabins driveway, which leads directly to the facility.

From the east via Brownville: Approach the K-I Rd. on ME 11 either 26 mi. southbound from Millinocket or 5.5 mi. northbound from Brownville Junction. Signage for the Katahdin Iron Works Historic Site (KIW) may be missing, so check your mileage. Turn west onto K-I Rd. The KIW checkpoint at the entrance to KI–Jo Mary Forest is 6.3 mi. from ME 11. Stop and register (fee charged).

To Little Lyford: From the gate, go 10.6 mi. Bear right and go 1.1 mi., then bear left, and go another 1.0 mi. to the Little Lyford Lodge and Cabins entrance on the right. Follow the blue squares with reflective arrows to the guest parking area a short distance from the lodge area.

To Gorman Chairback: From the gate, go 7.3 mi. Turn left onto Chairback Mtn. Rd. Continue for 1.3 mi., and turn right onto the Gorman Chairback Lodge and Cabins driveway, which will lead you directly to the facility.

Mountain Brook Pond Trail (AMC)

This short walk leads to the south shore of pretty Mountain Brook Pond. Park on the left side of Baker Pond Rd. in a small parking lot, 1.3 mi. west of Upper Valley Rd. and 4.4 mi. north of the jct. of Greenville Rd. and K-I Rd.

The trail to the pond (sign) leaves the road about 20 ft. east of the lot. Cross the road and head north, down the bank on a wooded path, which leads into a small clearing just short of Mountain Brook Pond. Log bridges lead down to the shore. Canoes are available here for use by AMC guests.

Note: From the same parking lot for Mountain Brook Pond Trail, a spur trail heads south for 0.2 mi. to a jct. with Pearl Ponds Trail.

Mountain Brook Pond Trail (AMC map 2: E2)

Distance from parking lot on Upper Valley Rd. (1,550 ft.) to
  • Mountain Brook Pond (1,550 ft.): 0.2 mi., 10 min.

Baker Pond Trail (AMC)

Parking for this trail is the same as for Mountain Brook Trail. From the parking lot, walk 0.3 mi. west along Baker Pond Rd. Turn right and walk around the large gate, and then up an old rocky roadbed. Shortly, where an older grown-in roadbed branches to the left, Baker Pond Trail heads to the right. The old road crests over three small hills until it then straightens out. It then crosses a brook and bears to the right. The trail then reaches a jct., where a sign indicates that Baker Pond is 0.4 mi. to the left, and Mountain Brook Pond is 0.7 mi. straight ahead and then quickly right.

To Baker Pond. From the jct., the trail to Baker Pond follows a graded path, bears to the left, and then crosses a wooden bridge. This lowland trail can often be wet and muddy. Ahead, the path narrows, and bog bridges are around the pond. The trail ends at Baker Pond Campsite. Just below the campsite is a nice view across the pond.

To Mountain Brook Pond. From the jct., the trail to Mountain Brook Pond continues along the rocky roadbed. It quickly reaches a jct. with an old logging road. Here the trail turns right (sign). Ahead, the road becomes overgrown and passes through a small clearing with good views of Baker Mtn. The trail turns into a grassy path as it heads down into the woods. Continuing on, the trail descends to Mountain Brook Pond and a small clearing with pond views.

Baker Pond Trail (AMC map 2: E2)

Distances from parking lot on Baker Pond Rd. (1,550 ft.) to
  • start of trail (via Baker Pond Rd.) (1,550 ft.): 0.3 mi., 10 min.
  • jct., trail north to Baker Pond and trail south to Mountain Brook Pond (1,650 ft.): 1.1 mi., 30 min.
  • Baker Pond Campsite (1,650 ft.): 1.5 mi., 45 min.
  • Mountain Brook Pond (1,550 ft.): 1.8 mi., 55 min.

Grassy Pond Trail (AMC)

Parking for this trail is the same as for Mountain Brook Trail. From the parking lot, walk 0.4 mi. west along Baker Pond Rd. to a grassy trail entrance on the right. Pass between three large boulders, following a wide path. The trail goes up uphill briefly, then drops down a set of log stairs to the east shore of Grassy Pond. Canoes are available here for AMC guests.

Grassy Pond Trail (AMC map 2: E2)

Distances from parking lot on Baker Pond Rd. (1,550 ft.) to
- start of trail (1,500 ft.) (via Baker Pond Rd.): 0.4 mi., 10 min.
- Grassy Pond (1,550 ft.): 0.5 mi., 15 min.

Horseshoe Pond Trail – West Section (AMC)

From the jct. of Greenville Rd. and K-I Rd., drive 2.1 mi. north on Upper Valley Rd. to the jct. with Baker Pond Rd. Turn left onto Baker Pond Rd. and follow this to its end at a parking lot (sign) and Pearl Ponds Campsite number 4.

From the lot, follow the wide, graded trail. The route is flat and winding, and leads gradually uphill. The trail ends at a tiny inlet on the north shore of Horseshoe Pond. Wooden stairs lead down to the water. Canoes are available here for AMC guests.

Horseshoe Pond Trail – West Section (AMC map 2: E2)

Distance from parking lot at end of Baker Pond Rd. (1,450 ft.) to
- Horseshoe Pond (1,450 ft.): 0.6 mi., 15 min.

Horseshoe Pond Trail – East Section (AMC)

This section of Horseshoe Pond Trail leaves from a logging road just south of Baker Pond Rd., at a point 0.7 mi. west of Upper Valley Rd. and 3.8 mi. north of the jct. of Greenville Rd. and K-I Rd. From Baker Pond Rd., walk south on the logging road for 100 yd. to a trail jct. Here, Horseshoe Pond Trail leaves the road to the right (west), while Indian Mtn. Circuit leaves the road to the left (east).

Horseshoe Pond Trail is a wide, grassy forest path. Cross four log bridges through a wet area to reach the jct. with Pearl Ponds Trail on the right at 0.3 mi. Continuing ahead on Horseshoe Pond Trail, the route follows a contour around the base of Indian Mtn. on an increasingly rough foot trail, crossing 29 bog bridges. Heading gradually downhill, the trail crosses a small stream just before a large wooden bridge. There is a view of Pearl Ponds to the right. The wide path climbs a small rise, then descends to a jct. just above the pond at 0.9 mi. A spur trail to the right leads 50 yd. to Horseshoe Pond Campsite and the pond, where a grassy clearing offers a beautiful view across the pond to Elephant Mtn.

Continuing on Horseshoe Pond Trail, the path leads north, away from the pond, climbing gradually to its end on a logging road at 1.4 mi. To the left (north), this road may be followed for 0.8 mi. to the start of the trail just south of Baker Pond Rd., thus making a loop hike possible.

Horseshoe Pond Trail – East Section (AMC map 2: E2)

Distances from Baker Pond Rd. (1,550 ft.) to
- Pearl Ponds Trail jct. (1,500 ft.): 0.3 mi., 10 min.
- Horseshoe Pond and Campsite (1,450 ft.): 0.9 mi., 25 min.
- end of trail at logging road (1,650 ft.): 1.4 mi., 40 min.
- complete loop (via logging road): 2.2 mi., 1 hr. 5 min.

Pearl Ponds Trail (AMC)

Parking for this trail is the same as for Mountain Brook Trail. From the parking lot, hike south 0.2 mi. on Grassy Pond Trail to a jct., then turn west. After crossing two small wooden bridges, the trail soon intersects with a short side trail on the left, which leads to the Pearl Ponds. Continuing straight on wide and grassy Pearl Ponds Trail, the trail soon bears left over a bridge, then reaches a wooden bench with a view of the Pearl Ponds. Ahead, the trail continues left and uphill to another jct. at 0.4 mi. To the right, a side trail leads to Pearl Ponds Campsites numbers 2 and 3. Continuing straight on the main trail, a jct. with a gravel road is reached at 0.6 mi. Cross the gravel road, and continue to Grassy Pond, where the trail ends at 0.7 mi.

Pearl Pond Trails (AMC map 2: E2)

Distances from parking lot on Baker Pond Rd. (1,550 ft.) to
- side trail to Pearl Ponds: 0.3 mi., 15 min.

- jct. with gravel road: 0.6 mi., 30 min.
- Grassy Pond: 0.7 mi., 35 min.

Indian Mtn. (2,338 ft.)

Indian Mtn. rises prominently from the valley west of the West Branch of the Pleasant River. Its open summit ledges (reached via Laurie's Ledge Trail) provide hikers with excellent views of AMC's Maine Woods property in the heart of the 100-Mile Wilderness.

Indian Mtn. Circuit (AMC)

This trail extends across the northern flank of Indian Mtn., just west of Little Lyford Ponds. The trail starts on Upper Valley Rd., diagonally across from the entrance to Little Lyford Lodge and Cabins, at a point 2.1 mi. north of the jct. of Greenville Rd. and K-I Rd. Parking is in a small lot at the trailhead.

The trail ascends gradually through the forest to the jct. with Laurie's Ledge Trail (sign) at 0.4 mi. The two trails share the same route for the next 0.3 mi. Ahead, where Laurie's Ledge Trail leaves to the left (south), Indian Mtn. Circuit Trail continues its westerly course around the mountain, generally on a contour. At 1.7 mi., the trail ends at a logging road 100 yd. south of Baker Pond Rd. Directly across the road is the east end of Pearl Ponds Trail.

Indian Mtn. Circuit (AMC map 2: E2)

Distances from trailhead parking on Upper Valley Rd. (1,300 ft.) to

- Laurie's Ledge Trail, east jct. (1,500 ft.): 0.4 mi., 20 min.
- Laurie's Ledge Trail, west jct. (1,600 ft.): 0.7 mi., 30 min.
- end of trail at logging road (100 yd. south of Baker Pond Rd.) (1,550 ft.): 1.7 mi., 1 hr.

Laurie's Ledge Trail (AMC)

Built by AMC in 2003 and named for its former Board of Directors president, Laurie Burt, the trail offers fine views to the north from its easterly overlook. White Cap and Gulf Hagas mountains are visible, and on a clear day Katahdin can be seen. From the westerly outlook there are good views of Elephant Mtn. and many of the area's ponds.

Parking for the trail is located on the left side of Upper Valley Rd., about 2.3 mi. north of the jct. of Greenville Rd. and K-I Rd. (soon after the entrance to Little Lyford Lodge and Cabins).

Follow the trail up the bank, then head left across a log bridge. The trail leads along the edge of a large boulder, where there is a view of Little Lyford Ponds and the ridge beyond before the trail switchbacks to the left. After a gradual but steady ascent, a jct. with Indian Mtn. Circuit is reached at 0.3 mi. The two trails share the same route, a grassy old logging road, for the next 0.3 mi. Ahead, at 0.6 mi., where Indian Mtn. Circuit continues straight, Laurie's Ledge Trail turns left.

The trail ascends moderately, soon passing through an interesting rock formation at about 0.7 mi. Beyond, the trail climbs to the base of a large cliff band and runs along the lower part of this for 100 yd. It then turns right and climbs steeply to a narrow ledge with a fine view to the east and south. Ahead, it reaches a side trail on the right leading 50 yd. to the easterly overlook and views to the north. Beyond, the trail continues to climb steadily, steeply at times, for 0.4 mi. The angle finally eases and the trail leads over the upper slopes to reach the westerly overlook below the true summit.

Laurie's Ledge Trail (AMC map 2: E2)
Distances from trailhead parking on Upper Valley Rd. (1,300 ft.) to
- Indian Mtn. Circuit, east jct. (1,500 ft.): 0.3 mi., 20 min.
- Indian Mtn. Circuit, west jct. (1,600 ft.): 0.6 mi., 30 min.
- Laurie's Ledge, westerly overlook (2,300 ft.): 1.5 mi., 1 hr. 15 min.

River Trail (AMC)

This trail runs south from AMC Little Lyford Lodge and Cabins along the west bank of the West Branch of the Pleasant River to a bridge crossing the river. Here the trail joins Head of the Gulf Trail, which runs southward to Gulf Hagas and Rim Trail and Pleasant River Tote Rd.

The trail leaves from behind Mountain View Cabin in the Little Lyford Lodge and Cabins area. Start by crossing a wet area on bog bridges before reaching a jct. with a spur trail (leads to the Pleasant River at the site of an old dam). Just ahead, at 0.1 mi., Nation's Nature Trail diverges to the right.

River Trail continues ahead at a moderate grade, following a ridge parallel to the river. Dropping down, it crosses a spot next to the river, and then climbs gradually, crossing a minor drainage. The trail then continues south, bearing away from the river. Pass Forrest's Folly, a winter ski trail, on the right at 0.7 mi. Ahead, reach a woods road at 1.0 mi. A bridge crossing the West Branch of the Pleasant River is visible on the left. Cross the bridge to connect with Head of the Gulf Trail, which provides access to Gulf Hagas.

River Trail (AMC map 2: E2–F2)
Distance from AMC Little Lyford Lodge and Cabins (1,250 ft.) to
* end of trail at woods road and bridge over West Branch of Pleasant River (1,150 ft.): 1.0 mi., 35 min.

Pond Loop Trail (AMC)

Utilizing a portion of Pleasant River Trail, Pond Loop Trail circles the uppermost of the Little Lyford Ponds. Numerous side trails provide opportunities for wildlife watching from vantage points along the shore of the upper and lower ponds. Trailhead parking is on Upper Valley Rd. at a point about 2.6 mi. north of the jct. of Greenville Rd. and K-I Rd.

A short spur trail connects the road and parking with Pond Loop Trail in about 0.3 mi. At the jct., turn right to circle the pond in a counterclockwise direction. There are views of the upper pond through the trees as the path winds over a few small rises. Shortly the trail crosses the pond's inlet on bog bridges. Climbing gradually uphill, the trail bears away from the pond to reach an old grassy road, which it follows through a clearing. Soon, the lower pond is visible through the trees on the right. Pass a large old stone chimney marked Gerry's Gazebo. Pryor's Path crosses the trail, leading left to a dock on the upper pond, and right to a dock on the lower pond.

Pond Loop Trail continues to a jct. with Pleasant River Trail at 1.0 mi. The two trails share the route for the next 0.5 mi. Turn left and climb gradually. Follow a small brook before dropping down to the upper pond and views of Baker Mtn. through the trees. The trail descends the ridge and crosses a large wooden bridge, known as Kendall's Crossing, over the outlet of the upper pond. Beyond the bridge, the trail climbs again, bearing away from the pond. At a jct. at 1.5 mi., bear left off Pleasant River Trail to continue on Pond Loop Trail. There is a quick downhill before the trail levels off and winds through the forest, passing a side trail on the left to the upper pond. Cross a dozen bog bridges to reach a jct. at 1.8 mi. On the left is a clearing on the shore of the upper pond. Canoes are available here for use by AMC guests. Turn right (west) to return to the trailhead parking lot at 2.1 mi.

Pond Loop Trail (AMC map 2: E2)
Distances from Upper Valley Rd. (1,350 ft.) to
- Pond Loop Trail jct. (1,200 ft.): 0.3 mi., 10 min.
- Pleasant River Trail, south jct. (1,100 ft.): 1.0 mi., 30 min.
- Pleasant River Trail, north jct. (1,250 ft.): 1.5 mi., 45 min.
- complete loop (via spur trail and Pleasant River Trail): 2.1 mi., 1 hr.

Nation's Nature Trail (AMC)

This 1.3-mi. yellow-blazed loop trail circles the area around Little Lyford Lodge and Cabins, passing through woodlands, wetlands, to The Pinnacle, and to the West Branch of the Pleasant River.

Park at the Laurie's Ledge Trail parking lot and cross Upper Valley Rd. to access a spur trail leading 0.2 mi. east to Nation's Nature Trail.

The trail is over level ground except for one short moderately steep climb up to The Pinnacle. Each area that the trail passes through has its own distinct ecological communities. Twelve interpretive stations en route offer more information. A detailed trail brochure is available at Little Lyford Lodge and Cabins.

Nation's Nature Trail (AMC map 2: E2)
Distances from Upper Valley Rd. parking lot (1,300 ft.) to
- start of Nature Trail (1,300 ft.): 0.2 mi., 5 min.
- Nature Trail loop: 1.3 mi., 40 min.
- complete loop from road: 1.7 mi., 50 min.

Henderson Brook Trail (AMC)

This trail winds along the banks and through the gorge of Henderson Brook just east of Long Pond. To reach the trailhead, drive south from the jct. of Greenville Rd. and K-I Rd. for 3.4 mi. Turn right (south) onto Chairback Mtn. Rd. and follow this for about 0.9 mi. to a small parking lot on the left.

The trail heads east and descends to the edge of Henderson Brook, which it follows down-valley past a series of pretty waterfalls and pools, crossing it several times. (*Note:* A rope strung across the brook in two places offers some assistance.) The trail merges with the AT at 0.9 mi. Continue ahead on the AT to reach the K-I Rd. in another 50 yd.

Henderson Brook Trail (AMC map 2: F3)

Distances from parking lot on Chairback Mtn. Rd. (1,110 ft.) to

- AT jct. (800 ft.): 0.9 mi., 40 min.
- K-I Rd. (via AT) (750 ft.): 0.9 mi., 45 min.

Chairback Mtn. (2,190 ft.)

This craggy peak in Bowdoin College East Grant Township rises south of the West Branch of the Pleasant River and forms the eastern end of the Barren–Chairback Range, which is traversed by the Appalachian Trail.

To reach the trailhead parking, drive north on ME 11 from Brownville Junction for 5.5 mi. Turn left (west) on Katahdin Iron Works Rd. and drive 6.8 mi. to the KI–Jo Mary Forest KIW Checkpoint. A fee is charged to pass through the gate. Beyond the gate, take the right fork. At 3.4 mi. from the gatehouse, the road reaches a second fork. Stay left here, crossing the West Branch of the Pleasant River on a bridge. K-I Rd. reaches the trailhead parking area on the right at 6.7 mi. from the gatehouse.

From the parking area, follow the spur trail downhill to a jct. with the AT at 0.2 mi. Turn left (west) and hike uphill to cross K-I Rd. at 0.7 mi. Beyond, climb moderately up the mountainside, passing a spring at 1.4 mi. Ahead at 1.9 mi., a side trail leads downhill off the ridge 0.2 mi. to East Chairback Pond. Proceeding south on the AT, continue climbing at a moderate grade to reach the base of the peak at 3.0 mi. Then climb more steeply over open ledges and up a talus slope to reach the summit of Chairback Mtn., with its outstanding views of the White Cap Range, Baker Mtn., and Elephant Mtn., at 4.1 mi.

Farther south on the AT, it is 0.5 mi. to Chairback Gap Lean-to, 0.9 mi. to the wooded summit of Columbus Mtn., 2.2 mi. to a short side trail leading to West Chairback Pond, 2.8 mi. to Monument Cliff on Third Mtn., and 3.3 mi. to a jct. with Third Mtn. Trail leading 1.4 mi. to Chairback Mtn. Rd.

Chairback Mtn. via AT (AMC map 2: F3, MATC map 3)

Distances from K-I Rd. trailhead parking area (650 ft.) to
- side trail to East Chairback Pond (1,500 ft.): 1.9 mi., 1 hr. 20 min.
- Chairback Mtn. summit (2,190 ft.): 4.1 mi., 3 hr. 10 min.

Third Mtn. (2,061 ft.)

Park in the parking lot (on the left) just past the trailhead (sign) on Chairback Mtn. Rd. at a point 2.4 mi. from its jct. with K-I Rd. Leaving the Chairback Mtn. Rd., the trail makes a short, steep ascent through a stand of birch.

Follow the blue blazes as the trail winds through the hardwood forest over the lower slopes of Third Mtn. Cross several small streams on wooden bridges and a wet area on bog bridges. Beyond, the trail begins to climb steadily on a number of long switchbacks. The trail makes its way toward several large boulders before climbing several steep rock staircases and then a wooden ladder. Views begin to open up through the trees and soon the angle eases and the trail reaches a jct. with the AT at 1.9 mi. at a height-of-land. To the left (east), it is 0.5 mi. via the AT to grand views atop Monument Cliff on Third Mtn. To the right (west), it is 2.0 mi. via the AT to the wooded summit of Fourth Mtn., and 5.0 mi. to the abandoned fire tower atop Barren Mtn.

Third Mtn. Trail (AMC map 2: F3, MATC map 3)

Distances from trailhead on Chairback Mtn. Rd. (1,200 ft.) to
- AT jct. (1,850 ft.): 1.4 mi., 1 hr. 20 min.
- Third Mtn. summit (2,061 ft.) at Monument Cliff (via AT): 2.1 mi., 1 hr. 40 min.

Barren Mtn. (2,650 ft.)

Barren Mtn. in Elliotsville Township, the highest and most accessible of the five mountain peaks of the rugged Barren–Chairback Range, is traversed by the AT. From Barren Slide and Barren Ledges are excellent viewpoints overlooking Bodfish Intervale, Lake Onawa, and Borestone Mtn. The abandoned summit fire tower is in disrepair. There are two approaches to Barren Mtn., from Monson and from Greenville.

Approach from Monson

From ME 15 in Monson, drive north 0.5 mi. to Elliotsville Rd. Turn right and drive 7.7 mi. to a bridge over Big Wilson Stream. Cross the bridge and take an immediate left. Follow this road (locally known as Bodfish Valley Rd.) across the Montreal, Maine & Atlantic Railway tracks at 8.4 mi. Pass the trailhead for Borestone Mtn. at 8.5 mi. Just beyond, the road turns to dirt. Follow it over the crest of the hillside then descend. At 10.5 mi., the road narrows and enters the former site of Bodfish Farm. At 10.7 mi., bear left at the fork, and cross a bridge over Long Pond Stream. Continue and turn left onto a dirt road at 11.3 mi. Pass Otter Pond at 11.4 mi., and reach a parking area at 12.0 mi.

A spur trail leaves this parking area and goes north and then east for 0.7 mi. to a jct. with the AT just east of Long Pond Stream Lean-to. The trail is flagged most of the way and is easy to follow. Bear right (east) on the AT at the jct.

The AT climbs the northwestern slope of Barren Mtn. At 1.8 mi., a blue-blazed side trail leads south to the head of Barren Slide, an interesting mass of boulders with a view west. At 2.0 mi., the AT reaches the open Barren Ledges and a striking view. The route then bears left and winds along the northern slope of the range over rough terrain to the base of the summit cone at 3.0 mi. The trail then climbs steeply through boulders for a short distance to the summit at 3.8 mi.

The AT continues 12.2 mi. northeast over the remaining peaks of the range (including Fourth, Third, Columbus, and Chairback mountains) to the valley of the West Branch of the Pleasant River. This hike is a backpacking trip of several days over rough terrain. Please refer to MATC's

Appalachian Trail Guide to Maine if you plan to make the trek across the range.

Approach from Greenville

From ME 15 in the center of Greenville, head east on Pleasant St. to where the road bears right around the airport. Continue on the gravel road and eventually cross Big Wilson Stream at the south end of Lower Wilson Pond. The road turns into K-I Road (marked by a small blue street sign). Continue on this and pass access roads for Rum Ridge and Rum Pond. At 7.3 mi., turn right onto another gravel road just before Indian Pond (this road is known locally as Indian Pond Rd., but is not marked as such). After the turn, drive over the pond outlet. At 7.5 mi., turn left onto another gravel road. Continue on this road, making sure to stay straight at 9.2 mi. where other spur roads come in. At a fork at 11.3 mi., bear right. Major logging activity is on the left of this intersection. At about 13.0 mi., the AT crosses and the road leads right and goes down a hill. Park in the area of the AT sign.

The AT leaves the road and descends 0.1 mi. to cross Long Pond Stream at the normally knee-deep ford. A fixed guide rope is available for assistance in crossing. Beyond, the trail turns east, passing Slugundy Gorge. At 0.9 mi., the trail reaches a blue-blazed side trail leading 150 yd. to Long Pond Stream Lean-to. Just ahead, the unmarked spur trail from the parking area north of Otter Pond enters from the right. See the previous description for the Monson approach for the AT route to the summit of Barren Mtn. from this point.

Barren Mtn. (AMC map 2: G1–G2, F1–F2, MATC map 3)

Distances from trailhead parking area north of Otter Pond (Monson approach) (650 ft.) to

- AT jct. near Long Pond Stream Lean-to (950 ft.): 0.7 mi., 30 min.
- side trail to Barren Slide (1,900 ft.): 1.8 mi., 1 hr. 30 min.
- Barren Ledges (2,000): 2.0 mi., 1 hr. 40 min.
- Barren Mtn. summit (2,650 ft.): 3.8 mi., 3 hr.

Distances from trailhead parking at AT crossing (Greenville approach) (700 ft.) to
- Long Pond Stream (650 ft.): 0.1 mi., 5 min.
- side trail to Long Pond Stream Lean-to (900 ft.): 0.9 mi., 35 min.

- jct., spur trail to parking area north of Otter Pond (950 ft.): 1.0 mi., 40 min.
- side trail to Barren Slide (1,900 ft.): 2.1 mi., 1 hr. 40 min.
- Barren Ledges (2,000 ft.): 2.3 mi., 1 hr. 50 min.
- Barren Mtn. summit (2,650 ft.): 4.1 mi., 3 hr. 10 min.

Borestone Mtn. (1,981 ft.)

This relatively low but rugged mountain in Elliotsville Township is the central natural feature of the 1,693-acre Borestone Mountain Sanctuary, a wildlife preserve owned and managed by Maine Audubon. Rising steeply above Lake Onawa, Borestone offers 360-degree views from its two alpine-like peaks. Three small ponds are found high on its southwestern slope. Two trails, Base and Summit, combine to reach the top of the mountain, and the access road may be used to form a nice loop hike.

To reach the sanctuary, drive north on ME 15 from the center of Monson for 0.5 mi. Turn right on Elliotsville Rd. and drive 7.7 mi. to Big Wilson Stream. Cross the bridge and immediately turn left on Bodfish Valley Rd. and go uphill. Cross the railroad tracks and proceed another 0.1 mi. to the trailhead (sign) on the right. A small parking area is on the left side of the road.

Base Trail (MA)

Follow the access road through a gate. A toilet is on the right. Just beyond is an information kiosk on the left and the start of Base Trail. (*Note:* A small day-use fee is charged, and no dogs are allowed.) The trail winds upward through the forest, gently at first, then more steeply, to reach the access road and toilet facilities at 0.9 mi. (*Note:* About halfway along Base Trail, a side trail leads right [south] to a viewpoint overlooking Little Greenwood Pond.) Turn left on the access road and follow it to Sunrise Pond and the Robert T. Moore Visitor Center at 1.0 mi. The center features wildlife displays and information on the interesting history of the mountain. A side trail leaves the center and leads 0.4 mi. northwest to viewpoints overlooking Midday and Sunset ponds.

Summit Trail (MA)

Leaving from the visitor center, Summit Trail follows the south shore of Sunrise Pond. Bearing away from the pond at its eastern edge, the trail begins a steep ascent that includes more than 140 stone steps. After a brief level area, the trail rises steeply again to reach the west peak of Borestone Mtn. at 0.7 mi. In several spots, fixed iron bars are available to assist hikers in the scramble up the rocks. Beyond, the trail dips down into a saddle before the final ascent to the higher east peak at 1.0 mi. Views are spectacular in all directions.

Borestone Mtn. (Barren Mtn. West quad, DeLorme map 41)
Distances from Bodfish Valley Rd. trailhead (850 ft.) to
- Sunrise Pond and visitor center (via Base Trail) (1,350 ft.): 1.0 mi., 40 min.
- Borestone Mtn., west peak (via Summit Trail) (1,950 ft.): 1.7 mi., 1 hr. 20 min.
- Borestone Mtn., east peak (via Summit Trail) (1,981 ft.): 2.0 mi., 1 hr. 30 min.

Little Wilson Falls

A worthwhile side trip in the Elliotsville Township area is to Little Wilson Falls, a striking 57-ft. waterfall in a deep slate canyon. From the center of Monson, drive north on ME 15, and in 0.5 mi., turn right on Elliottsville Rd. Take this road for 7.7 mi. to Big Wilson Stream, and turn left just before reaching the bridge. Drive for 0.8 mi. to the end of the road and park.

Just past the waterfall and large pool, follow the left bank of the stream uphill. The trail is rough in places, with slippery rocks and roots, so use caution. Continue to follow the route of the stream, angling steadily up the hillside. Eventually the angle eases, and the trail proceeds through the forest along the top of the gorge. At about 1.0 mi., a jct. with the AT is reached. Continue south on the AT, climbing moderately. Pass several viewpoints into the gorge before reaching the top of the falls at 1.3 mi.

Little Wilson Falls (USGS Barren Mtn. West, Monson East quads, DeLorme map 41)
Distance from trailhead off Elliotsville Rd. (550 ft.) to
- Little Wilson Falls (950 ft.): 1.3 mi., 1 hr.

Little Moose Public Reserved Land

This 13,500-acre unit of the Maine's public lands system straddles the town lines of Big Moose and Moosehead Junction townships near the southwest corner of Moosehead Lake just west of Greenville. The main natural feature is Big Moose Mtn., a sprawling mountain peak with a narrow summit that provides outstanding views of the Moosehead Lake region. This is also the site of the first fire tower in Maine. Nestled into the long ridge of Little Moose Mtn. are five scenic ponds known for their wildlife watching and fishing. A system of trails wends through the preserve, connecting the ponds and leading to numerous outlooks, as well as climbing to the peak of Big Moose Mtn.

Little Moose Mtn. (2,126 ft.)

Little Moose Mtn. is a long and undulating ridgeline extending for more than 5.0 mi. from east to west just west of Moosehead Lake. This mostly wooded mountain offers a surprising number of fine viewpoints along its length. Five scenic mountain ponds tucked into its north and south slopes provide for wildlife watching and primitive camping. The trail system on Little Moose Mtn. can be reached from three points in the unit.

Greenwood Trail (MBPL)

To reach the eastern trailhead and the approach to Little Moose Mtn., travel 2.9 mi. north on ME 15/6 from the blinking light in the center of Greenville. Turn left into the Moose Mountain Inn and proceed to the trailhead parking at the left (south) end of the lot (sign).

The trail ascends moderately to the southwest along the undulating ridgeline of Little Moose Mtn. Frequent outlooks en route provide extensive views eastward to Borestone Mtn., the peaks of the Barren–Chairback Range, and Baker Mtn. North across Moosehead Lake, and take in wide views of Big and Little Spencer mountains and Mt. Kineo. Crest the eastern ridge of Little Moose Mtn. at 1.6 mi.. Then descend steeply to Papoose Pond at 2.4 mi., and a view of Big Moose Mtn. rising impressively in the distance. At 2.6 mi., reach the jct. with Loop Trail. To the right, it is

1.3 mi. to the Mtn. Rd. trailhead via Loop Trail past Little and Big Moose ponds. To the left, it is 2.6 mi. via Loop and Notch Ponds trails to Big and Little Notch ponds, and 3.5 mi. to the Notch Ponds trailhead.

Greenwood Trail (AMC Little Moose Mtn. and Big Moose Mtn. map, USGS Big Squaw Pond quad, DeLorme map 41)

Distances from Moose Mountain Inn trailhead on ME 15/6 (1,050 ft.) to
- Highpoint on east ridge (2,050 ft.): 1.6 mi., 1 hr. 15 min.
- Papoose Pond (1,650 ft.): 2.4 mi., 1 hr. 40 min.
- jct. Loop Trail (1,600 ft.): 2.6 mi., 1 hr. 45 min.
- Little Moose Pond (1,550 ft.): 2.9 mi., 1 hr. 55 min.
- Big Moose Pond outlet (1,500 ft.): 3.6 mi., 2 hr. 10 min.
- Mtn. Rd. trailhead (1,650 ft.): 3.9 mi., 2 hr. 20 min.
- Notch Ponds trailhead (1,400 ft.): 6.1 mi., 4 hr.

Loop Trail (MBPL)

To reach the trailhead for Big and Little Moose ponds, drive north on ME 15/6 from Moose Mountain Inn for 2.1 mi. Turn left (southwest) on North Rd. Pass the trailhead for Big Moose Mtn. on the right at 1.4 mi. from ME 15/6. Reach the jct. of North Rd. and Mtn. Rd. at 1.6 mi. Turn left onto Mtn. Rd., and drive another 1.0 mi. to the trailhead on the left.

Leaving the road, Loop Trail descends to cross Moose Brook at 0.25 mi. and reaches Big Moose Pond at 0.4 mi. Following the north shore, the trail splits at 0.75 mi. Continue left Little Moose Pond at 1.0 mi and Greenwood Trail on the left at 1.2 mi. Loop Trail climbs to a highpoint on Little Moose Mtn., offering occasional views of the Little and Big Moose ponds. Reach a jct. with Notch Ponds Trail at 2.0 mi. Turn right here and descend to reach Big Moose Pond. Continue on to the point where Loop Trail originally split at 2.5 mi. Turn left to reach the Mtn. Rd. trailhead. [*Note:* There are several campsites in this area. Visit outdoors.org/bookup-dates for more information.]

Little Moose Mtn. from the north (AMC Little Moose Mtn. and Big Moose Mtn. map, USGS Big Squaw Pond quad, DeLorme map 41)

Distances from Mtn. Rd. trailhead (1,650 ft.) to
- Big Moose Pond outlet (1,500 ft.): 0.4 mi., 15 min.
- Little Moose Pond (1,550 ft.): 1.0 mi., 30 min.
- jct. Greenwood Trail (1,600 ft.), 1.2 mi., 1 hr. 15 min.

- jct. Notch Ponds Trail (1,700 ft.), 2.0 mi., 2 hrs.
- jct. Loop Trail (1,550 ft.), 2.5 mi., 2.5 hrs.

Notch Ponds Trail (MBPL)

To reach the Notch Pond trailhead, turn right at the jct. of Mtn. Rd. and North Rd. and follow North Rd. to a jct. at 4.5 mi. Turn left here for Notch Pond. (Straight ahead 100 yd. is Big Indian Pond.) At 0.4 mi., bear right at a fork. The Notch Pond trailhead is on the right in another 0.5 mi. Parking is on the left.

Follow the outlet stream of Little Notch Pond uphill for 0.6 mi. to the pond itself. Skirting the north shore, reach a jct. at 0.9 mi. To the right, it is 0.1 mi. to Big Notch Pond. To the left, climb steeply away from the jct. to reach the ridgeline of Little Moose Mtn. At 1.7 mi., the trail ends at the jct. with Loop Trail.

Little Moose Mtn. from the west (AMC Little Moose Mtn. and Big Moose Mtn. map, USGS Big Squaw Pond quad, DeLorme map 41)

Distances from Notch Ponds trailhead (1,400 ft.) to
- jct. between Little and Big Notch ponds (1,600 ft.): 0.9 mi., 35 min.
- jct. Loop Trail (1,700 ft.), 1.7 mi., 2 hrs.

Big Moose Mtn. (3,196 ft.)

Big Moose Mtn. dominates the country to the southwest of Moosehead Lake. Located in Big Moose and Moosehead Junction townships just west of Greenville, the mountain is well-known for its exceptional views of the Moosehead Lake Region and Katahdin. The original 1919 steel fire tower still stands on the summit, marking the site of the first fire lookout in the state (then made of logs), established in 1905.

From the blinking traffic light in the center of Greenville, drive north on ME 15/6 for 5.2 mi. Turn left (west) on North Rd. and enter Little Moose PRL (sign). Proceed 1.5 mi. to trailhead parking on the right.

The well-marked trail leaves from the back of the parking lot near an information kiosk. The trail meanders westerly at a moderate grade to reach the old fire warden's cabin on the right at 1.4 mi. Beyond the cabin, the trail crosses Middle Moose Brook and begins to climb steeply over a

Little Moose Mtn. and Big Moose Mtn.

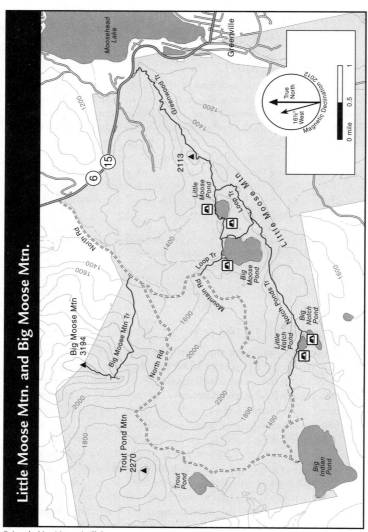

© Appalachian Mountain Club

long staircase of rock steps. A short side trail to the left at 1.6 mi. leads to a scenic viewpoint. Continuing the steady ascent, the trail reaches the narrow crest of the high ridgeline and turns right (north) to climb the final distance to the summit, which is achieved at 2.1 mi. The old fire tower and several small antennae and accompanying buildings occupy the summit area.

From the tower, a short trail leads north toward a helipad and a ledge with a view down over Mirror Lake, an isolated pond on the northeastern spur of the mountain. Another trail continues north to the top of the now defunct Squaw Mountain ski area.

Big Moose Mtn. (AMC Little Moose Mtn. and Big Moose Mtn. map, USGS Big Squaw Pond quad, DeLorme map 41)

Distances from North Rd. trailhead (1,350 ft.) to
- old fire warden's cabin (2,050 ft.): 1.4 mi., 1 hr. 5 min.
- Big Moose Mtn. summit (3,196 ft.): 2.1 mi., 2 hr.

Eagle Rock (2,350 ft.)

The long ridgeline of Big Moose Mtn. extends northwest for several miles toward Indian Pond and the Kennebec River, where the ridgeline culminates at a large, bald outcropping known as Eagle Rock, where there are spectacular views.

From the blinking traffic light at the junction of ME 15/6 and Lily Bay Rd. in the center of Greenville, drive north on ME 15/6 for 8.5 mi. Turn left (west) on Burnham Pond Rd., and go 3.7 mi. to a fork. Bear left at the fork, and drive 1.2 mi. to the trailhead on the left (marked by pink flagging and a handmade sign). Park just ahead along the road on the right.

The trail proceeds easterly for a distance at an easy grade before starting to climb via switchbacks. This is a well-used and well-marked path, but you will have occasional blowdowns to contend with. A wooden ladder and a rope aid in scrambling up a steep section. After leveling off for a time, the trail ascends steeply again, dips briefly, then gains the huge open ledge at Eagle Rock with its panoramic views.

Eagle Rock (USGS Indian Pond North, DeLorme map 40)

Distance from Burnham Pond Rd. (1,050 ft.) to
• Eagle Rock (2,350 ft.): 1.5 mi., 1 hr. 20 min.

Elephant Mtn. (2,636 ft.)

Unlike other mountains in Maine of the same name, this Elephant Mtn. actually does resemble an elephant's head, minus the tusks. Its sloping southern face and small ledge that appears as an eye are recognizable from many surrounding peaks. Though no foot trail reaches its summit, a short trail on its lower slopes leads hikers to the historic 1963 crash site of a B-52 bomber. Of the nine crew members, only the pilot and navigator survived the tragic accident.

From the blinking light in the center of Greenville on ME 15/6, drive north on Lily Bay Rd. for 6.7 mi. Turn right (east) on Prong Pond Rd. Begin new mileage. At 1.8 mi., bear right; at 3.8 mi., bear left at a fork. Cross North Brook on a bridge at 5.4 mi., and just ahead, bear left at jct. At 6.7 mi., bear right at a fork, and at 7.1 mi., the road makes a sharp right turn. The trailhead is here on the left. Parking is along the right side of the road.

The trail to the crash site is an easy and very accessible 0.2 mi. Pieces of the wreckage line both sides of the trail route, which culminates at an information kiosk and a large slate memorial leaning against a big piece of the cabin of the downed plane. Visitors have left a variety of flags and wreaths over time. It is a moving experience and a different kind of hike.

Elephant Mtn. B-52 Memorial Crash Site (USGS Number Four Mtn. quad, DeLorme 41)

Distance from trailhead parking (1,600 ft.) to
• B-52 memorial site (1,750 ft.): 0.2 mi., 10 min.

Number Four Mtn. (2,890 ft.)

Rising south of First Roach Pond in Frenchtown Township, Number Four Mtn. offers excellent views from the open ledges and the abandoned fire tower on its summit.

From the blinking light in the center of Greenville on ME 15/6, drive north on Lily Bay Rd. for 18.2 mi. Turn right onto Frenchtown Rd. and follow this for 2.2 mi. Turn right onto Lagoon Brook Rd., and go 1.3 mi., then turn left onto Meadow Brook Rd. Follow this road south for 0.9 mi. to the signed trailhead on the left. The road passes over Lagoon Brook about 500 ft. before reaching the trailhead. Ample parking is found along the road.

The trail runs easterly for 0.25 mi. to reach Lagoon Brook, where the trail then bears right and runs almost due south. In typical fire warden trail fashion, the path climbs steeply up the mountainside to the upper ridge, which the path then follows to the old fire tower. The lower portion of the trail is through an old logging clear-cut, and the upper third is through pretty woods. The tower provides excellent views that include Katahdin, Moosehead Lake, the Bigelow Range, Green Mtn., and Big and Little Spencer mountains. From the summit, a side trail leads 250 ft. south to a ledge and views ranging from White Cap Mtn. to Lily Bay Mtn. to Moosehead Lake and Moose Mtn.

Number Four Mtn. (USGS Number Four Mtn. quad, DeLorme map 41)
Distance from Meadow Brook Rd. trailhead (1,500 ft.) to
• Number Four Mtn. summit (2,890 ft.): 1.5 mi., 1 hr. 30 min.

Mt. Kineo (1,789 ft.)

Mt. Kineo rises dramatically from a peninsula jutting out from the eastern shore of Moosehead Lake in Kineo Township just north of Rockwood. The sheer 800-ft. southeastern face of this iconic mountain makes it visible from points throughout the region. Hikers to the summit ridge and fire tower are rewarded with remarkable views of the remote north woods. The quickest and most scenic way to reach Kineo is by ferry from Rockwood.

From the blinking traffic light in the center of Greenville, travel north on ME 15/6 for 19.6 mi. to the village of Rockwood. Turn right onto a road marked with signs for the Rockwood Public Landing. From the landing, it is about a 10-min. boat ride to Mt. Kineo. The Kineo Shuttle is the sole provider of ferry services to Kineo for hikers, sightseers, and golfers. The shuttle operates from late May through mid-October and charges a $10 fee per person round-trip. In the high summer months of July and August, the shuttle runs hourly. In the shoulder months of May, June, September, and October, the schedule is less frequent. Call the Kineo Shuttle at 207-534-9012 for schedule information (no website).

North, Bridle, and Indian trails can be used to summit the mountain and form a loop hike. The three trails (all blue-blazed) share a common start at the boat landing. From here, follow the old carriage road along the base of the mountain to the left.

Indian Trail

Indian Trail is the shortest route to the summit and fire tower and provides the most views. Indian Trail diverges right from the old carriage road at 0.8 mi. from the landing, and follows the edge of the cliffs. Indian Trail then rises steeply to where it joins Bridle Trail 0.4 mi. from the fire tower. Continue northeast to reach the top of the mountain.

Bridle Trail

This is the original fire warden trail to the summit. The trail begins 0.3 mi. north of Indian Trail, or 1.1 mi. along the carriage road from the landing. Bridle Trail is longer than Indian Trail and has no views en route but does offer easier grades. Bridal Trail merges with Indian Trail 0.4 from the summit of Kineo. Continue northeast to reach the top of the mountain.

North Trail

The longest trail is North Trail, which includes the entire length of the carriage road. The trail initially follows the shore of Moosehead Lake all the way to Hardscrabble Point. From here, the trail continues along the shoreline over rough ground consisting of rocks and roots, and then begins a strenuous climb through a stand of old hardwoods to the summit. Only limited views are available along this trail.

Mt. Kineo (USGS Mt. Kineo quad, DeLorme map 41)
Distances from dock at Kineo Cove (1,030 ft.) to
  • Bridle Trail and Indian Trail jct.: 0.8 mi.

- Mt. Kineo summit (1,789 ft.) (via Indian Trail): 1.6 mi., 1 hr. 10 min.
- Mt. Kineo summit (1,789 ft.) (via Bridle Trail): 2.0 mi., 1 hr. 20 min.
- Mt. Kineo summit (1,789 ft.) (via North Trail): 4.1 mi., 2 hr. 20 min.

Little Kineo Mtn. (1,927 ft.)

Rising prominently east of North Bay on Moosehead Lake and Mt. Kineo, Little Kineo Mtn. in Days Academy Grant Township is remote and takes some doing to get to, but rewards hikers for the effort with outstanding views from its summit ledges.

From the blinking light in the center of Greenville on ME 15/6, drive north on Lily Bay Rd. for 19 mi. to the village of Kokadjo on the west end of First Roach Pond. Begin new mileage. At 0.4 mi. beyond the village, the road turns to dirt and forks. Bear left at the fork onto Sias Hill Rd., and follow this for 1.1 mi. Turn left onto Spencer Bay Rd. At 8.2 mi., pass a sign for Spencer Pond Camps, and at 9.4 mi., cross a bridge over the outlet of Spencer Pond. At 11.2 mi., bear left at a fork, and at 15.0 mi., go right at a fork. The road comes to a T intersection at 17.8 mi. Turn left here, and soon cross a bridge. At 18.0 mi., turn right (sign for Kelly Wharf). Go left at a fork at 18.7 mi., and soon the cliffs of Little Kineo Mtn. come into view. Reach the trailhead (sign) on the right at 20.2 mi. from Kokadjo. Park along either side of the road.

The trail leaves the north side of the road and crosses a low area before beginning to climb northeasterly over the ledges composing the precipitous southeast face of the mountain. The trail is well-marked with blazes, flagging, and rock cairns. It is steep in sections but overall is a moderate climb. Views are good on the way up and get better with each step. The final 0.5 mi. along the summit ridgeline is superb, with vistas taking in the expanse of Moosehead Lake, Mt. Kineo, Big Moose Mtn., Big and Little Spencer mountains, Katahdin, and countless more peaks of the vast north woods.

Little Kineo Mtn. (USGS Mt. Kineo quad, DeLorme map 41)

Distance from trailhead parking (1,400 ft.) to
- Little Spencer Mtn. summit (1,927 ft.): 1.0 mi., 50 min.

Big Spencer Mtn. (3,230 ft.)

Rising sharply from the countryside north of Kokadjo and First Roach Pond, Big Spencer Mtn. is a prominent landmark in the area northeast of Moosehead Lake. An abandoned fire tower sits on the northeastern end of its 2.0-mile-long summit ridge. The true summit is 0.3 mi. southwest of the tower. Panoramic views are possible from both points. The mountain lies within the 4,244-acre Big Spencer Ecological Reserve managed by MBPL.

From the blinking light in the center of Greenville on ME 15/6, drive north on Lily Bay Rd. for 19 mi. to the village of Kokadjo at the west end of First Roach Pond. At 0.4 mi. beyond Kokadjo, turn left onto Sias Hill Rd. Follow this for 8.0 mi. to a narrow, one-lane bridge over Bear Pond Brook. Turn left after crossing the bridge, and take this road 6.1 mi. to the trailhead (sign) on the left. Parking is alongside the road.

The trail proceeds south and climbs moderately then more steeply up the north ridge of the mountain. At 0.8 mi., the old fire warden's cabin is reached (this cabin is scheduled to be removed in 2012). Beyond the cabin, the trail is very steep, gaining more than 1,000 ft. of elevation over the final 0.7 mi. to the summit. Wooden ladders aid in climbing some of the more slippery areas. Hikers are asked to please respect the solar panels, small communications building, and wood platform on the mountaintop.

Big Spencer Mtn. (USGS Big Spencer Mtn. quad, DeLorme map 49)
Distance from Spencer Mtn. Rd. trailhead (1,400 ft.) to
 • Big Spencer Mtn. summit (3,230 ft.): 2.0 mi., 2 hr. 30 min.

Little Spencer Mtn. (3,040 ft.)

The elongated mass of Little Spencer Mtn. in East Middlesex Canal Township, with its steep flanks and rock faces, is a distinctive landmark in the Moosehead Lake region. Its summit and nearby open ledges offer outstanding views.

From the blinking light in the center of Greenville on ME 15/6, drive north on Lily Bay Rd. for 19.0 mi. to the village of Kokadjo at the west end of First Roach Pond. At 0.4 mi. beyond Kokadjo, turn left onto Sias Hill Rd. and follow this for 1.2 mi., then turn left onto Spencer Bay Rd. Follow this for 7.4 mi. Turn right at the sign for Spencer Pond Camps, and continue 2.2 mi. to the Little Spencer trailhead on the right (sign).

A short distance into the woods is a commemorative plaque labeling the trail, "The Ram Trail." This is in honor of Richard Manson, who in the 1960s explored various routes to the summit from Spencer Pond Camps. The trail is well-marked and well-maintained. Beyond, the trail rises gently for 0.25 mi., and then begins a steep ascent. After passing a viewpoint over Spencer Pond and Moosehead Lake, the trail traverses east to the south face of the mountain and soon begins to climb over ledges and slides to reach a 70-ft. chimney. One person at a time is the recommended approach in the chimney, and care should be exercised not to dislodge any rocks. The fixed rope may be used for assistance. (*Note:* Because of the difficulty of the chimney, this hike may not be a good choice when the rocks are wet, or at any time with young children or dogs.)

Little Spencer Mtn. (USGS Lobster Mtn. quad, DeLorme map 49)
Distance from Spencer Bay Rd. trailhead (1,200 ft.) to
• Little Spencer Mtn. summit (3,040 ft.): 2.0 mi., 2 hr. 15 min.

Green Mtn. (2,395 ft.)

An old fire tower stands atop the highest peak of Green Mtn., located in Dole Brook and Comstock townships northwest of Pittston Farm and northeast of Boundary Bald Mtn.

From ME 15/6 just west of the village of Rockwood, turn north on Northern Rd., immediately crossing Moose River. Follow this road for 20.0 mi. to the North Maine Woods checkpoint at Pittston Farm, where a fee is charged to pass through. Begin new mileage. At 1.9 mi. west of the gate, go left at a fork. Reach a jct. with South Branch Access Rd. at 3.3 mi. and turn left (west). At 5.5 mi., bear right onto Old Boundary Rd. (marked with a faded sign). Follow this to the trailhead (sign) on the right (north) side of the road at 8.7 mi. from Pittston Farm.

The trail starts immediately uphill, but levels off until reaching the site of the old warden's cabin at 0.3 mi. Beyond, the trail contours across the side of the mountain until the trail reaches a brook. Here the trail turns uphill and crosses a wooded ridge before dropping into a slight depression, then rising again across the contours. The trail rises up the mountain in steps, using a series of old logging haul roads en route.

About 400 ft. below the summit, reach a small, disintegrating cabin on the left. From there to the peak, the trail is worn and marked by faint light-blue blazes and orange flagging. On top, 360-degree views can be had by climbing the fire tower, which has a ladder but no cab.

Green Mtn. (USGS Foley Pond quad, DeLorme map 48)
Distance from Old Boundary Rd. trailhead (1,900 ft.) to
  • Green Mtn. summit (2,395 ft.): 1.5 mi., 1 hr. 15 min.

Little Russell Mtn. (2,376 ft.)

An old fire tower caps Little Russell Mtn., which rises just west of the Piscataquis County line in Russell Pond Township.

From ME 15/6 just west of the village of Rockwood, turn north on Northern Rd., immediately crossing Moose River. Follow this road for 20 mi. to the North Maine Woods checkpoint at Pittston Farm, where a fee is charged to pass through. At 1.9 mi. west of the gate, bear right, and at 5.0 mi., reach Golden Rd. Turn right, and travel east on Golden Rd. for 14.7 mi. to 490 Rd. Turn left (north) here, and drive 9.7 mi. Turn right onto Russell Mtn. Rd., and take this 5.7 mi. to the town line separating St. John Township and Russell Pond Township. The trail is the town line and is liberally blazed with yellow paint. Ample parking is found along the road.

The trail follows the brushed-out boundary line eastward, rising at a steady but moderate grade through the cutover forest. Near the crest of the north ridge, reach a jct. that is well-marked with orange flagging. Here, the route bears right (south) and ascends easily up the ridge, taking advantage of a series of old logging haul roads cutting through the dense forest growth. Continue to follow the orange flagging markers, bearing left at all intersections, to reach the heavily wooded summit and its fire tower (no cab). Climb the ladder to get splendid 360-degree views that include Moosehead Lake, Big and Little Spencer mountains, and Katahdin.

Little Russell Mtn. (USGS Russell Mtn. quad, DeLorme map 48)
Distance from Russell Mtn. Rd. trailhead (1,950 ft.) to
- Little Russell Mtn. summit (2,376 ft.): 1.2 mi., 1 hr.

SUGGESTED HIKES

Easy

Elephant Mtn. [rt: 0.6, 20 min.]. A short hike on the lower slopes of the mountain leads hikers to a memorial at the 1963 crash site of a B-52 bomber.

Henderson Brook [rt: 2.6 mi., 1 hr. 20 min.]. A nice stroll along the gorge and cascades of Henderson Brook.

Nation's Nature Trail [lp: 1.7 mi., 50 min.]. A great hike for the whole family just south of Little Lyford Lodge that leads past 12 interpretive stations.

Little Wilson Falls [rt: 2.6 mi., 2 hr.]. A fun hike up a wooded valley to a 57-ft. waterfall in a deep slate canyon.

River Trail [rt: 2.2 mi., 1 hr. 10 min.]. A pleasant woods walk along a former tote road that follows the West Branch of the Pleasant River.

Nesuntabunt Mtn. [rt: 2.4 mi., 1 hr. 30 min]. Follow the AT to get far-reaching views over Nahmakanta Lake and the 100-Mile Wilderness from the summit ledges.

Moderate

Laurie's Ledge [rt: 3.4 mi., 3 hr.]. Hike Indian Mtn. Circuit, then Laurie's Ledge Trail to several great viewpoints. From the easterly outlook, you can see as far north as Katahdin on a clear day.

Big and Little Moose ponds [lp: 3.8 mi., 3 hr.]. Visit two wilderness ponds on this scenic circuit hike through Little Moose PRL.

Borestone Mtn. [rt: 4.0 mi., 3 hr.]. The Base and Summit trails lead to Sunrise Pond and its nature center, then on to the alpine peaks of Borestone Mtn. and excellent wilderness vistas.

Third Mtn. [rt: 4.8 mi., 3 hr. 20 min.]. Climb to a high ridge on the Barren–Chairback Range and a jct. with the AT, and then finish with great views from Monument Cliff.

Mt. Kineo [lp: 3.6 mi., 3 hr. 30 min.]. Take a scenic ferryboat ride on Moosehead Lake, and then hike a pleasant loop on the Indian and Bridle trails to the bare summit of Mt. Kineo and far-reaching views over the lake.

Gulf Hagas [lp: 8.0 mi., 4 hr.]. A spectacular circuit hike on Rim Trail and the historic Pleasant River Tote Rd. that leads to the "Grand Canyon of Maine" and a series of scenic waterfalls in a long slate canyon.

Big Moose Mtn. [rt: 4.2 mi., 4 hr.]. A well-marked trail leads steeply to the summit of Big Moose and its historic fire tower, the first in the state, and fine views.

Little Spencer Mtn. [rt: 4.0 mi., 4 hr. 30 min.]. A challenging hike that ascends through a narrow chimney and over steep terrain to the ledges of Little Spencer Mtn., with excellent views of the Moosehead Lake region.

White Cap Mtn. [rt: 6.0 mi., 4 hr. 50 min]. A short, steep hike on White Brook Trail leads to the summit of White Cap Mtn., where the view is one of the finest in the state.

Big Spencer Mtn. [rt: 4.0 mi., 5 hr.]. The hike to the summit and fire tower is steep and challenging, but the outstanding wilderness vistas are worth the effort.

Strenuous

Turtle Ridge [lp: 9.3 mi., 6 hr.]. Four pretty ponds and several scenic ridgetops are featured on this loop hike into the Nahmakanta backcountry.

Debsconeag Backcountry [lp: 12.5 mi., 6 hr. 15 min.]. Make it a full day hike or spread the mileage over a two-day backpack trip to enjoy the many remote ponds and scenic ridges of the Debsconeag Backcountry Trail east of Nahmakanta Lake.

Chairback Mtn. [rt: 8.2 mi., 6 hr. 20 min.]. A hike along the AT past East Chairback Pond reaches a craggy summit with fine views to the north and west.

Barren Mtn. [rt: 7.2 mi., 6 hr. 20 min.]. A rewarding hike on the AT leads to the remote summit of Barren Mtn., passing lovely viewpoints at the Barren Slide and Barren Ledges en route.

Third, Columbus, and Chairback Mtn. Loop [lp: 10.2 mi., 7 hr. 20 min.]. A fine traverse of the north end of the Barren–Chairback ridge can be made by ascending Third Mtn. Trail, following the AT across the ridge to Third, Columbus, and Chairback mountains, and returning via Henderson Brook Trail and Chairback Mtn. Rd.

SECTION THREE
Western Lakes and Mountains

Grafton Notch State Park 108

Mahoosuc Public Reserved
  Land........................109

Old Speck Mtn. 110

Goose Eye Mtn. 113

Mt. Carlo 116

Baldpate Mtn., East Peak and
  West Peak 121

Grafton Loop Trail.......... 124

Mt. Will 131

Rumford Whitecap 131

Old Blue Mtn. 133

Bemis Mtn. 133

Tumbledown Public Reserved
  Land 135

Tumbledown Mtn. 136

Little Jackson Mtn. 140

Jackson Mtn. 141

Blueberry Mtn. 142

Mt. Blue State Park 143

Mt. Blue................. 143

Bald Mtn. (Weld). 144

Sugarloaf 144

Aziscohos Mtn. 145

Bald Mtn. (Oquossoc)....... 146

West Kennebago Mtn. 147

Snow Mtn. 147

Kibby Mtn. 148

Saddleback Mtn. and The Horn ..149

Mt. Abraham 151

AMC map 3: Bigelow Range

AMC map 6: Mahoosuc Range

AMC Tumbledown Mtn. map (p. 138)

Crocker Mtn., North Peak and
  South Peak 152

Sugarloaf Mtn. 154

Spaulding Mtn. 155

Burnt Mtn. 155

Bigelow Preserve............ 156

Avery Peak, West Peak, South Horn,
  North Horn, and Cranberry
  Peak 157

Little Bigelow Mtn. 161

Maine Huts & Trails 162

Suggested Hikes 164

The Western Lakes and Mountains section includes, from west to east, the central and northern areas of Oxford County, all of Franklin County, and the western part of Somerset County. The Canadian border forms the northern boundary of all three counties, and the New Hampshire border forms the western boundary of Oxford County. To the south, the section is bounded by the Androscoggin River and US 2. The region west of Rangeley features a number of large lakes, including Rangeley, Cupsuptic, Mooselookmeguntic, and Upper and Lower Richardson lakes. Much of this area is drained by the Ellis, Swift, and Sandy rivers, all of which empty into the Androscoggin River. To the northeast are Flagstaff Lake and its feeder, the Dead River. The Carrabassett River and Sandy Stream drain this area and flow south into the Kennebec River.

This section describes 35 mountains and 56 trails in the nearly continuous chain of mountain peaks extending from the New Hampshire border northeast to Flagstaff Lake. Many of these trails are located on large swaths of public land, including Grafton Notch State Park, Mahoosuc PRL, Tumbledown PRL, Mt. Blue State Park, and Bigelow Preserve. Outside of those areas, the trails are mostly on private property and are open for public use through the generosity of the various landowners.

The Mahoosuc Range rises east and north of the Androscoggin River and extends across the border of Maine and New Hampshire. Fourteen peaks exceed 3,000 ft., including Bald Cap, Mt. Success, Mt. Carlo, Goose Eye Mtn. and its three summits, Fulling Mill Mtn., Mahoosuc Arm, Old Speck Mtn., Slide Mtn., Sunday River Whitecap, Puzzle Mtn., and the two peaks of Baldpate Mtn. At 4,170 ft., Old Speck Mtn. is the highest in the range. The highest body of water in Maine is Speck Pond, which lies tucked in between Old Speck Mtn. and Mahoosuc Arm at an elevation of 3,400 ft. South of Grafton Notch, the low peaks of Mt. Will and Rumford Whitecap are local favorites that rise above the Androscoggin River valley. North of Black Brook Notch is Old Blue Mtn. and the six summits on the long ridge of Bemis Mtn. Just east, concentrated in a semicircular ring around the village of Weld, are the 3,000-ft. peaks and great cliffs of Tumbledown Mtn.; the summits of Little Jackson, Jackson, and Blueberry mountains; the conical form of Mt. Blue; and, finally, Bald Mtn. West of the Rangeley Lakes along ME 16 are the lightly traveled summits of Aziscohos and West Kennebago mountains, and the popular Bald Mtn. In the 30-mi. stretch between ME 17 and ME 4 west of Rangeley and Stratton are a string of 4,000-ft. summits, from Saddleback and The Horn, to Spaulding, Abraham, and Sugarloaf, to the north and south peaks of Crocker Mtn. North of ME 27 is the Bigelow Range and the craggy 4,000-ft. summits of Avery Peak and West Peak, and the subsidiary peaks of North and South Horn, Cranberry Peak, and Little Bigelow Mtn., all overlooking Flagstaff Lake. Northwest of the Bigelows are the scattered high peaks in the remote region east and west of the Dead River extending north to the Canadian border, which includes Snow and Kibby mountains.

The AT traverses this section, extending 113 mi. from the Maine–New Hampshire border to Long Falls Dam Rd. on the east side of Flagstaff Lake.

Camping

Nineteen lean-tos and campsites along the AT provide for trailside camping. There is trailside camping along Grafton Loop Trail and at sites in the Mahoosucs. AMC sites at Carlo Col, Full Goose, Speck Pond, Bull Run, Slide Mtn., Sergeant, and Bald Mtn. require pre-notification from large groups for use, which helps to lessen impact and minimize overcrowding. Visit outdoors.org/group_notification or call 603-466-2721 ext. 8150. Public campgrounds are available at Mt. Blue State Park in Weld (136 campsites) and Rangeley Lake State Park in Rangeley Plantation (50 campsites). Three backcountry huts operated by Maine Huts & Trails are located east of the Bigelows and offer lodging and meals. Numerous privately operated campgrounds are throughout this section.

Grafton Notch State Park

Grafton Notch State Park comprises 3,191 acres of mountainous terrain on the east and west sides of ME 26 from the Newry–Grafton Township town line to about 1.5 mi. north of the height-of-land in Grafton Notch at the AT crossing. The park includes the summit and northeastern slopes of Old Speck Mtn. and the lowest western and southwestern slopes of the Baldpates, including Table Rock.

In addition to the AT, there are trails to The Eyebrow, an impressive cliff forming the great western wall of Grafton Notch, and to Table Rock high on the east side. A number of short graded trails and paths leading to interesting natural features are along ME 26, including Step Falls, Screw Auger Falls, Mother Walker Falls, and Moose Cave. A large trailhead parking area with a pit toilet, trail register, and information kiosk is found on the west side of ME 26 at the head of Grafton Notch. The AT to Old Speck and Baldpate Mtn. and Eyebrow and Table Rock trails leave from this point. No camping is allowed in the park.

Trail Access from ME 26

Distances from jct. ME 26 and US 2 in Newry via ME 26 to
- Grafton Loop Trail (southern trailhead): 4.6 mi.
- Step Falls Preserve: 7.6 mi.
- Screw Auger Falls: 9.1 mi.
- Mother Walker Falls: 10.1 mi.
- Moose Cave: 10.9 mi.
- Trailhead parking at Grafton Notch and AT crossing: 11.5 mi.
- Spruce Meadow Picnic Area: 12.5 mi.
- North Rd. (access to Success Pond Rd. trailheads): 16.3 mi.

Mahoosuc Public Reserved Land

The Mahoosuc Range extends for about 30 mi. in a northeast-southwest direction from the Androscoggin River in Gorham, New Hampshire, to Old Speck and Grafton Notch in Grafton Township, Maine. The range is generally bounded by NH 16 in the west, US 2 in the south, and ME 26 in the east. More than two dozen summits are in the Mahoosucs, including eleven peaks over 3,000 ft. The highest is Old Speck Mtn. at 4,170 ft. The deep defile of Mahoosuc Notch is traversed by the AT, and Grafton Notch is bisected by ME 26.

The Mahoosuc PRL comprises 31,764 acres of the Mahoosuc Range in Maine, and essentially surrounds Grafton Notch State Park. North of the park, the Mahoosuc PRL unit encompasses the entirety of West and East Baldpate mountains. South of the state park, the unit extends to the Maine–New Hampshire border and encompasses the summits of Old Speck, Mahoosuc Arm, Fulling Mill, and Goose Eye mountains, and Mt.

Carlo. The AT crosses most of the major summits of the Mahoosuc Range, and much of the western section of Grafton Loop Trail runs through Mahoosuc PRL. Backcountry camping is available at thiteen sites within the unit.

Trail Access from the west

Access to the peaks of Mahoosuc Range from the west is possible via Success Pond Rd., which extends the length of the lower western slopes of the range. From the trailhead parking area on ME 26 in Grafton Notch at the AT crossing, drive north for 4.9 mi. Turn left on North Rd., and follow this for 4.0 mi. to a jct. with Success Pond Rd. and York Pond Rd. (*Note:* The former access from ME 26 was via York Pond Rd. In 2011, this road washed out and was closed.) Bear right on Success Pond Rd., and continue south to reach the Speck Pond, Notch, Carlo Col and Goose Eye, and Success trailheads. Refer to following summary table for detailed mileages between points.

Trailhead Access from the west (AMC map 6: C12–D12, DeLorme ME map 18, NH map 49)

Distances from ME 26 via North Rd. and Success Pond Rd. to
- Speck Pond Trail trailhead: 9.4 mi.
- Notch Trail spur road to trailhead: 10.7 mi.
- Carlo Col and Goose Eye trailhead: 13.5 mi.
- Success Trail trailhead: 16.2 mi.
- Hutchins St., Berlin, NH: 21.6 mi.

Old Speck Mtn. (4,170 ft.)

Old Speck Mtn., so named for its speckled appearance caused by large areas of exposed rock and tree cover and to distinguish it from the Speckled Mountains in Stoneham and Peru, dominates the western side of Grafton Notch. Long thought to be the second-highest peak in the state, after Hamlin Peak on Katahdin, Old Speck Mtn. is now considered fourth, after Hamlin, Sugarloaf Mtn., and Crocker Mtn., North Peak. The open observation tower on the wooded summit offers outstanding views of Grafton Notch, West and East Baldpate to the north, the jumbled peaks of the Mahoosuc Range to the south, and beyond to the Presidential Range.

Old Speck Trail (AMC)

This trail, part of the AT, ascends Old Speck Mtn. from a well-signed parking area (small fee) on ME 26 at the height-of-land in Grafton Notch. From a kiosk on the north side of the parking lot, follow the trail leading to the left (the right-hand trail goes to Baldpate Mtn.). In 0.1 mi., Eyebrow Trail leaves right to circle over the top of an 800-ft. cliff (shaped like an eyebrow) and rejoin Old Speck Trail.

The main trail crosses a brook and soon begins to climb, following a series of switchbacks with many rock steps to approach the falls on Cascade Brook. Above the falls, the trail, now heading more north, crosses the brook for the final time (last water), turns left at a ledge with a view up to Old Speck, and, at 1.1 mi., passes the upper terminus of Eyebrow Trail on the right. Old Speck Trail bears left and ascends gradually to the north ridge, where the trail swings more to the left and follows the ridge, with frequent ledgy footing and numerous short descents interspersed through the ascent. At 3.0 mi. is an outlook east from the top of a ledgy hump. The trail descends again briefly, then ascends steadily to the south, passing the abandoned and closed Link Trail on the left. Old Speck Trail climbs a fairly steep and rough pitch and passes an excellent north outlook just before its jct. with Mahoosuc Trail, where Old Speck Trail ends. The flat, wooded summit of Old Speck—where an observation tower and the recently cleared summit plateau affords fine views—is 0.3 mi. left (east). Speck Pond Shelter is 1.1 mi. to the right.

Old Speck Trail (AMC map 6: B13–C13, MATC map 7)

Distances from ME 26 (1,450 ft.) to

- Eyebrow Trail, upper jct. (2,480 ft.): 1.1 mi., 1 hr. 5 min.
- Mahoosuc Trail (4,030 ft.): 3.5 mi., 3 hr. 5 min.
- Old Speck Mtn. summit (4,170 ft.) (via Mahoosuc Trail): 3.8 mi., 3 hr. 20 min.

Eyebrow Trail (MBPL)

This trail provides a steep and rough alternative route to the lower part of Old Speck Trail, passing along the edge of the cliff called The Eyebrow that overlooks Grafton Notch. Eyebrow Trail is better suited for ascent than descent. The trail leaves Old Speck Trail on the right 0.1 mi. from the parking area off ME 26. Eyebrow Trail climbs moderately northwest and north for 0.4 mi., then swings left and ascends more steeply with the aid of cable handrails. It turns right at the base of a rock face, crosses a rock slab where iron rungs and a small ladder have been placed to assist hikers (but is still potentially dangerous if icy), then turns sharply left and ascends steeply, bearing right where a side path leaves straight ahead for an outlook. Soon the trail runs at a moderate grade along the top of the cliff (with good views), then descends to an outlook and runs mostly level until it ends at Old Speck Trail.

Eyebrow Trail (AMC map 6: B13, MATC map 7)
Distance from Old Speck Trail, lower jct. (1,525 ft.) to
• Old Speck Trail, upper jct. (2,480 ft.): 1.2 mi., 1 hr. 10 min.

Speck Pond Trail (AMC)

This trail ascends to Speck Pond from Success Pond Rd. at a point 9.4 mi. southwest of ME 26 via North and Success Pond roads. Parking is on the left before the trailhead, opposite the entrance to Speck Pond Rd.

The trail leaves Success Pond Rd., enters the woods, and in 100 yd. crosses Sucker Brook. In another 75 yd., the trail crosses the brook again. (In high-water conditions, it may be best to walk 100 yd. up Speck Pond Rd. and then bushwhack south back to the trail on the near side of the brook.) The trail follows the north side of the brook at easy then moderate grades for 1.4 mi., then turns left away from the brook and traverses northward across an area of recent logging, crossing several skid roads and the top of an open brushy area. Follow markings carefully here, especially where the trail bears right at a cairn as it leaves the open area. The trail then swings right (east) and climbs moderately, crosses a relatively level section, then bears left and climbs rather steeply and roughly, with one wooden ladder, up an often-wet ledge, to the jct. at 3.1 mi. with the May Cutoff, which diverges right.

May Cutoff (AMC). This short trail runs 0.3 mi. (50-ft. ascent, 10 min.) from Speck Pond Trail to Mahoosuc Trail with only minor ups and downs, ascending across a scrubby hump along the way that is probably the true summit of Mahoosuc Arm.

Speck Pond Trail continues over a height-of-land, passes an outlook over the pond and up to Old Speck Mtn., then descends steeply to the pond and reaches the campsite and Mahoosuc Trail.

Speck Pond Trail (AMC map 6: C12–C13, MATC map 7)
Distance from Success Pond Rd. (1,730 ft.) to
  • Speck Pond Campsite (3,400 ft.): 3.6 mi., 2,000 ft., 2 hr. 50 min.

Goose Eye Mtn. (3,870 ft.)

This striking mountain in Riley Township offers excellent panoramic views—including the Presidential Range and the surrounding peaks of the Mahoosuc Range—from its rocky alpine summit. Goose Eye and its subsidiary East Peak (3,794 ft.) and North Peak (3,675) can be reached from the east via Wright and Mahoosuc trails, from the north via Notch and Mahoosuc trails, from the west via Goose Eye Trail, and from the south via Carlo Col and Mahoosuc trails.

Notch Trail (AMC)

This trail ascends at easy grades to the southwest end of Mahoosuc Notch, providing the easiest access to that wild and beautiful place. The trail begins on Shelter Brook Rd. (sign for Notch Trail), a spur road that leaves Success Pond Rd. 10.7 mi. southwest of ME 26 via North and Success Pond roads and runs 0.3 mi. to a jct., where there is limited parking on the left. Shelter Brook Rd. turns right here (the road ahead is blocked off) and crosses two bridges (the second of which has been deteriorating and should be checked before you drive across). At 0.6 mi. from Success Pond Rd., a parking area is on the right, and 50 yd. farther, the trail leaves the road on the left (sign).

The trail ascends easily, following old logging roads along Shelter Brook, crossing to its north side and then back to the south side at 1.1 mi. Here, the trail swings left (northeast), soon crosses the brook again, and continues up to the height-of-land, where it meets Mahoosuc Trail; turn left to traverse the notch. A short distance along Mahoosuc Trail, the valley, which has been an ordinary one, changes sharply to a chamber formation, and the high cliffs of the notch, which have not been visible at all on Notch Trail, come into sight.

Notch Trail (AMC map 6: C12–C13, MATC map 7)

Distance from parking area on Shelter Brook Rd. (1,650 ft.) to
  • Mahoosuc Trail (2,460 ft.): 1.9 mi., 800 ft., 1 hr. 20 min.

Goose Eye Trail (AMC)

This trail ascends Goose Eye Mtn. from Carlo Col Trail (see p. 117), 0.2 mi. from Success Pond Rd. at a point 13.7 mi. southwest of ME 26 via North and Success Pond roads. Goose Eye Trail ends at Mahoosuc Trail 0.1 mi. beyond the summit. Goose Eye Trail has easy-to-moderate grades for most of its length, then climbs very steeply, with some ledge scrambling, to the scenic summit. The lower part of the trail must be followed with care through logged areas.

From the gravel logging road that Carlo Col Trail follows, Goose Eye Trail diverges left at a sign, drops down an embankment, follows a new section of trail for 90 yd., and turns right onto the original route, an old logging road. Goose Eye Trail quickly crosses a brook, runs through a brushy, overgrown area, crosses another brook, and bears left onto a gravel road at 0.3 mi. from Carlo Col Trail. Goose Eye Trail follows this road for 0.1 mi., then diverges right (watch carefully for sign) and passes through a clear-cut area where the footway may be very obscure through an area of tall grass. The trail swings to the right (southeast) across a wet spot at 0.6 mi. and climbs gradually through woods between logged areas, crossing an overgrown skid road at an angle.

At 1.2 mi., the trail reaches the Maine–New Hampshire state line and enters a fine hardwood forest. The trail swings right at 1.7 mi. and angles up the south side of a ridge at a moderate grade, climbs more steeply uphill, then becomes gradual at the crest of the ridge in dense conifers; at 2.4 mi., there is a glimpse of the peak of Goose Eye ahead. The trail ascends moderately along the north side of the ridge, then climbs steeply, swinging left to bypass a very difficult ledge, then scrambling up a somewhat less difficult ledge. The trail soon comes out on the open ledges below the summit, to which it makes a steep, scrambly ascent. From the summit, which is reached at 2.9 mi. and has magnificent views in all directions, the trail descends over ledges 0.1 mi. to Mahoosuc Trail, which turns right (southbound) and runs straight ahead at the jct. (northbound).

Goose Eye Trail (AMC map 6: C12–C13, MATC map 7)

Distances from Carlo Col Trail (1,660 ft.) to

- Goose Eye Mtn. summit (3,870 ft.): 2.9 mi., 2,200 ft., 2 hr. 35 min.
- Mahoosuc Trail (3,800 ft.): 3.0 mi., 2,200 ft., 2 hr. 40 min.

Wright Trail (MBPL)

This trail, steep and rough in places, provides access to Goose Eye Mtn. and the Mahoosuc Range via a scenic route from the east that begins in a place known as Ketchum, located on a branch of the Sunday River. The upper part of the trail formerly had two separate branches, but the north branch, which ascended through a small glacial cirque, has been closed because of erosion and safety concerns. The south branch, which follows a ledgy ridge, is now the sole route up to the main ridge crest.

To reach the trailhead, leave US 2, 2.8 mi. north of Bethel, Maine, and follow Sunday River Rd. At a fork at 2.2 mi., bear right (signs for Jordan Bowl and covered bridge), and at 3.3 mi., bear right again (sign for covered bridge) and continue past Artist Covered Bridge (left) at 3.8 mi. from US 2. At 6.5 mi., the road becomes gravel. At 7.8 mi., turn left across two new bridges, then immediately take the first right, which is Bull Branch Rd. (As of 2011, both of these turns had signs reading, "Frenchmans, Goose Eye." Frenchman's Hole is a popular swimming area on Bull Branch Rd.) At 9.3 mi., Goose Eye Brook is crossed on a bridge, and the trailhead is on the left at 9.5 mi. from US 2. There was no trail sign at the trailhead in 2011; the trail starts at a small signboard behind a boulder. Parking is available here, or a short distance farther up the road.

Leaving Bull Branch Rd., the blue-blazed trail descends toward Goose Eye Brook, then follows its north side upstream past several cascades and pools and a 30-ft. gorge. At 0.5 mi., the trail makes a left turn onto a woods road and follows it for 0.2 mi., then makes a right turn onto an older road. At 0.9 mi., the trail bears left off the road and descends gradually 100 yd. to Goose Eye Brook at its confluence with a tributary, where the trail bears right and follows the tributary for 0.1 mi., then turns sharply left and crosses it. From this point, the trail roughly follows the north side of Goose Eye Brook, with minor ups and downs, crossing two small tributaries, until the trail reaches the former loop jct. at 2.5 mi. A designated MBPL tentsite is on the right just before the jct.

From the former loop jct., where the north branch (now closed) continued ahead across a tributary brook, the south branch of the trail immediately crosses Goose Eye Brook to the left and climbs, gradually at first and then moderately by switchbacks with rough sections and wooden steps, to the ridge crest at 3.1 mi. At 3.4 mi., after a rough ascent, the trail reaches an open spot, then descends slightly back into the woods. The trail then resumes a steep, rough ascent on ledges to an open knob with beautiful views at 3.6 mi. The trail continues along the ridge with several open areas and occasional minor descents to cross small sags, then finally climbs moderately to Mahoosuc Trail in the small gap between East Peak and West Peak (main summit) of Goose Eye Mtn. at 4.4 mi. The main summit can be reached in 0.4 mi. by following Mahoosuc Trail to the left (southbound) and then Goose Eye Trail. The ledgy East Peak is reached by climbing steeply for 0.1 mi. on Mahoosuc Trail to the right (northbound).

Wright Trail (AMC map 6: C13, MATC map 7)
Distances from parking area on Bull Branch Rd. (1,240 ft.) to
- MBPL tentsite and former loop jct. (2,300 ft.): 2.5 mi., 1,150 ft., 1 hr. 50 min.
- Mahoosuc Trail (3,630 ft.): 4.4 mi., 2,600 ft., 3 hr. 30 min.
- West Peak of Goose Eye Mtn. (3,870 ft.) (via Mahoosuc Trail and Goose Eye Trail): 4.8 mi., 2,850 ft., 3 hr. 50 min.
- East Peak of Goose Eye Mtn. (3,794 ft.) (via Mahoosuc Trail): 4.5 mi., 2,750 ft., 3 hr. 35 min.

Mt. Carlo (3,565 ft.)

Mt. Carlo in Riley Township is situated just east of the Maine–New Hampshire border, roughly in the middle of the Mahoosuc Range. Mt. Carlo can be climbed from the west via Carlo Col Trail and from the north via either Goose Eye and Mahoosuc trails or Wright and Mahoosuc trails.

Carlo Col Trail (AMC)

This trail ascends to Mahoosuc Trail at the small box ravine called Carlo Col, and, in combination with Goose Eye Trail, makes possible a scenic loop over Mt. Carlo and Goose Eye Mtn. Carlo Col Trail leaves Success Pond Rd. on a gravel logging road (AMC trail sign and road sign for Carlo Col trailhead) that begins 16.2 mi. southwest of ME 26 via North and Success Pond roads. Parking for several cars is available a few yards up the road on the left.

From the parking area, the trail follows the road southeast, and in 0.2 mi. Goose Eye Trail (sign) diverges left down an embankment, and Carlo Col Trail continues straight ahead on the road, climbing easily through a logged area. At 0.7 mi., the trail takes the left-hand road at a fork, descends on the road for 0.1 mi., then turns left (sign) onto a footpath into the woods and immediately crosses the brook that flows from Carlo Col (may be difficult to cross at high water). The trail ascends easily, and at 1.0 mi. turns right onto a relocated section where the older route climbed left into a brushy clear-cut area. The trail runs through woods between the brook and the clear-cut, swings right to cross the brook at 1.3 mi., and recrosses it in another 100 yd. The trail then skirts the edge of the clear-cut, crosses the brook again, and climbs moderately, turning right onto the original route at 1.8 mi. At 2.2 mi., the trail approaches a small mossy brook on the left and climbs alongside it, with rocky footing, to a side path on the left at 2.4 mi. that climbs 50 yd. to Carlo Col Campsite. Here, the main trail swings right across the small brook (last water, perhaps for several miles) and ascends moderately to Mahoosuc Trail at Carlo Col. The summit of Mt. Carlo is 0.4 mi. to the left on this trail, and to the right a fine outlook ledge is reached in a short distance via a fairly difficult scramble.

Carlo Col Trail (AMC map 6: C12, D12–D13, MATC map 7)

Distances from Success Pond Rd. (1,630 ft.) to

- Goose Eye Trail (1,660 ft.): 0.2 mi., 50 ft., 10 min.
- Carlo Col Shelter (2,960 ft.): 2.4 mi., 1,350 ft., 1 hr. 55 min.
- Mahoosuc Trail (3,170 ft.): 2.7 mi., 1,550 ft., 2 hr. 10 min.

Mahoosuc Trail (AMC)

This trail route extends across the length of the Mahoosuc Range from Gorham, New Hampshire, to the summit of Old Speck Mtn. Beyond its jct. with Centennial Trail, Mahoosuc Trail is a link in the AT. Camping is limited to the tentsites at Trident Col and to four shelters: Gentian Pond, Carlo Col, Full Goose, and Speck Pond (all of which also have tentsites). These sites may have a caretaker, in which case a fee is charged (group notification required; see p. 108). Water may be scarce, particularly in dry weather.

This trail route is among the most rugged and strenuous of its kind in the White Mountains, with numerous minor humps and cols and many ledges, some of them quite steep and likely to be slippery when wet. Parts of the trail may require significantly more time than that provided by the formula, particularly for backpackers with heavy packs.

Mahoosuc Notch, in particular, may require several hours to traverse. The notch is regarded by experienced hikers to be one the most difficult sections of the entire AT. It can be hazardous in wet or icy conditions and can remain impassable because of snow through the end of May and perhaps longer.

The entirety of Mahoosuc Trail is described in detail in AMC's *White Mountain Guide*. The trail is also shown from end to end on AMC map 6: Mahoosuc Range, included in this guide. The Maine section of the trail, from Carlo Col just east of the Maine–New Hampshire border, to the summit of Old Speck Mtn., is described here.

From Carlo Col, 0.3 mi. east of Carlo Col Shelter and 2.6 mi. from Success Pond Rd., the trail climbs steadily to the bare summit of Mt. Carlo at 0.4 mi., where there is an excellent view. The trail then passes a lower knob, descends through a meadow, and reaches a col at 1.0 mi. The trail turns more northerly and climbs steeply to a knoll below Goose Eye, then passes through a sag and climbs steeply again to the narrow ridge of the main (west) peak of Goose Eye Mtn. at 1.8 mi. (*Caution:* Use care on the ledges.) Here, Goose Eye Trail branches sharply left, reaching the open summit and its spectacular views in 0.1 mi., and continues to Success Pond Rd. in 3.2 mi. Mahoosuc Trail turns sharply right (east) here and follows the ridge through mixed ledge and scrub to a col at 2.1 mi., where the trail meets Wright Trail (leads 1.9 mi. to a campsite and 4.4. mi. to Bull Branch Rd. in Ketchum).

Beyond, Mahoosuc Trail climbs steeply through woods and open areas to the bare summit of East Peak of Goose Eye Mtn. at 2.2 mi. The trail then turns north and switchbacks downhill through scrub to a col. Ahead, the trail runs in the open nearly to the foot of North Peak of Goose Eye Mtn., except for two box ravines, where there is often water. At the summit of North Peak at 3.4 mi., the trail turns sharply right (east) along the ridge, then swings northeast down the steep slope, winding through several patches of scrub. At the foot of the steep slope, the trail enters the woods and angles down the west face of the ridge to the col and Full Goose Campsite at 4.4 mi. A spring is located 80 yd. to the right (east of the campsite).

The trail then turns sharply left and ascends, coming into the open below the summit of the south peak of Fulling Mill Mtn., which is reached at 4.9 mi. Here, the trail turns sharply left and runs through a meadow. The trail descends northwest through woods, first gradually, then steeply, to the head of Mahoosuc Notch at 5.9 mi. Here, Notch Trail diverges sharply left (southwest) and leads 2.2 mi. to Success Pond Rd.

From the head of Mahoosuc Notch, Mahoosuc Trail turns sharply right (northeast) and descends the length of the narrow notch along a rough footway, passing through a number of boulder caverns, some with narrow openings where progress may be slow and where ice remains into summer. The trail is marked with white blazes on the rocks.

At the lower end of the notch, at 7.0 mi., the trail bears left and ascends moderately but roughly up the east side of Mahoosuc Mtn. to cross a brook. The trail then winds upward among rocks and ledges on the very steep wooded slope of Mahoosuc Arm on rough footway. At 8.6 mi., a few yards past the top of the flat ledges near the summit of Mahoosuc Arm, May Cutoff diverges left and leads 0.3 mi. to join Speck Pond Trail.

Mahoosuc Trail swings right, crosses the semi-open summit plateau, then drops steeply to Speck Pond (3,430 ft.), the highest pond in Maine. The trail crosses the outlet brook and continues around the east side of the pond to Speck Pond Campsite at 9.5 mi. (in summer, there is a caretaker and a fee for overnight camping). Here, Speck Pond Trail leaves to the left, leading 3.1 mi. to Success Pond Rd.

Beyond the pond, Mahoosuc Trail climbs over a hump, and then runs across the east face of a second small hump. The trail then climbs the west shoulder of Old Speck, reaching an open area where the footway is well defined on the crest. Near the top of the shoulder, the trail bears right, re-enters the woods, and follows the wooded crest.

Old Speck Trail, which continues the AT north, diverges left to Grafton Notch at 10.6 mi. Mahoosuc Trail leads straight ahead to the summit of Old Speck Mtn. and its observation tower at 10.9 mi. Grafton Loop Trail leaves from this point and heads south.

Mahoosuc Trail in New Hampshire (AMC map 6: E10–E11, D11–D12)

Distances from Hogan Rd. parking area north of Androscoggin River in Gorham (820 ft.) to

- Mt. Hayes summit (2,555 ft.): 2.5 mi., 2 hr. 10 min.
- Centennial Trail (2,550 ft.): 2.7 mi., 2 hr. 15 min.
- Cascade Mtn. summit (2,631 ft.): 4.5 mi., 3 hr. 30 min.
- Trident Col (2,030 ft.): 5.7 mi., 4 hr. 5 min.
- Page Pond (2,220 ft.): 6.7 mi., 4 hr. 50 min.
- Wocket Ledge viewpoint (2,700 ft.): 7.3 mi., 5 hr. 20 min.
- Dream Lake, inlet brook crossing (2,620 ft.): 8.4 mi., 6 hr. 5 min.
- Austin Brook Trail (2,155 ft.): 10.5 mi., 7 hr. 15 min.
- Mt. Success summit (3,565 ft.): 13.3 mi., 9 hr. 35 min.
- Success Trail (3,170 ft.): 13.9 mi., 9 hr. 55 min.
- Carlo Col Trail at Carlo Col (3,170 ft.): 15.7 mi., 11 hr. 5 min.

Mahoosuc Trail in Maine (AMC map 6: D13, C13, B13, MATC map 7)

Distances from Carlo Col (3,170 ft.) to

- Mt. Carlo summit (3,565 ft.): 0.4 mi., 25 min.
- Goose Eye Trail jct. (3,800 ft.): 1.8 mi., 1 hr. 25 min.
- Wright Trail jct. (3,630 ft.): 2.1mi., 1 hr. 35 min.
- Goose Eye Mtn., East Peak (3,794 ft.): 2.2 mi., 1 hr. 45 min.
- Goose Eye Mtn., North Peak (3,675 ft.): 3.4 mi., 2 hr. 30 min.
- Full Goose Campsite (2,950 ft.): 4.4 mi., 3 hr.
- Notch Trail (2,460 ft.): 5.9 mi., 4 hr.
- foot of Mahoosuc Notch (2,150 ft.): 7.0 mi., 4 hr. 45 min.
- Mahoosuc Arm and May Cutoff (3,750 ft.): 8.6 mi., 6 hr. 15 min.
- Speck Pond Campsite (3,400 ft.): 9.5 mi., 6 hr. 40 min.
- Old Speck Trail jct. (4,030 ft.): 10.6 mi., 7 hr. 35 min.
- Old Speck Mtn. summit (4,170 ft.): 10.9 mi., 7 hr. 50 min.

Distances from Old Speck Mtn. summit (4,170 ft.) to

- Old Speck Trail jct. (4,030 ft.): 0.3 mi., 10 min.

- Speck Pond Campsite (3,400 ft.): 1.4 mi., 50 min.
- Mahoosuc Arm summit (3,770 ft.): 2.3 mi., 1 hr. 25 min.
- foot of Mahoosuc Notch (2,150 ft.): 3.9 mi., 2 hr. 15 min.
- Notch Trail (2,460 ft.): 5.0 mi., 3 hr.
- Full Goose Campsite (2,950 ft.): 6.5 mi., 4 hr. 15 min.
- Goose Eye Mtn., North Peak (3,675 ft.): 7.5 mi., 5 hr. 5 min.
- Goose Eye Mtn., East Peak (3,794 ft.): 8.7 mi., 5 hr. 55 min.
- Wright Trail (3,630 ft.): 8.8 mi., 5 hr. 55 min.
- Goose Eye Trail (3,800 ft.): 9.1 mi., 6 hr. 10 min.
- Mt. Carlo (3,565 ft.): 10.5 mi., 7 hr. 5 min.
- Carlo Col Trail at Carlo Col (3,170 ft.): 10.9 mi., 7 hr. 20 min.

Baldpate Mtn., East Peak (3,780 ft.) and West Peak (3,662 ft.)

Baldpate Mtn. rises to the east of Grafton Notch. The two main peaks are the alpine summit of East Peak and the more wooded West Peak. Access is via the AT, which traverses both. Table Rock is an interesting side hike to airy ledges high above Grafton Notch.

Table Rock Trail (MBPL)

Table Rock Trail offers a short but steep climb to the prominent rock ledge of Table Rock on Baldpate Mtn. on the east side of Grafton Notch and spectacular views of Old Speck Mtn. across the notch. From the ledge, the trail continues on to rejoin the AT. Table Rock Trail also features an extensive slab cave system, possibly the largest in the state.

The trail leaves the AT to the right (south) 0.1 mi. from the trailhead on ME 26 (see p. 124). From this jct., Table Rock Trail rises gently for 0.3 mi. along the side of a hill above a marsh until reaching a dropoff. From here, the trail climbs to reach a rocky, caribou moss–covered area at 0.6 mi. After several switchbacks along ledges, the trail enters a deep ravine between two rock faces. At the top of the ravine, bear right. The trail climbs less steeply to a prominent outlook at 0.8 mi. At 0.9 mi., the trail reaches the base of the ledges that form Table Rock, where the slab caves begin. (*Caution:* Be careful if you explore the caves. Some are quite deep, and a fall could mean serious injury.)

On the trail, continue around the bottom of Table Rock. (Note the weather-formed rock that looks like a shark's fin on the ledges above.) At 1.0 mi., after swinging behind Table Rock, reach a side trail leading left 20 yd. to Table Rock. To the right, the upper part of Table Rock Trail continues with little change in elevation to reach the AT in 0.5 mi. Turn right (east) to reach Baldpate; go left (west) to return to the trailhead on ME 26.

Table Rock Trail (AMC map 6: B13, MATC map 7)
Distances from trailhead parking area on ME 26 (1,450 ft.) to
  - start of trail (1,500 ft.) (via AT): 0.1 mi., 5 min.
  - Table Rock and jct. with upper trail (2,350 ft.): 1.0 mi., 1 hr.
  - complete loop: 2.4 mi., 2 hr.

Baldpate Mtn. via Appalachian Trail from the south (MATC)

The trail leaves the north side of the parking area on ME 26 in Grafton Notch. At a fork, take the trail to the right. It soon crosses ME 26 and then runs briefly through woods and beside a marsh until, at 0.1 mi., the trail crosses a brook on a log footbridge. Just ahead, the AT passes Table Rock Trail, which leaves right. The AT rises gradually on an old woods road. At 0.8 mi., the AT passes the upper end of Table Rock Trail. Ahead, the AT climbs steadily and then more steeply to the western knob of Baldpate, where there are good views to the northwest. The AT then angles up the north side of the knob to a ridge extending toward West Peak, soon descending to a brook where, at 2.3 mi., a side trail leads south to Baldpate Lean-to.

Beyond, the trail climbs steeply to West Peak and good views at 3.1 mi. The trail continues north to dip several hundred feet before climbing to East Peak at 4.0 mi., marked by a large cairn. The alpine summit offers extensive views of the western Maine mountain and lake country. Also at the summit, Grafton Loop Trail enters from the right (south). From here, the AT continues 6.3 mi. to East B Hill Rd.

Baldpate Mtn. via Appalachian Trail from the south (AMC map 6: B13–B14, MATC map 7)
Distances from trailhead parking area on ME 26 (1,450 ft.) to
  - lower side trail to Table Rock (1,500 ft.): 0.1 mi., 5 min.

- upper side trail to Table Rock (2,100 ft.): 0.8 mi., 45 min.
- side trail to Baldpate Lean-to (2,600 ft.): 2.3 mi., 1 hr. 45 min.
- Baldpate Mtn., West Peak (3,662 ft.): 3.1 mi., 2 hr. 40 min.
- Baldpate Mtn., East Peak (3,780 ft.) and Grafton Loop Trail jct.: 4.0 mi., 3 hr. 10 min.
- East B Hill Rd. (1,450 ft.): 10.3 mi., 6 hr. 40 min.

Baldpate Mtn. via Appalachian Trail from the north (MATC)

The trail leaves the left (south) side of East B Hill Rd. about 8 mi. west of Andover village. The trail descends from the road, crosses a small brook, then turns south along the edge of a progressively deeper gorge cut by this brook, which the AT follows for 0.5 mi. before turning west into the mouth of Dunn Notch. At 0.8 mi., the trail crosses the West Branch of the Ellis River (a large stream at this point) at the top of a double waterfall plunging 60 ft. into Dunn Notch. You can reach the bottom of the falls via an old logging road across the stream. (Upstream, you will find a small, rocky gorge and the beautiful upper falls.) The AT crosses the old road and climbs steeply up the eastern rim of the notch. The AT then climbs moderately to the south.

At 1.3 mi., the trail turns left and climbs gradually through open hardwoods along the edge of the northern arm of Surplus Mtn. At 3.0 mi., the trail angles right (southwest) around the nose of Surplus, climbs gently along a broad ridge, and passes near the summit. Beyond, the trail descends steeply over rough ground to reach Frye Notch Lean-to, near the head of Frye Brook at 4.5 mi. From the lean-to, the trail climbs gradually, then more steeply, gaining more than 1,300 ft. in less than 1 mi. to the open summit of East Peak of Baldpate Mtn. at 6.3 mi. The trail then drops down, then climbs West Peak at 7.2 mi. Beyond, the AT descends into Grafton Notch via the trail from the south (see p. 124), passing the upper and lower jct. with Table Rock Trail and Baldpate Lean-to en route.

Baldpate Mtn. via Appalachian Trail from the north (USGS B Pond and Old Speck quads, MATC map 7, DeLorme map 18)

Distances from East B Hill Rd. (1,450 ft.) to
- Dunn Notch, West Branch of Ellis River (1,300 ft.): 0.8 mi., 55 min.
- Frye Notch Lean-to (2,250 ft.): 4.5 mi., 3 hr.
- Baldpate Mtn., East Peak (3,780 ft.): 6.3 mi., 4 hr. 30 min.

- Baldpate Mtn., West Peak (3,662 ft.): 7.2 mi., 5 hr. 10 min.
- trailhead parking area on ME 26 (1,450 ft.): 10.3 mi., 7 hr.

Grafton Loop Trail

This major new trail was constructed over a six-year period by AMC and other members of the Grafton Loop Trail Coalition, including MBPL, MATC, ATC, Maine Conservation Corps, Hurricane Island Outward Bound School, several timber management companies, Sunday River Ski Resort, and other private landowners. The goal was to develop multiday hiking opportunities that offer alternatives to heavily used sections of the AT. This unique public-private partnership was the first major AMC new-trail construction project in the White Mountains since Centennial Trail was opened in 1976. About 30 mi. of new trail have been constructed on either side of Grafton Notch, which, along with an 8-mi. section of the AT between Old Speck Mtn. and Baldpate Mtn., has created a 38-mi. loop that connects a series of scenic peaks and other natural features.

Parking for the southern trailhead (used for both eastern and western sections) is located on the east side of ME 26, 4.9 mi. north of its jct. with US 2 in Newry and just north of Eddy Rd. To reach the western section trailhead, walk 0.6 mi. south on the shoulder of ME 26 to a sign for Grafton Loop Trail. (*Note:* No parking is allowed at the western trailhead. The northern trailhead is located on ME 26 in the Grafton Notch parking area, 11.5 mi. north of US 2 where the AT crosses ME 26.)

Grafton Loop Trail (eastern section) (AMC/MATC)

The eastern section of Grafton Loop Trail was completed and opened to the public in 2003. This consists of a 20.8-mi. route that leaves ME 26 in Newry and returns to the road in Grafton Notch State Park via a 3.7-mi. section of the AT. The trail traverses four mountain peaks and includes five primitive campsites. About half of the trail crosses private lands, and the remainder is located on public lands managed by MBPL as part of the Mahoosuc PRL and Grafton Notch State Park.

Grafton Loop Trail begins at a post with a blue blaze on it. Leaving the parking lot, the trail heads through a young forest, crosses a small brook, and then an overgrown logging road. The trail switchbacks several times on a gradual incline along parts of an old logging road, passing through an area of young spruce and white birch before passing into an area thick with downed balsam fir. The trail continues gradually uphill, using sections of a logging road and switchbacks. The trail is clearly marked with blue blazes and cairns. Avoid turning left onto smaller unmarked paths. At about 2 mi., turn left and begin a steep climb. At about 2.4 mi., the trail crosses over several exposed granite boulders and ledges offering views of the Sunday River ski area, Grafton Notch, and the distant Presidentials. The trail cuts back into the woods before climbing a steep boulder staircase with some mild rock scrambling. (*Caution:* The exposed granite areas are very slippery in wet weather.)

Reach the south summit of Puzzle Mtn., marked by a large rock cairn, at 3.2 mi. Excellent views appear in all directions. The lower end of Woodsum Spur Trail enters from the right (not recommended from this direction). Ahead, at 3.6 mi., the trail reaches the rocky ledge top of Puzzle Mtn. Here, the upper end of Woodsum Spur Trail diverges to the right.

Descend the mountain to the north, following cairns. Grafton Loop Trail traverses rolling terrain with a few boulder scrambles and a steel ladder. Beyond, the trail descends gradually on stone steps. At 4.9 mi., it reaches the jct. with the spur trail leading 300 ft. to Stewart Campsite.

After the jct., Grafton Loop Trail makes a winding descent on switchbacks. The trail crosses an overgrown road before leveling out as the trail approaches Chase Hill Brook. Take care to follow only the blue trail blazes in this area. At 6.3 mi., cross Chase Hill Brook (crossing may be difficult during times of high water). At the base of the mountain (6.7 mi.), the trail intersects an old road. Turn right, walk 0.25 mi., and reenter the woods at the cairn on the left side of the road. The trail winds up Long Mtn., crossing, following, and leaving the woods road several times. The trail eventually leaves the woods road for good and continues through mature forest. The trail contours up a ridge on long, gradual switchbacks with occasional steep sections. As the trail gains altitude, gaps in the trees afford views of the Sunday River ski area and the summit of Mt. Washington. The trail becomes steeper and uses a stone staircase and wooden staircase/ladder to assist with the ascent.

At 9.4 mi, a short spur trail near the summit of Long Mtn. leads north to a viewpoint. Grafton Loop Trail reaches a highpoint on Long Mtn. at 9.5 mi. Beyond, the trail winds easily downhill, crossing several small streams. At 10.4 mi., the trail reaches the 440-ft. spur trail to Town Corner Campsite. At 11.1 mi., the trail crosses a snowmobile trail and a log bridge. The trail then descends along a brook to the jct. at 11.9 mi., where a 400-ft. spur trail leads to Knoll Campsite. Ahead, the trail follows Wight Brook through a level area, crossing the brook several times (may be difficult to cross in high water).

At 13.2 mi., reach the jct. with a spur trail leading 450 ft. to Lane Campsite on Wight Brook. The spur continues beyond the campsite to a lovely waterfall and pool. Beyond the spur trail, the trail climbs steeply to reach a short spur to Lightening Ledge at 14.2 mi., where there are good views of Puzzle Mtn. and the Bear River valley. At 14.5 mi., the trail reaches the knob of Lightening Ledge (2,644 ft.), where there are good views of the Baldpates.

The trail heads back into the woods and descends through the forest with rugged rock faces to the left. A short, moderate descent brings the trail back to Wight Brook, and at 14.9 mi. the trail crosses the brook. A short ascent leads to a jct. at 15.0 mi. with a spur trail leading 300 ft. to East Baldpate Campsite. Grafton Loop Trail then continues on, passing a huge glacial erratic at 16.4 mi. At 17.1 mi., the trail reaches the open summit of East Peak of Baldpate and spectacular views of the mountains and lakes in all directions. (Care should be taken to stay on the trail to avoid disturbing the fragile alpine vegetation.) Grafton Loop Trail joins the AT on the summit for the descent 4.0 mi. down to ME 26 and the Grafton Notch parking area.

Grafton Loop Trail (eastern section) (AMC map 6: B13–B15, C15)

Distances from southern trailhead on ME 26 (730 ft.) to
- Woodsum Spur Trail, west jct. (2,900 ft.): 3.2 mi., 2 hr. 45 min.
- Puzzle Mtn. (3,133 ft.): 3.6 mi., 3 hr.
- Stewart Campsite spur trail (2,500 ft.): 4.9 mi., 4 hr.
- Long Mtn. spur trail (2,950 ft.): 9.4 mi., 6 hr. 30 min.
- Town Corner Campsite spur trail (2,400 ft.): 10.4 mi., 7 hr.
- Knoll Campsite spur trail (1,850 ft.): 11.9 mi., 7 hr. 45 min.
- Lane Campsite spur trail (1,950 ft.): 13.2 mi., 8 hr. 30 min.

- East Baldpate Campsite spur trail (2,350 ft.): 15.0 mi., 9 hr. 30 min.
- Baldpate Mtn., East Peak (3,780 ft.): 17.1 mi., 11 hr. 30 min.
- Grafton Notch parking area on ME 26 (1,450 ft.) (via AT): 21.1 mi., 13 hr. 45 min.

Woodsum Spur Trail (MLT)

This loop trail on the south side of Puzzle Mtn. is part of the Stewart Family Preserve, a 485-acre parcel of land protected by a conservation easement held by the MLT. The trail is fairly rugged with significant elevation gains and losses for its relatively short length. MLT recommends hiking the trail in a clockwise direction.

The northern end of the spur leaves Grafton Loop Trail and heads easterly below the true summit of Puzzle Mtn. Woodsum Spur Trail passes through a wet area, then descends to the col on the southeastern ridge. A short, steep pitch climbs to the southeast peak with limited views. The trail then drops off the peak to the south and west, descending through shrub and forest with occasional open ledges. The trail passes through a wet area before crossing a stream. Gradually ascending as it traverses westward, the trail turns sharply to the northeast and climbs steeply to a boulder field. The trail intersects Grafton Loop Trail on an open ledge at 1.4 mi.

Woodsum Spur Trail (AMC map 6: C15)
Distances from Grafton Loop Trail, northern jct. (3,100 ft.) to
- low point on loop (2,600 ft.): est. 1.0 mi., 50 min.
- Grafton Loop Trail, southern jct. (2,900 ft.): 1.4 mi., 1 hr. 15 min.

Grafton Loop Trail (western section) (AMC)

The western section of the trail opened in 2007 and provides access to spectacular views from Sunday River Whitecap (though views from the rest of this section are limited). Grades are mostly easy to moderate with a few short, steep pitches. The first 7.0 mi. of this section pass through private land (some of which is under conservation easement), where landowners have generously granted public access. Camping is allowed only at the four designated campsites, and fires are not permitted.

Parking for the western section of the trail is allowed only at the trailhead for the eastern section. This parking area is on the east side of ME 26, 4.9 mi. north of its jct. with US 2 at Newry and almost opposite Eddy Rd. To reach the western section trailhead, walk 0.6-mi. south on the shoulder of ME 26 to a sign for Grafton Loop Trail on the west side of the road. By agreement with the landowner, parking is prohibited at the western section trailhead. Mileages are given from the eastern section trailhead parking area, and so include the 0.6-mi. road walk to the western trailhead.

From ME 26, the trail follows a farm road along the left edge of a field for 90 yd., then bears left off the road (sign), and, in another 125 yd., turns right to cross the Bear River on a snowmobile bridge. Marked with snowmobile trail arrows, the trail crosses two fields and enters the woods, following an old road south. At 1.2 mi., the road swings left, and in another 50 yd., the trail turns right (west) off the road (sign) onto a footpath. In 20 yd., the blue-blazed trail crosses a small brook and swings right to follow it, climbing at mostly easy grades and crossing the brook three more times in the next 0.4 mi.; between the second and third of these crossings, the trail passes a small flume. The trail continues following the brook at moderate grades up the northeast slope of Bald Mtn., occasionally making use of old woods roads. The main trail crosses the brook twice more, and at 2.2 mi., just beyond the second of these crossings, a spur path leads 60 yd. left across the brook to Bald Mtn. Tentsite, with two tent platforms (group notification required; see p. 108).

At 2.4 mi., the main trail turns left, crosses the brook for the last time, and climbs steadily by switchbacks to the broad crest of Bald Mtn. The trail continues at easy grades across the plateau, crosses a small sag, and reaches its highpoint on Bald Mtn. at 3.2 mi. The trail then descends moderately to a flat saddle, then runs nearly level to the right of a brushy logged area. The trail soon begins the ascent of Stowe Mtn., first at easy grades, then steeply with many rock steps as the trail enters spruce woods. At 4.3 mi., the trail ascends a series of wooden ladders. The grade eases as the trail crosses the flat, wooded crest of Stowe Mtn. at 4.5 mi. The trail then descends to a minor col at 4.8 mi., crosses a small brook, and ascends briefly to the semi-open ledges of the west knob of Stowe Mtn., where there are limited views. Marked by cairns, the trail runs across the ledges for 0.1 mi., then reenters the woods. It follows a winding course through dense growth, then swings north and descends at mostly easy grades. The trail now traverses the southwestern slope of Sunday River Whitecap through open woods, with minor ups and downs, crossing several small, unreliable brooks.

At 6.0 mi., a spur path diverges left and descends 0.2 mi. to Sargent Brook Tentsite, crossing a small brook (reliable) in 50 yd. Here, there are three tent pads. The main trail traverses to the west, then turns right (north) at 6.2 mi. and ascends moderately along the west slope of Sunday River Whitecap, gaining the ridge crest in a small col at 6.7 mi. The trail follows the ridge over a hump, descends to another col, then climbs again, emerging on open ledges at 7.0 mi., where AMC trail crews have used innovative construction techniques—including scree walls and raised wooden walkways—to protect the fragile alpine vegetation. Hikers are urged to stay on the defined trail and outlook areas. At 7.1 mi., just before the summit is reached, a side path descends 25 yd. right to a designated viewing area looking east. In another 20 yd., a similar path leads 20 yd. left to a western outlook with a fine view of the northern Mahoosucs and the distant Presidentials.

The main trail crosses the summit and descends steeply north over open ledges, then swings more to the northeast, winding down over ledges and through patches of scrub with excellent views of the peaks around Grafton Notch. The trail descends into a belt of woods, then in 125 yd. swings left (west) and emerges on an open shoulder. At 7.6 mi., the trail enters the woods for good and descends steadily west, then southwest through an area where some yellow blazes remain from a former unofficial trail. The grade eases in open woods, and at 8.3 mi., the trail swings left (south) on the broad floor of Miles Notch, runs nearly level for 0.1 mi., then bears right (west) and ascends through partly logged areas onto the lower slope of Slide Mtn. The trail turns left (south) again and contours along the slope, with occasional rough footing, then descends through a bouldery area to a low point at 9.1 mi.

Ahead, the trail soon swings west and ascends briefly, then runs northwest at easy grades, with minor ups and downs, passing to the left of a large boulder at 9.5 mi. The trail runs at easy grades through fine hardwood forest for some distance along the base of Slide Mtn., then rises gradually into mixed woods. At 10.4 mi., a spur on the right ascends 110 yd. to Slide Mtn. Tentsite, where there are three tent pads (group notification required; see p. 108). About 35 yd. past this jct., Grafton Loop Trail crosses a small brook (the water source for the campsite), runs west, then soon swings right and ascends through a hardwood glade. The trail then bears left and winds gradually up the east side of a valley.

At 11.4 mi., a spur path leads 0.1 mi. left to Bull Run Tentsite (two tent platforms) (group notification required; see p. 108), crossing a brook that is the water source. The main trail enters conifers and climbs more steadily across the slope, gaining the crest of a southeastern spur of Old Speck Mtn. at 11.9 mi. Here, the trail swings left and ascends the ridge crest, then bears left again and climbs by easy switchbacks with good footing. At 12.2 mi., the trail climbs through a blowdown patch with restricted views south. The grade increases at 12.7 mi., and the footway becomes rough with rocks, roots, and holes as the trail angles the south slope of Old Speck. At 13.0 mi. is an outlook southeast toward Sunday River Whitecap and the Bear River valley. The trail soon swings right, and the footing improves. After one more steady climb, the trail levels, passes a trail sign, and 10 yd. farther emerges in the clearing at the summit of Old Speck Mtn. Here are fine views northeast, and a full panorama may be obtained from the observation tower, which is ascended by a metal ladder. From the summit, Old Speck Trail leads 0.3 mi. northwest to Mahoosuc Trail.

Grafton Loop Trail (western section) (AMC map: C13–C15)

Distances from Grafton Loop Trail (eastern section) trailhead parking area on ME 26 (730 ft.) to:

- start of western section via ME 26 (730 ft.): 0.6 mi., 20 min.
- spur path to Bald Mtn. Tentsite (1,370 ft.): 2.2 mi., 1 hr. 25 min.
- highpoint on Bald Mtn. (2,070 ft.): 3.2 mi., 2 hr. 15 min.
- Stowe Mtn. summit (2,730 ft.): 4.5 mi., 3 hr. 25 min.
- Sargent Brook Tentsite spur (2,650 ft.): 6.0 mi., 4 hr. 15 min.
- Sunday River Whitecap summit (3,335 ft.): 7.1 mi., 5 hr. 10 min.
- Miles Notch (2,350 ft.): 8.3 mi., 5 hr. 45 min.
- Slide Mtn. Tentsite spur (2,550 ft.): 10.4 mi., 7 hr. 10 min.
- Bull Run Tentsite spur (2,700 ft.): 11.4 mi., 7 hr. 45 min.
- Old Speck Mtn. summit (4,170 ft.): 13.3 mi., 9 hr. 25 min.
- Grafton Notch (1,450 ft.) (via Mahoosuc Trail and AT): 17.1 mi., 11 hr. 45 min.

Mt. Will (1,736 ft.)

This mountain is located in Bethel on the border of Newry. The blue-green-blazed trails are maintained by the Bethel Conservation Commission. The North Ledge Trail section goes through Bethel Town Forest, but the rest of the trail is on private land. The marked trailhead is on the western side of US 2, 1.9 mi. north of the highway rest area, just opposite the Bethel transfer station. A parking area is on the west side (north) of the road.

Not far from the trailhead, the trail divides. The right fork goes up a nature trail to the North Ledges. This section of the trail provides good views of the valley and surrounding mountains from the relatively open ledges. From the North Ledges, the trail proceeds through a series of higher ledges on the way to the South Cliffs. The trail has numerous overlooks of the Androscoggin and Bear valleys north and east. At South Cliffs are fully open views south and east. From the cliffs, the trail drops steeply and then more easily back to the jct. and out to ME 2.

Mt. Will (USGS Bethel quad, DeLorme map 10)

Distances from ME 26 (700 ft.) to
- North Ledges (1,350 ft.) (via Nature Trail): 0.75 mi., 45 min.
- South Cliffs (1,450 ft.): 2.25 mi., 1 hr.
- complete loop: 3.25 mi., 2 hr. 30 min.

Rumford Whitecap (2,214 ft.)

The 751-acre Rumford Whitecap Preserve in Rumford, managed by MLT, is a conservation property that includes the bald summit ridge and south slopes of Rumford Whitecap Mtn., which offers panoramic views and plenty of blueberries in season. Two maintained trails ascend the mountain from the southwest.

From the jct. of US 2 and ME 5, 0.5 mi. west of Rumford Point, go north on ME 5 toward Andover. At 2.8 mi., turn right (east) and cross the Ellis River. At 3.2 mi., turn left onto East Andover Rd. and, in another 0.2 mi., reach the trailhead parking area on the left. Orange/Red Trail begins at a red gate directly across the road. Starr Trail begins about 100 yd. north on East Andover Rd. at a gray gate.

Orange/Red Trail (MLT)

From the gate (orange/red markers), follow the woods road and soon reach a register box on the right. Pass through a log yard and bear left. Climb gradually to reach a trail jct. on the left at 0.3 mi. This trail (green markers) leads northwest about 0.1 mi. to cross a stream on a bridge before joining Starr Trail.

Beyond the jct., the woods road climbs moderately. Ahead, the road narrows in a level area and bears left (sign: "to foot trail"). Climb steeply on switchbacks and rock steps, contour to the east for a short distance, then resume climbing. Cross a semi-open area, then cross a wide track (the old trail route to the summit, more direct but steep and eroded). Ahead, follow cairns over ledges to finally merge with the old trail route. Turn right on the wide, eroded trail and climb easily to a jct. with Starr Trail (yellow markers) on the left at 1.8 mi. Continuing ahead on Orange/Red Trail, climb gradually up the ridgeline in semi-open terrain to reach the ledges of open summit at 2.5 mi.

Orange/Red Trail (USGS East Andover quad, DeLorme map 18)

Distances from red gate on East Andover Rd. (850 ft.) to
- Starr Trail jct. (1,900 ft.): 1.8 mi., 1 hr. 25 min.
- Rumford Whitecap Mtn. summit (2,214 ft.): 2.5 mi., 1 hr. 45 min.

Starr Trail (MLT)

Pass beyond the gray gate and follow the logging road to a clearing (sign) and then a register box on the right. At 0.3 mi., a short connector trail on the right (green markers) crosses a bridge over a stream to join Orange/Red Trail in about 0.1 mi.

Continue straight ahead on the logging road and proceed up a long hill. At a small rock wall and yellow flagging tape, Starr Trail turns left and climbs moderately on a cleared skidder trail, levels off, then turns sharply right. Beyond, the trail turns left (cairn) to follow the logging road again, up another long hill. At 1.2 mi., the trail takes a sharp right off the road onto a footpath. Follow this to a large ledge with views. Ahead, follow cairns and blazes through woods and over ledges to a jct. with Orange/Red Trail at 1.8 mi. The summit of Rumford Whitecap is 0.7 mi. left (northeast) via this trail.

Starr Trail (USGS East Andover quad, DeLorme map 18)
Distances from gray gate on East Andover Rd. (850 ft.) to
 • Orange/Red Trail jct. (1,900 ft.): 1.8 mi., 1 hr. 25 min.
 • Rumford Whitecap Mtn. summit (2,214 ft.): 2.5 mi., 1 hr. 45 min.

Old Blue Mtn. (3,600 ft.)

This mountain in Township D rises steeply above Black Brook, south of Elephant Mtn. and west of Lower Richardson Lake. Access is gained from the south or north via the AT. To reach the AT from ME 5 in Andover, go 0.6 mi. east on ME 120 to South Arm Rd. Turn left onto South Arm Rd., and drive north for 7.7 mi. to the AT crossing at Black Brook Notch. Limited parking is available on the right side of the road.

Leaving South Arm Rd., the AT climbs steeply up the north wall of Black Brook Notch, gaining 900 ft. in 0.6 mi. At the top of the climb are good views south to Black Brook Notch and the peaks beyond. Ahead, the trail climbs gradually to the base of the upper south slope of Old Blue Mtn., reaching it at 2.3 mi. Beyond, the trail makes the final ascent to the summit at 2.8 mi., where there are outstanding views in every direction.

From the summit, the AT descends north into the high valley between Old Blue Mtn. and Elephant Mtn. At 4.3 mi., the AT reaches a col and an impressive stand of old-growth spruce. Bemis Stream Trail enters from the right at 6.0 mi. It is 6.1 mi. to ME 17 via this trail. Ahead on the AT, it is 7.3 mi. to ME 17.

Old Blue Mtn. (USGS East Andover quad, MATC map 7, DeLorme map 18)
Distances from South Arm Rd. (1,450 ft.) to
 • top of Black Brook Notch (2,350 ft.): 0.6 mi., 45 min.
 • Old Blue Mtn. summit (3,600 ft.): 2.8 mi., 2 hr. 25 min.

Bemis Mtn. (3,592 ft.)

Bemis Mtn. in Township D rises south of Mooselookmeguntic Lake and its long ridge crest extends in a northeast-southwest direction. The AT traverses the range, and outstanding views can be had from the five peaks en route, including East and West peaks, and First, Second, and Third peaks.

West Peak is the highest. Bemis Stream Trail is an alternate route for ascent or descent and, combined with the AT, makes a loop hike over the range possible.

Bemis Mtn. via Appalachian Trail

Access to the AT is a from spot known as Height of the Land on ME 17, 11.0 mi. south of Oquossoc and 26.0 mi. north of Rumford. Parking is available 0.5 mi. south on ME 17, opposite the trailhead for Bemis Stream Trail (see p. 135). (*Note:* In 2011, the widening of ME 17 in this area was under construction and its impact on the AT crossing at the Height of Land was uncertain.)

The trail descends 0.8 mi. to Bemis Stream. Ford the stream at a point where the stream divides around an island (may be difficult to cross in high water). At 1.0 mi., cross the gravel Bemis Rd., a former railroad grade. Just ahead, pass a small spring, the last water source southbound for 3.5 mi. Ahead, climb steeply through woods to emerge on open ledges at 1.5 mi., then cross a series of rocky knobs, the first at 1.7 mi. Beyond, the trail follows the ridge crest marked by cairns and white blazes to reach First Peak at 2.2 mi. and then Second Peak at 3.1 mi.

Bemis Mtn. Lean-to is reached at 4.6 mi., and then Third Peak at 5.0 mi. Cross East Peak of Bemis Mtn. at 6.2 mi., and West Peak at 6.3 mi. Arrive at the jct. with Bemis Stream Trail at 7.3 mi. Ahead on the AT, it is 3.2 mi. to the summit of Old Blue Mtn. and 6.0 mi. to South Arm Rd. Via Bemis Stream Trail, it is 6.3 mi. back to ME 17.

Bemis Mtn. (USGS Houghton and Metallak Mtn. quads, MATC map 7, DeLorme map 18)

Distances from ME 17 (2,200 ft.) via AT to
- Bemis Mtn., First Peak (2,604 ft.): 2.2 mi., 1 hr. 20 min.
- Bemis Mtn., Second Peak (2,915 ft.): 3.1 mi., 2 hr.
- Bemis Mtn. Lean-to (2,800 ft.): 4.6 mi., 2 hr. 45 min.
- Bemis Mtn., Third Peak (3,115 ft.): 5.0 mi., 3 hr. 10 min.
- Bemis Mtn., West Peak (3,592 ft.): 6.3 mi., 4 hr. 10 min.
- Bemis Stream Trail jct. (3,300 ft.): 7.3 mi., 4 hr. 45 min.
- complete loop (via AT, Bemis Stream Trail, and ME 17): 13.6 mi., 8 hr.

Bemis Mtn. via Bemis Stream Trail

This trail, the former route of the AT, provides an alternate route to the peaks of the Bemis Range, and using the AT, makes a loop hike possible. Bemis Stream Trail starts from ME 17 at a point 0.5 mi. south of the AT crossing, 11.5 mi. south of Oquossoc, and 25.5 mi. north of Rumford. The trailhead parking lot is located directly across the road from the start of the trail.

Following blue blazes, cross three small side streams at 0.1 mi., then descend gradually on a wide trail. At 0.8 mi., the forest opens up, affording views of Bemis Mtn. to the west and Brimstone Mtn. to the east. Descend steeply, and at 1.0 mi., cross the gravel Bemis Rd., a former railroad grade. Cross the road and follow a wide trail past a pool in Bemis Stream at 1.3 mi., then climb to finally cross Bemis Stream (may be difficult in high water) at 2.2 mi. Continue to climb, with the stream on the left, and cross several side streams. At 4.2 mi., reach a gravel logging road. Turn left to cross a bridge, then reenter the woods on the right immediately after. Follow Bemis Stream and cross it again at 5.2 mi. Ascend steadily through a mature spruce forest, and pass several glacial erratics. Reach the jct. with the AT at 6.3 mi. To the north, it is 1.0 mi. to the summit of West Peak of Bemis Mtn., 2.7 mi. to Bemis Mtn. Lean-to, and 7.3 mi. to ME 17 via the AT. To the south, it is 3.2 mi. to the summit of Old Blue Mtn. and 6.0 mi. to South Arm Rd.

Bemis Mtn. (USGS Houghton and Metallak Mtn. quads, MATC map 7, DeLorme map 18)

Distances from ME 17 (2,050 ft.) via Bemis Stream Trail to

- Bemis Rd. (1,700 ft.): 1.0 mi., 35 min.
- AT jct. (3,300 ft.): 6.3 mi., 4 hr.
- Bemis Mtn., West Peak (3,592 ft.): 7.3 mi., 4 hr. 40 min.

Tumbledown Public Reserved Land

This large swath of public land encompasses more than 10,000 acres in Township 6 North of Weld. Owned and managed by MBPL, the parcel includes Tumbledown Mtn., Little and Big Jackson mountains, and the top of Blueberry Mtn. MBPL holds conservation easements on an additional 12,000 acres in the vicinity. Nine trails provide miles of hiking opportunities in this scenic mountain region.

Tumbledown Mtn. (3,068 ft.)

Tumbledown Mtn. features an extensive alpine area on its high ridges and an impressive 700-ft. cliff on its south face, which has attracted rock climbers for years. Another natural feature of the mountain is Tumbledown Pond, a pretty tarn tucked into a bowl beneath the peaks of Tumbledown and Little Jackson mountains. The views from the open summit ridges are exceptional. Loop, Brook, Parker Ridge, and Pond Link trails reach the high terrain on Tumbledown.

Loop Trail (MBPL)

Ascent of this interesting trail requires rock scrambling at its upper end before reaching Tumbledown Ridge Trail high on the mountain, just west of the summit of Tumbledown.

To reach the Loop trailhead from the west, leave ME 17 in Byron at a point 22.0 mi. south of Oquossoc and 13.0 mi. north of Mexico. Travel east on Dingle Hill Rd. to cross over Coos Canyon and the Swift River. Stay on this road for 4.5 mi. to trailhead parking on the left, noting that the road changes names to Weld Rd., and then to Byron Rd. en route.

From the east, begin at the jct. of ME 156 and ME 142 in Weld village. Go north on ME 142 for 2.3 mi. Turn left onto West Side Rd. At 2.7 mi., where the paved West Side Rd. bears left, continue straight on the gravel-surfaced Byron Rd. Pass the Brook trailhead on the right at 6.4 mi. Reach the Loop trailhead at 7.7 mi.

The blue-blazed trail rises gradually to the north, crossing a brook twice, and at 1.0 mi. passes the huge Tumbledown Boulder. From here, the trail rises steeply to emerge in the open at Great Ledges, where there are splendid views of the impressive 700-ft. cliffs of Tumbledown Mtn. On the ledges, at a large cairn, Loop Trail turns right. Ahead, the trail crosses a brook and then climbs steeply up a gully. Near the top of the gully, a side trail leads right to a fissure cave known as Fat Man's Misery. Above this is an opening in the boulders with iron rungs to aid in the ascent. (This section makes the trail unsuitable for dogs.) At 0.6 mi. from the Great Ledges cairn, reach the saddle between the peaks of Tumbledown, and a spring (unreliable in dry weather). From this jct. at 1.9 mi., Tumbledown Ridge Trail leads west to the main summit of Tumbledown and east to Tumbledown Pond and the jct. with Brook Trail.

Loop Trail (AMC Tumbledown Mtn. map, USGS Roxbury quad, DeLorme map 19)

Distance from Byron Rd. (1,350 ft.) to
• saddle and Tumbledown Ridge Trail jct. (2,950 ft.): 1.9 mi., 1 hr. 45 min.

Brook Trail (MBPL)

This trail along Tumbledown Brook provides an easy and direct route to scenic Tumbledown Pond, where the trail connects with Tumbledown Ridge, Parker Ridge, and Pond Link trails.

To reach the Brook trailhead from the west, leave ME 17 in Byron at a point 22.0 mi. south of Oquossoc and 13.0 mi. north of Mexico. Travel east on Dingle Hill Rd. to cross over Coos Canyon and the Swift River. Stay on this road for 5.8 mi. to trailhead parking on the left, noting that the road changes names to Weld Rd. and then to Byron Rd. en route.

From the east, begin at the jct. of ME 156 and ME 142 in Weld village. Go north on ME 142 for 2.3 mi. Turn left on West Side Rd. At 2.7 mi., where the paved West Side Rd. bears left, continue straight on the gravel-surfaced Byron Rd. Reach the Brook Trailhead on the right at 6.4 mi., noting that Byron Rd. changes names to Weld Rd. en route.

The trail follows an old woods road for the first 1.0 mi. After crossing Tumbledown Brook, the trail turns right and parallels the brook as it climbs. Ahead, cross the brook a final time before arriving at a jct. with Parker Brook Trail, which enters from the right at 1.5 mi. Just ahead, Brook Trail reaches Tumbledown Pond and a jct. Here, Tumbledown Ridge Trail leads left 0.6 mi. to Loop Trail and 0.7 mi. to the west peak of Tumbledown Mtn.

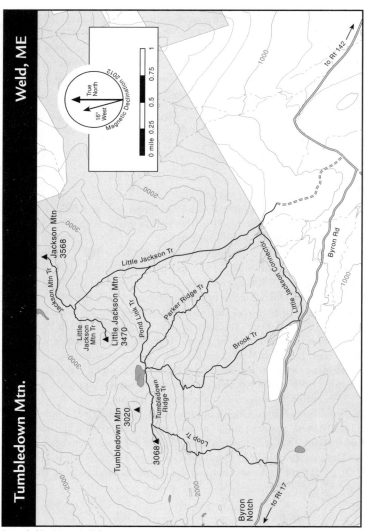

Weld, ME

Tumbledown Mtn.

© Appalachian Mountain Club

Brook Trail (AMC Tumbledown Mtn. map, USGS Roxbury quad, DeLorme map 19)

Distance from Byron Rd. (1,100 ft.) to
  • Tumbledown Pond (2,650 ft.): 1.5 mi., 1 hr. 30 min.

Tumbledown Ridge Trail (MBPL)

From the outlet of Tumbledown Pond and the jct. with Brook and Parker Ridge trails, Tumbledown Ridge Trail ascends west over mostly open ledges to the jct. with Loop Trail at 0.6 mi. Just beyond at 0.7 mi. is the west peak of Tumbledown Mtn. and great views of the Swift River valley and Old Blue and Elephant mountains to the west.

Tumbledown Ridge Trail (AMC Tumbledown Mtn. map, USGS Roxbury quad, DeLorme map 19)

Distances from Tumbledown Pond outlet (2,650 ft.) to
  • Loop Trail jct. (2,950 ft.): 0.6 mi., 30 min.
  • Tumbledown Mtn., west peak (3,068 ft.): 0.7 mi., 35 min.

Little Jackson Connector (MBPL)

From Brook trailhead, this trail heads easily east across the lower slopes of Tumbledown to its end at 1.1 mi. at a large clearing (former trailhead and parking area which is now permanently closed to vehicles and camping) and the jct. with Parker Ridge and Little Jackson trails.

Little Jackson Connector (AMC Tumbledown Mtn. map, USGS Roxbury quad, DeLorme map 19)

Distance from Brook trailhead on Byron Rd. (1,100 ft.) to
  • jct., Parker Ridge and Little Jackson trails (1,150 ft.): 1.1 mi., 35 min.

Parker Ridge Trail (MBPL)

Parker Ridge Trail is one of oldest trails up Tumbledown Mtn., and access is via the 1.1-mi. Little Jackson Connector from Brook trailhead. In a clearing, where Little Jackson Trail bears to the right, Parker Ridge Trail bears left (west) into the woods and crosses a brook. The trail then turns northwest to join an old woods road. For 1.0 mi., the trail rises gently through second-growth forest, then steeply for a short distance over three ledges. Beyond, the trail continues to climb steadily. It then crosses the open ledges of Parker Ridge with views of the peaks of Tumbledown ahead, then descends west, passing a jct. with Pond Link Trail on the right at 2.1 mi. Tumbledown Pond and the jct. with Brook and Tumbledown Ridge trails are just ahead at 2.2 mi.

Parker Ridge Trail (AMC Tumbledown Mtn. map, USGS Roxbury quad, DeLorme map 19)

Distances from Byron Rd. (1,100 ft.) to
- start of Parker Ridge Trail (1,150 ft.) (via Little Jackson Connector): 1.1 mi., 35 min.
- Tumbledown Pond (outlet) (2,650 ft.): 2.2 mi., 1 hr. 55 min.

Pond Link Trail (MBPL)

From Parker Ridge Trail at a point 0.1 mi. east of Tumbledown Pond, Pond Link Trail leaves to the left (north) and skirts the east end of the pond for about 100 yd. The trail then turns east to ascend to a height-of-land between Parker Ridge and Little Jackson Mtn. at 0.3 mi. from the pond. The trail continues generally east to a jct. with Little Jackson Trail at 0.9 mi.

Pond Link Trail (AMC Tumbledown Mtn. map, USGS Roxbury quad, DeLorme map 19)

Distances from Tumbledown Pond (2,650 ft.) to
- start of trail (via Parker Ridge Trail): 0.1 mi., 3 min.
- height-of-land (2,850 ft.): 0.3 mi., 15 min.
- Little Jackson Trail jct. (2,250 ft.): 0.9 mi., 40 min.

Little Jackson Mtn. (3,470 ft.)

This mountain features an extensive alpine area and fine views east to Jackson Mtn. and Mt. Blue, west overlooking Tumbledown Pond and the peaks of Tumbledown Mtn., and southeast to Webb Lake.

Little Jackson Trail (MBPL)

Gain access to Little Jackson Trail via the 1.1-mi. Little Jackson Connector from Brook trailhead. In a clearing, where Parker Ridge Trail bears left (west), Little Jackson Trail bears right. You'll soon cross a stream, and just beyond, the trail takes a sharp right (sign) onto an old woods road, which climbs steadily at a moderate grade. Ahead, the road becomes steeper and more eroded before reaching the jct. with Pond Link Trail on the left at 2.6 mi., which leads 1.0 mi. to Tumbledown Pond via Parker Ridge Trail.

Little Jackson Trail continues to climb, getting progressively steeper with a rough footway. Soon after crossing a brook, the trail reaches the open ledges of the col between Jackson and Little Jackson mountains at 3.4 mi. and the jct. with Jackson Mtn. Trail, which leads right (north) 0.7 mi. to the summit of Jackson Mtn.

Just ahead, Little Jackson Trail turns left and ascends over ledges with many fine outlooks to the summit of Little Jackson Mtn. at 4.4 mi.

Little Jackson Trail (AMC Tumbledown Mtn. map, USGS Roxbury quad, DeLorme map 19)

Distances from Byron Rd. (1,100 ft.) to

- start of trail (1,150 ft.) via Little Jackson Connector: 1.1 mi., 35 min.
- Pond Link Trail jct. (2,250 ft.): 2.6 mi., 1 hr. 55 min.
- Little Jackson Mtn. summit (3,470 ft.): 4.4 mi., 3 hr.

Jackson Mtn. (3,568 ft.)

Jackson is a rambling, heavily forested mountain with a 100-sq.-ft. clear-cut, a helicopter landing pad, and a radio structure on its top. Limited views can be had to the west from the summit, but excellent views looking south, east, and west are available from open ledges about halfway up. The trail is narrow, and caution should be exercised in following it.

Jackson Mtn. Trail diverges right (north) from Little Jackson Trail in the col between Little Jackson and Big Jackson mountains, about 120 ft. west of the first open ledges on Little Jackson Trail. From the jct., continue over open ledges for about 300 ft., where the trail turns sharply left (west) and descends gradually into the woods on a snowmobile trail. In another 180 ft., the trail turns right (north), leaving the snowmobile trail, and begins to climb toward Jackson Mtn. The trail is well defined and marked by a few cairns, but there are no blazes. Reach an open ledge with views southeast to Little Jackson. Beyond, the path is less defined and there are numerous small blowdowns. Reach the mostly wooded summit of Jackson Mtn. at 0.7 mi.

Jackson Mtn. (AMC Tumbledown Mtn. map, USGS Jackson Mtn. quad, Delorme map 19)
Distance from Little Jackson Trail jct. (3,050 ft.) to
  • Jackson Mtn. summit (3,568 ft.): 0.7 mi., 40 min.

Blueberry Mtn. (2,962 ft.)

This mountain is located east of Jackson, Little Jackson, and Tumbledown mountains and north of Webb Lake. To reach the trail, drive north on ME 142 from its jct. with ME 156 in Weld village. Pass West Side Rd. on the left at Weld Corner at 2.2 mi. At 3.5 mi., turn left onto a gravel road at a sign for Blueberry Mtn. Bible Camp and Conference Center. Pass a gate at 0.3 mi. along the gravel road, and reach the main building and parking at 1.5 mi. from ME 142.

Blueberry Mtn. Trail (MBPL)

Follow the road beyond the parking area and buildings to the east to an athletic field. Cross to the far end of the field, and at 0.5 mi., continue into the woods on an old road. The blue-blazed trail follows the old woods road, which rises steeply and crosses a recently logged area. Beyond, the trail forks right from the road and climbs steeply. After a series of ledges, the grade moderates and the trail passes through a section of large boulders. The bare summit is reached at 2.0 mi., where there are interesting geological formations and excellent views in all directions.

Blueberry Mtn. (USGS Madrid quad, DeLorme map 19)
Distance from parking at bible camp (1,350 ft.) to
  • Blueberry Mtn. summit (2,962 ft.): 2.0 mi., 1 hr. 45 min.

Mt. Blue State Park

Located in Weld, Mt. Blue State Park is Maine's largest state park at about 8,000 acres in size. The bulk of the park lies east of Webb Lake and includes the iconic peak of Mt. Blue and a nature trail on Center Hill. A campground, beach, and nature center are found on the southwest shore of Webb Lake.

Mt. Blue (3,190 ft.)

Rising steeply east of Webb Lake in Weld, Mt. Blue is known for its conical profile which, when viewed from surrounding summits, is unmistakable. The former fire tower on the summit has been replaced with an observation tower and offers outstanding panoramic views.

Mt. Blue Trail (MBPL)

To reach the trail from the jct. of ME 156 and ME 142 in Weld village, drive east on Center Hill Rd. At 3.0 mi., where Center Hill Rd. bears left, continue straight ahead on Mt. Blue Rd. Follow this for another 3.5 mi. to the trailhead parking area (sign and kiosk).

The well-worn path ascends steadily up the fall line of the mountain at moderate-to-steep grades, passing through thick woods en route. Reach an outlook just below the summit and then quickly top out at the new (2011) observation tower set in a small grassy field. A number of scenic outlooks ring the summit, offering views of Saddleback Mtn. and The Horn; Mt. Abraham and Spaulding and Sugarloaf mountains; the sprawling mass of the Presidential Range; the Carters and Mahoosucs; and nearby Bald Mtn.

Mt. Blue Trail (USGS Weld quad, DeLorme map 19)
Distance from Mt. Blue Rd. (1,350 ft.) to
 • Mt. Blue summit (3,190 ft.): 1.7 mi., 1 hr. 45 min.

Center Hill Nature Trail (MBPL)

This interesting and scenic self-guiding nature trail loop leads around Center Hill at a consistent contour, passing eleven interpretive stations that describe the natural history and ecology of the area. Outstanding views of the peaks of Tumbledown and the Jacksons are possible from ledges along the trail.

Center Hill Nature Trail (USGS Weld quad, DeLorme map 19)
Distance from Center Hill picnic area (1,550 ft.) to
  • complete loop: 0.5 mi., 20 min.

Bald Mtn. (Weld) (2,370 ft.)

The trail up Bald Mtn. leaves the west side of ME 156 about 9 mi. northwest of the jct. of ME 4 and ME 156 in Wilton and about 5.5 mi. southeast of the jct. of ME 142 and ME 156 in Weld. Parking is on the broad shoulder on the south side of the road.

Immediately cross Wilson Stream on stepping-stones (last sure water) and enter the woods. The well-defined, but unmarked trail climbs steeply through the young woods of a recent logging operation. Ahead, the trail reaches open ledges at 0.9 mi. (Use caution, as the ledges can be slippery when wet.) From this point to the summit, the trail is marked by blue blazes and cairns. At the peak at 1.5 mi., there are fine views in all directions.

Bald Mtn. (Weld) (USGS Mt. Blue quad, DeLorme map 19)
Distance from ME 156 (1,050 ft.) to
  • Bald Mtn. summit (2,370 ft.): 1.5 mi., 1 hr. 25 min.

Sugarloaf (1,521 ft.)

Sugarloaf in Dixfield is conspicuous because of its two prominent summits. The mountain offers fine vistas from its open northern summit. En route to Sugarloaf, a side trail leads to Bull Rock and good views of the Dixfield area.

From the jct. of US 2 and ME 142 in Dixfield, drive north on ME 142 for 1.2 mi. Turn right (east) on Holt Hill Rd. and continue 0.5 mi. to Moxie Heights Rd. Turn left, then immediately right onto Red Ledge Rd. Go 0.1 mi. and park along the side of the road where it narrows and a private driveway goes left. (*Note:* The road ahead is rough and may not be passable by passenger cars.)

Walk uphill on Red Ledge Rd., which soon turns left at a sharp, steep curve. At 0.2 mi., where the road bears right (white house visible on left), the trail to Sugarloaf Mtn., an old woods road/snowmobile trail, continues straight ahead. At about 0.4 mi., an ATV track leaves left. This is the side trail to the ledges of Bull Rock, which is reached in about 0.4 mi. and offers nice views.

Continuing ahead to on the trail to Sugarloaf, cross a large log yard at 0.5 mi.. At 0.8 mi., leave the old road and bear sharply right uphill on a footpath (maroon blazes). Climb steadily up the steep slope to a col at 1.0 mi. (*Note:* The trail may be hard to follow through this area because of recent logging.) Proceed straight across the col to a large rock with a maroon blaze on the left. Climb steeply from this point to the summit ledges of Sugarloaf at 1.1 mi.

Sugarloaf (USGS Dixfield quad, DeLorme map 19)

Distances from parking on Red Ledge Rd. (850 ft.) to
- side trail to Bull Rock (950 ft.): 0.4 mi., 15 min.
- Sugarloaf summit (1,521 ft.): 1.1 mi., 55 min.

Aziscohos Mtn. (3,215 ft.)

This mountain in Lincoln Plantation is located just south of Aziscohos Lake and offers excellent views of the Rangeley Lakes region. Fifteen lakes are visible from the summit. The abandoned fire tower on the summit was removed in 2004.

The trail begins on ME 16, 1 mi. east of the bridge over Magalloway River at Aziscohos Dam. About 100 ft. east of a gravel logging road, the trailhead is marked with a sign that may be obscured by heavy growth. The trail leads gradually uphill on an old tote road through open hardwood and mixed forest. The trail then turns sharply left at 0.5 mi. At 1.0 mi., the trail enters conifers, and it crosses a brook at 1.1 mi. Beyond, the trail continues more steeply, becoming rough as it leads over boulders and exposed roots. The trail reaches the abandoned Tower Man's Trail coming in from the northwest at 2.0 mi. Ahead, it is 0.1 mi. over ledges to the open summit.

Aziscohos Mtn. (USGS Richardson Pond and Wilsons Mills quads, DeLorme maps 27, 28)

Distance from ME 16 (1,550 ft.) to
- Aziscohos Mtn. summit (3,215 ft.): 2.1 mi., 1 hr. 55 min.

Bald Mtn. (Oquossoc) (2,443 ft.)

This small mountain in Oquossoc, a village of Rangeley, occupies a scenic location between Mooselookmeguntic and Rangeley lakes and is part of the Maine PRL system managed by MBPL. Views from its summit observation tower range from the surrounding lakes to Saddleback and Elephant mountains to Mt. Washington and the Presidential Range.

To reach the trail from the jct. of ME 4 and ME 17 in Oquossoc, drive west on ME 4 for about 1 mi. to the terminus of ME 4 at Haines Landing. Turn left (south) onto Bald Mtn. Rd. before the landing and follow the road for 0.9 mi. to the parking area and trail on the left.

The trail climbs gradually through the forest on a wide, well-worn path that is marked with blue blazes. Ahead, the trail ascends steeply for a short distance over a rough trail of rocks and roots. It soon levels off, and after some minor boulder scrambling, the summit tower and a picnic table are reached at 1.0 mi.

A slightly longer alternative route on Bald Mtn. leaves from the boater's parking lot on ME 4, just east of Haine's Landing. The trail leaves the rear of the lot and crosses the gentle northwest slopes of the mountain, merging with the main trail in 1.0 mi., at a point 0.2 mi. east of the Bald Mtn. Rd. trailhead. Turn left (east) to reach the summit of Bald Mtn. in another 1.0 mi.

Bald Mtn. (USGS Oquossoc quad, DeLorme map 28)

Distance from Bald Mtn. Rd. (1,500 ft.) to
- Bald Mtn. summit (2,443 ft.): 1.0 mi., 1 hr.

Distances from boater's parking lot on ME 4 (1,450 ft.) to
- jct. main trail (1,600 ft.): 1.0 mi., 30 min.
- Bald Mtn. summit (2,443 ft.): 2.0 mi. 1 hr. 30 min.

West Kennebago Mtn. (3,705 ft.)

This isolated mountain in Upper Cupsuptic Township, north of the Rangeley lakes and west of Kennebago Lake, is the highest of the several summits of the north–south ridge that forms the mountain.

To reach the start of the trail, turn right (north) from ME 16 onto Morton Cutoff Rd., 4.8 mi. west of the ME 4 and ME 16 jct. in Oquossoc and 0.3 mi. west of the MFS buildings at Cupsuptic Lake. Drive 3.2 mi. from ME 16 to a jct. with Lincoln Pond Rd. Turn right (east), and in 5.5 mi., the road reaches a parking area on the left. The trail begins at the right end of the parking area.

The red-blazed trail starts as a woods road. It soon narrows to a footpath and climbs rather steeply. At 0.9 mi., it levels out among conifers and bears left. Then it begins to climb again, crosses a small stream, and turns sharply right. Beyond, the trail becomes heavily eroded. At 1.4 mi., it reaches the site of the old fire warden's camp. A spring is 100 yd. to the left of the site of the camp.

The trail leaves the site of the old camp from the upper right (northwest) corner of the clearing. At 1.7 mi., the trail reaches the ridge, where the trail turns left (south) and follows the ridge to the fire tower (not accessible).

West Kennebago Mtn. (USGS Kennebago quad, DeLorme map 28)

Distances from Lincoln Pond Rd. (1,950 ft.) to
- site of old fire warden's camp (3,186 ft.): 1.4 mi., 1 hr. 20 min.
- West Kennebago Mtn. summit (3,705 ft.): 2.1 mi., 1 hr. 55 min.

Snow Mtn. (3,948 ft.)

Snow Mtn. is located in Alder Stream Township in the remote terrain northwest of Flagstaff Lake. An abandoned fire tower (no cab) is on the wooded summit, and views can be had by climbing the ladder. The mountain and the land around it are owned by the Penobscot Indian Nation. Day use is permitted, but overnight camping is not allowed without advance permission.

From its jct. with ME 16 in Stratton, drive north on ME 27 for 13.7 mi. Turn left (west) onto North Rd., and at 2.2 mi. from ME 27, pass a gravel road on the left. Pass Bag Mtn. Rd. on the right at 2.7 mi., and Sports Carry Rd. on the left at 3.1 mi. At a fork at 3.8 mi., bear right and drive to the parking area at the end of the road at 4.9 mi.

Follow the two-wheel track—the trail—into the woods. Cross a bridge at 0.1 mi. and ascend gradually. At 1.1 mi., cross a second bridge. Cross a third bridge at 1.5 mi., and at 1.7 mi., reach a fork. A small sign to the right reads "Snow Mtn. Trail." This is the former trail route and is very hard to follow.

Ignore the right at the fork and proceed straight ahead for 200 ft. to the jct. of another two-wheel track. Proceed straight ahead up a rocky gully. Soon, cross a skidder trail (blue flagging) and continue ahead to reach Snow Mtn. Pond on the left at 2.1 mi. Follow the muddy track along the north shore of the pond. At 2.3 mi., with the far end of the pond still in sight through the trees, look for a small wooden sign on a tree with an arrow pointing to the right. Immediately beyond it is a very obscure trail. Turn right here and follow this old fire warden's trail.

A short distance above the jct., the footway becomes more defined. Climb moderately then more steeply to reach a spring at 2.8 mi. Just above, turn sharply left and scramble up and over the rock face of an overhanging boulder. Continue to climb steeply to reach the old fire tower and abandoned warden's cabin on the summit at 3.3 mi.

Snow Mtn. (USGS Chain of Ponds and Jim Pond quads, DeLorme map 28)

Distances from parking area (1,800 ft.) to
- Snow Mtn. Pond (2,800 ft.): 2.1 mi., 1 hr. 35 min.
- Snow Mtn. summit (3,948 ft.): 3.3 mi., 2 hr. 45 min.

Kibby Mtn. (3,638 ft.)

This remote mountain in Skinner Township lies in the heart of the vast forestlands north of Flagstaff Lake, and east of the Canadian border and Chain of Ponds. From the platform on the old fire tower on the summit, superb views may be had of the jumble of mountain peaks in this region, as well as the turbines of the Kibby Wind Power Project (New England's largest wind farm) just to the south.

From its jct. with ME 16 in Stratton, drive north on ME 27 for 16.8 mi. and turn right onto Gold Brook Rd. (sign for Kibby Wind Power Project). Pass the Series B access road on the right at 3.6 mi., Wahl Rd. on the right at 6.0 mi., and Spencer Ball Rd. (Series A access road) on the right at 7.6 mi. Continue straight at a fork at 8.9 mi. Pass mile marker 9 (Beaudry Rd.) on the right and reach the crest of a hill at 9.4 mi. Turn right on a wide gravel road, then right again on a narrower road with a wind turbine visible ahead. Park in the large clearing on the left. A two-wheel track—the trail—heads into the woods beyond the clearing.

Ascend gradually on the woods track. At 0.9 mi., bear right off the main track (flagging and a small cairn). Ahead, the old road narrows to a grassy trail occasionally marked by pink flagging. In a clearing, bear right and continue on the well-defined path. In the final 0.5 mi., the trail climbs at a moderate-to-steep grade before leveling off to reach the old fire tower (platform, no cab) at 2.3 mi.

Kibby Mtn. (USGS Kibby Mtn. quad, DeLorme maps 28, 38, 39)
Distance from parking area (2,550 ft.) to
• Kibby Mtn. summit (3,638 ft.): 2.3 mi., 1 hr. 30 min.

Saddleback Mtn. (4,120 ft.) and The Horn (4,041 ft.)

Saddleback Mtn. sprawls across Sandy River Plantation and Madrid and Redington townships southeast of Rangeley. Its long ridge crest extends in a northeast-southwest direction for more than 3 mi., with pronounced saddles separating its high peaks. Two of the summits exceed 4,000 ft.: Saddleback and The Horn. The Saddleback Mtn. ski area is located on the northwestern slope of the mountain. The bare alpine summits of both offer extensive views in all directions. Saddleback, with its widespread areas above treeline, is also unusually exposed. Hikers should proceed with caution during periods of high winds and low visibility.

Saddleback via Appalachian Trail from the south (MATC)

To approach Saddleback Mtn. from the south, follow ME 4 for 32.0 mi. north from the jct. of ME 4 and US 2 in Farmington. From the jct. of ME

4 and ME 16 in Rangeley, it is 9.9 mi. south on ME 4 to the trailhead. The AT crosses ME 4 at a steep, winding section of the road. A large trailhead parking lot is off the west side of the highway.

From ME 4, the AT descends and crosses the Sandy River via a bridge at 0.1 mi. The trail climbs out of the valley, crossing a gravel logging road at 1.1 mi. At 1.8 mi., the trail passes Piazza Rock Lean-to. A side trail leads left 200 yd. to the top of Piazza Rock, a large granite slab protruding from the cliff. Just ahead along the trail are the Caves, a series of boulder caves with narrow passages.

The AT then climbs steeply, skirting the west shore of Ethel Pond. Turning sharply left at the end of the pond, the trail climbs to pass Mud Pond, then descends slightly to reach Eddy Pond (last reliable water). Watch for a point near the east shore of Eddy Pond about 3.7 mi. from ME 4 where the trail, after turning left onto a gravel road for a few feet, turns sharply right from the road onto a trail. Beyond, the trail rises steeply through conifers, emerging on a scrub-covered slope.

The exposed open crest of Saddleback, which extends for the next 3.0 mi., is a particularly scenic hike on a good day, but can be difficult in bad weather. Use care to follow the rock cairns and blazes marking the route. After a long stretch over rocky slopes and heath, the trail descends slightly into a sag, then climbs ahead to reach the summit at 5.7 mi.

The AT continues ahead over the open alpine slopes, descending steeply into the col between Saddleback and The Horn, before climbing to reach the summit of The Horn 1.6 mi. from the main summit and 7.3 mi. from ME 4. For the continuation of the AT beyond The Horn, refer to the *Appalachian Trail Guide to Maine* (MATC).

Saddleback via Appalachian Trail from the south (USGS Saddleback Mtn. and Redington quads, MATC map 6, DeLorme maps 19, 29)

Distances from ME 4 (1,600 ft.) to
- jct. with logging road: 1.1 mi., 35 min.
- Piazza Rock Lean-to: 1.8 mi., 1 hr.
- Saddleback Mtn. summit (4,120 ft.): 5.7 mi., 3 hr. 30 min.
- The Horn summit (4,041 ft.): 7.3 mi., 4 hr. 15 min.

Mt. Abraham (4,049 ft.)

Mt. Abraham (or "Abram") in Mt. Abram Township lies to the south of Sugarloaf and Spaulding mountains in the Mt. Abraham PRL unit. Mt. Abraham has an impressive ridgeline that extends for about 4.5 mi. in a northwest-southeast direction and consists of about eight peaks ranging from 3,400 to more than 4,000 ft. The highest peak lies north of the middle of the ridge. The extensive areas above timberline on Mt. Abraham gives it an impressive alpine appearance for its height.

Two trails ascend to the summit: Fire Warden's Trail approaches the mountain from the Kingfield side in the southeast, and Mt. Abraham Trail approaches from the northwest via the AT over Spaulding Mtn.

Fire Warden's Trail (MBPL)

From the jct. of ME 27 and ME 16 in Kingfield, drive north on ME 27 for 0.5 mi., crossing a bridge over the Carrabassett River en route. Turn left (west) onto West Kingfield Rd. At 3.3 mi. from ME 27, the road becomes gravel. At a crossroads at 3.5 mi., proceed straight ahead on what is now called Rapid Stream Rd. At 6.0 mi., reach a major fork. Take the left fork, and in about 100 yd., cross the first of two bridges over Rapid Stream. Cross the second bridge; the road forks again immediately after the bridge. Follow the right fork for 0.5 mi. to a T intersection. The trail starts here (sign). Parking is on the side of the road to the left or right. (*Note:* The bridges over Rapid Stream may not be passable by smaller vehicles because of the wide width of the bridge's wooden beams. If in doubt, park in a grassy pullout on the right before the bridges and walk to the trailhead, about 0.5 mi.)

The trail passes through deciduous forest to cross a logging road in about 1 mi. Beyond, the trail eventually reaches the site of the former fire warden's cabin (removed in 2011). A good spring can be found to the right of the old cabin site. At this point, the trail turns left. A short distance above the old cabin site, a side trail leads left to a brook (last reliable water). Then the trail climbs steadily and steeply for about 1 mi. to emerge into the open at treeline. Beyond this point, the trail is exposed for the last 0.5 mi., and care should be taken in the event of bad weather. The trail, marked by cairns, rises steadily up and across a huge talus field—at 350 acres this is the second-largest alpine zone in Maine—to the summit and the site of the former fire tower. Here, Mt. Abraham Trail leads 1.7 mi. to connect with the AT about 1 mi. south of Spaulding Mtn. Lean-to. (*Note:* MBPL has plans to establish a new campsite and privy somewhere in the area of the old fire warden's cabin site in the near future.)

Fire Warden's Trail (USGS Mt. Abraham quad, MATC map 6, DeLorme map 29)
Distances from trailhead (1,150 ft.) to
- former fire warden's cabin site (2,127 ft.): 3.0 mi., 2 hr.
- Mt. Abraham summit (4,049 ft.): 4.5 mi., 3 hr. 45 min.

Mt. Abraham Trail (MATC)

This trail leaves from the AT at a point 6.3 mi. south of Caribou Valley Rd. Refer to the descriptions for Sugarloaf and Spaulding mountains to reach the start of the trail (see pp. 154 and 155).

Mt. Abraham Trail leads 1.7 mi. southeast following a very old tote road, climbing gradually then steeply up the densely forested northern ridge of Mt. Abraham. The trail emerges from the trees and ascends a talus field to the alpine summit and site of the former fire tower. Extensive views are possible in all directions.

Mt. Abraham Trail (USGS Mt. Abraham quad, MATC map 6, DeLorme map 29)
Distances from Caribou Valley Rd. (2,250 ft.) to
- Spaulding Mtn. side trail (3,900 ft.): 4.4 mi., 3 hr.
- Spaulding Mtn. Lean-to: 5.2 mi., 3 hr. 30 min.
- Mt. Abraham Trail (3,350 ft.): 6.3 mi., 4 hr. 5 min.
- Mt. Abraham summit (4,049 ft.): 8.0 mi., 5 hr. 15 min.

Crocker Mtn., North Peak (4,228 ft.) and South Peak (4,050 ft.)

The peaks of Crocker Mtn. are located just west of Sugarloaf Mtn. and are separated from it by Caribou Valley and the South Branch of the Carrabassett River. North Peak of Crocker Mtn., despite its height, is heavily wooded to the top and has few views. South Peak of Crocker Mtn., in comparison, has a distinct summit cone with fine views. Hikers can approach the mountain via the AT from ME 27 or from Caribou Valley Rd.

Crocker Mtn. via Appalachian Trail from ME 27 (MATC)

From the jct. of ME 27 and the access road to the Sugarloaf ski area in Carrabassett Valley, travel north on ME 27 for 2.6 mi. to the AT crossing, where there is a trailhead parking lot on the left.

Follow the AT southbound, climbing steadily through woods for 1.4 mi. to reach a knoll on the north ridge of Crocker Mtn. Beyond, pass through a long section of coniferous forest. Ahead, the trail angles up the western side of the ridge through hardwood forest. The trail continues up the ridge, reenters softwoods at about 3.5 mi., and crosses a small stream at 4.2 mi. (usually reliable; last water). Then the trail rises more steeply to the crest and reaches North Peak of Crocker Mtn. at 5.2 mi. The descent into the col begins immediately. The trail leads to the low point of the col and soon begins to climb toward the rocky South Peak of Crocker. The true summit is reached via a 50-yd. side trail (sign) to the right (west), where the AT makes a sharp left turn for the descent to Caribou Valley Rd.

Crocker Mtn. via Appalachian Trail from ME 27

Distances from ME 27 (1,450 ft.) via AT to
- Crocker Mtn., North Peak (4,228 ft.): 5.2 mi., 4 hr.
- Crocker Mtn., South Peak (4,050 ft.): 6.2 mi., 4 hr. 25 min.
- Caribou Valley Rd. (2,250 ft.): 8.3 mi., 5 hr. 30 min.

Crocker Mtn. via Appalachian Trail from Caribou Valley Rd. (MATC)

Caribou Valley Rd. leads south from ME 27 from a point 1.0 mi. northwest of the entrance to the Sugarloaf ski area. Follow the road to the AT crossing at 4.3 mi. from ME 27 (Caribou Valley Rd. is a rough road and a high-clearance vehicle is recommended.) Parking is available at the AT crossing. This trailhead is also used to reach Sugarloaf to the east.

The AT leaves the road to the right (west) and climbs steadily but not too steeply. At 1.0 mi., a side trail leads right 0.2 mi. to Crocker Cirque

Campsite. On the side trail to this campsite is the last reliable water. Beyond the turnoff to the campsite, the AT begins a steep climb to a high shoulder of the mountain, which the AT then follows toward the summit. Where the trail turns sharply right, a side trail (sign) on the left leads 50 yd. to South Peak of Crocker Mtn. Beyond, the AT descends into a col, and then climbs steadily to North Peak of Crocker Mtn.

Crocker Mtn. via Appalachian Trail from Caribou Valley Rd.
Distances from Caribou Valley Rd. (2,250 ft.) to
- side trail to Crocker Cirque Campsite (2,700 ft.): 1.0 mi., 35 min.
- Crocker Mtn., South Peak (4,050 ft.): 2.1 mi., 2 hr.
- Crocker Mtn., North Peak (4,228 ft.): 3.1 mi., 2 hr. 45 min.

Sugarloaf Mtn. (4,250 ft.)

Sugarloaf Mtn., the second-highest mountain in Maine, is best known and most frequented for the Sugarloaf ski area on its northern slopes. For the hiker, the view from the symmetrical, bare cone is well worth the climb. The number of peaks visible may be unequaled in the state, except perhaps from Katahdin. Spaulding Mtn. is about 2.1 mi. to the south of Sugarloaf Mtn. and is connected to it by a high ridge.

The approach to Sugarloaf is via the AT from the north, which leaves Caribou Valley Rd. at a point 4.3 mi. south of ME 27. (Caribou Valley Rd. is a rough road and a high-clearance vehicle is recommended.) Parking is available at the AT crossing. This trailhead is also used to reach the north and south peaks of Crocker Mtn. to the west and north.

Leaving the road to the east (left), the trail soon crosses the South Branch of the Carrabassett River (dangerous in high water). The trail follows the stream for a time, and then begins to climb, at first gently and then more steeply. Ahead, the trail crosses ledges and skirts the top of a cirque on the western side of Sugarloaf. The last water is a stream at 1.8 mi. At 2.3 mi., reach a jct. Here, the AT turns right toward Spaulding Mtn., and Sugarloaf Mtn. Trail leaves left, climbing steadily for 0.6 mi. to the summit of Sugarloaf.

Sugarloaf Mtn. (USGS Sugarloaf Mtn. quad, MATC map 6, DeLorme map 29)
Distances from Caribou Valley Rd. (2,250 ft.) via AT to
  • Sugarloaf Mtn. Trail jct. (3,550 ft.): 2.3 mi., 2 hr.
  • Sugarloaf Mtn. summit (4,250 ft.): 2.9 mi., 2 hr. 30 min.

Spaulding Mtn. (4,010 ft.)

Spaulding Mtn. rises above along the long ridge extending southwest between Sugarloaf and Lone mountains. The final mile of the AT was cut here in 1937.

From its jct. with Sugarloaf Mtn. Trail, at a point 2.3 mi. from Caribou Valley Rd., the AT continues southbound, traversing the crest of the ridge between Sugarloaf and Spaulding mountains, with views and steep cliffs on the left. At 3.8 mi., the trail begins the ascent of Spaulding, first steeply, then more gradually. At 4.4 mi., a side trail leads left 0.1 to the summit of Spaulding.

Continuing south on the AT, the trail descends to reach Spaulding Mtn. Lean-to (via a 150-ft. side trail) at 5.2 mi. Ahead, the jct. of Mt. Abraham Trail is reached at 6.3 mi. For a description of the AT south of this point, refer to the *Appalachian Trail Guide to Maine* (MATC).

Spaulding Mtn. (USGS Sugarloaf Mtn. quad, MATC map 6, DeLorme map 29)
Distances from Caribou Valley Rd. (2,250 ft.) via AT to
  • Sugarloaf Mtn. Trail jct. (3,550 ft.): 2.3 mi., 2 hr.
  • Spaulding side trail (3,900 ft.): 4.4 mi., 3 hr.
  • Spaulding Mtn. summit (4,010 ft.) via side trail: 4.5 mi., 3 hr. 5 min.
  • Spaulding Mtn. Lean-to: 5.2 mi., 3 hr. 30 min.
  • Mt. Abraham Trail jct. (3,350 ft.): 6.3 mi., 4 hr. 5 min.

Burnt Mtn. (3,600 ft.)

This little-visited peak, also known as Burnt Hill, lies just east of Sugarloaf and offers extensive views from its open alpine summit, including Sugarloaf and Spaulding mountains, the long ridge of Mt. Abraham, and the Bigelow Range. From the jct. of ME 16 and ME 27 in Kingfield, drive about 15 mi. north to Carrabassett Valley. Turn left onto the access road to the Sugarloaf ski area. Parking is available at several lots near the main base lodge and the Grand Summit Hotel. From behind the hotel, it is a short walk to the trailhead, following Adams Mtn. Rd., Mountainside Rd., and finally Bigelow Mtn. Rd. to its end, where there is a sign for "Burnt Mtn. Trail."

A wide ski trail (No. 21) leads into the woods a short distance to the trail, which starts on the right just after crossing the West Branch of Brackett Brook. Follow the blue-blazed trail along the brook, crossing it several times. The trail veers away from the brook and begins to climb steadily, reaching the col between Burnt Mtn. and Sugarloaf. The remainder of the hike is above treeline, marked by cairns and blue blazes. The summit is reached at 2.8 mi.

Note: In 2010, Sugarloaf expanded its ski trail system to the east into the basin of Brackett Brook. Burnt Mtn. Trail is now crossed by two 30-ft. swaths cleared for skiing. The first swath is located 0.8 mi. from the start; the second at 1.1 mi. Although the trail route remains intact, the removal of the trees in these cleared areas has affected the blazing. Sugarloaf has plans to continue expansion in this area and expects to minimize impact to the trail.

Burnt Mtn. (USGS Sugarloaf Mtn. quad, DeLorme map 29)
Distance from start of trail at Brackett Brook (1,750 ft.) to
  • Burnt Mtn. summit (3,600 ft.): 2.8 mi., 2 hr. 20 min.

Bigelow Preserve

The Bigelow Preserve was established by citizen referendum in 1976 and is managed by MBPL. The 36,000-acre preserve encompasses the entire Bigelow Range, which extends in a generally east–west direction for about 12 mi. just south of Flagstaff Lake. The central features are the high alpine summits of Avery and West peaks, the symmetrical twin peaks of North Horn and South Horn, and the bare ledges of Cranberry Peak. East of Avery Peak, separated by Safford Notch, is the long ridge of Little Bigelow Mtn. Trailhead access from the south is via ME 27 in Stratton and Wyman Township and from the east via East Flagstaff Rd. Backcountry camping is available at two campsites and three tentsites, and drive-in campsites are found at Round Barn on Flagstaff Lake.

Avery Peak (4,088 ft.), West Peak (4,145 ft.), South Horn (3,805 ft.), North Horn (3,792 ft.), and Cranberry Peak (3,194 ft.)

From Avery Peak, there is a spectacular outlook over the rugged wilderness of mountains and lakes, ponds, and streams ranging north to Katahdin and BSP, and south to Sugarloaf and the Crockers. Flagstaff Lake, an artificially constructed lake and Maine's fourth-largest body of water, lies just north of the Bigelow Range. Like the range, the lake stretches east–west. West of the Horns lies Horns Pond, a picturesque tarn. Cranberry Pond and Arnold's Well are farther west along the range.

Three trails approach the range from the south. Fire Warden's Trail is the most direct, albeit steep, approach to the main peaks of the Bigelow Range, but Horns Pond Trail provides quick access to Horns Pond, where the trail joins the AT to follow the ridge between the Horns, over South Horn and West Peak, and on to Avery Peak. A third approach is via the AT, which extends from ME 27 to the ridge west of Horns Pond. A fourth and longer approach is by way of Bigelow Range Trail, which leads east from Stratton to join the AT east of Cranberry Pond. This route involves considerable ridge travel up and down the many peaks of the range. The route extends the range's full length, from the western end to Avery Peak. From East Flagstaff Rd. at Flagstaff Lake, gain access to the high peaks via Safford Notch Trail and the AT.

Via Appalachian Trail from the south (MATC)

The AT leaves ME 27 2.6 mi. northwest of the Sugarloaf ski area access road. Trailhead parking is available on the left (south side of road).

The trail descends gradually and crosses Stratton Brook Rd. at 0.8 mi. Shortly after, cross Jones Pond Rd., and then descend to cross Stratton Brook on a footbridge. Beyond, the trail joins an old tote road, turns left, and soon crosses a stream. At 1.9 mi., turn right off the road and soon reach Cranberry Stream Tentsite. Cross a tote road at 2.5 mi., and beyond, pass an old beaver pond. Then climb gradually but steadily into the basin of Cranberry Pond, and pass a spring (last reliable water before Horns Pond). At 3.2 mi., reach a jct. Here, the AT turns sharply right (north).

Bigelow Range Trail (sign) continues straight ahead (west) to reach Cranberry Peak in 1.8 mi., and the trailhead at the end of Curry St. in Stratton at 5.0 mi.

Ahead on the AT, the trail climbs steeply through a boulder field, and at 4.0 mi., reaches the crest of the ridge. Here, the trail turns right (east) and follows the ridge, crossing a minor summit. Where the trail takes a sharp left, there is a lookout a few yards to the right over Horns Pond to the Horns. The trail descends steeply, and at 5.2 mi., Horns Pond Trail comes in on the right. The AT continues along the south shore of Horns Pond, passing a side trail to the Horns Pond Lean-tos at 5.4 mi.

From Horns Pond, the AT continues east, climbing South Horn. At 5.9 mi., the blue-blazed North Horn Trail leads 0.2 mi. left to North Horn. Ahead, the AT crosses the peak of South Horn (6.0 mi.) and continues along the undulating crest of the range, reaching West Peak at 8.2 mi. The trail then descends to the Bigelow Col and Myron Avery Tentsite at 8.5 mi. Here, Fire Warden's Trail comes in on the right. The AT continues east, climbing to the summit of Avery Peak at 8.9 mi. From Avery Peak, the AT descends east 2.2 mi. to its jct. with Safford Brook Trail.

Via Appalachian Trail from the south (AMC map 3: B2–B3, MATC map 5)
Distances from ME 27 (1,450 ft.) to
- Stratton Brook Pond Rd. (1,250 ft.): 0.8 mi., 25 min.
- Cranberry Stream Tentsite: 1.9 mi., 1 hr.
- Bigelow Range Trail jct. (2,450 ft.): 3.4 mi., 2 hr. 5 min.
- Horns Pond Trail jct. (3,150 ft.): 5.2 mi., 3 hr. 15 min.
- Horns Pond Lean-tos (3,150 ft.): 5.4 mi., 3 hr. 20 min.
- South Horn summit (3,805 ft.): 5.9 mi., 4 hr. 10 min.
- West Peak summit (4,145 ft.): 8.2 mi., 5 hr. 40 min.
- Bigelow Col, Fire Warden's Trail jct., Myron Avery Tentsite (3,800 ft.): 8.5 mi., 5 hr. 55 min.
- Avery Peak (4,088 ft.): 8.9 mi., 6 hr. 15 min.
- Safford Brook Trail jct. (2,250 ft.): 11.1 mi., 7 hr. 30 min.

Fire Warden's Trail (MATC)

This trail provides direct and steep access to Avery and West peaks from the south.

To reach the trail, turn north onto Stratton Brook Pond Rd. from ME 27 at a point about 3.2 mi. northwest of the Sugarloaf ski area access road and 4.5 mi. southeast of Stratton. The road crosses the AT in 1.0 mi., and continuing ahead, turns left at 1.6 mi., where there is trailhead parking. From the parking area, follow the rough road to Stratton Brook. Cross the brook (use caution in high water) and continue on the old road. At 0.7 mi., reach a fork and go left. From this point, Fire Warden's Trail leads north and then runs east on the level.

Ahead, the trail then climbs steeply over ledges to a shelf. The grade is moderate for the next 1.5 mi., during which the trail crosses several brooks. At 2.5 mi., Horns Pond Trail leaves left (northwest). At 3.5 mi., Fire Warden's Trail becomes increasingly steep as it climbs north-northeast on rock steps to Bigelow Col. The trail passes Moose Falls Tentsite at 3.5 mi., and joins the AT in the col at 4.7 mi. Myron Avery Tentsite is located here.

From the col, go right (east) on the AT and climb 0.4 mi. to reach Avery Peak and the remains of the old fire tower. To reach West Peak from the col, go left (west) on the AT and climb 0.3 mi.

Fire Warden's Trail (AMC map 3: B2–B3, MATC map 5)

Distances from Stratton Brook Pond Rd. (1,450 ft.) to

- Horns Pond Trail jct. (1,800 ft.): 2.5 mi., 1 hr. 10 min.
- Moose Falls Tentsite (2,500 ft.): 3.5 mi., 2 hr. 15 min.
- Bigelow Col, AT jct., Myron Avery Tentsite (3,800 ft.): 4.7 mi., 3 hr. 30 min.
- Avery Peak summit (4,088 ft.) via AT: 5.1 mi., 4 hr.
- West Peak summit (4,145 ft.) via AT: 5.0 mi., 4 hr.

Horns Pond Trail (MATC)

Horns Pond is a scenic tarn at the western base of the Horns, and this trail provides the most direct access. The trail starts from Fire Warden's Trail, diverging left at a point 2.1 mi. from the parking area west of Stratton Brook Pond. Horns Pond Trail heads northwest, climbing gradually. It skirts the southern edge of an old bog with a good view of South Horn. Beyond, the trail continues to rise gradually, and then gets increasingly steeper. At 4.6 mi., the trail intersects the AT. Bear right onto the AT for 0.2 mi. to reach Horns Pond and Horns Pond Campsite.

Horns Pond Trail (AMC map 3: B2–B3, MATC map 5)

Distances from Stratton Brook Pond Rd. (1,250 ft.) to
- start of trail (1,800 ft.) (via Fire Warden's Trail): 2.1 mi., 1 hr. 20 min.
- AT jct. (3,150 ft.): 4.6 mi., 3 hr. 15 min.
- Horns Pond Campsite (3,150 ft.): 4.8 mi., 3 hr. 25 min.

Bigelow Range Trail (MATC)

This blue-blazed trail starts from the village of Stratton at the western end of the range. From the center of Stratton, drive 0.8 mi. south on ME 27 to Curry St. (opposite the town ball field). Take Curry St. for 0.7 mi. to its end, where there is trailhead parking.

The trail proceeds easily through the woods, then climbs gradually on an old woods road. The trail crosses a brook at 1.0 mi. and climbs to reach Arnold's Well (a deep cleft in the rocks, no drinking water) at about 1.5 mi. Beyond, the trail reaches open ledges and good views. Ahead, pass a short side trail to a cave. The summit of Cranberry Peak is reached at 3.2 mi. after a short, steep ascent. Beyond the peak, the trail descends steeply then more gradually to reach the north shore of Cranberry Pond. The trail ends at a jct. with the AT at 5.0 mi.

Bigelow Range Trail (AMC map 3: B1–B2, MATC map 5)

Distances from Curry St. (1,150 ft.) to
- Cranberry Peak (3,194 ft.): 3.2 mi., 2 hr. 40 min.
- AT jct. (2,450 ft.): 5.0 mi., 3 hr. 40 min.

Safford Brook Trail (MATC)

This trail affords access to Little Bigelow Mtn. and Avery Peak from the north at Flagstaff Lake. To reach the trail, turn north off ME 16 onto Long Falls Dam Rd. in New Portland. At 17.3 mi., turn left (northwest) onto Bog Brook Rd. (gravel). From here, drive 0.7 mi. and bear left onto East Flagstaff Rd. Cross the AT in 0.1 mi. At about 4.3 mi., the road crosses Safford Brook and, just ahead, reaches the trailhead parking area. (*Note:* The trail officially starts 0.3 mi. to the northeast at Round Barn Campsite on the shore of Flagstaff Lake, but most hikers headed for Bigelow skip this short stretch and start from the parking lot on East Flag-staff Rd.)

At first, Safford Brook Trail follows a graded tote road, then climbs steeply, crosses Safford Brook, and enters Safford Notch. At 2.3 mi., the trail reaches a jct. with the AT. Fifty yd. east (left) on the AT is a blue-blazed trail that leads south (right) 0.2 mi. to Safford Notch Campsite. Continuing in this direction, the AT reaches the highest peak of Little Bigelow Mtn. at 5.5 mi.

Ahead, the AT rises steeply west toward Avery Peak, with several excellent vistas en route. At 3.2 mi., the AT reaches the crest of the ridge. Here, a side trail leads left 0.1 mi. to the top of Old Man's Head, a huge cliff on the south side of the mountain. From this jct., the AT continues to climb steeply, reaching the timberline and, shortly thereafter, the alpine summit of Avery Peak and the concrete and stone base of the old fire tower. Outstanding views appear in all directions.

Safford Brook Trail (AMC map 3: A4, B3–B4, MATC map 5)

Distances from East Flagstaff Rd. (1,200 ft.) to

- AT jct. (2,250 ft.) (via Safford Brook Trail): 2.3 mi., 1 hr. 40 min.
- Little Bigelow Mtn. summit (3,070 ft.) (via AT north): 5.5 mi., 3 hr. 40 min.
- Avery Peak (4,088 ft.) (via AT south): 4.5 mi., 3 hr. 40 min.

Little Bigelow Mtn. (3,070 ft.)

Little Bigelow Mtn. lies to the east of the main Bigelow Range, separated from it by a deep notch, known as Safford Notch. The ridge is long and narrow, with steep cliffs along its southern side. The northern slope descends steadily for some 2 mi. to Flagstaff Lake. Access to the summit is via the AT from the east or Safford Brook Trail and the AT from the north and west.

To reach the trail, turn north off ME 16 onto Long Falls Dam Rd. in New Portland. At 17.3 mi., turn left (northwest) onto Bog Brook Rd. (gravel). From here, drive 0.7 mi. and bear left onto East Flagstaff Rd. Reach the AT crossing in 0.1 mi.

The AT climbs through hardwoods alongside a brook. At 1.4 mi., a blue-blazed side trail leads right 0.1 mi. across the brook to Little Bigelow Lean-to. The trail continues through the woods, leaving the brook, and climbs a series of open ledges. At 3.0 mi., the trail reaches a viewpoint at the southeastern end of the summit ridge. The true summit is about 0.5 mi. farther along the trail. Beyond, the trail continues to a jct. with Safford Brook Trail in Safford Notch at 6.7 mi.

Little Bigelow Mtn. (AMC map 3: B3–B4, MATC map 5)

Distances from East Flagstaff Rd. (1,150 ft.) via AT to
- Little Bigelow Lean-to (1,800 ft.): 1.4 mi., 1 hr.
- Little Bigelow summit (3,070 ft.): 3.5 mi., 2 hr. 45 min.
- Safford Brook Trail jct. (2,250 ft.): 6.7 mi., 4 hr. 15 min.

Maine Huts & Trails

A new addition to this region is the Maine Huts & Trails system, a network of backcountry huts connected by miles of nonmotorized trails. The three existing huts and 45 mi. of trails are located between ME 27/16 in Carrabassett Valley and US 201 in West Forks and are open for year-round use. The huts provide comfortable overnight lodging (private or shared rooms) and meals during the full-service seasons (summer through fall and winter). The trails accommodate a variety of nonmotorized uses, including hiking and mountain biking in summer and fall months, and groomed cross-country skiing and snowshoeing in winter. Paddling access is available to Flagstaff Lake and the Dead River. Plans call for expanding the system to 180 mi. of trails and twelve backcountry huts between the Mahoosucs and Moosehead Lake.

Maine Hut Trail

This is the primary trail corridor of the MHT system. The current southern trailhead is on Gauge Rd. in Carrabassett Valley, just off ME 27/16 near the town office. The current northern trailhead is on US 201 just north of West Forks. The trail is an 8-to-10-ft.-wide track that is groomed in winter for classic cross-country skiing and makes a pleasant hiking route in summer. Some sections are open and built to accommodate mountain biking.

Starting at the Gauge Rd. trailhead, climb gradually along the lower slopes of Little Poplar Mtn. to reach Poplar Stream Falls Hut at 2.4 mi. Occasional views of the Bigelow Range are possible to the north and west en route.

Beyond Poplar Stream Falls Hut, the trail comes to a jct. with Larry's Loop at 2.7 mi., crosses Carriage Rd., and, beyond, crosses the southeast corner of Bigelow Preserve. Cross East Flagstaff Rd. at 5.9 mi. Ahead at 6.8 mi., reach a jct. with Hemlock Trail. Turn left here and continue on Hemlock Trail, a narrow trail leading through a stand of mature hemlock trees, to a jct. with the AT at 7.5 mi. Cross the AT and continue along the shore of Flagstaff Lake. Hemlock Trail merges with Maine Hut Trail at 9.6 mi. A jct. with Shore Trail is reached at 11.0 mi. (Shore Trail is an alternate route along the shore of Flagstaff Lake to Flagstaff Lake Hut.) Continue on Maine Hut Trail, and the hut appears in a birch grove above the lake at 12.3 mi.

Beyond Flagstaff Lake Hut, the trail follows the Dead River and finally crosses it at 18.3 mi. at the 210-ft. Tom and Kate Chappell Footbridge. Just after, take a right to stay along the river and see the views of Grand Falls, then continue on to the Grand Falls Hut at 20.3 mi.

From Grand Falls Hut, Maine Hut Trail follows the north bank of the Dead River to a trailhead parking area at US 201 in West Forks, which is reached at 33.8 mi.

Maine Hut Trail can be hiked in segments, in either direction and in any season. Additional side trails are planned at various points along the route. An additional trailhead parking area providing access to this area can be found along the east shore of Flagstaff Lake just off Long Falls Dam Rd., a few miles south of an area known as Big Eddy.

Maine Hut Trail (AMC map 3: A4–A5, B4–B5, C4, USGS Poplar Mtn., Little Bigelow, Basin Mtn., Pierce Pond, The Forks quads, DeLorme maps 29, 30, 40)

Distances from Gauge Rd. trailhead (850 ft.) off ME 27/16 in Carrabassett Valley to
- Poplar Stream Falls Hut (1,300 ft.): 2.4 mi., 1 hr. 30 min.
- Flagstaff Lake Hut (1,150 ft.): 12.3 mi., 6 hr.
- Grand Falls Hut (1,000 ft.): 20.3 mi., 10 hr.
- US 201 in West Forks (600 ft.): 33.8 mi., 17 hr.

Larry's Loop Trail

This 5.0-mi. loop hike starts and ends at Gauge Rd. trailhead off ME 27/16 in Carrabassett Valley. Start out on Maine Hut Trail to reach the jct. with Larry's Loop at 1.0 mi. Turn left onto Larry's Loop Trail, which follows Poplar Stream and leads to two pretty waterfalls known as Poplar Stream Falls. At about 2.2 mi., just past the first set of falls at the top of a rock staircase, turn left and continue another 0.2 mi. Turn left again, cross a bridge, and turn left once again to complete the loop. Once you reach the end of Larry's Loop Trail and the Carriage Rd. footbridge, cross the bridge to the left and take a right onto Maine Hut Trail to return to the trailhead.

Larry's Loop Trail (AMC map 3: B4, USGS Poplar Mtn. quad, DeLorme map 29)
Distances from Gauge Rd. trailhead (850 ft.) off ME 27/16 in Carrabassett Valley to
- start of trail via Maine Hut Trail (1,000 ft.): 1.0 mi., 35 min.
- Poplar Stream Falls (1,100 ft.): 2.2 mi., 1 hr. 10 min.
- complete loop: 5.0 mi., 2 hr. 30 min.

SUGGESTED HIKES

Easy Hikes

Center Hill Nature Trail [lp: 0.5 mi., 20 min.]. This self-guiding nature trail loop leads around Center Hill and offers outstanding views of the peaks of Tumbledown and the Jacksons from ledges en route.

Bald Mtn. (Oquossoc) [rt: 2.0 mi., 2 hr.]. This trail climbs steadily on easy grades to the summit of Bald Mtn., where there are excellent lake and mountain views from the ledges of the summit.

Table Rock [lp: 2.4 mi., 2 hr.]. A moderately steep but spectacular climb to a prominent rock ledge and extensive slab cave system on Baldpate Mtn. Return via the AT for a nice loop hike.

Mt. Will [lp: 3.25 mi., 2 hr. 30 min.]. The first part of Mt. Will Trail loop is a nature trail with markers identifying trees and providing history of the area. The North Ledges and South Cliffs offer good views of the Androscoggin River valley.

Larry's Loop [lp: 5.0 mi., 2 hr. 30 min.]. Larry's Loop Trail, part of the Maine Huts & Trails system, follows Poplar Stream and leads to two pretty waterfalls. A short 0.4-mi. side hike halfway along leads to Poplar Stream Falls Hut.

Bald Mtn. (Weld) [rt: 3.0 mi., 2 hr. 50 min.]. Although the first part of this trail is through a recently lumbered area, the fine views from the ledges and summit of Bald Mtn. make for a satisfying hike.

Moderate Hikes

Kibby Mtn. [rt: 6.6 mi., 3 hr.]. A delightful hike up an old woods road with some steep sections to the summit of Kibby Mtn., where an old fire tower platform provides extensive views of the western Maine and southern Québec mountains.

Rumford Whitecap [lp: 5.0 mi., 3 hr. 30 min.]. Ascend via Orange/Red Trail to the long bald summit ridge of Rumford Whitecap, which offers panoramic views and plenty of blueberries in season. On the descent, bear right and take Starr Trail over more ledges back to the start.

Mt. Blue [rt: 3.4 mi., 3 hr. 30 min.]. A steady, steep climb to a summit observation tower offers outstanding panoramic views. Several ledge outcrops also provide viewpoints.

Blueberry Mtn. [rt: 4.0 mi., 3 hr. 30 min.]. A fine hike to the bare summit and views of the Jacksons, Tumbledown Range, and Mt. Blue. Look for interesting geological formations in the rocks on top.

Aziscohos Mtn. [rt: 4.2 mi., 3 hr. 50 min.]. A steady, moderate climb through varied terrain to the alpine summit of the east peak, where fifteen lakes of the Rangeley lakes region can be seen.

Tumbledown Mtn. [rt: 5.2 mi., 4 hr. 40 min.]. Make a steep ascent through boulder fields on Loop Trail to reach the alpine summit of Tumbledown Mtn. Then follow Tumbledown Ridge Trail to the delightful Tumbledown Pond.

Burnt Mtn. [5.6 mi., 4 hr. 40 min.]. Hike this little-visited peak just east of Sugarloaf and enjoy extensive views from its alpine summit, including Sugarloaf and Spaulding mountains, the long ridge of Mt. Abraham, and the Bigelow Range.

Old Blue Mtn. [rt: 5.6 mi., 4 hr. 50 min.]. A steep initial climb out of Black Brook Notch via the AT leads to the summit of Old Blue Mtn. and outstanding views of the surrounding mountainous countryside east of Lower Richardson Lake.

Strenuous Hikes

Old Speck Mtn. [rt: 7.6 mi, 6 hr. 40 min.]. Follow Old Speck Trail, part of the AT, on a winding ascent to the summit of Old Speck (the final 0.3 mi. is via Mahoosuc Trail). The observation tower affords a panoramic view of the peaks around Grafton Notch, the Mahoosuc Range, and the Presidential Range beyond.

Mt. Abraham [rt: 9.0 mi., 7 hr. 30 min.]. Hike Fire Warden's Trail and cross a steep talus field to reach the extensive alpine area high on the mountain and panoramic views.

Goose Eye Mtn. [rt: 9.6 mi., 7 hr. 40 min.]. Follow Wright and Mahoosuc trails to the high alpine terrain on Goose Eye Mtn. From the summit of West Peak, enjoy outstanding views of the Mahoosuc Range, the White Mountains, and the Androscoggin River valley.

Avery Peak and West Peak [lp: 11.7 mi., 9 hr. 30 min.]. This loop hike ascends via Horns Pond Trail to the crest of the Bigelow Range at Horns Pond, then heads east on the AT, climbing South Horn. Beyond, a long ridge walk leads to the alpine summits of West and Avery peaks. Descend from Bigelow Col via Fire Warden's Trail to close the loop. Excellent views are possible from many points along the route.

Grafton Loop Trail (eastern section) [ow: 20.8 mi., 2 days]. Take in the great views from the alpine summits of Puzzle Mtn. and West Peak of Baldpate Mtn. on this fine backpacking route, which features four primitive campsites along the way.

Grafton Loop Trail (western section) [ow: 17.1 mi., 2 days]. Enjoy excellent vistas from the open summit of Sunday River Whitecap and the observation tower on Speck Mtn. Fine hiking leads to four primitive campsites en route.

SECTION FOUR
EVANS NOTCH AND OXFORD HILLS

Streaked Mtn. 171

Singepole Ridge 171

Crocker Hill 172

Bear Mtn. 173

Black Mtn. 173

Bald Mtn. 174

Speckled Mtn. 175

Mt. Zircon 176

Bucks Ledge and Lapham
Ledge. 177

Maggie's Park. 178

Mt. Christopher 179

Mt. Tire'm 180

Sabattus Mtn. 181

The Roost. 182

Caribou Mtn. 184

Speckled Mtn. 187

Blueberry Mtn. 191

East Royce Mtn. and West
Royce Mtn. 194

Durgin Mtn., Butters Mtn., and
Red Rock Mtn. 197

AMC map 7: Evans Notch

Albany Mtn. 200

Harndon Hill, Lord Hill, and
Pine Hill. 205

Little Deer Hill and Deer Hill . . . 207

Suggested Hikes 210

The Evans Notch and Oxford Hills section includes all of southern Oxford County and that part of Androscoggin County west of the Androscoggin River. To the north, the area is bounded by US 2 and the Androscoggin River, which also constitutes the eastern boundary as it makes its 178-mi. journey to merge with the Kennebec River at Merrymeeting Bay in Topsham. The Cumberland County line and US 302 form the southern boundary, and to the west, the area is bounded by ME/NH 113 and the state of New Hampshire.

This section describes 30 mountains and 45 trails in the Evans Notch and Oxford Hills region. Most of the peaks in the Oxford Hills are on private property and are open for public use through the generosity of the various landowners. Nearly all of the trails in the Evans Notch region are in the WMNF.

The Oxford Hills extend west from the Androscoggin River to the WMNF southwest of Bethel and, along with scattered lakes and ponds, account for the bulk of the terrain in the region. These mountains, ranging in elevation from about 1,000 ft. to just over 2,200 ft., include Streaked Mtn.; Singepole Ridge; Crocker Hill; Bear, Black, Bald, and Speckled mountains; and Mt. Zircon. Southeast of Bethel, in and around Bryant Pond and Locke Mills, are a number of scenic hills and ledges, including Bucks and Lapham ledges, Ring Hill, Peaked Mtn., and Mt. Christopher. Sandwiched between ME 5 in the east and ME/NH 113 in the west are the peaks of the Maine section of the WMNF. Evans Notch, in the midst of a jumble of mountain peaks, is the primary natural feature. The mountains east of the notch range from 1,250 ft. on Pine Hill to 2,906 ft. on Speckled Mtn. Other mountains are Caribou Mtn. and The Roost; Spruce Hill; and Blueberry, Durgin, Butters, Red Rock, and Albany mountains. Just south are Little Deer, Deer, Harndon, and Lord hills. To the west of Evans Notch is East Royce Mtn. Nearby is West Royce Mtn., just across the NH border. At 3,210 ft., it is the highest in the area and in this section. South of the WMNF are the peaks of Mt. Tire'm and Sabattus Mtn.

White Mountain National Forest

Most of the trails in the Evans Notch region are within the boundaries of the WMNF. Established in 1918, the WMNF features a diverse landscape of mountains, forests, lakes, rivers, and streams totaling 728,150 acres in New Hampshire and 49,346 acres in Maine.

The WMNF is not a national park but, rather, a national forest. Whereas parks are established primarily for preservation and recreation, national forests are managed for multiple use. In the administration of national forests, the following objectives are considered: recreation management, timber production, watershed protection, and wildlife habitat management. About 45 percent of the WMNF is open to timber harvesting on a carefully controlled basis. The USFS manages logging operations so that trails, streams, camping places, and other spots of public interest are protected. The boundaries of the WMNF are usually marked wherever they cross roads or trails, often by red-painted corner posts and blazes. Hunting and fishing are permitted in the WMNF under state laws, and licenses are required. Organized groups, including those sponsored by nonprofit organizations, must apply for outfitter-guide permits to conduct trips on WMNF land for which a fee is charged.

Camping

The WMNF operates four campgrounds in this section, at Crocker Pond just west of ME 5 in Albany Township, and at Hastings, Wild River, Cold River, and Basin along ME/NH 113 in Evans Notch. Numerous privately operated campgrounds with a variety of amenities are also available.

Camping and wood fires are restricted in many areas under the Forest Protection Area (FPA) program to protect vulnerable areas from damage. These protected areas can change from year to year. Contact the WMNF for updated information.

Current restrictions include the following:

- No camping above treeline (where trees are less than 8 ft. tall), except in winter, and then only in places that have at least 2 ft. of snow cover on the ground—but not on any frozen body of water. The point where the restricted area begins is marked on most trails with small signs, but the absence of such signs should not be construed as proof of the legality of a site.
- No camping or wood fires within a quarter-mile of any trailhead, picnic area, hut, cabin, shelter, developed tent site, campground, or day-use site. In this section, camping is also prohibited within a quarter-mile on either side of Wild River Rd.
- No motorized equipment or mechanical transport.
- No storing of equipment, personal property, or supplies, including geocaching and letter boxing.
- Hiking group size may not exceed ten people, and no more than ten people may occupy any designated or non-designated campsite.

Trailhead Parking Fees

Where parking sites in the WMNF have a posted fee sign, hikers will need to display an annual or weekly parking pass on their windshield or dashboard, or should be prepared to purchase a daily parking pass at the trailhead. This is the case at Brickett Place Day Use Site in Evans Notch. Almost all the proceeds from these passes are used for improvements in the WMNF. Annual and weekly parking passes are available at WMNF ranger stations.

For more information on the WMNF, Forest Protection Areas, backcountry camping rules, parking fees, and related items, visit fs.fed.us/r9/forests/white_mountain.

Caribou–Speckled Mtn. Wilderness

This 14,000-acre wilderness area east of Evans Notch, established in 1990 and managed by the USFS, encompasses the peaks of Caribou, Red Rock, Butters, Durgin, Speckled, Ames, and Blueberry mountains and Spruce Hill. Twelve trails lead into the wilderness and provide extensive opportunities to explore this unique mountain environment.

In accordance with USFS Wilderness policy, the trails in Caribou–Speckled Mtn. Wilderness are generally maintained to a lower standard than are non-Wilderness trails. The trails may be rough, overgrown, or essentially unmarked with minimal signage, and considerable care may be required to follow them.

Wilderness regulations, intended to protect wilderness resources and promote opportunities for challenge and solitude, prohibit use of motorized equipment or mechanical means of transportation of any sort. Camping and wood fires are not allowed within 200 ft. of any trail except at designated campsites. Hiking and camping group size is limited to ten persons. Camping and fires are also prohibited above treeline (where trees are less than 8 ft. tall) except in winter, when camping is permitted above treeline in places where snow cover is at least 2 ft. deep, but not on any frozen body of water.

Streaked Mtn. (1,770 ft.)

The distinctive west face of Streaked Mtn. in Hebron can be seen for miles in the Norway–South Paris area. The mountain offers a short but steep half-mile hike to the open ledges on its top. Hebron Academy maintains the trail. To reach it, turn southeast from ME 117 onto Streaked Mtn. Rd. about 2.9 mi. from the jct. of ME 117 and ME 119 in South Paris and 5.3 mi. southwest of Buckfield. At 0.5 mi., the trail (sign) starts left by a brook. Parking is along either side of the road.

Start by following a brook and an old telephone line along the edge of a field. The trail quickly becomes steep, rocky, and eroded. It passes through a section of dense forest before emerging onto smooth rock slabs. Soon the grade moderates and the trail crosses under the phone line. Beyond, the trail climbs to reach the broad summit and a complex of communication towers and buildings. ATV trails crisscross the mountaintop. Follow these tracks right (east) to more viewpoints and ledges. Descending, leave the phone line at the second pole to drop down to the ledges to the left.

Streaked Mtn. (USGS Oxford quad, DeLorme map 11)

Distance from Streaked Mtn. Rd. (1,030 ft.) to
* Streaked Mtn. summit (1,770 ft.): 0.6 mi., 45 min.

Singepole Ridge (1,420 ft.)

Across the valley southwest of Streaked Mtn. is Singepole Ridge in Paris. Although the trail does not reach the actual summit, open ledges offer broad views to the south and west. The trailhead is on Brett Hill Rd., 0.5 mi. south of ME 117 and about 2.5 mi. from the jct. of ME 117 and ME 119 in South Paris. At the point where Brett Hill Rd. turns northwest, park alongside the road.

Follow the dirt Durrell Hill Rd. uphill on foot. In 0.4 mi., bear left off the road onto a driveway and reach a residence and a garage in another 350 ft. Beyond the garage, the trail—an ATV trail—heads into the woods. The numerous side roads/trails can be confusing; follow the main track. At 1.1 mi., reach an obscure fork, which can easily be missed. To the right is a steep shortcut leading to the top of the ridge. The left fork—the main trail—winds up past an old quarry. (Both routes converge on the ridge above.) Just past the quarry, the trail emerges on an open ledge with tailings from the mine. Turn right and descend briefly into the woods, then follow a track to open ledges. Cairns lead to the cliff edge overlooking Hall Pond.

Singepole Ridge (USGS Oxford quad, DeLorme map 11)
Distance from jct. of Brett Hill Rd. and Durrell Hill Rd. (890 ft.) to
  • Singepole Ridge ledges and overlook (1,300 ft.): 1.1 mi., 45 min.

Crocker Hill (1,374 ft.)

Crocker Hill in Paris, the site of the 1868 panorama of the White Mountains painted by George L. Vose, Bowdoin College professor of civil engineering, offers fine views of the surrounding countryside and other mountains. Leave from Paris Hill Rd. in Paris just north of Paris Hill Country Club, and turn right (east) onto Lincoln St. (which soon becomes Mt. Mica Rd.). At 1.1 mi., turn left onto Thayer Rd., and proceed 0.7 mi. to where the road turns left. Limited parking is on the shoulder.

The Old Crocker Hill carriage road leaves straight ahead from beyond the gate. At 0.2 mi., the road makes a sweeping left turn where a snowmobile trail continues straight ahead. Ahead, the trail ascends gradually, and then veers sharply right on a switchback. A few yards after the switchback is the old mine shaft. Soon, the trail switchbacks to the left once more. The view to the left is partially obscured by trees, but a short walk toward the overlook affords an open vantage point. Leave the carriage road at 0.6 mi. by turning right onto a foot trail marked by a small cairn. Climb steadily for 0.2 mi. to the western viewpoint. Yellow blazes mark the trail. To reach the eastern viewpoint, follow the trail 0.1 mi. past a cairn on left. A bench sculpted out of a fallen tree adorns the outlook.

Crocker Hill (USGS West Sumner quad, DeLorme map 11)
Distance from Thayer Rd. (900 ft.) to
  • Crocker Hill summit (1,374 ft.): 0.9 mi., 40 min.

Bear Mtn. (1,208 ft.)

This mountain in Hartford offers fine views overlooking Bear Pond and the surrounding countryside of the upper valley of the Androscoggin River.

From ME 4 at North Turner, turn west onto ME 219 (Bear Pond Rd.). Follow this for 4.0 mi. to Pratt Hill Rd. Turn left and drive 0.9 to the jct. of Berry Rd. (right) and Mahoney Rd. (left). Proceed straight ahead through this intersection to trailhead parking in a grassy field immediately on the right.

The trail follows a dirt road past several houses, crossing a brook along the way. Ascend gradually as the wide road deteriorates to a woods road. At a fork, bear right and continue up the rocky, eroded route.

Partway up the hill, a narrow trail leaves the dirt road to the right and heads for the western summit. Turn right onto this trail and contour easily along the ridgeline. The path makes a sharp right at a metal culvert, and, a short distance beyond, breaks out onto open ledges. Just ahead is an outlook at a large boulder and good views to the southeast.

To reach the main summit, where the narrow trail leaves the dirt road to the right, continue straight ahead on the dirt road toward the height-of-land. At about 1.1 mi., a road from the north comes in on the left, and the trail (road) swings around to the right (south). Ahead are good views to the west, south, and southeast from the summit.

Bear Mtn. (USGS Buckfield quad, DeLorme map 11)

Distances from parking area (400 ft.) to
- side trail to western summit (1,100 ft.): est. 0.9 mi., 35 min.
- Bear Mtn. main summit (1,208 ft.): 1.9 mi., 1 hr. 20 min.

Black Mtn. (2,133 ft.)

This mountain in Sumner and Peru, just east of Speckled Mtn., is a broad, flat mass with about five definite summits running roughly east–west. A trail climbs to the easternmost summit from the Sumner side.

From the jct. of ME 26 and ME 219 in West Paris, go 8.0 mi. east on ME 219 to Greenwood Rd. Turn left and follow Greenwood Rd. 1.5 mi. to Black Mtn. Rd. Turn left again and proceed 0.2 mi. to a fork. Bear left at the fork and go straight on Black Mtn. Rd. for another 2.1 mi. Where a driveway leaves right, turn left and park ahead on the left.

Hike up the road 0.25 mi. and diverge right from the road onto an old woods road. Follow this to a small open area. Bear left here (marked by white triangle) and cross a brook on a stone culvert. Beyond, go right (marked by white triangle), uphill, crossing a skidder track. Continuing on, the trail has been affected by logging in this area and the woods road may be difficult to follow. Beyond, cross a large brook. Follow a wide, rocky path, ascending gradually. An occasional cairn marks the path. The road eventually narrows to a footpath. At the next fork, bear left at a rock cairn. At the next cairn at 0.6 mi., turn right uphill. (*Note:* If you come to a steep gully with a small stream, you've missed the turn.) Climb steadily up an eroded path. Cross a small brook in a level area, then resume climbing. Finally, break out onto the rocky summit with fine views to the southeast. Bear left and walk along the plateau, noting the old carvings in the rock (dating to 1889) on the left, just steps from the trail. The summit ridge is crisscrossed with paths, and several lead to outcroppings with views.

Black Mtn. (USGS Worthley Pond quad, DeLorme map 11)

Distance from Black Mtn. Rd. (950 ft.) to

- Black Mtn., eastern summit (2,133 ft.): 1.8 mi., 1 hr. 30 min.

Bald Mtn. (1,692 ft.)

This mountain is in the northeastern corner of Woodstock near Shagg Pond. Together with neighboring Speckled Mtn. to the east, Bald Mtn. offers interesting hiking with good cliff-top and summit views.

From the jct. of ME 26 and ME 219 in West Paris, go east on ME 219 about 4.1 mi. to Tuell Hill Rd. and turn left. Take this road to where it dead-ends and turn left onto Redding Rd. Follow Redding Rd. past Shagg Pond and continue along the road for 0.5 mi. to a parking area on the left at the top of the hill.

Follow an old road into the woods gradually uphill for 0.4 mi. As Little Concord Pond comes into view, reach a jct. Straight ahead, a short side trail leads to the pond. The main route turns sharply right onto a foot trail and, just ahead, takes another sharp right, climbing up over the rocks.

The trail levels off near the ridge crest and soon reaches the wooded summit at 1.0 mi. Scramble out to the cliff top overlooking Shagg Pond, where there are fine views beyond to the White Mountains. (*Note:* See below for the trail route from this point to Speckled Mtn.)

Bald Mtn. (USGS Mt. Zircon quad, DeLorme map 11)

Distances from Redding Rd. (970 ft.) to
- Little Concord Pond jct. (1,110 ft.): 0.4 mi., 10 min.
- Bald Mtn. summit and ledges (1,692 ft.): 1.0 mi., 1 hr.

Speckled Mtn. (2,183 ft.)

Speckled Mtn. lies to the east of Bald Mtn. in Peru. The route to Speckled Mtn. from the summit of Bald Mtn. drops steeply into a col and then follows the ridge to the Speckled Mtn. summit, with extensive views in all directions. Speckled Mtn. can also be climbed from the north via Speckled Mtn. Pasture Trail.

Route from Bald Mtn.

From the ledge viewpoint on Bald Mtn. (see p. 174), continue in and out of the trees on the edge of the precipice before bearing left at the cliff's end and descending steeply on recently hardened trail to a col and a small stream. Beyond, climb gradually along the rolling ridge on an old woods road (snowmobile trail), following blue blazes and rock cairns, with the cone of Speckled Mtn. often visible ahead through the trees. After a right turn off the old road onto a footpath, ascend a series of ledges and slabs, alternating through openings in the forest canopy and dense conifers. Make a final steep climb to the summit ridge, and then walk easily along to the metal pole marking the top of the mountain.

Speckled Mtn. (USGS Mt. Zircon quad, DeLorme map 11)

Distance from Bald Mtn. ledges (1,692 ft.) to
- Speckled Mtn. summit (2,183 ft.): 1.3 mi., 1 hr. 10 min.

Speckled Mtn. Pasture Trail

Speckled Mtn. Pasture Trail offers a direct approach to the mountain instead of the traverse from Bald Mtn.

From ME 108 in West Peru, turn right onto Main St. Go through West Peru, staying on Main St., which becomes Dickvale Rd. in 4.3 mi. Continue on Dickvale Rd. until the pavement ends at 4.8 mi. Park to the side of the road. The trail starts to the left behind a gate.

The trail starts as a well-graded logging road leading to a log yard at about 0.5 mi., where the trail degrades to an ATV trail. At a four-way jct. at 0.9 mi., bear right onto the roadbed and emerge into an area that has been recently harvested. At 1.2 mi., at a red sign reading "Speckled Mtn.," the ATV trail leaves right and the route ahead becomes a heavily rutted skidder road. At 1.6 mi., another skidder road comes in from the right at an old stone wall. Bear left here, and in another 0.1 mi. emerge onto a wide haul road. Jog right on the road for 100 ft. (red posts are on both sides of the road), then turn left into the woods on an ATV trail. In 50 ft., reach a property boundary marked with yellow paint and climb steeply up the mountainside, still following ATV tracks, to the east ridge of Speckled Mtn. at 2.2 mi. Continue up the ridge to a ledgy knob. Ahead, emerge onto a shrubby ledge. Here, the ATV track leaves right and the trail continues to another ledgy knob (yellow blazes end here). Beyond, follow the ridge over ledges, moving in and out of the trees. Occasional cairns mark the route, but the trail can be difficult to follow. Reach the summit at 3.2 mi.

Speckled Mtn. Pasture Trail (USGS Mt. Zircon quad, DeLorme map 11)
Distances from Dickvale Rd. (800 ft.) to
- logging haul road (1,200 ft.): 1.7 mi., 1 hr. 5 min.
- base of east ridge (1,600 ft.): 2.2 mi., 1 hr. 35 min.
- Speckled Mtn. summit (2,183 ft.): 3.2 mi., 2 hr. 25 min.

Mt. Zircon (2,240 ft.)

This mountain, straddling the town lines of Milton Township and Peru, rewards hikers with exceptional views to the south and east from its craggy alpine summit. To reach Mt. Zircon from the south, from the jct. of ME 26 and ME 232 in Woodstock, go north on ME 232 for 6.8 mi. to Abbotts

Mill. Turn right onto South Rumford Rd. and drive 6.4 mi. to a gated gravel road on the right where a Rumford Water District tree farm sign is located. Park in the grassy area along South Rumford Rd. From the east, from the jct. of US 2 and ME 108 in Rumford, drive west on US 2 for 0.5 mi. Turn left and cross the Androscoggin River, then follow South Rumford Rd. west for 3.2 mi. to the trailhead.

Begin by walking south on the gravel road (old Zircon Rd.) past the locked red gate, then uphill on an easy but steady grade. At 0.9 mi., just past a logging operation on the left, a snowmobile trail leaves right. Bear left here, and follow the gravel road to a gated spring house at 1.5 mi. This remnant of the old Zircon Water Bottling Company is fenced in, but just across the road, cold, clear water gushes from a spring pipe. Nearing the height-of-land, look for a white Mt. Zircon Trail sign on the left at 2.1 mi. Turn off the road here and follow the footpath, moderately at first, then more steeply with rough footing. Finish by climbing over slabs to the top. A large cairn and the downed, rusting old fire tower mark the summit.

Mt. Zircon (USGS Mt. Zircon and Rumford quads, DeLorme maps 10, 11, 18, 19)
Distances from South Rumford Rd. (600 ft.) to
- Mt. Zircon spring house (1,200 ft.): 1.5 mi., 1 hr.
- start of trail (via old Zircon Rd.) (1,400 ft.): 2.1 mi., 1 hr. 30 min.
- Mt. Zircon summit (2,240 ft.): 2.9 mi., 2 hr. 10 min.

Bucks Ledge (1,200 ft.) and Lapham Ledge (1,100 ft.)

On the southwest ridge of Moody Mtn. in Woodstock, Bucks Ledge offers good views west over North and South ponds to the ski trails on Mt. Abram and farther to the peaks of Evans Notch and the White Mountains beyond.

From the post office in Bryant Pond, drive 1.4 mi. north on ME 26 to a gravel woods road (the trail) on the right just before a small camp. Park along the side of the road south of the camp and the woods road, taking care not to block the woods road.

Immediately pass a small sign and register box. Beyond, pass through an old gate and follow the woods road north uphill. At 0.5 mi., reach a jct.

with a foot trail on the right (sign and orange flagging) that leads an easy 0.5 mi. to Lapham Ledge and good views south to Bryant Pond and the surrounding hills.

Continuing ahead on the woods road, pass through a clearing (old log yard) and bear left off the road at a sign for Bucks Ledge at 0.6 mi. At 0.7 mi., bear sharply right onto the wide trail and soon begin to climb moderately. After a short, steep climb, reach the top of the ledges at 1.2 mi. Continue along the ledges, passing several viewpoints, before descending steeply to a jct. with Mann Rd. at 1.5 mi., just above the shore of North Pond. Turn left and follow the road south. Reach a jct. with Rocky Rd. at 2.5 mi. and ME 26 just ahead. Walk the shoulder of ME 26 to return to the trailhead at 2.8 mi.

Bucks Ledge and Lapham Ledge (USGS Bryant Pond quad, DeLorme map 10)
Distances from ME 26 (750 ft.)
- side trail to Lapham Ledge (900 ft.): 0.5 mi., 15 min.
- Lapham Ledge (1,100 ft.) via side trail: 1.0 mi., 40 min.
- Bucks Ledge (1,200 ft.): 1.2 mi., 50 min.
- complete loop: 2.8 mi., 1 hr. 30 min.

Maggie's Park

This 86-acre woodland park in Greenwood was donated to the town by Maggie Ring, a lifelong resident. Local residents maintain an interconnected system of six color-coded trails on Ring Hill and Peaked Mtn.

From the post office in Bryant Pond, drive 3.4 mi. north on ME 26 to a jct. with Howe Hill Rd. (sign for Mt. Abram ski area). Turn left onto Howe Hill Rd., cross the railroad tracks, then turn left onto Greenwood Rd. Follow this for 1.4 mi. to trailhead parking on the right (sign).

Ring Hill Trail

Starting to the right of the kiosk at the back of the parking lot, follow orange blazes 50 ft. to a jct. and bear right to hike the loop counterclockwise. At 0.2 mi., Abner's Path (blue blazes) leaves right. Just ahead, pass Mae's Path (green blazes) on the right. Ahead, cross the upper end of Abner's Path and head gradually uphill, switchbacking several times. At 0.6 mi., the trail levels off and soon reaches an open ledge with good views of Mt. Abram. Cross the ledge and descend to the left. After several switchbacks, cross Abner's Path again at 0.8 mi. At 1.0 mi., Maggie's Path (purple blazes) leaves left. Beyond, close the loop and reach the parking area at 1.1 mi.

Ring Hill Trail (USGS Bryant Pond quad, Delorme map 10)

Distances from Greenwood Rd. (750 ft.) to

- ledges (1,050 ft.): 0.7 mi., 25 min.
- complete loop: 1.1 mi., 40 min.

Peaked Mtn. Trail

Leave the parking lot to the left of the kiosk, following yellow blazes. In 100 yd., turn right off the woods road and head uphill into the woods on a foot trail. Climb gradually via switchbacks to a jct. with Harriet's Path (red blazes) on the left at 0.2 mi. Pass Abner's Path (blue blazes) on the right at 0.3 mi., and the upper end of Harriet's Path at 0.4 mi. Arrive at a blue-painted stake at 0.5 mi that marks the boundary of Maggie's Park. Beyond, the ridge levels off and a jct. with the summit loop is reached at 0.6 mi. Continue straight ahead on the old woods road, trending easily up along the ridgeline. At 0.9 mi., make a sharp left (unmarked trail to right). The summit and a series of ledges with nice views of Mt. Abram are just ahead. Beyond, leave the ledges and descend briefly, then remain on a contour before closing the loop at the jct. at 1.2 mi. Turn right and retrace your steps to the parking area, which is reached at 1.8 mi.

Peaked Mtn. Trail (USGS Bryant Pond quad, DeLorme map 10)

Distances from Greenwood Rd. (750 ft.) to

- Peaked Mtn. summit (1,230 ft.) and ledges: 0.9 mi., 40 min.
- complete loop: 1.8 mi., 1 hr. 5 min.

Mt. Christopher (1,200 ft.)

Ledges high on the east face of Mt. Christopher provide nice views of Bryant Pond and the Oxford Hills beyond. From the post office in Bryant Pond, drive 0.6 mi. north on ME 26 to a jct. with Lakeside Dr. (ball field on left). Turn left on Lakeside Dr. and drive 0.6 mi. Turn left on Conservation Ln. at a sign for the University of Maine 4-H Camp & Learning Center. In another 0.1 mi., bear left into a parking lot amid the camp buildings.

Odyssey Trail

Leave the parking lot and walk steeply uphill on the gravel road past a cabin and a trail on the left at 0.1 mi. Just beyond, where the road turns left, go straight ahead on an old woods road, following blue blazes. Ascend gradually on the grassy road (also a snowmobile trail) and, at 0.7 mi., bear right onto a footpath At 0.8 mi., bear left in a mossy area, then descend briefly and cross an old woods road. Beyond, ascend at a moderate grade to a boulder on the ridge top (carvings in the rock date to 1887) and reach a small TV antenna atop a ledge at 1.0 mi. A viewpoint overlooking Bryant Pond is just ahead.

After the outlook, descend through the woods along the cliff edge and pass through a parklike stand of pines and hemlocks. At 1.5 mi., leave the cliff edge and descend more steeply to cross a dirt road (sign for Kinsman Cemetery). Pass to the right of the Kinsman Family mausoleum at 1.8 mi. to reach the shore of Bryant Pond. Bear left to continue along the shore, passing a camp at 2.0 mi., to a trail sign at 2.2 mi. Turn left here and proceed uphill to the camp road at 2.4 mi. Turn right onto the road for the parking lot, which is reached in another 0.1 mi.

Odyssey Trail (USGS Bryant Pond quad, DeLorme map 10)
Distances from parking lot (750 ft.) to
- ledges atop Mt. Christopher (1,200 ft.): 1.0 mi., 45 min.
- complete loop: 2.5 mi., 1 hr. 30 min.

Mt. Tire'm (1,104 ft.)

Mt. Tire'm in Waterford offers an easy hike that yields good views of the Long Lake region. To reach the trailhead, follow ME 35 to the center of Waterford, then turn left (northwest) onto Plummer Hill Rd. for about

100 yd. A plaque marks the start of Daniel Brown Trail on the left. Parking is along the road.

Take the wide Daniel Brown Trail (Old Squire Brown Trail) uphill into the woods, following a stone wall on the left. The path is not blazed but is well defined and easy to follow. Contour up the east side of the hill through the forest, with occasional glimpses of Keoka Lake. Soon after, reach a viewpoint overlooking Bear Pond, Bear Mtn., and Long Lake. Just ahead on the summit ledges are views to Pleasant Mtn. and the ski trails on Shawnee Peak.

Mt. Tire'm (USGS Waterford Flat quad, DeLorme map 10)
Distance from Plummer Hill Rd. (510 ft.) to
  • Mt. Tire'm summit (1,104 ft.): 0.7 mi., 40 min.

Sabattus Mtn. (1,253 ft.)

From the top of the immense cliffs on the southwest face of Sabattus Mtn. in Lovell, hikers will enjoy extensive views ranging from Pleasant Mtn. to the Baldfaces on the eastern edge of the White Mountains. The trail and protection of the mountain is a joint partnership between MBPL and Greater Lovell Land Trust. To reach the trail, follow ME 5 north from Lovell to Center Lovell. At 0.7 mi., take Sabattus Rd. right (east) past Center Lovell General Store and continue to a fork at 1.5 mi. Bear right onto Sabattus Trail Rd. at the fork and drive 0.7 mi. on this dirt road to the parking lot (sign) on the right.

The yellow-blazed trail splits a short distance into the woods. Take the left fork, climbing gradually with occasional switchbacks. At the ridge top, traverse right on level trail to reach an outlook and a large outcrop of white quartzite. Pass another viewpoint to reach the site of the old fire tower on the summit. (Attached to one of the concrete stanchions is a memorial to Steven Hickey, a local young man who died while trying to save his brother after a boating accident.) Views here take in numerous ponds and Pleasant Mtn. Farther along are a park bench, an unusual find on a mountaintop, and views west as far as Mt. Washington and the Presidential Range. To descend, return to the tower site and bear left. Descend steeply at first then more gradually back to the parking area.

Sabattus Mtn. (USGS North Waterford quad, DeLorme map 10)

Distances from Sabattus Trail Rd. (700 ft.) to
- Sabattus Mtn. summit (1,253 ft.): 0.8 mi., 40 min.
- complete loop: 1.6 mi., 1 hr. 5 min.

Evans Notch Rd. (ME/NH 113)

This scenic auto road extends from the jct. of US 302 in Fryeburg north to the jct. of US 2 in Gilead. The road generally follows the Maine–New Hampshire border, bisecting the Evans Notch region. Three WMNF campgrounds—Basin, Cold River, and Hastings—are located along this route. A number of trailheads are also found en route, to the east and west of the road. To assist in locating these points, the following summary is provided:

Evans Notch Rd. (ME/NH 113)

Distances from jct. US 302 in Fryeburg to
- Stow village: 11.3 mi.
- AMC Cold River Camp (east): 16.7 mi.
- Baldfaces trailhead (east): 16.8 mi.
- Cold River Campground and access road to Basin Campground (west): 18.9 mi.
- Brickett Place (east): 19.2 mi.
- Royce Trail (west): 19.2 mi.
- Laughing Lion trailhead (west): 21.3 mi.
- East Royce (west) and Spruce Hill (east) trailheads: 22.3 mi.
- Haystack Notch (east) trailhead: 23.6 mi.
- Caribou/Mud Brook trailhead (east): 24.9 mi.
- Wheeler Brook Trail (Little Lary Brook Rd.) (east): 25.8 mi.
- The Roost south trailhead (east): 25.9 mi.
- Hastings Campground (east): 26.3 mi.
- Wild River Campground (via Wild River Rd.) (west): 26.7 mi.
- The Roost north trailhead (east): 26.8 mi.
- US 2 in Gilead: 29.7 mi.

The Roost (1,364 ft.)

This small hill in Batchelders Grant Township offers fine views of the Wild River and Evans Brook valleys.

Roost Trail (WMNF)

This trail starts from two trailheads 0.9 mi. apart on the east side of ME 113. The north trailhead (sign, parking on shoulder) is 0.1 mi. north of a bridge over Evans Brook and 0.2 mi. north of the jct. of ME 113 and Wild River Rd. at Hastings. The south trailhead is just south of another bridge over Evans Brook.

Leaving the north trailhead, the trail ascends a steep bank for 90 yd., then bears right (east) and ascends gradually along a wooded ridge, rejoining an older route of the trail at 0.1 mi. Roost Trail crosses a small brook at 0.3 mi., then rises somewhat more steeply, swings right, and emerges on a ledge at the summit (no views) at 0.5 mi. Here, a side trail descends 0.1 mi. and 100 ft. west through woods to spacious open ledges, where the views are excellent. The main trail descends generally southeast from the summit at a moderate grade and crosses a small brook, then turns right (west) on an old road (no sign) and follows it past a cellar hole and a brushy area back to ME 113.

The Roost (AMC map 7: E13)

Distances from ME 113, north trailhead (820 ft.) to
- The Roost (1,374 ft.): 0.5 mi., 30 min.
- ME 113, south trailhead (850 ft.): 1.2 mi., 55 min.

Wheeler Brook Trail (WMNF)

The trailheads for this wooded, viewless trail are on the south side of US 2 (sign; limited roadside parking), 2.3 mi. east of the jct. of US 2 and ME 113, and on Little Lary Brook Rd. (FR 8), 1.6 mi. from its jct. with ME 113, which is 7.0 mi. north of the road to the WMNF Cold River Campground and 3.8 mi. south of the jct. of US 2 and ME 113. The trail is lightly used and requires care to follow.

From US 2, the trail follows a gated, grassy logging road south, soon crossing an old woods road and then passing junctions with another woods road on the right and a snowmobile trail on the left. Wheeler Brook Trail enters the WMNF at 0.4 mi., bears left on a grassy road, and joins and follows Wheeler Brook, crossing it four times. The trail turns left (arrow) at a logging road fork at 1.0 mi., just before the third crossing of the brook. The trail rises steadily to its highest point, just over 2,000 ft., at the crest of the northwest ridge of Peabody Mtn. (2,462 ft.) at 2.1 mi. (There is no trail to the wooded summit of Peabody Mtn.) The trail then descends generally southwest, merges onto an old logging road (FR 8) that comes down from the left, and reaches Little Lary Brook Rd. Turn left onto Little Lary Brook Rd. and continue about 100 yd. to a locked gate near the bridge over Little Lary Brook, 1.6 mi. from ME 113.

In the reverse direction, proceed along Little Lary Brook Rd. about 100 yd. from the locked gate, then turn right onto FR 8 at the jct. where FR 185 continues straight ahead. The trail (arrow) leaves the left side of the road in another 0.3 mi.

Wheeler Brook Trail (AMC map 7: E13)

Distance from US 2 (680 ft.) to
  • gate on Little Lary Brook Rd. (1,220 ft.): 3.5 mi., 2 hr. 25 min.

Caribou Mtn. (2,850 ft.)

This mountain is in the townships of Batchelders Grant and Mason. The bare summit ledges afford excellent views. The Caribou and Mud Brook trails make a pleasant loop. The Caribou summit and much of the surrounding area are part of the Caribou–Speckled Mountain Wilderness Area.

Caribou Trail (WMNF)

This trail provides access to the attractive ledges of Caribou Mtn. The middle section of this trail is in the Caribou–Speckled Mtn. Wilderness. Caribou's west trailhead, which it shares with Mud Brook Trail, is located at a parking area on the east side of ME 113, 6.0 mi. north of the road to WMNF Cold River Campground and 4.8 mi. south of US 2. The east trailhead is on Bog Rd. (FR 6), which leaves the south side of US 2 at 1.3 mi. west of the West Bethel Post Office (a sign for Pooh Corner Farm and a road sign are located at this jct.) and leads 2.8 mi. to the trailhead, where a gate ends public travel on the road.

From the parking area on ME 113, the trail runs north, ascending slightly and then descending. It crosses Morrison Brook at 0.4 mi. (no bridge) and turns east to follow the brook, crossing it five more times and entering the Wilderness. The third crossing, at 2.0 mi., is at the head of Kees Falls, a 25-ft. waterfall. A side path descends steeply on the north side of the brook to a good view of the falls. Ahead, the trail climbs steadily, then levels off at the height-of-land as the trail crosses the col between Gammon and Caribou mountains at 2.9 mi. Soon, Mud Brook Trail leaves right to reach the summit of Caribou in 0.6 mi. and ME 113 in 3.9 mi.

Caribou Trail continues ahead at the jct., descending steadily into a ravine and swinging left to cross a small brook. The trail leaves the Wilderness at 3.4 mi., continues down the valley of Bog Brook, and turns northeast, crossing Bog Brook at 4.3 mi. and a tributary in another 0.2 mi. The trail continues at easy grades, bears right across a brook, and at 5.2 mi., just after crossing another brook, the trail turns left onto a logging road (FR 6). At 5.4 mi., the trail turns right at a jct. with another logging road and continues to the gate on Bog Rd. (Ascending, turn left at 0.1 mi. and bear right off the logging road at 0.3 mi.)

Caribou Trail (AMC map 7: E13–E14)
Distances from ME 113 (960 ft.) to
- Mud Brook Trail (2,420 ft.): 3.0 mi., 2 hr. 15 min.
- Caribou Mtn. summit (2,850 ft.) (via Mud Brook Trail): 3.6 mi., 2 hr. 45 min.
- Bog Rd. (860 ft.): 5.5 mi., 3 hr. 30 min.

Mud Brook Trail (WMNF)

This trail begins on ME 113 at the same point as Caribou Trail, 6.0 mi. north of the road to WMNF Cold River Campground, then passes over the summit of Caribou Mtn. and ends at Caribou Trail in the pass between Caribou Mtn. and Gammon Mtn. Despite the ominous name, the footing on Mud Brook Trail is generally dry and good. The eastern section of this trail is in the Caribou–Speckled Mtn. Wilderness.

From ME 113, the trail runs generally south, then turns east along the north side of Mud Brook, rising gradually. The trail crosses the brook at 1.5 mi., then crosses it again at 1.9 mi., and swings left (north) uphill, climbing more steeply. The trail crosses several smaller brooks and, at 3.0 mi., comes out on a small bare knob with excellent views east. The trail turns left into the woods and makes a short descent into a small ravine, then emerges in the open, passing a short side path on the right leading to ledges with excellent views east. Scramble up to open ledges on the south summit knob, with views south and west (hikers should walk only on bare rock in the summit area to preserve fragile vegetation).

The trail, which is poorly marked and requires care to follow, runs northeast across the broad summit ledges, descending slightly and generally keeping to the right (southeast) side of the crest. At 3.4 mi., the trail turns left up a short scramble, then turns right (sign) with the open ledges of the north summit knob a few steps to the left. The trail enters the woods and descends north to meet Caribou Trail in the col.

Mud Brook Trail (AMC map E13–F13)

Distances from ME 113 (935 ft.) to
- Caribou Mtn. summit (2,850 ft.): 3.4 mi., 2 hr. 40 min.
- Caribou Trail (2,420 ft.): 3.9 mi., 2 hr. 55 min.

Haystack Notch Trail (WMNF)

This trail, with mostly easy grades but some potentially difficult brook crossings, runs through Haystack Notch. The trail is lightly used and in places requires care to follow. The middle section of this trail is in the Caribou–Speckled Mtn. Wilderness.

The west trailhead is on the east side of ME 113, 4.7 mi. north of the road to WMNF Cold River Campground. Roadside parking is available a short distance to the north or south. To reach the east trailhead, follow Flat Rd. south from US 2 opposite the West Bethel Post Office, and at 3.2 mi. turn right (west) on Grover Hill Rd. This road is paved for 1.0 mi., then changes to a narrow, rough, gravel road with few opportunities for parking; many vehicles will not be able to drive all the way to the trailhead. Small parking spots are on the left at 1.2 mi. from Flat Rd., and on the right at 1.7, 2.0, and 2.4 mi. The road then rises steeply, bears right at a fork, descends to cross Miles Brook on a bridge, then rises again to a clearing at 2.5 mi. with a hiker symbol and arrow, where the road continues to the left (southwest) past a WMNF gate; in the future, there may be a trail sign by the gate.

Continue on foot up the road past the gate for 0.1 mi., where the trail emerges in a large, grassy clearing with a sign for Miles Notch Trail on the right. Haystack Notch Trail begins as a faint track leading to the right (west) along the north side of the clearing.

From the west trailhead on ME 113, the trail runs generally east along the east branch of Evans Brook, crossing the branch and its south fork, then following its north fork, with three more crossings. The first crossing, in particular, may be difficult at high water. The trail enters the Wilderness at 1.3 mi. and climbs under the cliffs of Haystack Mtn. to the broad height-of-land in Haystack Notch at 2.1 mi. The trail then descends moderately into the valley of the Pleasant River's West Branch, where the grade becomes easy. The trail leaves the Wilderness at 3.4 mi., and at 4.4 mi., after crossing a WMNF boundary line and then a tributary brook, makes the first of three crossings of the West Branch, which may be difficult at high water. The trail now rises slightly into a recently logged area (added to the WMNF in 2009) and bears left onto a logging road at 5.2 mi. The trail follows this road into the grassy clearing and meets the northern end of Miles Notch Trail at a trail sign, 0.1 mi. south of the WMNF gate. In the reverse direction, bear right and downhill (arrow and cairn) off the logging road, 0.2 mi. from the trail sign in the grassy clearing.

Haystack Notch Trail (AMC map 7: E14, F13–F14)

Distances from ME 113 (1,070 ft.) to
- Haystack Notch (1,810 ft.): 2.1 mi., 1 hr. 25 min.
- WMNF gate (900 ft.): 5.5 mi., 3 hr. 5 min.

Speckled Mtn. (2,906 ft.)

This mountain lies east of Evans Notch, in Batchelders Grant and Stoneham. Speckled Mtn. is one of at least three mountains in Maine that are known by this name. The open summit ledges have excellent views in all directions. A spring is about 0.1 mi. northeast of the summit, just off Red Rock Trail. Subsidiary peaks include Spruce Hill, and Blueberry and Ames mountains.

Spruce Hill Trail (WMNF/CTA)

This trail begins on the east side of ME 113, 3.4 mi. north of the road to WMNF Cold River Campground, opposite the start of East Royce Trail, and ascends to Bickford Brook Trail, with which Spruce Hill Trail forms the shortest route to the summit of Speckled Mtn. Most of this trail is in the Caribou–Speckled Mtn. Wilderness. The trail ascends moderately through woods, passing the Wilderness boundary sign at 0.6 mi., to the summit of Spruce Hill at 1.5 mi. The trail then descends into a sag and climbs to meet Bickford Brook Trail on the ridge crest west of Ames Mtn.

Spruce Hill Trail (AMC map 7: F13)

Distances from ME 113 (1,425 ft.) to

- Bickford Brook Trail (2,400 ft.): 1.9 mi., 1 hr. 30 min.
- Speckled Mtn. summit (2,906 ft.) (via Bickford Brook Trail): 3.1 mi., 2 hr. 25 min.

Bickford Brook Trail (CTA)

This trail ascends Speckled Mtn. from Brickett Place (a historical brick building that serves as a WMNF visitor center during summer) on ME 113, 0.3 mi. north of the road to WMNF Cold River Campground. Most of this trail is in the Caribou–Speckled Mtn. Wilderness. The trail enters the woods near the garage adjacent to Brickett Place, climbs moderately, then, at 0.3 mi., turns to the right onto an old WMNF service road (built for access to the former fire tower on Speckled Mtn.), and follows this road for the next 2.5 mi. The trail soon enters the Wilderness, and at 0.7 mi., Blueberry Ridge Trail leaves on the right (east) for the lower end of the Bickford Slides and Blueberry Mtn.; this trail rejoins Bickford Brook Trail 0.5 mi. below the summit of Speckled Mtn., affording the opportunity for a loop hike. At 1.1 mi., the upper end of Bickford Slides Loop enters on the right. Bickford Brook Trail soon swings away from the brook and rises to the crest of the main west ridge of Speckled Mtn., where Spruce Hill Trail enters left at 3.1 mi. Bickford Brook Trail then passes west and north of the summit of Ames Mtn. into the col between Ames Mtn. and Speckled Mtn., where Blueberry Ridge Trail rejoins right at 3.8 mi. Bickford Brook Trail then continues upward to the summit.

Bickford Brook Trail (AMC map 7: F12–F13)

Distances from ME 113 (600 ft.) to

- Blueberry Ridge Trail, lower jct. (970 ft.): 0.7 mi., 30 min.
- Spruce Hill Trail (2,400 ft.): 3.1 mi., 2 hr. 25 min.
- Blueberry Ridge Trail, upper jct. (2,585 ft.): 3.8 mi., 2 hr. 55 min.
- Speckled Mtn. summit (2,906 ft.): 4.3 mi., 3 hr. 20 min.

Cold Brook Trail (WMNF)

This trail ascends Speckled Mtn. and affords fine views from numerous open ledges in its upper part, which is in the Caribou–Speckled Mtn. Wilderness. Below its jct. with Evergreen Link Trail, Cold Brook Trail is mostly on private land. Its trailhead is reached from ME 5 in North Lovell, 2.0 mi. south of Keewaydin Lake, by following West Stoneham Rd. for 1.9 mi. and turning right onto Adams Rd. (Evergreen Valley Inn sign), just after the bridge over Great Brook, then continuing to gravel Enid Melrose Rd. on the right 2.2 mi. from ME 5. The WMNF sign is on the paved road, where parking is very limited. It may be possible to drive 0.5 mi. on the rough gravel road to a small parking area on the right. Cold Brook Trail can also be approached via Evergreen Link Trail, a shorter and more attractive alternative to the lower section of this trail.

Beyond the parking spot, where hikers should proceed on foot, the road becomes rougher, and 0.7 mi. from the paved road, Cold Brook Trail bears left past a gate. The next 1.0 mi. is on a road (muddy in places) that climbs, then levels off to reach a cabin (the Duncan McIntosh House). Continuing ahead on the road, take the left fork, then the right. The trail descends to Cold Brook and crosses it at 1.9 mi., then crosses a logging yard, bearing right on the far side. The trail climbs moderately, bears right at a fork, crosses a branch brook, and passes west of Sugarloaf Mtn. The trail climbs easily past the WMNF boundary to a jct. left at 2.7 mi. with Evergreen Link Trail from Evergreen Valley.

Beyond, Cold Brook Trail ascends moderately, then swings left and climbs rather steeply up the southeast side of Speckled Mountain's south ridge. The grade eases as the trail swings more to the north and emerges on semi-open ledges at 3.5 mi.; follow cairns and blazes carefully as the trail winds over ledges and through patches of scrub. The trail crosses open ledges with excellent views south, dips, and passes a small pond on the left, then climbs to another open ledge. Above this fine viewpoint, the trail swings left across a craggy shoulder and reenters the woods at 4.4 mi. The trail descends slightly, then ascends through dense conifers. At 4.9 mi., the trail emerges on semi-open ledges again and soon reaches a jct. with Red Rock Trail right and Bickford Brook Trail left, where Cold Brook Trail follows Bickford Brook Trail left 30 yd. to the summit of Speckled Mtn.

Cold Brook Trail (AMC map 7: F13–F14)

Distances from Adams Rd. (485 ft.) to

- Evergreen Link Trail (1,175 ft.): 2.7 mi., 1 hr. 45 min.
- Speckled Mtn. summit (2,906 ft.): 4.9 mi., 3 hr. 40 min.

Evergreen Link Trail (WMNF)

This trail provides the easiest access to Speckled Mtn. via the scenic ledges on the upper Cold Brook Trail. Evergreen Link Trail is lightly used but easily followed by experienced hikers. To reach the trailhead, leave ME 5 in North Lovell, 2.0 mi. south of Keewaydin Lake, and follow West Stoneham Rd. northwest for 1.9 mi. Just beyond the bridge over Great Brook, turn right onto Adams Rd. (sign for Evergreen Valley) and follow it for 1.5 mi., passing the trailhead for Cold Brook Trail. Then turn right onto Mountain Rd. (sign for Evergreen Valley Inn); Evergreen Link Trail begins as a gravel road diverging right 0.5 mi. from Adams Rd. Trailhead parking is available in a snowmobile trailer parking area (signs) located a short distance along a side road to the left off Mountain Rd., 0.3 mi. from Adams Rd. You may be able to park at the inn (with permission) at 0.4 mi.

From either parking area (distances are given from the snowmobile lot), follow paved Mountain Rd. uphill on foot; where it bears left, take the gravel road (soon blocked by a cable) straight ahead and continue climbing steeply. At 0.5 mi., turn left onto a grassy logging road (sign: LINK), then right onto Link Trail proper at 0.8 mi. (sign: Speckled Mtn. via Cold Brook Trail). The trail, blazed in yellow, leads off at a bearing of 70 degrees. It crosses a woods road at 1.1 mi. and reaches Cold Brook Trail at 1.3 mi.; turn left for the ledges and Speckled Mtn.

Evergreen Link Trail (AMC map 7: F13)
Distances from snowmobile parking area (550 ft.) to
• Cold Brook Trail (1,175 ft.): 1.3 mi., 1 hr.
• Speckled Mtn. summit (2,906 ft.) (via Cold Brook Trail): 3.5 mi., 2 hr. 55 min.

Blueberry Mtn. (1,781 ft.)

This mountain, a long outlying spur running southwest from Speckled Mtn., has mostly open ledges offering fine views.

Blueberry Ridge Trail (CTA)

This trail begins and ends on Bickford Brook Trail, leaving at a sign 0.7 mi. from its trailhead at Brickett Place on ME 113 and rejoining 0.5 mi. below the summit of Speckled Mtn. (The upper part of Blueberry Ridge Trail may also be reached from Stone House Rd. via Stone House or White Cairn trails.) The entire Blueberry Ridge Trail is in the Caribou–Speckled Mtn. Wilderness.

Leaving Bickford Brook Trail, Blueberry Ridge Trail descends toward Bickford Brook, and at 0.1 mi., a graded spur path descends 50 yd. to the right to a view of the Lower Slide from a high bank. In a short distance, the lower end of Bickford Slides Loop diverges left from the main trail, just before the latter crosses Bickford Brook. Care should be taken to avoid several unofficial side paths in this area.

Bickford Slides Loop. This short side path, 0.5 mi. long, leaves Blueberry Ridge Trail on the left just before it crosses Bickford Brook, 0.1 mi. from its lower jct. with Bickford Brook Trail. About 20 yd. from its beginning, Bickford Slides Loop crosses Bickford Brook (may be difficult at high water) and climbs northeast alongside it for 0.2 mi., with three minor stream crossings. The loop climbs steeply over a low rise and descends to a jct. at 0.3 mi., where a short side path descends steeply left to a pool at the base of the Middle Slide. (The former continuation of this branching path up the steep west wall of the ravine has been abandoned.) Bickford Slides Loop now climbs on a narrow, rough footway past the Middle and Upper slides, then drops sharply to cross the brook above the Upper Slide. Here, the loop turns sharply left and climbs easily to Bickford Brook Trail, 0.4 mi. above that trail's lower jct. with Blueberry Ridge Trail.

From the junctions with the spur path to the Lower Slide and Bickford Slides Loop, Blueberry Ridge Trail crosses Bickford Brook (may be difficult at high water) and ascends steeply southeast past a good western outlook to an open area just over the crest of Blueberry Ridge, where White Cairn Trail enters right at 0.7 mi. Overlook Loop (0.4 mi. long), with excellent views to the south, leaves Blueberry Ridge Trail shortly after this jct. and rejoins the trail shortly before Stone House Trail enters on the right at 0.9 mi., a few steps past the highpoint of the trail on Blueberry Mtn. From the jct. with Stone House Trail, marked by signs and a large cairn, Blueberry Ridge Trail bears left and descends to a spring (unreliable) a short distance from the trail on the left (north). Here, the trail turns sharply right and ascends over ledges with fine views, marked by cairns, and through patches of woods, passing over several humps. The best viewpoints are passed at 1.5 mi., 1.8 mi., and 2.5 mi. After crossing one more ledge area at 2.8 mi., the trail swings right into spruce woods, climbs slightly, then turns right and descends to meet Bickford Brook Trail in the shallow pass at the head of the Rattlesnake Brook ravine, 0.5 mi. below the summit of Speckled Mtn.

Blueberry Ridge Trail (AMC map 7: F13)

Distances from Bickford Brook Trail, lower jct. (970 ft.) to
- Stone House Trail (1,780 ft.): 0.9 mi., 55 min.
- Bickford Brook Trail, upper jct. (2,585 ft.): 3.1 mi., 2 hr. 30 min.

Stone House Trail (CTA)

This trail ascends to the scenic ledges of Blueberry Mtn. from Stone House Rd. (formerly Shell Pond Rd.). The upper part of this trail is in the Caribou–Speckled Mtn. Wilderness. To reach the trailhead, leave NH 113 on the east side 1.3 mi. north of AMC's Cold River Camp and follow Stone House Rd. 1.1 mi. to a padlocked steel gate, where a parking area is on the right. The lower part of this trail, including Rattlesnake Flume and Rattlesnake Pool, is on private land, and hikers are requested to stay on the marked trails.

The trail leaves the road (which here is also Shell Pond Trail) on the left (north), 0.5 mi. beyond the gate, east of an open shed. The trail follows a logging road and approaches Rattlesnake Brook. At 0.2 mi. from Stone House Rd., the trail merges with a private road (descending, bear right at arrow) and immediately reaches the jct. with a spur path that leads right 30 yd. to a bridge overlooking Rattlesnake Flume, a small, attractive gorge.

The main trail soon swings right (arrow), and at 0.5 mi., just after crossing a bridge over a small brook, another spur leads right 0.1 mi. to the exquisite Rattlesnake Pool, which lies at the foot of a small cascade. The main trail soon enters the WMNF, and at 1.2 mi., the trail swings left and begins to climb rather steeply straight up the slope, running generally northwest to the top of the ridge, where Stone House Trail ends at Blueberry Ridge Trail only a few steps from the top of Blueberry Mtn. The eastern jct. with Overlook Loop is 30 yd. to the left up a ledge. For Speckled Mtn., turn right onto Blueberry Ridge Trail.

Stone House Trail (AMC map 7: F13)

Distance from Stone House Rd./Shell Pond Trail (615 ft.) to
• Blueberry Ridge Trail (1,780 ft.): 1.5 mi., 1 hr. 20 min.

White Cairn Trail (CTA)

This trail, steep in places, provides access to the open ledges on Blueberry Mtn. and, with Stone House Trail, makes a rewarding half-day circuit. The upper part of this trail is in the Caribou–Speckled Mtn. Wilderness. The trail begins on Stone House Rd. (formerly Shell Pond Rd.), which leaves NH 113 on the east side 1.3 mi. north of AMC's Cold River Camp and runs 1.1 mi. to a padlocked steel gate, where a parking area is on the right.

The trail leaves Stone House Rd. (which here is also Shell Pond Trail) at a small clearing 0.3 mi. beyond the gate. The trail follows an old logging road north across a flat area, then ascends moderately, entering the WMNF at 0.3 mi. At 0.8 mi., the trail climbs steeply up a well-constructed rock staircase, then turns sharply left and begins to climb on ledges along the edge of the cliffs that are visible from the road. The grade moderates as the trail runs northwest along the crest of the cliffs, with excellent views to the south. At 1.2 mi., the trail passes a spring, then swings right (north) at easy grades; follow cairns carefully as the trail winds through ledgy areas. The trail passes another spring just before ending at the jct. with Blueberry Ridge Trail, 0.2 mi. west of the upper terminus of Stone House Trail. Overlook Loop, which leaves Blueberry Ridge Trail just east of its jct. with White Cairn Trail, provides a scenic alternate route, 0.4 mi. long, to Stone House Trail.

White Cairn Trail (AMC map 7: F13)
Distance from Stone House Rd. /Shell Pond Trail (600 ft.) to
• Blueberry Ridge Trail (1,750 ft.): 1.4 mi., 1 hr. 15 min.

East Royce Mtn. (3,114 ft.) and West Royce Mtn. (3,210 ft.)

These mountains rise to the west of Evans Notch and the Cold River. East Royce Mtn. is located in Batchelders Grant Township, Maine, and West Royce Mtn. is in Bean's Purchase, New Hampshire.

East Royce Trail (AMC)

This trail climbs steeply to East Royce Mtn. from a parking area on the west side of ME 113 just north of the height-of-land in Evans Notch and 3.4 mi. north of the WMNF Cold River Campground. Leaving the parking area, the trail immediately crosses Evans Brook and ascends, soon swinging left to cross a brook on ledges at the top of a fine cascade. The trail continues ascending, steeply at times, crossing several other brooks in the first 0.5 mi. At the final brook crossing at 1.0 mi., Royce Connector Trail leaves on the left, leading in 0.2 mi. to Royce Trail for West Royce. After ascending a steep and rough section with several scrambles, East Royce Trail emerges on open ledges at 1.1 mi., with a view east to Speckled Mtn. The trail soon reaches a subsidiary summit with views to the south, turns right, and climbs to a broad open ledge with wide-ranging views, where the plainly marked trail ends. Here, a faintly marked, beaten path turns right (north), dropping down the steep edge of the ledge, and runs generally northeast over several more ledges, passing over the true summit of East Royce in 250 yd. and continuing another 180 yd. to a large open ledge with a beautiful outlook to the north and west.

East Royce Trail (AMC map 7: F12–F13)

Distances from ME 113 (1,420 ft.) to

- Royce Connector Trail (2,610 ft.): 1.0 mi., 1 hr. 5 min.
- ledge at end of East Royce Trail (3,070 ft.): 1.3 mi., 1 hr. 30 min.
- East Royce Mtn. summit (3,114 ft.): 1.5 mi., 1 hr. 35 min.
- northern viewpoint (3,090 ft.): 1.7 mi., 1 hr. 40 min.

Laughing Lion Trail (CTA)

This trail (sign) begins on the west side of ME 113, just north of a roadside picnic area and about 2.4 mi. north of the road to the WMNF Cold River Campground. The trail descends to and crosses the Cold River (here, a rather small brook), then ascends west to a ridge crest and follows it north, alternating moderate and steep sections, passing two outlooks on the left looking down the valley. The trail then swings west and levels off just before it ends at Royce Trail.

Laughing Lion Trail (AMC map 7: F12–F13)

Distance from ME 113 (1,370 ft.) to

- Royce Trail (2,200 ft.): 1.1 mi., 1 hr. 5 min.

Royce Trail (AMC)

This trail runs to the summit of West Royce Mtn. from the west side of ME 113, at a point opposite the Brickett Place about 0.3 mi. north of the access road to the WMNF Cold River Campground. The first two crossings of the Cold River are difficult in high water.

Leaving ME 113, the trail follows a narrow road for about 0.3 mi., bears right where another road joins from the left, then crosses the Cold River, and bears off the road to the right onto a yellow-blazed footpath. The trail recrosses the river at 0.7 mi., crosses a tributary at 1.1 mi., and crosses the river again at 1.3 mi. Then, after crossing the south branch of the Mad River, the trail rises more steeply and soon passes Mad River Falls, where a side path leads left 25 yd. to a viewpoint. Royce Trail climbs moderately up the valley, passing several cascades as it comes back near the Mad River, then becomes rather rough and rises steeply under the imposing ledges for which East Royce is famous. At 2.7 mi., Laughing Lion Trail enters on the right, and at a height-of-land at 2.9 mi., after a very steep and rough ascent, Royce Connector Trail branches right, leading to East Royce Trail for East Royce.

Royce Connector Trail (AMC). This short trail, 0.2 mi. long (10 min., ascent 50 ft.), links Royce Trail and East Royce Trail, permitting the ascent of either summit of Royce from either trail, crossing some ledges with restricted views. Royce Connector Trail has recently been improved with many new bog bridges.

Royce Trail bears left at this jct. and descends somewhat, crossing a small brook, then climbs to the height-of-land between the Royces at 3.6 mi., where Burnt Mill Brook Trail to Wild River Rd. bears right. Here, Royce Trail turns abruptly left (west) and zigzags up the steep wall of the pass, turns sharply left (southeast), then swings more to the southwest. The trail climbs moderately up the ridge over ledges and through stunted spruce, passing two outlooks to the east, to the summit of West Royce, where Royce Trail meets Basin Rim Trail. The best views in the summit area are from ledges to the left of the trail shortly before the trail reaches the mostly wooded highpoint and trail jct.

Royce Trail (AMC map 7: F12)

Distances from ME 113 (600 ft.) to

- Mad River Falls (900 ft.): 1.6 mi., 55 min.
- Laughing Lion Trail (2,200 ft.): 2.7 mi., 2 hr. 10 min.
- Royce Connector Trail (2,650 ft.): 2.9 mi., 2 hr. 30 min.
- Burnt Mill Brook Trail (2,610 ft.): 3.6 mi., 2 hr. 55 min.
- West Royce Mtn. summit (3,210 ft.): 4.3 mi., 3 hr. 30 min.
- East Royce Mtn. summit (3,114 ft.) (via Royce Connector and East Royce Trail): 3.6 mi., 3 hr. 5 min.

Burnt Mill Brook Trail (WMNF)

This trail ascends from a parking area off Wild River Rd. (FR 12), 2.7 mi. south of ME 113, to Royce Trail in the col between East Royce Mtn. and West Royce Mtn. From Wild River Rd., Burnt Mill Brook Trail ascends south at easy grades on old logging roads, passing a fine cascade on the left at 0.6 mi. The trail crosses two small tributary brooks, and at 1.4 mi., the trail begins to climb more steeply. It crosses Burnt Mill Brook at 1.7 mi., and ascends to the col between the Royces, where Burnt Mill Brook Trail meets Royce Trail.

Burnt Mill Brook Trail (AMC map 7: F12)

Distance from Wild River Rd. (990 ft.) to
- Royce Trail (2,610 ft.): 2.0 mi., 1 hr. 50 min.

Durgin Mtn. (2,440 ft.), Butters Mtn. (2,246 ft.), and Red Rock Mtn. (2,141 ft.)

These little-visited mountains compose the long ridge extending east from Speckled Mtn. into the heart of the Caribou–Speckled Mtn. Wilderness.

Miles Notch Trail (WMNF)

This trail runs through Miles Notch, giving access to the east end of the ledgy ridge that culminates in Speckled Mtn. The trail is lightly used and sparsely marked and requires great care to follow in places. To reach its south terminus, near which Great Brook Trail also begins, leave ME 5 in North Lovell on West Stoneham Rd. and follow that road northwest for 1.8 mi., then turn right onto Hut Rd. just before the bridge over Great Brook. Continue 1.5 mi. to the trailhead, where parking is on the left (the trail sign was missing as of 2011). For the northern trailhead of Miles Notch Trail, see directions for the eastern trailhead of Haystack Notch Trail on p. 186. From the trail sign in the grassy clearing, 0.1 mi. south of the WMNF gate, Miles Notch Trail begins as a faint track leading ahead (south) across the clearing.

From the south terminus, the trail climbs north on an old logging road, soon bearing left (sign: no ATVs) as a snowmobile trail bears right and downhill. At 0.3 mi., Miles Notch Trail bears left off the old road (arrow), then climbs over a small ridge and descends steadily into the valley of Beaver Brook. At 1.2 mi., at the bottom of the descent, the trail turns left onto another old logging road and follows it for 0.2 mi., then bears right off the road and soon crosses a branch of Beaver Brook. The trail climbs steadily, crosses Beaver Brook at 2.3 mi., and continues to ascend the east side of the valley through an ice-damaged area where undergrowth may obscure the footway. The trail runs along the gully of a small brook, then turns left away from the brook and reaches Miles Notch at 2.9 mi.; ascending to the notch, the cliffs of Miles Knob can be seen up to the left. The trail now descends gradually along the east side of a ravine, and at 3.2 mi., Red Rock Trail leaves on the left for the summit of Speckled Mtn. Miles Notch Trail then descends moderately, crossing Miles Brook and its branches six times. The trail enters a recently logged area that was added to the WMNF in 2009, crosses Miles Brook again at 5.1 mi, then follows a logging road to its northern terminus in the large grassy clearing where the trail meets the eastern end of Haystack Notch Trail at a trail sign, 0.1 mi. south of the WMNF gate.

Miles Notch Trail (AMC map 7: E14–F14)

Distances from south terminus (490 ft.) to
- Red Rock Trail (1,740 ft.): 3.2 mi., 2 hr. 30 min.
- WMNF gate (900 ft.): 5.5 mi., 3 hr. 40 min.

Red Rock Trail (WMNF)

This trail ascends to Speckled Mtn. from Miles Notch Trail 0.3 mi. north of Miles Notch, 3.2 mi. from its southern trailhead and 2.2 mi. from its northern trailhead. Red Rock Trail traverses the long eastern ridge of the Speckled Mtn. range, affording fine views of the surrounding mountains. The trail is lightly used, sparsely marked, and in places requires great care to follow. This entire trail is in the Caribou–Speckled Mtn. Wilderness.

Red Rock Trail leaves Miles Notch Trail, descends to cross Miles Brook in its deep ravine, then angles up the north slope of Miles Knob and gains the ridge crest northwest of that summit. Red Rock Trail descends to a col, then ascends to the east knob of Red Rock Mtn., where the trail passes an obscure side path that leads left 50 yd. downhill to a spectacular ledge viewpoint (potentially dangerous if wet or icy) at the top of the sheer south cliff of Red Rock Mtn.; the side path leaves the trail 10 yd. east of a more obvious path that leads to a ledge with a limited view. The main trail continues to the true summit of Red Rock Mtn. at 1.2 mi., which provides a view to the north.

A short distance beyond the summit, at a ledge with a view southwest, the trail swings right and descends over more ledges to the Red Rock–Butters col, where the trail turns left (avoid a beaten path leading to the right through the col), then in 10 yd. turns right (arrow) and ascends to the east knob of Butters Mtn. The trail follows the ridge, with several ups and downs, passing near the summit of Butters Mtn. at 2.5 mi. and then continuing on to the next sag to the west.

At 3.4 mi., Great Brook Trail diverges left (east) and descends southeast to its trailhead, which is very close to the southern trailhead of Miles Notch Trail. Red Rock Trail swings southwest and climbs to the summit of Durgin Mtn. and ledges with some outlooks, the best located on an obscure side path just before the highpoint—at 4.4 mi. The trail then descends easily to a notch, climbs sharply, then ascends generally southwest to the jct. with Cold Brook Trail and Bickford Brook Trail 30 yd. east of the summit of Speckled Mtn. A spring near the trail is located about 0.1 mi. east of the summit.

Red Rock Trail (AMC map 7: F13–F14)

Distances from Miles Notch Trail (1,740 ft.) to

- Red Rock Mtn. summit (2,141 ft.): 1.2 mi., 50 min.
- Butters Mtn. summit (2,246 ft.): 2.5 mi., 1 hr. 40 min.
- Great Brook Trail (2,000 ft.): 3.4 mi., 2 hr. 15 min.
- Speckled Mtn. summit (2,906 ft.): 5.6 mi., 3 hr. 55 min.

Great Brook Trail (WMNF)

This trail ascends to Red Rock Trail east of Speckled Mtn. The upper part of the trail is in the Caribou–Speckled Mtn. Wilderness; this section is sparsely marked, requires care to follow, and has poor footing in places. To reach its trailhead, leave ME 5 in North Lovell on West Stoneham Rd. and follow that road northwest for 1.8 mi. Turn right just before the bridge over Great Brook onto Hut Rd., and continue 1.5 mi. to the trailhead, which is about 100 yd. past the southern trailhead for Miles Notch Trail.

Great Brook Trail continues up the gravel road and bears right onto FR 4 at 0.8 mi., just after crossing Great Brook on a gated bridge. (It may be possible to drive vehicles to this point, where parking is available near a small cascade.) At 1.8 mi., the trail turns left onto an older, grassy road and follows Great Brook, passing a stone wall, a cellar hole, and a gravesite marking the mid-1800s homestead of the Butters family on the left at 2.0 mi., just before crossing a tributary brook. The trail narrows to a footpath and, at 3.0 mi., crosses Great Brook, with some interesting cascades below and above the crossing. The trail enters the Wilderness, then bears left (arrow) and climbs, steeply at times, keeping well above the brook. At the head of the valley, the trail crosses the brook twice and soon reaches the ridge crest, where the trail joins Red Rock Trail in the col between Butters Mtn. and Durgin Mtn.

Great Brook Trail (AMC map 7: F13–F14)

Distances from trailhead (500 ft.) to

- Red Rock Trail (2,000 ft.): 3.7 mi., 2 hr. 35 min.
- Speckled Mtn. summit (2,906 ft.) (via Red Rock Trail): 5.9 mi., 4 hr. 15 min.

Albany Mtn. (1,930 ft.)

On the eastern edge of the WMNF is a cluster of low hills, with Albany Mtn. being the highest. Views from its open summit ledges are excellent in all directions.

Albany Mtn. Trail (WMNF)

This trail provides access to ledges and views on Albany Mtn. from trailheads to the north and the south. Because of extensive beaver flooding north of Albany Notch, a 1.1-mi. section of Albany Notch Trail has been abandoned, and the remainder of that trail—0.6 mi. on the north end, 2.5 mi. on the south end, and a 0.4- mi. connecting path—has been combined with Albany Mtn. Trail into a single through route with a spur leading to the summit of Albany Mtn. (Trail signs for Albany Notch Trail may still be present until new signage is in place.) The southern section, which is located partly on old, rather overgrown logging roads, is poorly marked and requires much care to follow. Most use of this trail is on the northern end, which provides the easiest access to Albany Mtn.

To reach the north trailhead, follow Flat Rd., which leads south from US 2 opposite the West Bethel Post Office and becomes FR 7 when it enters the WMNF at 4.5 mi. At 5.8 mi., turn right onto FR 18, following signs for Crocker Pond Campground. The trailhead parking lot and kiosk are on the right in another 0.6 mi. The trailhead can also be reached from ME 5, just south of Songo Pond, by turning west onto Patte Brook Rd., which becomes FR 8. At 2.8 mi., turn left onto FR 18 and follow it for 0.6 mi. to the trailhead and parking on the right.

The south trailhead is reached by leaving ME 5 at the west end of Keewaydin Lake, 2.4 mi. west of the East Stoneham Post Office and 0.7 mi. east of the Lovell–Stoneham town line, and following Birch Ave. north. Bear right onto Birch Ave. at 0.4 mi. from ME 5; the trail begins at a sign at 1.0 mi., where pavement ends and the road ahead becomes gravel, narrow, and rough. The beginning of the trail is in a residential area, and no designated public parking is available; it may be possible to drive 0.2 mi. along the gravel road to a small parking area on the left. Parking is extremely limited beyond this point.

Leaving the parking area for the north trailhead on FR 18, the trail follows an old logging road, with one relocation to the left, and a beaver swamp crossing at 0.4 mi. where the trail may be flooded at times. At 0.6 mi., the trail bears left toward Albany Mtn., where the abandoned section of Albany Notch Trail continues ahead. Albany Mtn. Trail now ascends moderately, turns right at the foot of a small mossy rock face at 1.2 mi., and climbs to a jct. at 1.5 mi.

Here, the spur to the summit of Albany Mtn. diverges left, soon crossing a ledge with a view of the Baldfaces and Mt. Washington over the treetops. Albany Mtn. Trail winds upward at easy grades across ledges and through stands of red pine and reaches the northeast outlook near the summit of Albany Mtn. at 0.4 mi. from the main trail, where regular marking ends. The best view is found by descending 50 yd. east to ledges at the edge of the ridge crest. The true summit, wooded and reached by an obscure path marked by cairns, is about 100 yd. south. The summit area has other viewpoints not reached by the trail that repay efforts devoted to cautious exploration by experienced hikers. The best viewpoint on the mountain is about 0.2 mi. southwest of the true summit; a sketchy and incomplete line of cairns leads to the summit, with some bushwhacking required.

At the jct. with the summit spur trail, Albany Mtn. Trail turns sharply right, rises slightly, then descends moderately for 0.4 mi. to the height-of-land in Albany Notch; partway down, the trail crosses a ledge with a view west. In the notch, the trail turns sharply left (south) and descends moderately, with a steeper pitch just below the pass, and crosses two small brooks (this section may be overgrown). The trail then runs at easy grades until it reaches a logging road used as a snowmobile trail at 2.6 mi., and turns left on this road. (If ascending from the south, turn sharply right off the road onto a narrow footpath leading into the woods just before the road dips to cross a small brook; the arrow marking this turn is easily missed.) This road is fairly easy to follow, but is wet in places and overgrown with tall grasses and other vegetation that permit little evidence of a footway.

At 3.0 mi., the trail bears right off the logging road onto an older road (arrow), which is also wet and overgrown. At 3.3 mi., the newer road rejoins from the left. The trail soon passes a WMNF gate and then merges with a gravel road that joins from the left. The trail passes a branch road on the right (in the reverse direction, bear right at this fork) and a camp on the left, crosses Meadow Brook on a culvert at 3.8 mi., and climbs gradually past several private homes and camps to the end of Birch Ave.

Albany Mtn. Trail (AMC map 7: F14–F15)
Distances from FR 18 (820 ft.) to
- spur trail to summit of Albany Mtn. (1,740 ft.): 1.5 mi., 1 hr. 10 min.
- Albany Notch (1,500 ft.): 1.9 mi., 1 hr. 25 min.
- trailhead on Birch Ave. (750 ft.): 4.4 mi., 2 hr. 40 min.

Distances to summit outlook on Albany Mtn. (1,925 ft.) via Albany Mtn. Trail and spur trail from
- north trailhead (820 ft.): 1.9 mi., 1 hr. 30 min.
- south trailhead (750 ft.): 3.3 mi., 2 hr. 15 min.

Albany Brook Trail (WMNF)

This short, easy trail follows the shore of Crocker Pond and then leads to attractive, secluded Round Pond. WMNF plans to upgrade the first 0.3 mi.

for wheelchair accessibility. The trail begins at the turnaround at the end of the main road at Crocker Pond Campground (do not enter the actual camping area), reached by following Flat Rd., which runs south from US 2 opposite the West Bethel Post Office and becomes FR 7 when it enters the WMNF at 4.5 mi. At 5.8 mi., turn right onto FR 18, and follow signs 1.5 mi. to the campground entrance. The trailhead can also be reached from ME 5 just south of Songo Pond by turning west onto Patte Brook Rd., which becomes FR 8. At 2.8 mi., turn left onto FR 18 and follow it 1.5 mi. to the campground entrance.

Leaving the turnaround, the trail descends to a small brook and follows the west shore of Crocker Pond for 0.2 mi., makes a short, moderate ascent, then joins and follows Albany Brook, descending gradually. At 0.9 mi., the trail goes straight through a logging-road intersection with a clearing visible on the right, and soon reaches the north end of Round Pond.

Albany Brook Trail (AMC map 7: F15)
Distance from Crocker Pond Campground (830 ft.) to
  • Round Pond (790 ft.): 1.0 mi., 35 min.

Shell Pond Trail (CTA)

This trail runs between Stone House Rd. (formerly Shell Pond Rd.), at the locked gate 1.1 mi. from NH 113, and Deer Hill Rd. (FR 9), 3.5 mi. from NH 113 (limited roadside parking nearby). Stone House Rd. leaves NH 113 on the east side 1.3 mi. north of AMC's Cold River Camp. Much of this trail is on private property, and hikers are requested to stay on the marked trails, especially in the vicinity of the Stone House. The trail itself does not come within sight of the pond, but Shell Pond Loop provides access to a viewpoint on the shore.

From the gate on Stone House Rd., continue east on the road on foot. Shell Pond Loop leaves right at 0.2 mi., and in another 80 yd., White Cairn Trail leaves left. At 0.4 mi., the road emerges at the side of a large field and soon turns right onto a grassy airplane landing strip. Here, at 0.5 mi., Stone House Trail diverges left, and the road ahead (not open to hikers) leads to a private house. Shell Pond Trail leaves right, paralleling the road for a short distance. The trail then swings left and heads east across a field with good views of the surrounding mountains, passing to the right of the Stone House at 0.6 mi.

The trail leaves the landing strip at 0.8 mi., entering a patch of woods to the left, and follows a grassy old road through an orchard. Use care, as the trail is not clearly marked in this area. The trail crosses Rattlesnake Brook on a bridge at 1.1 mi., passes through a wet area, and turns left off the road at 1.2 mi., where Shell Pond Loop bears right. From here, Shell Pond Trail ascends gradually to Deer Hill Rd.

Shell Pond Trail (AMC map 7: G13)

Distance from gate on Stone House Rd. (600 ft.) to
  • Deer Hill Rd. (755 ft.): 1.8 mi., 1 hr.

Shell Pond Loop (CTA)

This trail skirts the south side of Shell Pond, making possible a pleasant loop hike in combination with Shell Pond Trail. Shell Pond Loop is located almost entirely on private property and also serves as an ATV trail; hikers are requested to stay on the marked trail, which leaves the south side of Shell Pond Trail 0.2 mi. east of the gate on Stone House Rd. (formerly Shell Pond Rd.) and leads through woods near the edge of a field, making several turns marked by yellow blazes.

At 0.2 mi., the trail turns right onto a grassy road, crosses a bridge over Shell Pond Brook, and soon swings left (east) on a well-worn woods road. It traverses the slope well above the south shore of Shell Pond, with several minor ups and downs. At 1.3 mi., the trail turns left off the road and descends, then meanders through the woods behind the east shore of the pond, crossing several small brooks. At 1.7 mi., a spur path leads 25 yd. left to a clearing and a bench with a fine view across the pond to the Baldfaces and Mt. Meader. The main trail bears right here and continues at easy grades to Shell Pond Trail, 0.6 mi. west of the latter's eastern trailhead on Deer Hill Rd. and 1.2 mi. from the gate on Stone House Rd.

Shell Pond Loop (AMC map 5: F13–G13)

Distance from western jct. with Shell Pond Trail (600 ft.) to
  • eastern jct. with Shell Pond Trail (610 ft.): 1.9 mi , 200 ft., 1 hr. 5 min.

Harndon Hill (1,395 ft.), Lord Hill (1,257 ft.), and Pine Hill (1,250 ft.)

This compact group of hills just west of Horseshoe Pond in Stoneham, Stow, and Lovell can be climbed via three trails.

Horseshoe Pond Trail (CTA)

This yellow-blazed trail starts from Deer Hill Rd. (FR 9), 4.7 mi. from NH 113 at a small pull-off at a curve in the road, and ends on Conant Trail, 0.2 mi. north of the ledges near the summit of Lord Hill. The former Horseshoe Pond Loop is now closed to public use, so there is no public access to the shore of this pond.

From Deer Hill Rd., the trail descends moderately, then turns right onto a gravel logging road. The trail follows this road, keeping straight at a jct. in 100 yd. At 0.3 mi., just before the gravel road ends, the trail turns right onto a grassy road that leads up into a brushy area, and ascends through a regenerating area. The trail continues ascending through woods to Conant Trail.

Horseshoe Pond Trail (AMC map 7: G13)
Distance from Deer Hill Rd. (700 ft.) to
• Conant Trail (1,115 ft.): 1.1 mi., 50 min.

Conant Trail (CTA)

This loop path to Pine Hill and Lord Hill is an interesting and fairly easy walk with several good outlooks. (*Note:* Because of significant beaver flooding on the south loop, it is currently recommended that hikers approach Lord and Pine hills via the north loop of Conant Trail, with the option for a return loop on Mine Loop. An alternate approach can be made via Horseshoe Pond Trail. For updates on this situation, visit the CTA website, chathamtrails.org.) Much of Conant Trail, especially the south loop, is on private land. The trail is frequently referred to (and may be signed as) Pine-Lord-Harndon Trail, though it does not go particularly close to the summit of Harndon Hill; this trail should not be confused with Conant Path, a short trail (not open to the public) near AMC's Cold River Camp.

Conant Trail is reached by following Deer Hill Rd. (FR 9) and making a right turn onto FR 9A, 1.5 mi. from NH 113; the best parking is at a four-way jct. a short distance from Deer Hill Rd., where a sign for North Barbour Rd. is located. There may not be a trail sign here.

Continue on foot along the road that leads east (left at the four-way jct.), soon descending to the dike across swampy Colton Brook. Beyond the dike, the yellow-blazed trail continues on a gravel road to the loop jct. at 0.4 mi., where the path divides. From here, the path is described in a counterclockwise direction. The south branch, also a snowmobile route, turns right and follows a logging road (Hemp Hill Rd.). At 0.7 mi., Conant Trail reaches a road section that has been flooded by beavers, where hikers must wade across or make a long and circuitous bushwhack to the left. Beyond, the road climbs to a level spot at 1.0 mi., then turns left onto a logging road, then left again in a few steps. The trail swings right and then left again at 1.2 mi. and ascends Pine Hill, rather steeply at times, passing a ledge with a fine view west at 1.4 mi. Here, the trail turns right and climbs to the west end of the summit ridge and continues to the most easterly knob, which has a good view north, at 2.0 mi.

Beyond, the trail swings left off the ledges and zigzags steeply down through hemlock forest. The trail crosses Bradley Brook at 2.3 mi., and in another 120 yd., crosses a logging road that can be followed 0.2 mi. left to Mine Loop, 0.4 mi. below the mine on Lord Hill. Conant Trail then climbs moderately to an outlook over Horseshoe Pond. Here, the trail turns left and climbs ledges to a jct. near the summit of Lord Hill at 3.0 mi., where Mine Loop leaves on the left.

Mine Loop. This path is 1.0 mi. long, 0.1 mi. shorter than the section of Conant Trail that Mine Loop bypasses. Except for the one critical turn mentioned later, it is fairly easy to follow. From the jct. with Conant Trail near the summit of Lord Hill, the path climbs briefly to the ledge at the top of an old mica mine, swings left and then quickly right onto a woods road, descends for 40 yd., and at 0.1 mi. turns left where a spur path leads right 30 yd. to the mine. The trail soon swings right, and at 0.3 mi., turns sharply left on a clear logging road. At 0.5 mi., the trail reaches a fork and turns sharply right back onto a less-used branch road (sign)—a turn that is easily missed. (The main road, continuing straight at this fork, crosses

Conant Trail between Pine Hill and Lord Hill in 0.2 mi. and continues south toward Kezar Lake.) Mine Loop descends to a flat area and climbs easily over a shoulder. At a clearing, the trail leaves the road on the right and descends 50 yd. to rejoin Conant Trail 1.1 mi. from its trailhead.

From Lord Hill, Conant Trail descends, with one tricky drop over a ledge, to the jct. with Horseshoe Pond Trail on the right at 3.2 mi. Here, Conant Trail bears left, then soon turns left again through a gap in a stone wall and runs at a fairly level grade, with minor ups and downs, along the south side of Harndon Hill. The trail passes a cellar hole, and Mine Loop rejoins on the left at 4.1 mi. At 4.5 mi., the trail passes a gate, becomes wider (in the reverse direction, avoid logging roads branching to the right), passes a cemetery on the right, reaches the loop jct., and continues straight ahead across the dike to the trailhead.

Conant Trail (AMC map 7: G13)

Distances from trailhead off Deer Hill Rd. (550 ft.) for

- complete loop over Pine Hill and Lord Hill on Conant Trail: 5.2 mi., 3 hr. 10 min.
- loop over Lord Hill via north branch of Conant Trail and Mine Loop: 4.3 mi., 2 hr. 35 min.

Little Deer Hill (1,090 ft.) and Deer Hill (1,367 ft.)

Rising southwest of Shell Pond, these low hills are crisscrossed by six interconnected trails that provide several miles of pleasant hiking in close proximity to AMC's Cold River Camp.

Deer Hills Trail (CTA)

This trail ascends Little Deer Hill and Deer Hill, providing a relatively easy trip that offers interesting views. The trail runs from a jct. by the Cold River, near AMC's Cold River Camp, to Deer Hill Rd. (FR 9), 1.4 mi. from NH 113, where limited roadside parking is available.

Access to the north end of the trail is from Baldface Circle Trail trailhead parking area on NH 113 (0.1 mi. north of the entrance to AMC's Cold River Camp) via the yellow-blazed Deer Hill Connector. This path leaves the east side of the lot, runs level for 150 yd., then turns left down a short pitch and descends gradually on the south side of Charles Brook, passing an unmarked private path on the right at 0.3 mi. and reaching a dam on the Cold River at 0.4 mi. Here, a trail from AMC's camp enters on the right (this trail is not open to the public). Distances given below include those traveled on the Deer Hill Connector.

Deer Hills Trail crosses Cold River on the dam abutments (may be difficult in high water). (In the reverse direction, after crossing the dam, turn right at a sign for "Baldface Parking Lot.") The trail soon passes the jct. on the left with Leach Link Trail, crosses the state line into Maine, and quickly passes the jct. on the right with Deer Hills Bypass. Deer Hills Trail continues straight ahead and climbs moderately past an outlook west, then bears left onto ledges and reaches the open summit of Little Deer Hill at 1.3 mi. Here, Frost Trail enters on the right, having ascended from Deer Hills Bypass.

The main trail descends into a sag, then climbs to a point near the summit of Deer Hill at 2.0 mi. Here, the trail turns right, descends 40 yd., and turns right again to a fine outlook 20 yd. to the left. The trail then descends the south ridge, passing another outlook, and turns left at 2.5 mi., where Deer Hills Bypass leaves on the right. Soon Deer Hills Trail turns left again, then turns right onto an old logging road at 2.7 mi. Here, a spur path (sign) follows the logging road left for 20 yd., then turns right and descends in 0.2 mi. and 150 ft. to Deer Hill Spring, a shallow pool with air bubbles rising through a small area of light-colored sand. The main trail descends from the jct. to Deer Hill Rd.

Deer Hills Trail (AMC map 7: G12–G13)

Distances from ME 113 at Baldface Circle Trail parking area (500 ft.) via Deer Hill Connector to

- Little Deer Hill summit (1,090 ft.): 1.3 mi., 1 hr.
- Deer Hill summit (1,367 ft.): 2.0 mi., 1 hr. 35 min.
- Deer Hills Bypass, eastern jct. (1,025 ft.): 2.5 mi., 1 hr. 50 min.
- Deer Hill Rd. (530 ft.): 3.3 mi., 2 hr. 10 min.

Deer Hills Bypass (CTA)

This trail skirts the south slopes of the Deer Hills, making possible various loop hikes over the summits. It leaves Deer Hills Trail just east of Cold River Dam and follows a level grassy road south along the river. At 0.4 mi., the trail turns left off the road and soon ascends a steep ledge with a view west. The trail swings left, and at 0.6 mi., Ledges Trail leaves left, and Deer Hills Bypass climbs steadily alongside a stone wall. At 0.8 mi., Frost Trail leaves left, climbing 0.15 mi. and 150 ft. to the summit of Little Deer Hill. Deer Hills Bypass descends into a shallow ravine, crossing two small brooks, and ascends again. The trail soon turns left onto a woods road, follows it for 0.1 mi., then turns left off the road (both turns are marked with signs and arrows). The trail then ascends easily to rejoin Deer Hills Trail on the south ridge of Deer Hill, 0.5 mi. below the summit.

Deer Hills Bypass (AMC map 7: G13)

Distance from western jct. with Deer Hills Trail (460 ft.) to
- eastern jct. with Deer Hills Trail (1,025 ft.): 1.4 mi., 1 hr.

Ledges Trail (CTA)

This trail passes interesting ledges and a cave but is very steep and rough, dangerous in wet or icy conditions, lightly used, and not recommended for descent. The trail diverges left from Deer Hills Bypass, 0.6 mi. from the Cold River Dam, and climbs steeply with several outlooks. At 0.2 mi., Ledges Trail divides; the left branch, signed "Ledges Direct," ascends through a small cave, and the slightly longer right branch, signed "By-Pass," loops out through the woods, then swings left across an excellent outlook ledge and rejoins the left branch in about 140 yd. About 40 yd. above the point where these branches rejoin, Ledges Trail meets Frost Trail, a connecting path from Deer Hills Bypass. The summit of Little Deer Hill is 70 yd. left on Frost Trail.

Ledges Trail (AMC map 7: G12)

Distance from Deer Hills Bypass (730 ft.) to
- Little Deer Hill summit (1,090 ft.): 0.3 mi., 20 min.

Leach Link Trail (CTA)

This trail gives access to Little Deer Hill and Deer Hill from Stone House Rd. (formerly Shell Pond Rd.), which leaves NH 113 on the east side 1.3 mi. north of AMC's Cold River Camp. The trail starts at a gated road on the right side of Stone House Rd. 0.3 mi. from NH 113. The northern part of the trail uses the former Shell Pond Brook Trail.

Beyond the gate, the trail follows a grassy road across a snowmobile bridge over Shell Pond Brook. At 0.2 mi., the trail turns right off the road (sign), then in another 50 yd. bears left and runs through hemlock woods along a bank high above the brook. The trail then descends, and at 0.5 mi., turns left at a point where the former route of the trail came across the brook from the right. The trail continues south along the Cold River at easy grades and ends at Deer Hills Trail a few steps east of Cold River Dam. To ascend the Deer Hills, turn left onto Deer Hills Trail.

Leach Link Trail (AMC map 7: G12)

Distance from Stone House Rd. (540 ft.) to
• Deer Hills Trail (450 ft.): 1.2 mi., 35 min.

SUGGESTED HIKES

Easy Hikes

Ring Hill [lp: 1.1 mi., 40 min.]. A woodland loop hike through Maggie's Park to ledges and views of Mt. Abraham. Several other options are possible on six color-coded trails.

The Roost [rt: 1.2 mi., 55 min.]. A short climb up Roost Trail from its northern trailhead to ledges offers views of Evans Notch and the Wild River valley.

Crocker Hill [rt: 1.8 mi., 1 hr. 20 min.]. Follow the Old Crocker Hill carriage road and then a footpath to fine views of the countryside in the central Oxford Hills.

Round Pond [rt: 2.0 mi., 1 hr. 10 min.]. An easy ramble to a pair of ponds along Albany Brook Trail.

Bucks Ledge [lp: 2.8 mi., 1 hr. 30 min.]. Enjoy great views overlooking pretty North Pond in Greenwood. A short side hike to Lapham Ledge adds more nice views to this easy hike.

Deer Hills These low hills provide good views of the Cold River valley and the Baldfaces. Options include a shorter out-and-back trip to **Little Deer Hill [rt: 2.6 mi., 1 hr. 40 min.]** or a longer loop over **Little Deer and Deer hills [lp: 4.3 mi., 2 hr. 45 min.]**. Use Deer Hill Connector, Deer Hills Trail, and Deer Hills Bypass.

Sabattus Mtn. [lp: 1.6 mi., 2 hr. 10 min.]. A fun loop hike to the summit of Sabattus Mtn. and its impressive cliffs with views ranging from Pleasant Mtn. to the Presidential Range.

Moderate Hikes

Albany Mtn. [rt: 3.8 mi., 2 hr. 25 min.]. A small mountain with good views over western Maine, reached by the north end of Albany Mtn. Trail.

Blueberry Mtn. [lp: 4.1 mi., 2 hr. 40 min.]. Many ledges have views on this loop combining Shell Pond and White Cairn trails, Overlook Loop, and Stone House Trail.

Bald Mtn. and Speckled Mtn. [rt: 4.6 mi., 4 hr. 20 min.]. A fine hike past Concord Pond to the cliffs of Bald Mtn. and on to the open ledges atop Speckled Mtn. and extensive views.

Mt. Zircon [rt: 5.6 mi., 4 hr. 20 min.]. Hike past the springhouse of the old Zircon Water Bottling Company on the way to a downed fire tower on the open summit of Mt. Zircon and exceptional views to the south and east.

Caribou Mtn. [lp: 6.9 mi., 4 hr. 25 min.]. A loop trip on Caribou and Mud Brook trails rewards with extensive views from the bare summit ledges of Caribou Mtn.

East Royce Mtn. and West Royce Mtn. [ow: 5.1 mi., 4 hr. 45 min.]. Hike Royce Trail past Mad River Falls to the summit of West Royce Mtn. Then head back east and climb East Royce Mtn. before dropping steeply down into scenic Evans Notch on East Royce Trail. Requires spotting a car at both trailheads.

Strenuous Hikes

Speckled Mtn. Loop [lp: 8.6 mi., 5 hr. 35 min.]. A scenic circuit along Blueberry Ridge and Bickford Brook trails, including the open summits of Blueberry and Speckled mountains.

Red Rock Mtn. Loop [lp: 10.3 mi., 6 hr. 35 min.]. An interesting valley and ridge loop for experienced hikers through a wild, less-visited area, with views from Red Rock Mtn., using Miles Notch, Red Rock, and Great Brook trails. The trails require care to follow in places.

SECTION FIVE
KENNEBEC AND MOOSE RIVER VALLEYS

Mt. Pisgah 214

Monument Hill 215

Kennebec Highlands 216

Round Top Mtn. 216

Sanders Hill 217

Mt. Phillip 218

The Mountain 219

French Mtn. 220

Moxie Bald Mtn. 220

Pleasant Pond Mtn. 222

Mosquito Mtn. 223

Kelly Mtn. 224

Coburn Mtn. 225

Sally Mtn. 226

Burnt Jacket Mtn. 227

Boundary Bald Mtn. 228

Suggested Hikes 229

The Kennebec and Moose River Valleys section includes all of Kennebec County and most of Somerset County and encompasses an area stretching roughly from the capital city of Augusta to the headwaters of the St. John River east of the Canadian border. The region is bordered by the coastal lowlands in the south and by Aroostook County and American Realty Rd. in the north. Along the eastern boundary are the interior hills and mountains, Moosehead Lake, and the forestlands between the Allagash and St. John River watersheds. To the west are the high peaks along the Québec frontier. From its source at Moosehead Lake, the Kennebec River flows south through the center of the region for 170 mi., emptying into the Atlantic Ocean east of Popham Beach. The Moose River originates near the Canadian border and flows generally east to its end at Moosehead Lake at Rockwood.

US 201 bisects the section north to south from Canada to Gardiner and is the primary travel route through the Kennebec Valley. ME 15 heads east from Jackman and follows the Moose River to Moosehead Lake.

This section describes 17 trails and 15 mountains. In the south are numerous low hills and mountains under 1,000 ft. in elevation, from Mt. Pisgah and Monument Hill adjacent to Androscoggin Lake to the Kennebec Highlands, where a small cluster of peaks dot the area around the Belgrade Lakes. Round Top Mtn. is the highest of these at 1,133 ft. The mountains reach over 2,000 ft. on both sides of the Kennebec River between Bingham and The Forks. Here, the AT crosses the Kennebec at Caratunk and leads to the craggy summits of Moxie Bald and Pleasant Pond mountains. Little-visited Mosquito Mtn., rising above the northwest end of Moxie Pond, is nearby. Northwest of the Kennebec River are the jumbled high peaks of the remote border region that reach to just under 4,000 ft. in elevation, many requiring travel over sometimes rough roads to reach the trailheads. Here is found Coburn Mtn., the highest in the section at 3,718 ft., and Boundary Bald Mtn. Nearby Sally and Burnt Jacket mountains, west of Jackman, rise to over 2,200 ft.

The AT traverses this section, extending 42 mi. from Flagstaff Lake at the foot of the Bigelows north to Bald Mtn. Pond east of Moxie Bald Mtn.

Camping

Thirteen lean-tos and campsites along the AT provide for trailside camping. No state parks or public reserved lands are available for either remote or roadside camping. A number of privately operated campgrounds, some operated by commercial whitewater rafting companies, offer a variety of camping and lodging choices and amenities.

Mt. Pisgah (809 ft.)

Located in the 700-acre Mt. Pisgah Conservation Area in Winthrop, this mountain features a 60-ft. fire tower on its summit, where fine views are possible to the west across Androscoggin Lake as far as the Presidential Range. The area is managed jointly by the Town of Winthrop and KLT.

From the jct. of US 202 and ME 132 in Monmouth, proceed east on US 202 for 0.5 mi. Turn left (north) onto North Main St. Drive 0.8 mi. to the crossroads in North Monmouth. Turn right onto Wilson Pond Rd. and go 0.2 mi. Turn left onto Mt. Pisgah Rd. and drive 1.6 mi. to the trailhead on the right (sign).

Tower Trail (KLT)

From the parking lot, take the old tower road about 200 ft. to a metal gate and a register box on the left. Leave the road and proceed easily on a well-defined trail marked with blue blazes. Cross a wet area on stepping-stones and bog bridges. Beyond, the trail climbs gradually, crossing several stone walls. At a jct., the main trail continues straight ahead. A short distance beyond, the trail climbs a small ledge, ascends a series of stone steps, and climbs to a large ledge. Reach the former MFS fire tower on the summit and the jct. with the old tower road at 1.0 mi.

For a loop option on the descent, follow the old tower road 1.0 mi. back to the trailhead.

Tower Trail (USGS Wayne quad, DeLorme map 12)
Distance from Mt. Pisgah Rd. (450 ft.) to
  • Mt. Pisgah summit (809 ft.): 1.0 mi., 40 min.

Monument Hill (660 ft.)

Monument Hill in Leeds is just west of Androscoggin Lake and offers pleasant views of the surrounding farms, forests, and lakes. A granite obelisk on the summit is dedicated to Leeds soldiers and sailors of the Civil War. The monument is inscribed with the words "Peace was sure 1865."

To reach the trail from US 202 between Lewiston and Augusta, take ME 106 north for 6.2 mi. to Leeds. Take Church Hill Rd. left (west) for 0.9 mi. to North Rd. on the right. Take this for 0.9 mi. to the trailhead on the right (sign) and roadside parking.

Occasional wooden signs with black arrows mark the well-worn trail route. Follow a woods road easily uphill to an old log yard in a level area. Here, the trail forks. The left fork and right fork rise gently east and southeast, respectively, to join at the summit, where there is a viewpoint to the east just beyond the monument.

Monument Hill (USGS Turner Center quad, DeLorme map 12)

Distance from North Rd. (450 ft.) to
  • Monument Hill summit (660 ft.) via left fork or right fork: 0.5 mi., 20 min.

Kennebec Highlands

The Kennebec Highlands encompasses the highest peaks in northwest Kennebec County and southeastern Franklin County. At 6,000 acres in size, this regionally significant block of conservation land is the result of a long-term partnership between MBPL and BRCA, which also manages 1,000 acres of preserved land in close proximity to the Kennebec Highlands.

Round Top Mtn. (1,133 ft.)

This mountain in Rome is the highest point in the Kennebec Highlands and offers spectacular views over Long and Great ponds, the village of Belgrade Lakes, and the surrounding hills. From the jct. of ME 27 and Watson Pond Rd., 4.4 mi. north of the village of Belgrade Lakes, turn left on Watson Pond Rd. and drive south 3.7 mi. Turn right at the MBPL sign and then immediately right again into the parking area.

Round Top Trail (BRCA)

This blue-blazed trail leaves the parking area just left of the kiosk. At 0.1 mi., the trail crosses a large slab of granite originally quarried for an old foundation. After a gradual rise, the trail winds through the woods, passing an opening in the trees with a view of Round Top Mtn. ahead. Beyond, the trail descends to a jct. with Kennebec Highlands Trail at 1.0 mi. Beyond the jct., Round Top Trail climbs steadily northward. Nearing the summit, limited views open up to the east and south. At 1.7 mi., a spur trail leads left (north) 0.3 mi. to a highpoint on Round Top Mtn. and several outlooks with spectacular views of the surrounding terrain of the Kennebec Highlands.

Continuing on, Round Top Trail passes a viewpoint before descending to reach a second viewpoint at some large rock slabs. Beyond, the trail descends steeply, between and over large rocks, to join Kennebec Highlands Trail at 2.1 mi. Turn right (south) onto this broad trail. At 2.9 mi., bear right at a three-way jct., marked by snowmobile trail signs. Just beyond (before a Y intersection of snowmobile trails), reach a jct. with Round Top Trail marked by a cairn. Turn left and follow the trail back to the parking area, which is reached at 3.9 mi.

Round Top Trail (USGS Belgrade Lakes quad, DeLorme map 20)
Distances from Watson Pond Rd. (550 ft.) to
- Round Top Mtn. spur trail: 1.7 mi., 1 hr. 5 min.
- Round Top Mtn. highpoint (1,100 ft.): 2.0 mi., 1 hr. 15 min.
- Complete loop (via highpoint): 4.5 mi., 2 hr. 30 min.

Sanders Hill (854 ft.)

This loop hike in Rome winds through the scenic northern part of the Kennebec Highlands just east of Watson Pond. From the jct. of ME 27 and Watson Pond Rd., 4.4 mi. north of the village of Belgrade Lakes, turn left onto Watson Pond Rd. and drive south 1.2 mi. to a parking area on the right. Sanders Hill Trail is described counterclockwise.

Sanders Hill Trail (BRCA)

Take the blue-blazed trail to the right of the kiosk and walk easily west. At 0.2 mi. there are nice views from the south end of Watson Pond, from atop a large boulder. The trail crosses the inlet for Watson Pond, follows an old logging road for a brief time, then bears left off the road. Ahead, the trail climbs moderately to cross a wet section. After a right turn, the trail reaches a ridgeline and crosses a rocky area and views east to Watson Pond, Mt. Phillip, and French Mtn. Ahead, the trail cuts between and climbs over several large granite slabs at 0.9 mi. and continues on to a semi-open area at 1.1 mi. with limited views to the east and south through the trees.

Just ahead, the trail crosses over the true summit before descending to join Kennebec Highlands Trail at 1.3 mi. Turn left (south) and follow this broad trail. At 1.9 mi., just before a wooden bridge over Beaver Brook, turn left (sign) into the woods and follow the brook. Just ahead, turn left again to reach Snapper Rock, a large glacial erratic. After crossing a woods road and passing several large boulders, the trail turns sharply left to reach an old logging road. Follow this back to the trailhead, which is reached at 2.9 mi.

Sanders Hill Trail (USGS Belgrade Lakes quad, DeLorme map 20)

Distances from Watson Pond Rd. (450 ft.) to

- Sanders Hill summit (854 ft.): 1.1 mi., 45 min.
- Complete loop: 2.9 mi., 1 hr. 50 min.

Mt. Phillip (755 ft.)

This summit overlooking Great Pond in Rome provides good views of the Kennebec Highlands to the west. From the jct. of ME 27 and ME 225 at Rome Corner, travel east on ME 225 for 1.5 mi. to a parking lot on the north side of the road, directly across from Starbird Ln.

Mt. Phillip Trail (BRCA)

Marked with blue blazes, this trail leaves from the northeast corner of the parking lot and heads east. At 0.1 mi., reach a jct. Bear right to follow the trail counterclockwise. The trail passes through a stand of mature pines before climbing at a moderate grade up the eastern slope of the mountain. The trail continues to a ledge at 0.6 mi. and then proceeds west across the ledge to a semi-open clearing at the summit at about 0.7 mi. Beyond, the loop continues, descending to the west, then turning in a southerly direction before dropping down into a stand of mature hemlock. Follow the trail back to the jct. and turn left for the parking lot.

Mt. Phillip Trail (USGS Belgrade Lakes quad, DeLorme map 20)

Distances from ME 225 (350 ft.) to

- Mt. Phillip summit (755 ft.): 0.7 mi., 35 min.
- complete loop: 1.4 mi., 1 hr. 5 min.

The Mountain (665 ft.)

The Mountain in Rome is situated on 207 acres owned and managed by BRCA and Belgrade Lakes Association. The Mountain rises between Long and Great ponds, offering fine views of the Kennebec Highlands and the surrounding lakes and woods. Drive about 1 mi. north of Belgrade Lakes village on ME 27. Turn right (east) onto Mountain Drive and proceed 0.3 mi. to a parking area on the left (north) side of the road.

The Mountain Trail (BRCA)

The Mountain Trail leads north from the parking area on an old logging road. At 0.4 mi., Great Pond Loop (marked by a green arrow) diverges to the right (east). Just ahead, at 0.5 mi., Long Pond Loop (white arrow) leaves the main trail on the left (west). The Mountain Trail continues upward straight ahead. Shortly before its end, Great Pond Loop rejoins The Mountain Trail from the right. Just ahead, Long Pond Loop rejoins The Mountain Trail from the left. All trails end here because private property lies ahead.

Great Pond Loop (BRCA)

Great Pond Loop (marked by green arrows) enters the woods on the right (east) at a point on The Mountain Trail 0.4 mi. from the parking area. Great Pond Loop winds through a boulder field before climbing to a small open area and the highest point on The Mountain. Beyond the summit, the loop continues north and west, descending to rejoin The Mountain Trail.

Long Pond Loop (BRCA)

Long Pond Loop leaves The Mountain Trail on the left (west) at a point 0.5 mi. from the parking area. The loop descends moderately, crossing over several slabs and boulders, before passing over a cliff with steep dropoffs and nice views of Long Pond and the Kennebec Highlands. Long Pond Loop continues northeast, rising to meet The Mountain Trail at its end.

The Mountain (USGS Belgrade lakes quad, DeLorme map 20)

Distances from Mountain Drive parking area (350 ft.) to
- The Mountain summit (665 ft.) via The Mountain Trail: 0.8 mi., 35 min.
- The Mountain summit (665 ft.) via The Mountain Trail and Great Pond Loop: 0.8 mi., 35 min.
- The Mountain summit (665 ft.) via The Mountain Trail and Long Pond Loop: 0.9 mi., 40 min.

French Mtn. (716 ft.)

From this summit in Rome, there are good views of the Belgrade Lakes area, including Whittier Pond to the east, Mt. Phillip to the northeast, and Long Pond to the southeast. From the jct. of ME 27 and Watson Pond Rd., proceed south on Watson Pond Rd. for 0.7 mi. to a paved parking apron on the east side of the road.

French Mtn. Trail (BRCA)

The trail immediately heads east, quickly passing the other end of its loop on the right. Continuing straight ahead, the trail swings south, climbing the northwest ridge of the mountain to reach a rocky precipice with nice views of Long Pond. Beyond the summit, the trail continues in the open to its end at the steep cliffs overlooking the north end of Long Pond, where there are views of Great Pond, The Mountain, and the village of Belgrade Lakes. Beyond, the trail descends and then swings north, angling down the west face of the mountain to close the loop not far from the parking area.

French Mtn. Trail (USGS Belgrade Lakes quad, DeLorme map 20)

Distances from Watson Pond Rd. (550 ft.) to
- French Mtn. summit (716 ft.) via right or left fork: 0.4 mi., 15 min.
- Complete loop: 0.8 mi., 25 min.

Moxie Bald Mtn. (2,630 ft.)

This mountain in Bald Mtn. Township features a long ridge extending north–south for about 4 mi. Its summit is alpine in nature, owing to its extensive area of open ledges. The views from the summit are excellent.

Katahdin is to the northeast; Bigelow, Sugarloaf, and Abraham are to the west; and Coburn and Boundary Bald are to the north.

The approach is via the AT, which leaves from a point on Moxie Pond Rd. just south of Joe's Hole, the southernmost point on Moxie Pond. The 0.7-mi. side trail to the north peak of Moxie, easy to reach from the AT, is worth exploring.

The trailhead can be reached from US 201 in The Forks in the north or from US 201 in Bingham in the south. From US 201 in The Forks just before the highway crosses the Kennebec River, turn right on Lake Moxie Rd. Follow this paved road for 5.3 mi. to Lake Moxie Station and a T intersection. Turn right onto Troutdale Rd. and follow the old railroad bed along Moxie Pond. (*Note:* This road can be rough and narrow in places, and many camps are located on this shore of the lake, so drive carefully.) At 12.6 mi., reach a small parking area on the right side of the road. The sign for the AT and Moxie Bald is on the left. From US 201 in Bingham, turn right (east) on ME 16 and drive 5.3 mi. Turn left (north) on Town Line Rd. Begin new mileage. At 0.7 mi., bear right at a fork. Turn right at a T intersection at 2.6 mi. At 4.8 mi., bear right at a fork. Reach the AT trailhead and parking (described above) at 11.2 mi. from ME 16.

Via Appalachian Trail from the west (MATC)

The AT to Moxie Bald leaves the east side of the road and immediately crosses Baker Brook near the inlet to Moxie Pond. (*Note:* Even in times of moderate water levels, this crossing may be difficult.) At 0.5 mi., the trail crosses a power line, and at 1.2 mi., crosses Joe's Hole Brook. Ahead, the AT reaches Bald Mtn. Brook at 2.6 mi. Cross the brook, pass a campsite, and, at 2.8 mi., reach a side trail leading 0.1 mi. to Bald Mtn. Brook Lean-to. Just beyond the side trail to the lean-to, cross a multi-use gravel road. Continue climbing to reach a jct. with the blue-blazed summit bypass trail at 4.2 mi., a good option in bad weather. (*Note:* The bypass trail rejoins the AT in 0.5 mi. at a point just north of the summit.) Ahead on the AT, ascend more steeply over ledges before fully breaking out into the open. At 4.8 mi., reach the open summit of Moxie Bald.

Moxie Bald Mtn. (USGS Moxie Pond and Dimmick Mtn. quads, MATC map 4, DeLorme map 30)
Distances from Troutdale Rd. (950 ft.) via AT to
- side trail to Bald Mtn. Brook Lean-to (1,350 ft.): 2.8 mi.
- Moxie Bald Mtn. summit (2,630 ft.): 4.8 mi., 3 hr. 15 min.

Pleasant Pond Mtn. (2,480 ft.)

Located on the AT between Moxie Pond and the Kennebec River in The Forks Plantation, Pleasant Pond Mtn. has open ledges that offer fine views in all directions. Hikers can approach the mountain from either the east or the west.

Via Appalachian Trail from the east (MATC)

For the east side trailhead, the approach by road is the same as for Moxie Bald Mtn. (see p. 220). Walk north along Troutdale Rd. from the parking area for 0.2 mi. to where the trail leads west up the mountain from a spot near Joe's Hole at the southern end of Moxie Pond. At 0.1 mi., the trail crosses under a power line, then passes through a low area of beaver bogs. The trail crosses a brook at 0.5 mi. Beyond, the trail ascends to the long southerly ridge of the mountain, which the trail follows until finally reaching the summit at 4.9 mi.

Via Appalachian Trail from the west (MATC)

The road approach from the west starts at US 201 in Caratunk at a point about 14 mi. north of the jct. of US 201 and ME 16 in Bingham. Leave the highway to the right at a sign for Caratunk and Pleasant Pond. Proceed 0.8 mi. to Caratunk village, then turn right and head uphill on Pleasant Pond Rd. At 3.9 mi., take the left fork onto North Shore Rd. At 4.2 mi. the pavement ends. At 5.3 mi., bear right into the woods where Boise Crossover Rd. bears left. Trailhead parking signs soon become evident as you proceed to a grassy opening and the AT at 5.5 mi.

The AT leaves the parking area and goes north toward Pleasant Pond Mtn. At 0.3 mi., reach a side trail leading 0.1 mi. to Pleasant Pond Lean-to. From the lean-to, a side trail leads an additional 0.2 mi. to a small sand beach on Pleasant Pond. Ahead on the AT, at 0.5 mi., another side trail leads 0.2 mi. to the aforementioned beach. Beyond, the rocky trail leads steeply uphill through dense woods. At 1.5 mi., the trail climbs over rock ledges and shortly thereafter, at 1.6 mi., breaks out onto open ledges at the summit and the site of the former fire tower.

Pleasant Pond Mtn. (USGS The Forks and Moxie Pond quads, MATC map 4, DeLorme map 30)

Distances from Troutdale Rd. (950 ft.) via AT (from the east) to
- power line: 0.1 mi.
- brook crossing: 0.5 mi.
- Pleasant Pond Mtn. summit (2,480 ft.): 4.9 mi., 3 hr. 10 min.

Distances from parking area (1,400 ft.) via AT (from the west) to
- side trail to Pleasant Pond Lean-to and beach: 0.3 mi.
- Pleasant Pond Mtn. summit (2,480 ft.): 1.6 mi., 1 hr. 15 min.

Mosquito Mtn. (2,215 ft.)

Rising just west of Moxie Pond in The Forks, this mountain offers excellent views in all directions from its summit ledges, from the many peaks ringing Moosehead Lake to Katahdin and the Bigelows.

From US 201 in The Forks just before the highway crosses the Kennebec River, turn right onto Lake Moxie Rd. Follow this paved road for 5.3 mi. to Lake Moxie Station and a T intersection. Turn right onto Troutdale Rd. and follow the old railroad bed along Moxie Pond. (*Note:* This road can be rough and narrow in places, and many camps are located on this shore of the lake, so drive carefully.) At 1.9 mi., just beyond where the road bears left away from the power line and enters the woods, is a small parking area on the right across from two camps. It is just large enough for several cars. (*Note:* Troutdale Rd. is narrow, and hikers should avoid parking along it.)

At about 0.1 mi., cross under a power line and soon reach an old woods road. Go left onto the woods road for 40 ft. before turning right onto the trail again. At a jct., turn left and follow the wide gravel road for 30 ft., then turn right uphill into the woods. Ahead, logging has reduced the forested trail corridor to a width of about 50 ft., and there are views north to Mt. Kineo. Beyond, the trail climbs steeply, passing a large boulder on the left, before leveling out for about 0.1 mi. After entering a stand of dense spruce, the eroded trail climbs steeply again, passing beneath a huge overhanging ledge to reach a long rock wall on the left. Follow this wall to its end, where a short side trail leads left onto ledges where there are fine views. The main trail continues to climb steeply over rocks and ledges to the open summit, which is reached at 1.9 mi.

Mosquito Mtn. (USGS Moxie Pond, DeLorme map 30)
Distance from Troutdale Rd. (950 ft.) to
  • Mosquito Mtn. summit (2,215 ft.): 1.9 mi., 1 hr. 35 min.

Kelly Mtn. (1,675 ft.)

This low mountain rises west of Bingham and the Kennebec River in Brighton Plantation, east of Bingham. On the summit, the 1925 fire tower still stands and continues to be accessible for good views of the area. Since use of the fire tower has ceased, the fire warden's trail has become overgrown and more recently has been obliterated by logging. The current trail follows an ATV route from the southwest.

To reach the trail from US 201 in Bingham, turn east on ME 16 and drive 10.4 mi. to the jct. of ME 151 at Mayfield Corner. Proceed 1.6 mi. south on ME 151 and turn right onto Iron Gate Rd. and follow it west. At 0.2 mi. from ME 151, bear left at the fork. At 1.3 mi., pass a gated road on the left that leads to the watchman's camp, now privately owned. Continue on (road name changes here to Smith Pond Rd. on DeLorme map 31) and bear left at 2.5 mi., where the road turns south. At 5.7 mi., turn left off Smith Pond Rd. onto a woods road and continue to another left at 6.9 mi. The road narrows, but is still passable. Follow this road to about 8.7 mi., where it dead-ends.

The unmarked trail leaves on the right as an ATV trail and initially traverses a wet area. At 0.2 mi., the trail forks left (marked with a sign for Kelley Mountain) and climbs gently for an additional 0.6 mi to the summit.

Kelly Mtn. (USGS Kingsbury quads, DeLorme map 31)
Distance from trailhead at end of road (1,250 ft.) to
   • Kelly Mtn. summit (1,675 ft.): 0.8 mi., 40 min.

Coburn Mtn. (3,718 ft.)

This mountain, west of US 201 between The Forks and Jackman, straddles the Upper Enchanted Township and Johnson Mtn. Township boundaries. Coburn Mtn. is the highest in the region, with spectacular views rivaling the best in Maine. The top of the old fire tower has been replaced with an observation deck. MBPL owns a portion of the mountain, including the summit and southeastern slopes.

At a point 10.6 mi. north of the bridge over the Kennebec River in The Forks and 14.3 mi. south of the jct. of US 201 and ME 15 in Jackman, turn west off US 201 onto Enchanted Mtn. Rd. This old logging road is passable by passenger vehicle for 0.2 mi. A high-clearance vehicle is required to drive the remaining 2.0 mi. to the site of the former Enchanted Mtn. Ski Area. (*Note:* If in doubt, vehicles may easily be parked on the wide shoulders at any point on the drive from US 201 to the mountain.) At the base of the mountain, a four-way intersection is found at a large clearing. Turn right and pass the old ski lodge foundation to find parking 100 yd. farther on the left, across from a second concrete foundation.

Leave the northwestern corner of this clearing (a compass reading of 280 degrees magnetic north is helpful). At a fork, follow the road to the left, which is signed "Coburn Mountain Trail Summit." Follow an old jeep trail steeply uphill, with the route alternating between a footpath and the former ski trail. About 0.7 mi. from the trailhead, reach the first of two solar-powered radio repeating stations. A snowmobile trail leaves the station coursing uphill to the summit. About 150 ft. along this trail, find the footpath exiting right and proceeding very steeply uphill. The trail exits the woods onto the summit at about 1.1 mi. at the solar panels of a second repeating station. The observation tower is just north on the ridge. The former fire warden's trail continues down the northeastern ridge but is in poor condition and is not recommended.

Coburn Mtn. (USGS Enchanted Pond and Johnson Mtn. quads, DeLorme map 40)

Distances from US 201 (1,700 ft.) to
- base of mountain at old ski area (via Enchanted Mtn. Rd.) (2,350 ft.): 2.2 mi., 1 hr. 40 min.
- first repeater station and summit footpath: est. 2.9 mi.
- Coburn Mtn. summit (3,718 ft.): est. 3.3 mi., 2 hr. 40 min.

Sally Mtn. (2,221 ft.)

Sally Mtn. is located in Attean Township between Wood and Attean ponds. The mountain has a long summit ridge extending northeast-southwest, with the highest point near its southwestern end. Although the trail is infrequently maintained, it gets sufficient use to keep the route clear.

Leave US 201 on Attean Rd., which is about 200 ft. south of the jct. of ME 6/15 and US 201, just south of Jackman. At 1.4 mi., the road turns to dirt. Park in an open area to the right, from where Sally Mtn. and the railroad trestle may be seen. From the parking area, backtrack along Attean Rd. a short distance to a gated camp road that leads to the railroad tracks of the Montreal, Maine & Atlantic Railway. Follow the railroad tracks west for about 1.8 mi., being careful when crossing the trestle over Moose River. Pick up Sally Mtn. Trail just beyond power pole #3112 and signal post #770. Look for a well-defined trail coming in from the left that can be followed across the tracks. A bright yellow sign marks the trailhead on the right side of the tracks.

The blue-blazed trail runs fairly level for a time before climbing steeply through the forest to the summit ridge. Among the rocks and scrub growth of the summit ridge, the trail becomes less distinct, but generally runs along the east-facing edge of the ridge on a gradual ascent toward the summit, passing the old fire watchman's spring (sign) en route. At the summit, four pieces of steel bolted to the rocks mark the site of the former fire tower. The views from the top are excellent, taking in several large ponds, and mountains ranging from Katahdin to Bigelow to the peaks along the Canadian border.

A pleasant alternative to the route along the railroad tracks is to approach the trail by canoe. Drive to the end of Attean Pond Rd. and a boat launch on Attean Pond. (*Note:* This is the start of the Moose River Bow

Trip.) Paddle along the north shore of the pond to reach the second established campsite in a small cove directly opposite Birch Island and Attean Lake Lodge. A trail leads through level forest for about 0.1 mi. to the railroad tracks and the start of the trail as described earlier.

Sally Mtn. (USGS Attean Pond quad, DeLorme map 39)
Distances from Attean Rd. (1,150 ft.) to
  • start of trail (via railroad tracks) (1,200 ft.): est. 1.8 mi., 50 min.
  • Sally Mtn. summit (2,221 ft.): est. 3.0 mi., 2 hr.

Burnt Jacket Mtn. (2,241 ft.)

Excellent views of the Moose River valley can be had from this open summit in Forsyth Township, which rises above Little Big Wood Pond west of Jackman. From the bridge over the Moose River on US 201 in Jackman, continue north on the highway for 1.0 mi. Turn left (west) on Sandy Stream Rd. and drive 0.3 mi. to a fork. Bear left onto Gander Brook Rd. and travel 4.2 mi. to a gated bridge over Wood Stream. Parking for several cars is available on the right side of the road.

Cross the bridge on foot and turn right onto an old logging road. Near the top of the first rise, look for a cairn and flagging tape on the left that mark the trailhead. The first 0.5 mi. is an eroded streambed. Beyond, the trail turns sharply to the right and climbs steeply. Flagging tape and old axe blazes mark the path in this area. At a ledge, the trail bears left and then quickly right. Ahead, cross two skidder trails and a seasonal brook, then climb steeply to a large ledge and a viewpoint amid a stand of red pines. Continuing on, the trail descends a steep rock chimney to a grassy swale and turns right. Follow pink flagging tape over several ledges with outlooks before reaching the summit at 1.8 mi.

Burnt Jacket Mtn. (USGS Jackman, Attean Pond and Stony Brook quads, DeLorme map 39)
Distance from bridge over Wood Stream (1,250 ft.) to
  • Burnt Jacket Mtn. summit (2,241 ft.): 1.8 mi., 1 hr. 25 min.

Boundary Bald Mtn. (3,640 ft.)

This rocky summit is north-northeast of Jackman and about 8.0 mi. southwest of the Canadian border. Its long, open summit ridge offers 360-degree views of the mountain and lake country of northern Somerset County, the Moosehead Lake Region, and southern Canada. The mountain and the collapsed fire tower at its top can be reached by a 1.2-mi. trail.

From the bridge on US 201 in Jackman, drive north toward Canada for 7.6 mi. Pass The Falls picnic area on the right at 7.2 mi. Take the second right after the picnic area at 7.6 mi. Bald Mtn. Rd. is an unmaintained gravel road leading 5.6 mi. to the trailhead. The road is generally suitable for high-clearance and four-wheel-drive vehicles. After leaving US 201, follow Bald Mtn. Rd. and bear right at the fork after the bridge over Heald Stream at 2.4 mi. Do not be drawn left by Heald Stream Rd. Ahead, bear left onto Notch Rd. at 4.1 mi. Park on Notch Rd. just beyond where Trail Rd. forks to the right at 4.3 mi. A small clearing on the right provides parking. From here, it is about 1.2 mi. to the trailhead, where an old wooden sign on the left reading "Bald Mt. Tower" marks the start of the footpath.

The blue-blazed trail heads up a seasonal slate streambed. The trail is easily followed at a steady grade to the high summit ridge. Proceed across the airy ridge to a communications tower facility where excellent views await. Next to the tower lies the wreckage of the 1937 fire tower. (*Note:* Although the trail is easily discerned above treeline, pay particular attention to the trail on the return trip, where it drops down into the trees.)

Boundary Bald Mtn. (USGS Boundary Bald Mtn. quad, DeLorme maps 39, 47)
Distances from parking on Notch Rd. (1,850 ft.) to
  • Boundary Bald Mtn. trailhead (2,450 ft.): 1.2 mi., 55 min.
  • Boundary Bald Mtn. summit (3,640 ft.): 2.4 mi., 2 hr. 10 min.

SUGGESTED HIKES

Easy Hikes

French Mtn. [lp: 0.8 mi., 25 min.]. Take this easy loop on French Mtn. Trail to steep cliffs and a lookout to Long and Great ponds, The Mountain, and the village of Belgrade Lakes.

Monument Hill [rt: 1.0 mi., 40 min.]. A fun hike to ledges offering pleasant views of Androscoggin Lake and the farms and woodlands to the east.

Mt. Pisgah [rt: 2.0 mi., 1 hr.]. An easy hike to a former MFS fire tower and good views to the west across Androscoggin Lake as far as the Presidential Range.

The Mountain [lp: 1.7 mi., 1 hr. 15 min.]. Rising between Long and Great ponds, a loop hike over The Mountain offers fine views of the Kennebec Highlands.

Sanders Hill [lp: 2.9 mi., 1 hr. 50min.]. This loop hike on Sanders Hill Trail in Rome winds through the scenic northern part of the Kennebec Highlands just east of Watson Pond.

Mt. Phillip [lp: 2.8 mi., 2 hr. 10 min.]. Enjoy views over Great Pond in Rome and the Kennebec Highlands to the west on this easy loop hike.

Moderate Hikes

Pleasant Pond Mtn. [rt: 3.2 mi., 2 hr. 30 min.]. Hike the AT from the west to the open summit ledges that offer views in all directions. A post-hike swim at the beach on Pleasant Pond is a nice bonus.

Round Top Mtn. [lp: 4.5 mi., 2 hr. 30 min.]. Take a loop hike on Round Top Trail to the highest summit in the Kennebec Highlands and spectacular views of the Belgrade Lakes region.

Burnt Jacket Mtn. [rt: 3.6 mi., 2 hr. 50 min.]. Enjoy excellent views of the Moose River valley and the peaks of the border region from this open summit west of Jackman.

Mosquito Mtn. [rt: 3.8 mi., 3 hr. 10 min.]. Enjoy panoramic views from the summit ledges of Mosquito Mtn., from the many peaks ringing Moosehead Lake to Katahdin and the Bigelows.

Sally Mtn. [rt: 6.0 mi., 4 hr.]. Although the first part of this hike is near railroad tracks, the views from the open ledges and the summit of the mountain are worth the hike. From the site of the former fire tower is a panoramic view that ranges from Katahdin to the Bigelows.

Strenuous Hikes

Boundary Bald Mtn. [rt: 4.8 mi., 4 hr. 20 min.]. Enjoy 360-degree views from the long, open summit ridge of Boundary Bald, including the lake country of northern Somerset County, the Moosehead Lake Region, and southern Canada.

Coburn Mtn. [rt: 6.6 mi., 5 hr. 20 min.]. Coburn is the highest mountain in the region and its summit observation tower offers spectacular views that rival the best in Maine.

Moxie Bald Mtn. [rt: 9.4 mi., 6 hr. 30 min.]. Hike the AT to the alpine summit ledges, where extensive views include the peaks of Katahdin, Bigelow, Sugarloaf, Abraham, Coburn, and Boundary Bald.

SECTION SIX
SOUTHWESTERN MAINE

Bradbury Mtn. 232

Rattlesnake Mtn. 233

Pleasant Mtn. 234

Douglas Mtn. 239

Bald Pate Mtn. 241

Mt. Tom. 242

Jockey Cap 243

Peary Mtn. 244

Burnt Meadow Mtn. 244

Stone Mtn. 246

Mt. Cutler 246

Sawyer Mtn. 250

Bauneg Beg Mtn. 251

Mt. Agamenticus 252

Suggested Hikes 255

AMC Pleasant Mtn. map (p. 235)

The Southwestern Maine section includes all of York and Cumberland counties and the southern part of Oxford County. The area is bordered by Casco Bay and miles of sandy beaches to the south, the Piscataqua and Salmon Falls rivers and the state of New Hampshire to the west, an abundance of natural lakes to the north, and low hills to the east. The predominant natural feature in this part of the state is Sebago Lake; at 46 square miles, it is the second-largest body of water in Maine.

The hills and mountains in this region are relatively low, rising to less than 1,000 ft. near the coast, and ranging from 1,000 to 2,000 ft. farther inland. Pleasant Mtn. is the highest peak at 2,006 ft. Many of the hills and mountains are wooded all of the way to the top, but others have open summits that provide fine views of the surrounding countryside northwest to the White Mountains and east and southeast to the coast.

This section describes 42 trails on 14 mountains. This is Maine's most populous region, and many of the trails are well used, though others, in contrast, see little use. Nearly half of the trails listed are on private property, and the rest are on lands protected by land trusts and public and private conservation agencies, including the state of Maine.

Camping

Camping is available at two state parks, as well as at many privately operated campgrounds. Bradbury Mtn. State Park in Pownal has 35 campsites, and Sebago Lake State Park in Casco has 129 sites. Both parks provide hot showers and restrooms and other amenities. No backcountry camping is available in this section.

Bradbury Mtn. (484 ft.)

The 800-acre Bradbury Mtn. State Park in Pownal offers a variety of short hiking trails, many of which lead to the summit of Bradbury Mtn. and good views of Casco Bay and the Portland skyline. To reach Bradbury Mtn., take I-95 to Exit 22 in Freeport. Drive west on ME 136 and immediately turn left onto Pownal Rd. Drive 4.0 mi. to Pownal Center and the jct. with ME 9. Turn right and go 0.8 mi. to Bradbury Mtn. State Park, where trailhead parking, a picnic area, pit toilets, and a campground are available.

Bradbury Mtn. Trails (MBPL)

Summit Trail is the shortest route to the summit and the most popular, climbing steeply 0.3 mi. to the peak via rock staircases. Northern Loop Trail follows the base of the mountain north before looping back to the south and the summit at 1.0 mi. Bluff Trail diverges from Northern Loop Trail on the upper mountain, offering a brief alternative route. Tote Road leaves Northern Loop Trail as it swings south, circling through the park before reaching the summit at 1.0 mi. Terrace Trail leaves Northern Loop Trail in the northeast corner of the park and climbs a ridge to join Bluff Trail. At 1.5 mi., Boundary Trail is the longest in the park. The trail splits from Northern Loop Trail and follows the north, west, and south boundaries of the park before climbing to the peak. South Ridge Trail is reached from the trailhead at the group area parking lot. From here, the trail winds up the south ridge of Bradbury to join with Boundary Trail to the top. (*Note:* Summit, Bluff, Terrace, and South Ridge trails are designated hiking only. All other trails are shared-use, and hikers may encounter mountain bikers and horseback riders.)

Bradbury Mtn. (USGS North Pownal quad, DeLorme map 5)

Distances from parking lot (250 ft.) to
  - Bradbury Mtn. summit (484 ft.) via Summit Trail: 0.3 mi., 15 min.
  - Bradbury Mtn. summit (484 ft.) via Northern Loop Trail: 1.0 mi., 30 min.
  - Bradbury Mtn. summit (484 ft.) via Bluff Trail and upper Northern Loop Trail: 1.0 mi, 30 min.
  - Bradbury Mtn. summit (484 ft.) via Tote Road and Northern Loop Trail: 1.0 mi., 30 min.
  - Bradbury Mtn. summit (484 ft.) via Terrace Trail, lower Northern Loop Trail, and upper Bluff Trail: 0.8 mi., 25 min.
  - Bradbury Mtn. summit (484 ft.) via Boundary Trail and lower Northern Loop Trail: 2.5 mi., 1 hr. 15 min.
  - Bradbury Mtn. summit (484 ft.) via Boundary Trail: 0.9 mi., 25 min.

Distance from group parking lot (200 ft.) to
  - Bradbury Mtn. summit (484 ft.) via South Ridge Trail and Boundary Trail: 0.7 mi., 30 min.

Rattlesnake Mtn. (1,035 ft.)

This summit in Casco offers fine ridge walking with views of Sebago Lake to the south and the White Mountains to the north. The mountain is privately owned by the Huntress family, which has maintained the trail to the top of the mountain since 1965. The trailhead is located on ME 85, 0.9 mi. south of its jct. with ME 11 in the hamlet of Webb's Mills in Raymond. Parking is in a small fenced-in area at the edge of the field. Please follow the rules posted at the start of the trail.

Bri-Mar Trail (Huntress Family)

Bri-Mar Trail crosses a field and enters the forest, following a woods road for a short distance. Shortly, bear right onto a foot trail and, following red markers, climb steadily up the hillside. The path levels off atop the ridge and reaches several lookouts with views to the south to Crescent Lake and Panther Pond. Ahead, a faint side trail marked by red dots leads right (north) 100 yd. to a small clearing with views through the trees to Mt. Washington and the Presidential Range. Beyond, climb over a rock knob to reach the wooded summit and the end of Bri-Mar Trail. (*Note:* A trail continues west to ledges with views to Sebago Lake, then descends the southwest side of the mountain following blue and orange flagging, but is obscure in places, is steep and rough, and is not recommended.)

Bri-Mar Trail (USGS Raymond quad, DeLorme map 5)
Distance from ME 85 (450 ft.) to
  • Rattlesnake main summit (1,035 ft.): 1.0 mi., 45 min.

Pleasant Mtn. (2,006 ft.)

This mountain on the Denmark–Bridgton town line rises abruptly from the comparatively flat surrounding countryside. This isolated mountain mass extends 4 mi. in a generally north–south line. The ten miles of hiking trails converge at the main summit, where there is an old fire tower. The summit was once known as House Peak because of the hotel that stood there from 1873 to 1907. The mountain was burned over in about 1860, and the forests and ledges remain open enough today for outstanding views. Mt. Washington, 29 mi. to the northwest, is particularly noticeable. The Shawnee Peak ski area operates on the slopes of the northern peak. LELT owns nearly 2,000 acres on the mountain, and TNC protects an additional 1,400 acres through conservation easements. Portions of the trail system and mountain are in private ownership and can be used thanks to the generosity of the landowners.

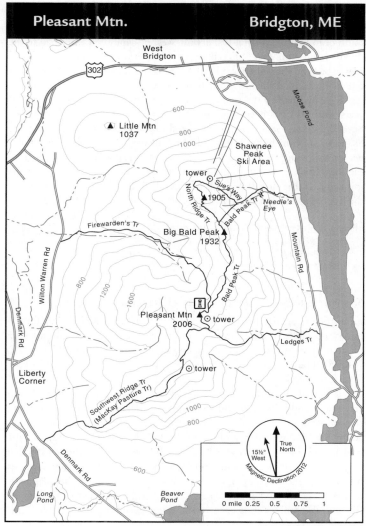

Pleasant Mtn.

Bridgton, ME

West
Bridgton

302

Moose
Pond

Little Mtn
1037

Shawnee
Peak
Ski Area

tower

Sue's Way

North Ridge Tr.

1905

Bald Peak Tr.

Needle's
Eye

Firewarden's Tr

Big Bald Peak
1932

Wilton Warren Rd

Bald Peak Tr

Mountain Rd

Denmark Rd

Pleasant Mtn
2006

tower

Ledges Tr

Liberty
Corner

tower

Southwest Ridge Tr
(MacKay Pasture Tr)

True
North

15½°
West

Magnetic Declination 2012

Denmark Rd

Long
Pond

Beaver
Pond

0 mile 0.25   0.5   0.75   1

© Appalachian Mountain Club

Firewarden's Trail (AMC, LELT)

This trail climbs to the main summit from the west. From US 302, turn south onto Wilton Warren Rd. 2.3 mi. west of Mountain Rd. (road to the ski area) and 7 mi. east of Fryeburg. A yellow farmhouse is on the left and a large barn on the right 1.2 mi. from US 302 with parking on the left. The trail starts at the right end of the parking area (sign).

The first half of the trail is old woods road with few views. In recent years, this road has been used for logging and is deeply rutted in places. Several logging roads cross the path and can be confusing. Follow the red blazes to stay on the trail. Beyond, the trail crosses a brook several times before narrowing to a rough old jeep road with exposed bedrock much of the way. The trail swings right (southeast), and climbs steadily to the summit ridge. In the final 0.2 mi., Bald Peak Trail (blue-blazed) comes in on the left (sign). An old storm shelter is just off the trail to the right.

Firewarden's Trail (AMC Pleasant Mtn. map)

Distances from parking area at farmhouse (450 ft.) to
- Bald Peak Trail jct. (1,900 ft.): 2.3 mi., 1 hr. 50 min.
- Pleasant Mtn. main summit (2,006 ft.): 2.5 mi., 2 hr.

Southwest Ridge (MacKay Pasture) Trail (AMC, LELT)

From the jct. of ME 117 and ME 160 in Denmark, take ME 160 for 0.3 mi. to the Moose Pond Dam. Turn right onto Denmark Rd. and drive 3.5 mi. to the parking area on the right, opposite the sign for Spiked Ridge Rd. (FR 78). The parking area may also be approached from US 302 in East Fryeburg by following Denmark Rd. for 3.4 mi.

The trail, marked by cairns and yellow blazes, begins on private property (sign) and follows an old woods road generally northeast, becoming steeper. At approx. 0.4 mi., the trail turns sharply right (southeast), angles across the hill, turns left, and reaches open ledges at 0.6 mi. Beyond, the trail ascends northeasterly along the mostly open ridge to the old wooden teepee at the southwestern summit (1,900 ft.) at 1.7 mi., with good views over Moose and Beaver ponds. The trail keeps to the ridge, then descends to a short saddle and angles across and down the hillside to a deep gully. Beyond, the trail ascends back to the ridge, becoming more gradual until the trail reaches Ledges Trail (blue-blazed) at 2.7 mi., which is 0.2 mi. from the summit.

Southwest Ridge (MacKay Pasture) Trail (AMC Pleasant Mtn. map)

Distances from Denmark Rd. (450 ft.) to

- Pleasant Mtn., southwestern summit (1,900 ft.): 1.7 mi.,1 hr. 20 min.
- Ledges Trail (1,810 ft.): 2.7 mi., 2 hr.
- Pleasant Mtn., main summit (2,006 ft.): 2.9 mi., 2 hr. 15 min.

Ledges Trail (AMC, LELT)

This trail leaves the west side of Mountain Rd. at a point 3.3 mi. south of US 302, 1.5 mi. south of Bald Peak Trail, and 0.6 mi. north of Walker's Bridge, which separates the two sections of Moose Pond. A small parking area is on the east side of the road next to FR 54.

The blue-blazed trail (sign) begins by climbing a stone stairway to an information kiosk, and beyond, gradually ascends along an old woods road. At 0.5 mi., cross two often dry streambeds. Continue to climb moderately for 0.6 mi., noting changes in direction as the trail traverses to the open ledges with views south and southeast. The trail follows the ledges, with the southwestern summit and cell tower visible ahead on the left. At 1.6 mi., Southwest Ridge Trail comes in on the left (sign). Ahead, the trail climbs through an area of ledges and scrub to the main summit and fire tower. Views to the west include Fryeburg, the Saco River Valley, and numerous ponds.

Ledges Trail (AMC Pleasant Mtn. map)

Distances from Mountain Rd. (500 ft.) to

- streambeds: 0.5 mi., 25 min.
- top of ledges: 1.1 mi., 1 hr.
- Southwest Ridge Trail jct. (1,810 ft.): 1.6 mi., 1 hr. 30 min.
- Pleasant Mtn. main summit (2,006 ft.): 1.8 mi., 1 hr. 40 min.

Bald Peak Trail (AMC, LELT)

This trail climbs the eastern side of Pleasant Mtn. to Big Bald Peak, and then runs south along the ridge to join Firewarden's Trail just below the main summit. When combined with Ledges Trail and a 1.5-mi. walk on

Mountain Rd., Bald Peak Trail forms an enjoyable circuit. Both trails follow blue blazes. There is no sure water on this trail during dry periods.

To reach the trail, follow Mountain Rd. along the western shore of Moose Pond to a point 1.8 mi. south of the road's jct. with US 302, and 1.2 mi. beyond the entrance to Shawnee Peak ski area. The trailhead is on the right between utility poles 49 and 50 (sign). Only limited roadside parking is available.

The trail starts westward, crosses a brook, and climbs steeply. At 0.2 mi., turn left and follow the north side of the brook. At 0.4 mi., a short but rough spur trail (sign) leads left to the Needle's Eye, a brook cascading through a cleft in the ledge. At 0.7 mi., just before the second of two small brooks, turn left (Sue's Way turns right; see sign). Climb 0.3 mi steeply over exposed bedrock, emerging onto ledges (cairn). Turn left and quickly reach Big Bald Peak (1,932 ft.) and excellent views at 1.1 mi. From Big Bald Peak, the trail follows the crest of the ridge, first south and then southwest over two humps, toward the main summit. At 2.2 mi., the trail joins Firewarden's Trail, which leads left (south) past the storm shelter to the top of Pleasant Mtn. and the fire tower.

Bald Peak Trail (AMC Pleasant Mtn. map)

Distances from Mountain Rd. (450 ft.) to
- Brook crossing and Sue's Way jct. (1,280 ft.): 0.7 mi., 50 min.
- Big Bald summit (1,932 ft.): 1.1 mi., 1 hr. 20 min.
- Firewarden's Trail jct. (1,900 ft.): 2.2 mi., 1 hr. 50 min.
- Pleasant Mtn. main summit (via Firewarden's Trail) (2,006 ft.): 2.4 mi., 1 hr. 55 min.

Sue's Way (AMC, LELT)

This orange-blazed trail starts 0.7 mi. up Bald Peak Trail and leads 0.5 mi. to the intersection of North Ridge Trail (sign). Turn right here and leave the woods. Go past the ski area summit warming hut and uphill a short distance to the top of Shawnee Peak ski area for views to the north. Combined, Sue's Way and North Ridge trails allow for an interesting loop hike. A spring can be found one-third of the way up Sue's Way, and the trail is often wet in season.

Sue's Way (AMC Pleasant Mtn. map)
Distance from Bald Peak Trail (1,300 ft.) to
  • North Ridge Trail (1,750): 0.5 mi., 25 min.

North Ridge Trail (AMC, LELT)

This white-blazed trail begins at the intersection with Sue's Way, 100 yd. downhill (southeast) from the top of Shawnee Peak ski area. North Ridge Trail heads due west on the level before turning left to pass through a granite slab. The trail then circles around the northwest side of North Peak before reaching the top. Beyond, the trail bears right to cross an open ledge where there are views of Big Bald Peak and the main summit of Pleasant Mtn. The trail then drops steeply into a col before ascending Big Bald Peak. Just below the top, Bald Peak Trail comes in from the left.

North Ridge Trail (AMC Pleasant Mtn. map)
Distance from Sue's Way (1,750 ft.) to
  • Bald Peak Trail jct. (1,840 ft.): 0.8 mi., 40 min

Douglas Mtn. (1,416 ft.)

This small mountain in Sebago is the highest of the Saddleback Hills that rise west of Sebago Lake. The 169-acre Douglas Mtn. Preserve was originally purchased by TNC, and was subsequently donated to the town of Sebago. Local stewards and volunteers maintain the preserve and its trails. A small fee is charged to help support these activities. The stone observation tower on the summit was built in 1925 and affords panoramic views of the surrounding countryside, including the Presidential Range, Pleasant Mtn., and the Atlantic Ocean. A nearby glacial erratic boulder is inscribed "Non sibi sed omnibus" (Not for one, but for all).

From the jct. of ME 113 and ME 11/107 in East Baldwin, turn north on ME 11/107. In 1.8 mi., ME 11 bears right. Continue on ME 107, and at 6.4 mi., reach Dyke Mtn. Rd. Turn left here (a small sign reads "Douglas Mtn.—1 mile"). In 1.0 mi., turn left onto Douglas Mtn. Rd., drive 0.2 mi., and turn left onto Ledges Rd. Just ahead is the parking lot for all trails.

Three routes lead to the top of Douglas Mtn. Eagle Scout Trail leaves from the parking lot and joins Nature Trail not far from the summit. Ledges Trail and Woods Trail are reached by walking 0.2 mi. on Ledges Rd. to Douglas Mtn. Rd. and following this uphill for another 0.2 mi. to the upper trailhead. Hikers may also drive to this point to drop off hikers, but no parking is allowed.

Eagle Scout Trail

This trail, delineated with orange markers, enters the woods and alternately follows a snowmobile trail/woods road and footpath, crossing several small brooks and wet areas. At a sign reading "To Nature Loop," the trail leaves the woods road and climbs steeply to a jct. with Nature Trail. To the right, a shortcut leads 0.25 mi. to the summit; to the left, it is 0.5 mi. to the top. Both routes are delineated with pink markers.

Eagle Scout Trail (USGS Steep Falls quad, DeLorme map 4)

Distances from Ledges Rd. parking lot (1,000 ft.) to
- Douglas Mtn. summit (1,416 ft.) via Nature Trail shortcut: 1.5 mi., 55 min.
- Douglas Mtn. summit (1,416 ft.) via Eagle Scout Trail and Nature Trail Loop: 1.75 mi., 1 hr. 5 min.

Ledges Trail

This is the shortest and most popular route to the summit. Start at the drop-off point 0.4 mi. from the parking area, proceed past two stone pillars and follow slabs and ledges an additional 0.5 mi. to the top of Douglas Mtn. The trail is delineated with lime-green markers.

Ledges Trail (USGS Steep Falls quad, DeLorme map 4)

Distances from Ledges Rd. parking lot (1,000 ft.) to
- Upper trailhead and drop-off point (1,100 ft.): 0.4 mi., 15 min.
- Douglas Mtn. summit (1,416 ft.): 0.9 mi., 40 min.

Woods Trail

This trail diverges from Ledges Trail soon after the trailhead and reaches the summit of Douglas Mtn. in 0.75 mi. The trail is delineated with dark-green markers.

> **Woods Trail (USGS Steep Falls quad, DeLorme map 4)**
> Distances from Ledges Rd. parking lot (1,000 ft.) to
> • Upper trailhead and drop-off point (1,100 ft.): 0.4 mi., 15 min.
> • Douglas Mtn. summit (1,416 ft.): 1.15 mi., 45 min.

Bald Pate Mtn. (1,150 ft.)

The Bald Pate Mtn. Preserve in South Bridgton, owned and managed by LELT, comprises 486 acres of forest, meadows, and craggy vistas. From the jct. of US 302 and ME 107/117 1.5 mi. south of Bridgton, turn left (west) onto ME 117. At 0.8 mi., ME 117 proceeds straight. Turn left (south) here onto ME 107. At 4.3 mi., pass Five Fields Farm on the left. Just ahead at the top of the hill at 4.6 mi., reach a dirt drive (sign) on the left leading to the main trailhead parking (kiosk).

Bald Pate Mtn. from the north (LELT)

Follow the wide, grassy track of Bob Chase Scenic Loop (blue markers) to a jct. at 0.2 mi. Here, Town Farm Brook Trail comes in from the left (leads 2.0 mi. north to Holt Pond Trail and on to Holt Pond), and Foster Pond Lookout Trail proceeds straight (leads 0.2 to a jct., where a spur trail leads 0.3 mi. east to a viewpoint over Foster Pond; to the right (south), the trail ascends easily to merge with Bob Chase Scenic Loop at 0.4 mi.).

Continuing on Bob Chase Scenic Loop, turn right (south), and climb gradually, crossing a wide track (ski trail in winter) to reach a jct. at 0.4 mi. where the trail splits. Both paths climb moderately past viewpoints to merge again at 0.6 mi. and a jct. with South Face Loop Trail. Follow this to reach the summit at 0.7 mi., where views can be seen through the trees and a bronze plaque honors conservation supporters of Bald Pate Mtn. Several loop possibilities from this point using South Face Loop, Pate, and Moose trails are described later.

Bald Pate Mtn. from the north (USGS North Sebago quad, DeLorme map 4)

Distances from Route 107 trailhead (800 ft.) to
- Bald Pate Mtn. summit (1,150 ft.) via Bob Chase Scenic Loop and South Face Loop Trail: 0.7 mi., 30 min.
- Bald Pate Mtn. summit (1,150 ft.) via Bob Chase Scenic Loop, Foster Pond Lookout Trail, and South Face Loop Trail: 0.9 mi., 35 min.

Bald Pate Mtn. from the south (LELT)

From the main trailhead, drive south on ME 107 for 0.9 mi. Turn left onto a dirt road (sign for Camp Micah), and go 0.5 mi. to a small parking lot on the left.

Follow Micah Trail (white markers) to a bridge over a creek, and then gradually up to a jct. To the right (east), South Face Loop Trail (orange markers) leads 0.6 mi. to the top, climbing the right side of the mountain's south face, past a viewpoint. To the left (west), South Face Loop Trail leads 0.9 mi. to the peak, climbing the left side of the mountain's south face, passing a viewpoint en route. At 0.1 mi., along this trail, Pate Trail (green markers) diverges right (north) and climbs 0.1 mi. at a moderate-to-steep grade past cliffs to the summit. At 0.4 mi., Moose Trail diverges left and leads 1.0 mi. along the base of the mountain at easy grades to the main trailhead parking lot on ME 107.

Bald Pate Mtn. from the south (USGS North Sebago quad, DeLorme map 4)

Distances from south trailhead (650 ft.) to
- Bald Pate Mtn. summit (1,150 ft.) via Micah Trail and South Face Loop Trail (right fork): 1.2 mi., 50 min.
- Bald Pate Mtn. summit (1,150 ft.) via Micah Trail, South Face Loop Trail, and Pate Trail: 0.8 mi., 40 min.
- Bald Pate Mtn. summit (1,150 ft.) via Micah Trail and South Face Loop Trail (left fork): 1.5 mi., 1.0 hr.

Mt. Tom (1,073 ft.)

Mt. Tom offers hikers a pleasant woods walk and rewarding views from the summit ledges overlooking the Saco River Valley and Pleasant Mtn. The top of the mountain is owned by TNC, and the trail leading up to the mountain is on land owned by the Carter family of Fryeburg. From the intersection of US 302 and ME 113 in Fryeburg, drive south on US 302 for 2.3 mi. Turn left onto Menotomy Rd., and proceed 2.3 mi. to a small parking area at a large barn and field on the right.

Mt. Tom Trail follows the Old Mountain Rd. south through the field to a dirt road. A short distance beyond the Mt. Tom Cabin (1883), the track turns to grass and ascends gradually. At a fork, bear left and continue easily upward through a mix of forest types, including a stand of old-growth hemlock. The trail emerges finally on the south-facing ledges of the mountain with fine views.

Mt. Tom (USGS Fryeburg quad, DeLorme map 4)

Distance from Menotomy Rd. (500 ft.) to
- Mt. Tom summit (1,073 ft.): 1.0 mi., 45 min.

Jockey Cap (600 ft.)

This ledge near Fryeburg rises 200 ft. above the valley and offers outstanding views for a small amount of time and effort. At the top, a bronze profile of the surrounding peaks is a monument to polar explorer Robert E. Peary, who lived in Fryeburg from 1878 to 1879. The profile affords a great way to identify neighboring mountains, including Mt. Washington. The trailhead is on the north side of US 302 at the Jockey Cap Store and Motel, 1.0 mi. east of the jct. of US 302 and ME 113 (traffic light) in the center of Fryeburg. Hikers may park at the south end of the lot, away from the store.

The trail begins through a gateway just to the right of the motel. The trail (blue-blazed) quickly bears left, then right, and soon reaches Molly Lockett's cave. The last of the Pequawket Indians, she is said to have used the cave for a shelter. Follow the trail to the left around the large rocks and circle up the west side of the cliff, which is visible through the trees. Climbing to the backside of the dome, emerge from the woods and scramble across the open summit to the monument and commanding views from Pleasant Mtn. to the Presidentials and Carter–Moriah Range to the peaks in the Evans Notch area.

Jockey Cap (USGS Fryeburg quad, DeLorme map 4)

Distance from US 302 (425 ft.) to
- Jockey Cap summit (600 ft.): 0.2 mi., 15 min.

Peary Mtn. (958 ft.)

The open ledges of this mountain in Brownfield afford good views of the White Mountains and the mountains of western Maine, including Mt. Chocorua, the Moats, Kearsarge, the Presidential Range, Carter–Moriah Range, and the peaks around Evans Notch. From the jct. of ME 160 and ME 113 in East Brownfield, proceed north on ME 113 for 2.2 mi. to Farnsworth Rd. Turn left (west) onto Farnsworth Rd. and drive 1.3 mi. to a bridge over Little Saco River. A small parking area is located on the right.

Follow the old woods road (snowmobile trail) past a gate on the south side of the river. Just ahead in a small clearing (old log yard), bear right. The trail heads south on the level and then climbs at a gradual grade to a saddle at 0.8 mi., in a small clearing with an old foundation and stone wall. Turn left (southeast) off the woods road, and immediately left again onto another woods road. In 100 ft., turn right (cairn) onto a footpath and ascend through open woods and over ledges (following cairns) 0.2 mi. to the south summit. Here are a granite bench and outstanding views to the north and west. To reach the main summit, follow the trail 0.4 mi. northeast across open ledges and through scrub. At trail's end are views to the east and north, including Pleasant Mtn. and Pleasant Pond.

Peary Mtn. (USGS Brownfield quad, DeLorme map 4)

Distances from Farnsworth Rd. (400 ft.) to
- saddle (800 ft.): 0.8 mi., 35 min.
- Peary Mtn., south summit (890 ft.): 1.0 mi., 45 min.
- Peary Mtn., main summit (958 ft.): 1.4 mi., 1 hr.

Burnt Meadow Mtn., North Peak (1,575 ft.)

Located in Brownfield, this mountain mass consists of three main summits and two lesser summits, all of nearly equal height. Deep cols separate Stone Mtn. from the North and South peaks of Burnt Meadow Mtn. Fine views may be had of the Saco River Valley, the western Maine mountains, and the White Mountains of New Hampshire. The mountain has been the site of considerable new trail construction and rehabilitation by AMC volunteers in recent years.

From the jct. of ME 113/5 and ME 160 in East Brownfield, drive west on ME 160 through Brownfield. In 0.9 mi., bear sharply left (south) past the Brownfield Community Church. Continue past Burnt Meadow Pond to trailhead parking (kiosk) on the right at 3.1 mi.

Burnt Meadow Mtn. Trail (AMC)

The trail (blue blazes) climbs west up the slope, staying on the southern edge of the ridge. At 0.4 mi., the trail passes over a small hump and drops slightly into a shallow col and the jct. with Twin Brook Trail at 0.5 mi. Beyond the col, Burnt Meadow Mtn. Trail continues up the crest of the spur, which becomes steeper and more open, with a sharp dropoff on the left. Cairns as well as blazes are used to mark the upper part of the route, which climbs a series of ledges to reach the open summit at 1.3 mi.

Burnt Meadow Mtn. Trail (USGS Brownfield quad, DeLorme map 4)
Distances from ME 160 (450 ft.) to
- Twin Brook Trail jct. (770 ft.): 0.5 mi., 40 min.
- Burnt Meadow Mtn., North Peak (1,575 ft.): 1.3 mi., 1 hr. 15 min.

Twin Brook Trail (AMC)

This trail forms a loop over the summit of Burnt Meadow Mtn. when combined with Burnt Meadow Mtn. Trail. The trail (yellow blazes) leaves Burnt Meadow Mtn. Trail at a point 0.5 mi. from the trailhead on ME 160. Twin Brook Trail follows a brook up the ravine between Stone Mtn. and the North Peak of Burnt Meadow Mtn. At 1.2 mi., the trail reaches a col and the jct. with Stone Mtn. Trail (leads left [south] 0.7 mi. to the 1,624-ft. summit of Stone Mtn.) Beyond, the trail climbs ledges on the southern flank of the North Peak of Burnt Meadow Mtn., reaching the summit at 2.0 mi. and the jct. with Burnt Meadow Mtn. Trail.

Twin Brook Trail (USGS Brownfield quad, DeLorme map 4)

Distances from jct. with Burnt Meadow Mtn. Trail (750 ft.) to
- jct. Stone Mtn. Trail (1,160 ft.): 1.2 mi., 50 min.
- Burnt Meadow Mtn., North Peak (1,575 ft.): 2.0 mi., 1 hr. 25 min.

Stone Mtn. (1,624 ft.)

This mountain is the highest of the three summits of the Burnt Meadow Mtn. mass in Brownfield. The new Stone Mtn. Trail to the peak was constructed by AMC and Friends of Burnt Meadow Mountains volunteers and opened in 2010. See the descriptions for Burnt Meadow Mtn. and Twin Brook trails for directions to the start of the trail.

Stone Mtn. Trail (AMC)

This trail heads south from close to the height-of-land between Stone Mtn. and Burnt Meadow Mtn., North Peak at a point 1.2 mi. from ME 160 via Burnt Meadow Mtn. and Twin Brook trails. The trail ascends the north shoulder of Stone Mtn., crosses a dry brook, and then switchbacks to reach ledges and the summit at 0.7 mi.

Stone Mtn. Trail (USGS Brownfield quad, DeLorme map 4)

Distance from jct. with Twin Brook Trail (1,150 ft.) to
- Stone Mtn. summit (1,624 ft.): 0.7 mi., 35 min.

Mt. Cutler (1,232 ft.)

The open ledges of this summit in Hiram offer good views of the Saco River Valley to the south and the White Mountains to the north. AMC volunteers have done significant trail building on Mt. Cutler in recent years, and a series of trails now lead to the summit. Future plans call for connecting Mt. Cutler's trails to those on Burnt Meadow Mtn.

At the jct. of ME 113/5 and ME 117 in Hiram, cross the bridge to the west side of the Saco River and immediately turn left onto River Rd. Turn right onto Mountain View Ave. at the Old Hiram Village Store. In 200 ft., the road turns left, and a parking lot is on the right at the site of the former railroad station. This is the trailhead for Barnes, Snowmobile, and Saco Ridge trails. Cross the abandoned railroad tracks (Old Mountain Division Line) and turn left (south). At the kiosk, Barnes Trail heads west into the woods.

Barnes Trail (AMC)

This is the original trail on Mt. Cutler, first marked in the 1950s by local resident Dr. Lowell "Bud" Barnes, who lived within sight of the current trailhead. In 100 yd., Barnes Trail forks to the right and Snowmobile Trail continues straight ahead. Continuing on Barnes Trail, enter the old Merrill Park and a grove of large white pines. Pass several open wells once used by the railroad. Now largely filled with debris and vegetation, they still hold water, so exercise caution with children. Beyond, climb steeply up the ravine between Mt. Cutler and the south shoulder of the mountain on rough trail. At the top of the ravine, take a sharp right and enter a rugged area of boulders. Pass under an overhanging ledge and ascend to open ledges. Turn sharply right and proceed to the top of the ledges at 0.4 mi. Continue along the ledges with viewpoints overlooking the Saco River and the village of Hiram. Leaving the ledges, Barnes Trail soon reaches a jct. with White Flag Trail (leads 0.25 mi. to North Trail) at 0.5 mi. Here, Barnes Trail makes a sharp left and ascends steadily to emerge on an open, south-facing ledge at 0.7 mi. At 0.8 mi., North Trail (blue blazes) comes in from the right (north). Ahead, Barnes Trail follows the ridgeline with alternating views southeast over the Saco River Valley and northwest to the Presidential Range. Cairns and red blazes mark the route. Crossing a secondary summit, the trail descends to a notch and an old woods road at 1.3 mi., and the jct. with Saco Ridge Trail. The true summit of Mt. Cutler is a short scramble to the west.

Barnes Trail (USGS Cornish and Hiram quads, DeLorme map 4)

Distances from Mountain View Ave. (400 ft.) to
- top of ledges (650 ft.): 0.4 mi., 20 min.
- White Flag Trail jct. (700 ft.): 0.5 mi., 25 min.
- south-facing ledge (950 ft.): 0.7 mi., 40 min.
- North Trail jct. (1,000 ft.): 0.8 mi., 45 min.
- notch below Mt. Cutler main summit (1,050 ft.): 1.3 mi., 1 hr.
- Mt. Cutler main summit (1,232 ft.): 1.4 mi., 1 hr. 5 min.

Snowmobile Trail

This trail leaves Barnes Trail 100 yd. from the Mountain View Ave. trail-head parking lot. The mostly level trail passes two houses below the trail on the left, then descends slightly to reach old, overgrown fields. Turning right, away from the fields, the trail reenters the woods, turns left, and crosses a small stream. Just beyond the stream at 0.5 mi., Saco Ridge Trail diverges right. Snowmobile Trail continues ahead, eventually following an old county road and ending in South Hiram.

Snowmobile Trail (USGS Cornish and Hiram quads, DeLorme map 4)

Distances from Mountain View Ave. (400 ft.) to

- Snowmobile Trail jct. (via Barnes Trail): 100 yd., 2 min.
- Saco Ridge Trail jct. (450 ft.): 0.5 mi., 20 min.
- notch below Mt. Cutler main summit (1,050 ft.) via Saco Ridge Trail: 1.3 mi., 1 hr.
- Mt. Cutler main summit (1,232 ft.): 1.4 mi., 1 hr. 5 min.

Saco Ridge Trail (AMC)

This trail (red blazes) leaves Snowmobile Trail at a point 0.5 mi. from Mountain View Ave. trailhead and climbs the prominent south ridge of Mt. Cutler. Soon after the jct., the trail begins a moderately steep ascent, on an old woods road. At a height-of-land, the trail turns sharply left and ascends a wooded slope to a jct. Here, Old South Ridge Trail leads 100 ft. to a view over the Saco River Valley, then continues downhill to join Snowmobile Trail in 0.2 mi. Continuing on Saco Ridge Trail, turn right and continue up the ridge with frequent views. Nearing the main ridge of Mt. Cutler, descend briefly to a notch, and then angle westward around the side of the mountain. Following cairns and red blazes, make the short, final ascent to the notch and the jct. with Barnes Trail at 1.3 mi. The summit of Mt. Cutler is a short scramble to the west.

Saco Ridge Trail (USGS Cornish and Hiram quads, DeLorme map 4)

Distances from Mountain View Ave. (400 ft.) to

- Saco Ridge Trail jct. (450 ft.) via Barnes Trail and Snowmobile Trail: 0.5 mi., 20 min.
- Old South Ridge Trail jct. (800 ft.): 0.8 mi., 35 min.

- notch below Mt. Cutler main summit (1,050 ft.) via Saco Ridge Trail: 1.3 mi., 1 hr.
- Mt. Cutler main summit (1,232 ft.): 1.4 mi., 1 hr. 5 min.

Old South Ridge Trail (AMC)

This trail is a former section of Saco Ridge Trail. Old South Ridge Trail is steep and can be slippery. It is not recommended for descent.

Old South Ridge Trail diverges right from Snowmobile Trail at a point 0.7 mi. from the Mountain View Ave. trailhead and climbs the steep face of the prominent south ridge of Mt. Cutler via switchbacks. About 100 ft. beyond an open ledge with views of the Saco River Valley, the trail merges with Saco Ridge Trail, which continues the ascent to the main ridge of Mt. Cutler.

Old South Ridge Trail (USGS Cornish and Hiram quads, DeLorme map 4)

Distances from Mountain View Ave. (400 ft.) to

- Old South Ridge Trail jct. (450 ft.) via Barnes Trail and Snowmobile Trail: 0.7 mi., 30 min.
- Saco Ridge Trail jct. (800 ft.): 0.9 mi., 40 min.
- notch below Mt. Cutler main summit (1,050 ft.) via Saco Ridge Trail: 1.4 mi., 1 hr. 5 min.
- Mt. Cutler main summit (1,232 ft.): 1.4 mi., 1 hr. 10 min.

North Trail (AMC)

This trail (blue blazes) ascends from the north to meet Barnes Trail high on the long east ridge of Mt. Cutler. From the jct. of ME 113 and River Rd. on the west side of the bridge over the Saco River, go north 0.6 mi. to Hiram Hill Rd. Turn left and go across the railroad tracks. The trailhead (unsigned, but marked by blue blazes on the twin pine trees) is on the left, 0.1 mi. from ME 113.

After entering the woods, pass a well house just uphill from the trail. Just beyond a brook crossing at 0.25 mi., White Flag Trail diverges left. At 0.3 mi., North Trail reaches the base of a steep grade and begins to switchback through thick hemlock forest. Above, emerge onto open ledges with good views north to Burnt Meadow Mtn. and Pleasant Mtn. The trail enters the woods once again, then comes out into the open and climbs to join Barnes Trail at 0.5 mi. (cairn).

North Trail (USGS Cornish and Hiram quads, DeLorme map 4)

Distances from Hiram Hill Rd. (450 ft.) to
- White Flag Trail jct. (600 ft.): 0.25 mi., 15 min.
- Barnes Trail jct. (1,000 ft.): 0.5 mi., 35 min.
- notch below Mt. Cutler main summit (1,050 ft.): 1.0 mi., 1 hr.
- Mt. Cutler main summit (1,232 ft.): 1.1 mi., 1 hr. 5 min.

White Flag Trail (AMC)

This short connector trail leaves North Trail 0.25 mi. from Hiram Hill Rd., just above the highest brook crossing. It runs east-southeast for 0.25 mi., skirting a small ridge then ascending gradually over ledges to join Barnes Trail just above the ledges overlooking Hiram village, at a point about 0.5 mi. from Mountain View Rd.

White Flag Trail (USGS Hiram and Cornish quads, DeLorme map 4)

Distances from Hiram Hill Rd. (450 ft.) to
- start of White Flag Trail via North Trail (600 ft.): 0.25 mi., 15 min.
- Barnes Trail jct. (700 ft.): 0.5 mi., 30 min.

Sawyer Mtn. (1,180 ft.)

The Sawyer Mtn. Highlands in Limington and Limerick are part of one of the largest blocks of undeveloped land in York and Cumberland counties. The FSHT owns 1,400 acres in this area, including the summit of Sawyer Mtn. The mountain may be reached from Limington in the east or from Limerick on the west side.

Sawyer Mtn. Trail (FSHT)

From the jct. of ME 25 and ME 117 in Limington, drive south on ME 117 for 2.5 miles to a parking area (sign) on the right.

The trail, marked by small wood blocks etched with the yellow outline of a turtle, follows the old Sawyer Mountain Rd. The road is rough, rocky, and severely eroded in places. Pass several camps on the right, and be sure to observe private property signs. Continue straight through several intersections (signed) and pass the Estes Cemetery on the right. At 1.5 mi. on the north shoulder of the mountain, reach a jct. A spur trail to the left leads 0.3 mi. to the summit and a large grassy clearing with views to the northwest.

Sawyer Mtn. Trail (USGS Steep Falls, Cornish and Limerick quads, DeLorme map 4)
Distances from ME 117 (500 ft.) to
- summit spur trail (1,080 ft.): 1.5 mi., 1 hr. 5 min.
- Sawyer Mtn. summit (1,180 ft.): 1.8 mi., 1 hr. 15 min.

Smith Trail (FSHT)

From the jct. of ME 11 and ME 5 in Limerick, drive east on ME 11 for 1.0 mi. Turn right (north) on Emery Corner Rd. In 1.5 mi., at Emery Corner, the road becomes Sawyer Mtn. Rd. Reach a parking lot (sign) and trailhead at 3.3 mi. from ME 11.

The trail ascends next to a ravine before leveling out and winding upward through several areas of forested ledges. Pass through openings in two stone walls and proceed on a grassy woods road to the jct. with the old Sawyer Mtn. Rd. and the foundations of the old Sawyer family homestead at 0.6 mi. Turn right, and at 1.2 mi. reach a spur trail on the right leading 0.3 mi. to the top of Sawyer Mtn.

Smith Trail (USGS Limerick quad, DeLorme map 4)
Distances from Sawyer Mtn. Rd. (650 ft.) to
- jct. old Sawyer Mtn. Rd. (925 ft.): 0.6 mi., 25 min.
- summit spur trail (1,080 ft.): 1.2 mi., 50 min.
- Sawyer Mtn. summit (1,180 ft.): 1.5 mi., 1 hr.

Bauneg Beg Mtn., Middle Peak (850 ft.)

This mountain in the 89-acre Bauneg Beg Mtn. Conservation Area in North Berwick is owned and managed by GWRLT. This is the only mountain in southern Maine without a communications tower, and the mountain offers fine views ranging from the White Mountains and western Maine to the Atlantic Ocean.

From North Berwick, drive north on US 4 for 2.1 mi. Turn left onto Boyle Rd. and continue straight as it turns into Ford Quint Rd., about 5.5 mi. from US 4. Turn left onto Fox Farm Rd., and proceed 0.3 mi. to trailhead on the left.

Bauneg Beg Trail (GWRLT)

The unmarked Bauneg Beg Trail trends uphill at a moderate grade, passing the lower end of North Peak Loop on the right. Ahead at a jct., the upper end enters from the right. Just ahead, Ginny's Way leads left (southeast) to the lookout atop the middle peak of the mountain. To the right (northwest), Linny's Way passes the upper end of North Peak Loop and leads through the rocks of Devils Den to the top. For the descent, retrace your steps or take the white-blazed North Peak Loop.

Bauneg Beg Mtn., Middle Peak (USGS Sanford quad, DeLorme map 2)
Distances from Fox Farm Hill Rd. (600 ft.) to
- Bauneg Beg Mtn., Middle Peak (via Ginny's Way or Linny's Way) (850 ft.): 0.6 mi., 25 min.
- Bauneg Beg Mtn., Middle Peak (via North Peak Loop) (850 ft.): 0.8 mi., 30 min.

Mt. Agamenticus (691 ft.)

The Mt. Agamenticus Conservation Region consists of more than 10,000 acres owned and managed by a cooperative of public and private agencies for conservation, watershed protection, and recreation. The central feature of these lands is the monadnock of Mt. Agamenticus, which rises distinctively above the coastal plain of southern York County.

From the Maine Turnpike, take Exit 7 onto Chases Pond Rd. Follow this west and north for 3.5 mi. Turn left onto Mountain Rd., and in 2.5 mi., reach the main trailhead parking on the right at the base of the summit auto road.

The paved auto road leads 0.7 mi. to the top of the mountain where there is a parking lot, two observation decks, a privately-operated fire tower, several communications towers, riding stables, and the old lodge of the long-defunct Big A ski area (now an environmental education center). Continuing ahead on Mountain Rd. (it shortly turns to dirt) leads around the west side of the mountain to two additional trailheads. Many paths, some maintained not only for hiking but also as bridle, mountain bike, or ATV trails, lead through the woods up to the grassy field on the open summit.

Ring Trail Loop (MACC)

Ring Trail circumnavigates the mountain and provides access to most of the short trails that lead to the summit. The route is an interpretive trail from the trailhead to the summit via Witch Hazel Trail. Along it are ten signed stations that describe the geology, wildlife, trees, and history on Mt. Agamenticus.

From the main trailhead on Mountain Rd. at the base of the auto road, follow the trail into the woods. At approximately 0.1 mi., Ring Trail forks. Bear left here, as the Ring Trail route and connecting trails are described from this point in a clockwise direction.

Follow Ring Trail and soon cross the auto road. At 0.4 mi., reach Blueberry Bluff Trail, which ascends 0.3 mi. to the peak over steep, exposed bedrock. Views to the south include Pawtuckaway Mtn. in New Hampshire and the Atlantic Ocean. At 0.7 mi., Wintergreen Trail merges from the left (leads downhill to a point on Mountain Rd. [parking] 0.7 mi. from the base of the auto road and main trailhead parking). At 0.8 mi., Horse Trail switchbacks 0.2 miles through a hemlock forest to the riding stable on top. Vulture View Trail departs right at 1.0 mi., reaching the summit in 0.5 mi. over steep, exposed bedrock. Mt. Washington, 90 mi. to the northwest, can be seen on a good day. Sweet Fern Trail leaves right at 1.25 mi. to follow an old ski trail and lift line 0.2 mi. to the top. Ahead, at 1.3 mi., the Goosefoot Trail comes in from the left, and just beyond, Chestnut Oak Trail also comes in from the left. Both trails end here and merge into Ring Trail. At 1.4 mi., Witch Hazel Trail climbs 0.1 to the summit. At 1.5 mi., Rocky Road joins from the left. This trail continues on 0.2 mi. to the auto road as Hairpin Turn Trail. A spur trail to the auto road leaves right at 1.85 mi. Ring Trail Loop is complete at 2.0 mi. From this jct., it is 0.1 mi. back to the main trailhead and parking area.

Ring Trail Loop (USGS York Harbor quad, DeLorme map 1)

Distance from Mountain Rd. (350 ft.) to
- Ring Trail fork (410 ft.): 0.1 mi., 5 min.

Distances clockwise (left) from Ring Trail fork (410 ft.) to
- Blueberry Bluff Trail (490 ft.): 0.4 mi, 10 min.
- Wintergreen Trail (470 ft.): 0.7 mi., 20 min.
- Horse Trail (505 ft.): 0.8 mi., 22 min.
- Vulture View Trail (485 ft.): 1.0 mi., 30 min.
- Sweet Fern Trail (490 ft.): 1.25 mi., 35 min.
- Goosefoot and Chestnut Oak trails (480 ft.): 1.3 mi., 40 min.
- Witch Hazel Trail (560 ft.): 1.4 mi., 45 min.
- intersection with Rocky Road and Hairpin Turn trails (560 ft.): 1.5 mi., 47 min.
- spur trail to auto road (475 ft.): 1.85 mi., 50 min.
- Ring Loop Trail fork (410 ft.): 2.0 mi., 1 hr.

Summit Trails (MACC)

Five trails leave Ring Trail at various points and climb to the Mt. Agamenticus summit, including Blueberry Bluff, Horse, Vulture View, Sweet Fern, and Witch Hazel trails.

Mt. Agamenticus (USGS York Harbor quad, DeLorme map 1)

Distances clockwise (left) from Mountain Rd. trailhead (350 ft.) to
- Mt. Agamenticus summit (691 ft.) via Blueberry Bluff Trail: 0.6 mi., 25 min.
- Mt. Agamenticus summit (691 ft.) via Horse Trail: 1.0 mi., 40 min.
- Mt. Agamenticus summit (691 ft.) via Vulture View Trail: 1.5 mi., 55 min.
- Mt. Agamenticus summit (691 ft.) via Sweet Fern Trail: 1.45 mi., 55 min.
- Mt. Agamenticus summit (691 ft.) via Witch Hazel Trail: 1.5 mi., 55 min.

SUGGESTED HIKES

Easy Hikes

Jockey Cap [rt: 0.4 mi., 25 min.]. An interesting short hike to the open summit where a monument to polar explorer Admiral Peary provides a 360-degree profile of the surrounding mountains.

Bradbury Mtn. via Summit Trail [rt: 0.6 mi., 30 min.]. An excellent family hike with views to Casco Bay and the Portland skyline from the open ledges on top.

Mt. Agamenticus via Blueberry Bluff Trail [rt: 1.2 mi., 50 min.]. A delightful stroll through blueberry patches to a great overlook with views of the White Mountains.

Mt. Tom [rt: 2.0 mi., 1 hr. 20 min.]. A fun hike on an old forest road through old-growth hemlocks with fine views to Pleasant Mtn. from the summit ledges.

Moderate Hikes

Mt. Cutler via Barnes Trail [rt. 2.8 mi., 2 hr. 10 min.]. A short, steep hike to ledges and good ridge walking with views south to the Saco River Valley and north to the White Mountains.

Douglas Mtn. via Eagle Scout Trail and Nature Loop [rt: 3.5 mi., 2 hr. 10 min.]. A satisfying woods hike to an old stone observation tower with excellent views to the north and east.

Burnt Meadow Mtn. via Burnt Meadow Mtn. Trail [rt: 2.6 mi., 2 hr. 30 min.]. A short, steep climb to ledges and an open summit with good views of the White Mountains in the north.

Pleasant Mtn. via Southwest Ridge (MacKay Pasture) Trail [rt: 5.8 mi., 4 hr.]. A steady, moderate climb to the summit of Pleasant Mtn., where there are excellent views, particularly to the west.

SECTION SEVEN
MIDCOAST

Mt. Battie. 257

Mt. Megunticook 259

Bald Rock Mtn. 265

Cameron Mtn. 265

Bald Mtn. 267

Ragged Mtn. 267

Beech Hill. 270

Frye Mtn. 271

Hogback Mtn. 272

Whitten Hill 273

Goose Ridge. 274

Mt. Waldo 275

Suggested Hikes 276

AMC map 4: Camden Hills

The Midcoast section includes the entirety of Waldo, Knox, Lincoln, and Sagadahoc counties. It is bounded by Penobscot Bay, its islands and coastal hills to the east, and forested peninsulas, craggy headlands, and bays on the Atlantic Ocean to the south. Scattered hills, farmlands, and lakes are to the north and west and characterize the interior of the region as well. The Androscoggin and Kennebec rivers merge at Merrymeeting Bay and flow into the ocean east of Popham Beach, and numerous other rivers, including the Damariscotta, Sheepscot, and Georges, slice across the landscape before emptying into the ocean.

This section, describing 30 trails and 12 mountains, features Camden Hills State Park, a 6,200-acre preserve encompassing the scenic Camden Hills. This compact and attractive group of mountains rises above the western shore of Penobscot Bay in the towns of Camden, Lincolnville, and Rockport. These mountains share many characteristics with the mountains of Acadia on Mt. Desert Island a few miles to the east: fine softwood forests, bold cliffs and ledges, and broad vistas of oceans, lakes, and mountains.

At 1,385 ft., Mt. Megunticook is the highest in the region and, with the exception of Cadillac Mtn., is the highest point along the Atlantic seaboard of the United States. A series of mountains continues northeast for several miles and includes Cameron Mtn. and Bald Rock Mtn. Mt. Battie lies just south of Megunticook, and a toll road climbs to its summit. Just outside the park to the west, trails lead to the popular Maiden's Cliff overlooking Megunticook Lake. More than 30 mi. of well-maintained, blue-blazed trails are in the park.

Megunticook Lake and Megunticook River separate the main peaks of the Camden Hills from the mountains extending to the southwest, which include Bald Mtn. and Ragged Mtn. Another area of low hills is located about 15 mi. northeast of the Camden Hills and includes Frye and Hogback mountains, Whitten Hill, and Goose Ridge.

Camping

Camping is available at Camden Hills State Park, where there are 106 campsites, hot showers, restrooms, trailhead parking, and other amenities. Numerous other privately operated campgrounds are also available. This section contains no backcountry camping.

Mt. Battie (800 ft.)

Located just south of Mt. Megunticook, this mountain features one of the most popular hikes in the Camden Hills because of its proximity to Camden village and its open ledges that offer outstanding views of the coast. In 1897, a toll road was built to the summit, and a hotel named the Summit House was built. The toll road (paved) remains but the hotel was torn down in 1920. A stone observation tower—a World War I memorial—was erected in its place the following year. The auto road leaves from Camden Hills State Park entrance on US 1 and climbs gradually to the top in 1.4 mi.

Mt. Battie Trail (MBPL)

This trail rises steeply over the rocky nose of Mt. Battie. Take ME 52 (Mountain St.) from its jct. with US 1 in Camden. Then take the fourth right, and then the first left onto Megunticook St. Continue steeply uphill to a small parking area.

The trail first climbs steadily and then more steeply north to emerge on open ledges before reaching the stone tower on top.

Mt. Battie Trail (AMC map 4: C1)

Distance from parking area on Megunticook St. (200 ft.) to
  • Mt. Battie summit (800 ft.): 0.5 mi., 30 min.

Carriage Road Trail (MBPL)

This trail climbs along the gradual western slopes of Mt. Battie via the route of an old carriage road. The trail leaves the right (northeast) side of ME 52 about 1.3 mi. from the jct. of US 1 and ME 52. Look for a small wooden sign: "Old Carriage Road—Mt. Battie Rd. 1 mile." Parking is along the road.

Old Carriage Rd. runs north 0.3 mi. to a jct. Here, Carriage Road Trail forks right, and Carriage Trail continues ahead to meet Tableland Trail. Carriage Road Trail rises gently on the old carriage road to join Mt. Battie Auto Rd. just north of the summit parking area. Cross the road to merge with Tableland Trail at 1.0 mi., turning right onto this trail to reach the summit of Mt. Battie in another 0.2 mi.

Carriage Road Trail (AMC map 4: C1)

Distances from ME 52 (250 ft.) to
  • Carriage Trail jct. (250 ft.): 0.3 mi., 10 min.
  • Tableland Trail jct. (700 ft.): 1.0 mi., 45 min.
  • Mt. Battie summit (800 ft.): 1.2 mi., 50 min.

Carriage Trail (MBPL)

This trail leaves Carriage Road Trail at a point 0.3 mi. from ME 52 and climbs gradually to reach Tableland Trail just north of the saddle between Mt. Battie and Mt. Megunticook at 1.0 mi. To the right, it is 0.8 mi. to the summit of Mt. Battie via Tableland Trail. To the left, it is 0.7 mi. to Ocean Lookout via Tableland Trail.

Carriage Trail (AMC map 4: C1–C2)

Distances from ME 52 (250 ft.) to
- Carriage Road Trail jct. (250 ft.): 0.3 mi., 10 min.
- Tableland Trail jct. (600 ft.): 1.0 mi., 40 min.
- Mt. Battie summit (800 ft.) (via Tableland Trail): 1.8 mi., 1 hr. 10 min.
- Ocean Lookout (1,250 ft.) (via Tableland Trail): 1.7 mi., 1 hr. 20 min.

Nature Trail (MBPL)

Nature Trail links the lower part of Megunticook Trail with Tableland Trail and provides access to both Mt. Battie (via Tableland Trail) and Mt. Megunticook (via either Megunticook or Tableland and Ridge trails). Nature Trail starts from the Mt. Battie hiker's parking lot, on the right 0.25 mi. up Mt. Battie Auto Rd. from the park entrance and US 1.

Nature Trail proceeds to a jct. at 0.1 mi. Turn left (west) to reach Tableland Trail in 0.7 mi. Turn right (north) to reach Megunticook Trail in 0.2 mi.

Nature Trail (AMC map 4: C2)

Distances from Mt. Battie Auto Rd. hiker's parking lot (250 ft.) to
- Tableland Trail jct. (650 ft.) via left fork: 0.8 mi., 30 min.
- Megunticook Trail jct. (450 ft.): 0.3 mi., 15 min.

Mt. Megunticook (1,385 ft.)

Mt. Megunticook, the highest peak in the Camden Hills, is a nearly 3-mi.-long mountain ridge extending in a northwest-southeast direction. The true summit is forested and has no view, but just to the southeast, Ocean Lookout takes in the expanse of Penobscot Bay and the nearby coastal hills. Several outlooks along Ridge Trail offer views over Megunticook Lake. Maiden Cliff is a prominent escarpment near the northwest end of the mountain.

Mt. Megunticook Trail (MBPL)

This trail leaves Nature Trail at a point 0.3 mi. from the Mt. Battie hiker's parking lot and climbs the east slope of the mountain. From this same jct., Multi-Use Trail leaves to the right, leading 5.0 mi. to trailhead parking on Youngstown Rd. At 0.6 mi., pass Adam's Lookout Trail on the left (leads 0.3

mi. to Tableland Trail). At 1.0 mi., the trail reaches Ocean Lookout, where Tableland Trail from Mt. Battie comes up from the left (south). From Ocean Lookout, follow Ridge Trail 0.4 mi. to the Mt. Megunticook summit.

Mt. Megunticook Trail (AMC map 4: B2, C2)

Distances from jct. with Nature Trail (450 ft.) to
- Ocean Lookout (1,250 ft.): 1.0 mi., 1 hr. 10 min.
- Mt. Megunticook summit (1,385 ft.) via Ridge Trail: 1.4 mi., 1 hr. 30 min.

Multi-Use Trail from the south (MBPL)

Multi-Use Trail leaves from the jct. of Mt. Megunticook Trail and Nature Trail 0.3 mi. from the hiker's parking lot on Mt. Battie Auto Rd. Multi-Use Trail, a gravel access road, heads north and then west around Mt. Megunticook. [*Note:* Due to improvements, the former Summer Bypass which left the trail to the left at 1.0 mi. and rejoined it at 1.8 mi. is no longer maintained or needed.] Reach the jct. with Slope Trail at 2.0 mi, immediately across from the renovated Megunticook Ski Shelter. To the left, Slope Trail ascends 1.0 mi. to the summit of Mt. Megunticook. Continuing ahead, Multi-Use Trail traverses the interior of the park, passing beneath Bald Rock Mtn. before reaching the Youngtown Rd. trailhead, 2.3 mi. from the jct. of ME 173 and US 1 in Lincolnville.

Multi-Use Trail from the south (AMC map 4: A2, B2, C2)

Distances from jct. with Nature and Mt. Megunticook trails (450 ft.) to
- Slope Trail jct. (550 ft.): 2.0 mi., 1 hr.
- Mt. Megunticook summit (1,385 ft.) (via Slope Trail): 3.0 mi., 1 hr. 55 min.
- Youngtown Rd. trailhead (250 ft.): 4.8 mi., 2 hr. 20 min.

Slope Trail (MBPL)

This trail leaves Multi-Use Trail at a point 2.0 mi. from its jct. with Nature and Mt. Megunticook trails and 2.3 mi. from the hiker's parking lot trailhead on Mt. Battie Auto Rd.

Slope Trail crosses over Spring Brook and climbs steeply to reach Ridge Trail at 1.0 mi. The true summit of Mt. Megunticook is 100 ft. up Ridge Trail from this jct.

Slope Trail (AMC map 4: B1–B2)

Distance from jct. with Multi-Use Trail (550 ft.) to
* Mt. Megunticook summit (1,385 ft.): 1.0 mi., 55 min.

Tableland Trail (MBPL)

This trail starts from the summit of Mt. Battie, crosses the parking area, and descends gradually to the north. The trail meets Carriage Road Trail coming in from the left (west) at 0.2 mi., and crosses Mt. Battie Auto Rd. at 0.5 mi. At 0.7 mi., pass Nature Trail on the right and, at 0.8 mi., Carriage Trail on the left. Beyond, Tableland Trail ascends and passes Adam's Lookout Trail on the right at 1.2 mi. The route keeps to the right (east) of two lines of cliffs and, again swinging to the northwest, climbs steeply to Ocean Lookout at 1.4 mi. The true summit of Mt. Megunticook is 0.4 mi. ahead via Ridge Trail.

Tableland Trail (AMC map 4: B2, C1–C2)

Distance from Mt. Battie summit (800 ft.) to
* Ocean Lookout (1,250 ft.): 1.4 mi., 1 hr.

Jack Williams Trail (MBPL)

This mostly wooded trail leaves Tableland Trail just below its jct. with Ridge Trail and contours across the southwest face of Mt. Megunticook. Near its end, Jack Williams Trail rises to meet Ridge Trail at a point 1.2 mi. west of the Mt. Megunticook summit and 1.0 mi. east of Maiden Cliff. Jack Williams Trail is named in honor of a local trail volunteer.

Jack Williams Trail (AMC map 4: B1–B2)

Distance from Tableland Trail (1,100 ft.) to
* Ridge Trail (900 ft.): 1.6 mi., 1 hr. 30 min.

Adam's Lookout Trail (MBPL)

This short trail connects Megunticook and Tableland trails while providing an excellent lookout over Penobscot Bay to the east.

Adam's Lookout Trail (AMC map 4: B2)

Distance from Megunticook Trail (850 ft.) to
  • Tableland Trail (1,100 ft.): 0.3 mi., 15 min.

Maiden Cliff Trail (MBPL)

Maiden Cliff rises abruptly above Megunticook Lake. A steel cross stands near the spot where 12-year-old Elenora French fell to her death in 1864. The trail starts from the northeast side of ME 52 at a signed parking area 2.8 mi. north of the jct. of ME 52 and US 1 in Camden, where the road passes above Barrett's Cove on Megunticook Lake.

The trail climbs north and west, at first following an eroded woods road along a small brook. At 0.4 mi., Ridge Trail continues ahead (north). Maiden Cliff Trail branches left (west) and climbs more steeply to open ledges and the cross at 0.8 mi. As an alternative, from Ridge Trail jct., continue to climb to the ridge. In 0.2 mi., turn left (north) on Scenic Trail and cross several open ledges with fine views of the lake before reaching the cliff in another 0.4 mi.

Maiden Cliff Trail (AMC map 4: B1)

Distances from ME 52 (150 ft.) to
  • Ridge Trail jct. (450 ft.): 0.4 mi., 30 min.
  • Maiden Cliff (700 ft.): 0.8 mi., 45 min.
  • Maiden Cliff (700 ft.) via Ridge and Scenic trails: 1.0 mi., 50 min.

Scenic Trail (MBPL)

This trail bears right (east) from Maiden Cliff Trail just above Maiden Cliff. Scenic Trail climbs over open ledges with good views, and then descends slightly to a jct. with Ridge Trail, at a point 0.6 mi. from ME 52 via Maiden Cliff and Ridge trails.

Scenic Trail (AMC map 4: B1)

Distance from Maiden Cliff (700 ft.) to
  • Ridge Trail jct. (850 ft.): 0.4 mi., 20 min.

Ridge Trail (MBPL)

Ridge Trail leaves Maiden Cliff Trail 0.4 mi. from ME 52 at a signed jct. and runs along the main ridge of Mt. Megunticook, over the wooded summit (1,385 ft.), and on to Ocean Lookout with its fine views of Penobscot Bay.

From the Maiden Cliff Trail jct., hike up to the right (south) and in 0.2 mi., Scenic Trail to Maiden Cliff diverges left. After a brief descent, Ridge Trail continues to climb, with occasional lookouts over Megunticook Lake. Pass Jack Williams Trail on the right at 0.6 mi. from Scenic Trail jct. In another 0.2 mi., Zeke's Trail comes in from the left (sign). Ahead, Ridge Trail crosses over a subsidiary summit (1,290 ft.), descends slightly, and then climbs gradually to the true summit of Mt. Megunticook, which is wooded. Just beyond, Slope Trail diverges left (north). In another 0.4 mi., Ridge Trail descends to its end at Ocean Lookout.

Ridge Trail (AMC map 4: B1–B2)

Distances from Maiden Cliff Trail jct. (450 ft.) to

- Scenic Trail jct. (850 ft.): 0.2 mi., 20 min.
- Jack Williams Trail jct. (900 ft.): 0.8 mi., 40 min.
- Zeke's Trail jct. (1,150 ft.): 1.1 mi., 55 min.
- Mt. Megunticook summit and Slope Trail jct. (1,385 ft.): 2.0 mi., 1 hr. 30 min.
- Ocean Lookout (1,250 ft.): 2.4 mi., 1 hr. 45 min.

Multi-Use Trail from the north (MBPL)

This trail, a gravel access road, serves as the approach to the mountains in the northern part of Camden Hills State Park, including Bald Rock, Cameron, Derry, and Frohock mountains. The trail may also be used to reach several trails that climb to the summit of Mt. Megunticook. At the base of Megunticook, a summer bypass avoids several low, wet areas. From the jct. of US 1 and ME 173 in Lincolnville, take ME 173 west. At 2.3 mi., bear left onto Youngtown Rd., and in 200 ft. turn left into a small parking area.

In 0.5 mi. from the trailhead, reach the jct. with Frohock Mtn. Trail, which leads left (south) to meet Bald Rock Mtn. Trail in 0.3 mi. and continues northeast over Derry Mtn. to its end atop the wooded Frohock Mtn. at 2.1 mi.

Continuing on Multi-Use Trail, reach the jct. of two trails at 1.2 mi. Here, Bald Rock Mtn. Trail heads left (south) 0.8 mi. to the summit of

Bald Rock Mtn., and Cameron Mtn. Trail leaves right and climbs 2.0 mi. to Cameron Mtn.

Ahead on Multi-Use Trail, Sky Blue Trail leaves right at 1.5 mi. At 2.4 mi. from Youngtown Rd., Multi-Use Trail passes Zeke's Trail on the right (leads 1.4 mi. to Ridge Trail), and at 2.8 mi., Multi-Use Trail reaches a jct. with Slope Trail (leads 1.0 mi. to the true summit of Mt. Megunticook). Multi-Use Trail continues to swing low around the northeast side of Mt. Megunticook to reach its end at the jct. of Nature Trail and Megunticook Trail at 4.8 mi., at a point 0.3 mi. from the hiker's parking lot trailhead on Mt. Battie Auto Rd.

Multi-Use Trail from the north (AMC map 4: A2, B2, C2)

Distances from Youngtown Rd. (250 ft.) to
- Frohock Mtn. Trail jct. (400 ft.): 0.5 mi., 15 min.
- Bald Rock Mtn. Trail and Cameron Mtn. Trail jct. (600 ft.): 1.2 mi., 50 min.
- Sky Blue Trail jct. (650 ft.): 1.5 mi., 1 hr.
- Zeke's Trail jct. (650 ft.): 2.4 mi., 1 hr. 30 min.
- Slope Trail jct. (550 ft.): 2.8 mi., 1 hr. 45 min.
- Mt. Megunticook Trail jct. (450 ft.): 4.8 mi., 2 hr. 45 min.
- Mt. Battie Auto Rd. (250 ft.) via Nature Trail: 5.1 mi., 3 hr.

Frohock Mtn. Trail (MBPL)

The trail leaves from Multi-Use Trail at a point 0.5 mi. from the Youngtown Rd. trailhead. From the jct. with Multi-Use Trail, turn left onto Frohock Mtn. Trail and head southeast. In 0.3 mi., reach a jct. with Bald Rock Mtn. Trail (leads 0.5 mi. to the summit of Bald Rock Mtn.). Frohock Mtn. Trail turns hard left (northeast) and climbs easily to the wooded summit of Derry Mtn. Beyond, the trail descends gradually to sag before a brief climb to its end atop Frohock Mtn. (454 ft.) at 2.1 mi.

Frohock Mtn. Trail (AMC map 4: A2–A3)

Distances from Multi-Use Trail (400 ft.) to
- Bald Rock Mtn. Trail jct. (650 ft.): 0.3 mi., 10 min.
- Frohock Mtn. (454 ft.): 2.1 mi., 1 hr. 5 min.

Bald Rock Mtn. (1,100 ft.)

Situated 2 mi. northeast of Mt. Megunticook, this mountain offers fine views from its summit ledges. Just below the summit is an old log lean-to that sleeps four persons. A second such shelter is found 0.1 mi. further north on Bald Rock Trail.

Bald Rock Mtn. Trail (MBPL)

Bald Rock Mtn. Trail diverges to the left (southeast) from Multi-Use Trail at a point 1.2 mi. from Youngtown Rd. Bald Rock Mtn. Trail climbs to the summit in 0.8 mi. at an easy-to-moderate grade. From the top of the mountain, there are excellent views of Penobscot Bay. Beyond, the trail descends to the west of Garey Mtn. to join Frohock Mtn. Trail at 1.3 mi.

Bald Rock Mtn. Trail (AMC map 4: A2, B2)
Distances from Multi-Use Trail (550 ft.) to
- Bald Rock Mtn. summit (1,100 ft.): 0.8 mi., 40 min.
- Frohock Mtn. Trail jct. (650 ft.): 1.3 mi., 55 min.

Cameron Mtn. (811 ft.)

In 2007, TNC acquired a 45-acre parcel that includes the open summit of Cameron Mtn. The following year the land was transferred to the state of Maine and is now part of Camden Hills State Park. Commercial blueberry fields are located on the summit, and hikers are asked to please stay on the trail.

Cameron Mtn. Trail (MBPL)

This trail diverges right (west) from Multi-Use Trail at its jct. with Bald Rock Mtn. Trail, 1.2 mi. from the Youngtown Rd. trailhead. Shortly, Cameron Mtn. Trail turns left (avoid the first left), following an old road. The trail crosses Black Brook and rises gradually past abandoned farmland, old cellar holes, and apple trees to a point just below the summit of Cameron Mtn., where a short side trail leads right (north) 0.1 mi. to its top. Beyond, the trail descends for a short distance before turning left (south) and starting to climb. Soon, Sky Blue Trail enters from the left, and just beyond at 2.0 mi., Cameron Mtn. Trail merges with Zeke's Trail.

Cameron Mtn. Trail (AMC map 4: A2, B1–B2)

Distances from Multi-Use Trail (600 ft.) to
- Cameron Mtn. summit (811 ft.): 1.1 mi., 35 min.
- Sky Blue Trail and Zeke's Trail jct. (950 ft.): 2.0 mi., 1 hr. 10 min.

Sky Blue Trail (MBPL)

Sky Blue Trail leaves Multi-Use Trail at a point 0.3 mi. beyond the start of Cameron Mtn. Trail and follows a course roughly parallel to that trail. At 1.5 mi., Sky Blue Trail merges with the upper end of Cameron Mtn. Trail, and just beyond, the jct. with Zeke's Trail is reached.

Sky Blue Trail (AMC map 4: B1–B2)

Distance from Multi-Use Trail (600 ft.) to
- Cameron Mtn. Trail jct. (950 ft.): 1.5 mi., 55 min.

Zeke's Trail (MBPL)

This trail diverges right (west) from Multi-Use Trail at a point 2.4 mi. from the Youngtown Rd. trailhead and ascends gradually. At 0.6 mi., Cameron Mtn. Trail enters from the right. At 0.9 mi., a spur trail leads right up to Zeke's Lookout (1,150 ft.), which offers views of Bald Rock Mtn. and Penobscot Bay through the trees. Zeke's Trail ends at its jct. with Ridge Trail at 1.4 mi., 0.9 mi. northwest of the summit of Mt. Megunticook.

Zeke's Trail (AMC map 4: B1–B2)

Distances from Multi-Use Trail (650 ft.) to
- Cameron Mtn. Trail jct. (950 ft.): 0.6 mi., 35 min.
- Zeke's Lookout spur trail (1,100 ft.): 0.9 mi., 1 hr.
- Ridge Trail jct. (1,150 ft.): 1.4 mi., 1 hr. 5 min.

Bald Mtn. (1,280 ft.)

This mountain in Camden is part of the 537-acre Bald Mtn. Preserve, which is owned and managed by CMLT. From Bald Mtn.'s attractive summit ledges, good views may be had of Penobscot Bay, Ragged Mtn., and the surrounding Camden Hills.

From US 1 at a point 0.8 mi. from the center of Camden, turn northwest on John St. At 0.8 from US 1, John St. becomes Hosmer Pond Rd. Follow this past the entrance to Camden Snow Bowl on the left (road name changes to Barnestown Rd. beyond). Continue to the height-of-land and a small trailhead parking lot on the right at 4.1 mi.

Bald Mtn. Trail (CMLT)

The trail enters the woods and immediately passes a kiosk. Cross a brook and quickly come to a jct. with Georges Highland Path (leads 2.4 mi. to a highpoint on Ragged Mtn.). Continuing straight ahead on Bald Mtn. Trail, climb steadily on switchbacks and rock steps. Leveling off, the trail reaches a viewpoint. Beyond, scramble up a short, steep pitch to an open ledge and views of Ragged Mtn. and Buzzard's Ledge across the notch.

After an easy traverse, Bald Mtn. Trail swings back toward the mountain and ascends steeply on rocks and ledges. At the top of the climb, hike along the cliff top with good views of the ocean and the peak of Bald Mtn. Bear left away from the cliffs and up to a knob. Cross a shallow col, then pass beneath the summit cliffs. Reach the base of a rock staircase and ascend steeply. (Trail to right is closed because of erosion and to protect fragile fauna.) Above, angle upward through woods and then climb switchbacks to the huge cairn on the summit at 0.9 mi.

Bald Mtn. Trail (USGS Camden quad, DeLorme map 14)

Distance from Barnestown Rd. (500 ft.) to
- Bald Mtn. summit (1,280 ft.): 0.9 mi., 50 min.

Ragged Mtn. (1,300 ft.)

This mountain rises to west of Camden and is the highest of the hills to the southwest of Megunticook Lake. The ski trails of the Camden Snow

Bowl are found on the northeast side of the mountain. Three trail sections of the GHP, an extensive system of footpaths developed and maintained by GRLT, ascend the mountain. Gain access via Thorndike Brook on Hope St., ME 17 west of Mirror Lake, and Barnestown Rd.

Georges Highland Path (Thorndike Brook Access) (GRLT)

GHP climbs the southwest ridge of Ragged Mtn., offering a series of good viewpoints en route. By traversing the entire ridge from north to south (or vice versa) and walking back to the start along ME 17, a fine loop hike of about 5 mi. can be had.

From the jct. of US 1 and ME 90 in Rockport, travel west on ME 90 for 2.7 mi. Turn right (northeast) on ME 17. Follow this for 5.4 mi. to Hope St. Turn right and reach the trailhead (sign and kiosk) on the right in 0.5 mi.

The initial going is easy through old fields and young woods, past stone walls and on and off old woods roads. Beyond, climb moderately to an overlook above Grassy Pond. Ahead, the trail switchbacks and then angles across the mountainside to a jct. with the GHP to Barnestown Rd. via Buzzard's Ledge at 1.2 mi. Continue along the ridge, climbing gradually to emerge onto ledges with broad views to the east. The trail remains out in the open for a fair distance before swinging back into a ravine.

Above the ravine, the trail is once again in the open with good walking over ledges and views over Mirror Lake and to Pleasant Mtn. and Spruce Peak. GHP climbs nearly to the summit of Ragged Mtn. at 2.3 mi. (there is a cluster of communication towers on top), but veers off into the woods just below. The trail continues ahead down the south ridge to meet an old carriage road, and then descends steadily toward Mirror Lake (the trail avoids the lake, a public water supply). Leveling off, the trail traverses north along the base of the mountain, bears left to cross a brook, and soon reaches the trailhead at 4.4 mi. at ME 17.

Georges Highland Path (Thorndike Brook Access) (USGS West Rockport quad, DeLorme map 14)

Distances from Hope St. trailhead (450 ft.) to
- jct., GHP to Barnestown Rd. (via Buzzards Ledge) (1,200 ft.): 1.2 mi., 55 min.
- Ragged Mtn. highpoint (1,250 ft.): 2.3 mi., 1 hr. 35 min.
- ME 17 trailhead (450 ft.): 4.4 mi., 2 hr. 35 min.

Georges Highland Path (ME 17 Access) (GRLT)

This trail ascends the southwest face of Ragged Mtn. and affords good views of the Camden village and the ocean, as well as the nearby peaks of Pleasant and Spruce mountains.

From the jct. of US 1 and ME 90 in Rockport, travel west on ME 90 for 2.7 mi. Turn right (northeast) on ME 17. Follow this for 1.1 mi. to trailhead parking (sign and kiosk) on the right, a short distance past Mirror Lake.

GHP enters the woods and, ahead, crosses a small brook. Turning right, the trail contours along the base of the mountain before ascending steadily with views through the trees to Mirror Lake. Reach an old carriage road and follow this easily north along the upper face of the mountain. Continue up the ridge on a foot trail, emerging on open ledges with views to the south. The trail ducks into scrub growth for a short distance before breaking into the open on ledges at 2.1 mi., a highpoint on Ragged Mtn. just beneath its summit. From here, the trail continues around the west face and along the north ridge to a jct. at 3.2 mi. To the left, it is 1.2 mi. via GHP to Hope St. (Thorndike Brook Access). To the right, it is 1.3 mi. via GHP to Barnestown Rd.

Georges Highland Path (ME 17 Access) (USGS West Rockport quad, DeLorme map 14)

Distances from ME 17 trailhead (450 ft.) to

- Ragged Mtn. highpoint (1,250 ft.): 2.1 mi., 1 hr. 30 min.
- Hope St. trailhead (450 ft.): 4.4 mi., 2 hr. 35 min.

Georges Highland Path (Barnestown Rd. Access) (GRLT)

This trail ascends Ragged Mtn. from the northeast, offering good views from Buzzard's Ledge, along the north ridge, and from the highpoint just below the summit.

From US 1 at a point 0.8 mi. from the center of Camden, turn northwest on John St. At 0.8 from US 1, John St. becomes Hosmer Pond Rd. Follow this past the entrance to Camden Snow Bowl on the left. Beyond this point, the road is known as Barnestown Rd. Continue to the height-of-land and a small trailhead parking lot on the right at 4.1 mi.

The trail enters the woods and immediately passes a kiosk. Cross a brook and come to a jct. Straight ahead, the Bald Mtn. Trail leads 0.9 mi. to the top of Bald Mtn. Turning right, GHP descends slightly, paralleling the brook. Below, recross the brook and cross Barnestown Rd. Ascend a short, steep pitch to a wide trail that winds up the hill at a moderate grade. Bear right at the lip of a ravine and soon reach Buzzard's Ledge and views northeast to Bald Mtn. Continue up the ridge over a series of open ledges. Reach a knob, then descend slightly to a jct. at 1.3 mi., where the GHP from Hope St. (Thorndike Brook Access) comes in from the right and merges. From here, it is 1.1 mi. to the highpoint on Ragged Mtn. and 3.2 to ME 17. To continue, follow the directions for GHP (Thorndike Brook Access).

Georges Highland Path (Barnestown Rd. Access) (USGS West Rockport quad, DeLorme map 14)

Distances from Barnestown Rd. trailhead (500 ft.) to
- Georges Highland Path (Thorndike Brook Access) jct. (1,190 ft.): 1.3 mi., 50 min.
- Ragged Mtn. highpoint (1,250 ft.): 2.4 mi., 1 hr. 35 min.

Beech Hill (530 ft.)

The 295-acre Beech Hill Preserve in Camden, owned and managed by CMLT, protects the only bald hilltop in the area, with panoramic views to Penobscot Bay and the Camden Hills. Atop the summit is Beech Nut, a historic sod-roofed stone hut.

Summit Road Trail (CMLT)

This trail climbs Beech Hill from the west through blueberry fields and grasslands. From the jct. of US 1 and ME 90, travel south 0.3 mi. to Beech Hill Rd. Follow this 1.7 mi. to trailhead parking on the left.

Follow a footpath through young woods and then through a field along the edge of the road. At a stone gate, turn right uphill on the wide track. Please observe signs asking hikers to remain on the trail. The road angles across the hillside in the open with fine views of the surrounding countryside, the Camden Hills, and the islands of Penobscot Bay. Reach the stone hut on top at 0.75 mi.

Summit Road Trail (USGS Camden quad, DeLorme map 14)

Distance from Beech Hill Rd. (350 ft.) to
  • Beech Hill summit (530 ft.): 0.75 mi., 25 min.

Woods Loop Trail (CMLT)

This trail ascends Beech Hill from the south through forest and fields. The trail forms a loop, providing hikers with an alternative route of about equal length for their ascent and descent. From the jct. of US 1 and ME 90, travel south on US 1 for 1.7 mi. Turn right onto Rockville Rd. and follow this 0.5 mi. to trailhead parking on the right.

Hike through a sugar maple grove and then bear left and soon reach a jct. The right fork makes an arc around the east side of the hill before reaching the summit. The left fork winds back and forth up the slope. The two trails meet at the edge of a field with views of the ocean to the east. The stone hut and the summit pines are visible up ahead to the west, and are reached at about 1 mi.

Woods Loop Trail (USGS Camden quad, DeLorme map 14)

Distance from Rockville Rd. (250 ft.) to
  • Beech Hill summit (530 ft.) via Woods Loop Trail: est. 1.0 mi., 40 min.

Frye Mtn. (1,139 ft.)

Frye Mtn. in Montville lies in the 5,240-acre FMWMA, managed by the Maine Dept. of Inland Fisheries & Wildlife. The wooded summit is reached via a loop trail that is part of GHP and maintained by GRLT.

From the jct. of ME 3 and ME 220 in Liberty, travel north on ME 220. Bear sharply right at Whites Corner at 3.2 mi. and reach Walker Ridge Rd. and the entrance to FMWMA on the right at 6.6 mi. Parking is available behind the maintenance building on the left.

To reach the start of the trail, walk north on ME 220 for 0.1 mi. The blue-blazed trail (a snowmobile trail for a short distance) heads right (east) into the woods. (*Note:* This is also the start of the trail to Hogback Mtn., which leaves in the opposite direction [west] from across ME 220.)

In about 50 ft., the trail diverges left, leaving the snowmobile trail, and climbs the ridge. Traversing east, the trail passes and crosses several stone walls and an old field before reaching Walker Ridge Rd. at 0.8 mi. Cross the road, reenter the woods, and quickly reach a kiosk. Ahead, cross a brook, continue on the trail, and cross a second brook. (*Note:* A high-water-crossing spur trail is reached on the left a short distance before the brook.) The trail follows the brook and then gradually bears away from it and heads south. Cross a number of stone walls and an old road before climbing to cross a third brook. Continue up a rocky ravine, and beyond, cross a gravel road and climb to a jct. at 2.8 mi. and the start of a loop over Frye Mtn.

Climb up to and across a series of ledges to reach the site of the old fire tower. Just beyond, the trail bears right off the large ledge (look for a small cairn and a blue blaze). Continue easily along to the east, then descend gradually before swinging back to the south and contouring along the southeast face of the mountain. Cross a brook and begin to climb. Cross over a ledge and descend briefly, reaching the loop trail jct. at 7.4 mi. Bear left and follow the trail 2.8 mi. back to ME 220, which is reached at 10.2 mi.

Frye Mtn. (USGS Mt. Liberty and Morrill quads, DeLorme map 14)

Distances from ME 220 (550 ft.) to

- Frye Mtn. summit (1,139 ft.): 3.0 mi., 1 hr. 50 min.
- entire loop hike: 10.2 mi., 5 hr.

Hogback Mtn. (1,115 ft.)

This mountain in Montville lies just west of Frye Mtn. The blue-blazed loop trail to its summit is part of the GHP system. Directions to the trailhead and parking are the same as for Frye Mtn.

Leave the west side of ME 220, and immediately cross a wet area on bog bridges. Beyond, follow a skidder trail for 50 ft., then bear left uphill. After a steep pitch, the grade moderates. Contour along the hillside with minor ups and downs. (*Note:* The trail is lightly used and can be obscure in places. Be sure to follow the blue blazes.) Pass a spring on the right, bear right to cross a small brook, and soon cross a woods road. Follow orange flagging across the cutover area beyond, picking up the trail again at the edge of the woods after about 150 ft. in the open. After a gentle ascent, and just past several gravestones and a massive oak tree on the left, reach the jct. of two woods roads and a trail jct. at 1.4 mi.

To the left, it is 0.7 mi. to Hogback Overlook. To the right, it is 0.4 mi. to Hogback Connector, a spur trail leading to the Sheepscot Headwaters Trail Network. Continue to the left and climb on a well-worn treadway, passing occasional cairns. Cross the rocky spine of the ridge in the semi-open with views to the north. Cross a jeep track, descend slightly, then proceed on the level. Cross a woods road and ascend easily to reach the steep south face of the mountain, where there are limited views through the trees. Ahead, reach the Hogback Overlook, a large cleared area with good views to the southeast, at 2.1 mi.

Soon the trail bears away from the south face, crosses a jeep track and passes over the wooded highpoint of the mountain. Beyond, descend easily to reach a woods road. Turn right to reach a jct. with the Hogback Connector, which leads left (west) to the Sheepscot Headwaters Trail Network. Continue to the right, following the grassy road and wooden marker posts. Descend on an eroded road to return to the jct. of the loop trail (watch carefully for the sign on the left) at about 2.7 mi. Bear left past the sign into the woods to return to ME 220, reaching it at about 4.1 mi.

Hogback Mtn. (USGS Mt. Liberty quad, DeLorme map 14)

Distances from ME 220 (550 ft.) to
- Loop trail jct. (850 ft.): 1.4 mi., 50 min.
- Hogback Overlook (1,050 ft.): 2.1 mi., 1 hr. 15 min.
- Entire loop hike: 4.1 mi., 2 hr. 15 min.

Whitten Hill (865 ft.)

The 410-acre Whitten Hill property in Montville, owned and managed by Sheepscot Wellspring Land Alliance, is part of a contiguous 1,100 acres of conservation lands. The alliance maintains a 26-mi. network of trails in Montville and Knox, the largest foot-travel-only system in the Midcoast region.

Northern Headwaters Loop Trail (SWLA)

This trail climbs easily over Whitten Hill and follows a portion of the headwaters of the Sheepscot River, making for a pleasant and interesting woods walk. From the jct. of ME 3 and ME 220 in Liberty, travel north on ME 220 to Whites Corner at 3.2 mi. Turn left onto Burnham Hill Rd. At 3.8 mi., bear right on Halldale Rd., which turns to dirt at 4.7 mi. Trailhead parking is reached on the left at 4.8 mi.

Follow the orange-blazed Whitten Hill Trail for 100 ft. to a jct. To the left, Bog Brook Trail leads to a series of trails south of Halldale Rd. Proceed to the right, following Northern Headwaters Loop Trail. At 0.1 mi., reach the main fork of the loop. Turn right and follow blue blazes easily along the ridgetop, passing a series of stone walls on the left. Cross the unmarked summit of Whitten Hill at 0.6 mi. Hemlock Hollow Trail joins from the right at 0.7 mi. Beyond, descend easily to the west, passing a spur trail leading right (north) to the Northern Headwaters trailhead on Whitten Hill Rd.

Ahead, pass Goose Ridge Trail on the right at 1.1 mi., and soon after, pass Mink Run Spur, also on the right. Continue downhill to reach the east bank of the Sheepscot River at about 1.5 mi. Cross the north side of Whitten Hill, following the course of the river with minor ups and downs. At about 2 mi., turn away from the river and ascend gradually to reach an old woods road. Leave the road and emerge into a large field with views to the south and west. Beyond, trend easily uphill to gain the ridge. Close the loop at the original jct. at 3.2 mi., and turn right (east) to reach the trailhead in another 0.1 mi.

Northern Headwaters Loop Trail (USGS Mt. Liberty quad, DeLorme map 14)

Distances from Halldale Rd. (750 ft.) to

- Whitten Hill summit (865 ft.): 0.6 mi., 20 min.
- Sheepscot River (450 ft.): 1.5 mi., 45 min.
- Entire loop hike: 3.4 mi., 1 hr. 45 min.

Goose Ridge (920 ft.)

This scenic hill in Montville features good ridge walking and several open fields with nice views of the rural countryside. Goose Ridge is part of the SWLA trail system.

From the jct. of ME 3 and ME 220 in Liberty, travel north on ME 220; bear sharply right at Whites Corner at 3.2 mi. Pass Walker Ridge Rd. and the entrance to FMWMA on the right at 6.6 mi. At 9.4 mi., turn left onto Freedom Pond Rd. Reach the trailhead on the left 10.5 mi. Parking is along the road.

Goose Ridge Trail (SWLA)

Follow the red-blazed trail into the woods, climbing easily. Begin a descent at 0.6 mi., pass an unsigned trail on the left, and then climb steadily. After a sharp right, reach a level area. Pass a sign for Spirited Horse Ranch (please stay on the trail). Bear left onto a two-wheel track, and soon reach an open field with good views at 1.2 mi. Climb to the top of the field and reenter the woods at 1.3 mi. Hike easily along the ridge, and at a second field, bear right over a stone wall at 1.5 mi. Cross the field with views to the Camden Hills. Reenter the woods at 1.6 mi. Immediately take a right onto a woods road and proceed on level ground. Pass through a stand of young birch and maple trees, then cross a swampy area. Pass through a stone wall at 1.8 mi., then ascend to the ridgetop. At 2.1 mi., reach the highpoint on Goose Ridge.

Beyond, continue along the level ridge, then begin a gentle descent next to a stone wall on the left. In a semi-open area, merge with a wide track coming in from the right. Reach a signpost at 2.7 mi., bear left, and follow a grassy road. At the next signpost, bear right into the woods and climb slightly over a knob. Reach a pipeline corridor at 2.9 mi. For the next 0.4 mi. the trail alternates between the woods and the pipeline. At 3.3 mi., bear left into the woods and, soon, cross a wet and overgrown area (*Caution:* trail is obscure in places here) with difficult footing. Emerge into a field and follow along the woods line. Bear left at a corner of the field, then right out to Penney Rd. at 3.6 mi.

Goose Ridge Trail (USGS Mt. Liberty quad, DeLorme map 14)

Distances from Freedom Pond Rd. (500 ft.) to
- Goose Ridge (920 ft.): 2.1 mi., 1 hr. 15 min.
- Penney Rd. (450 ft.): 3.6 mi., 2 hr.

Mt. Waldo (1,064 ft.)

This attractive mountain in Frankfort is best known for the granite quarries on its eastern side. Its many open ledges offer excellent views.

From the jct. of US 1A and ME 139 (Loggin Rd.) in Frankfort, head south on US 1A for 0.3 mi. Turn right onto Old Belfast Rd., pass beneath a railroad overpass, and at 0.5 mi., turn right onto Tyler Ln. At 0.7 mi., the road forks. Here, where Old Stage Rd. bears right, continue straight on Tyler Ln. Beyond, the dirt road gets rough. At 3.3 mi., pass a dirt road and old power line on the left. Park here on the side of the road.

Follow the eroded dirt road and the power line toward the mountain and its summit communication towers, and reach a large commercial blueberry field on the right. Ahead, where the old road goes sharply right at the upper corner of the field, bear left up into the woods to reach the old power line. Follow this track directly uphill over a series of ledges to the top. (*Note:* In 2011, a wind power project was proposed for the summit of Mt. Waldo. The status of the project was undetermined at the time this guide was published.)

Mt. Waldo (USGS Mt. Waldo quad, DeLorme map 23)
Distance from Tyler Ln. (500 ft.) to
• Mt. Waldo summit (1,064 ft.): est. 0.8 mi., 40 min.

SUGGESTED HIKES

Easy Hikes

Beech Hill [rt: 1.5 mi., 45 min.]. A short walk via Summit Road Trail to the open summit of Beech Hill, the historical Beech Nut stone hut, and sweeping coastal views.

Mt. Battie Trail [rt: 1.0 mi., 1 hr.]. Mt. Battie Trail is a short but steep hike gaining 600 ft. in 0.5 mi. The summit of Mt. Battie provides superb views of the Midcoast islands in Penobscot Bay.

Mt. Waldo [rt: 1.6 mi., 1 hr. 5 min.]. A short hike to the granite ledges of Mt. Waldo, where there are wonderful views southeast to Penobscot Bay as well as to the east and north.

Bald Mtn. Trail [rt: 1.8 mi., 1 hr. 30 min.]. A scenic loop hike with great cliff-top views of Ragged Mtn., Hosmer Pond, Camden village, and Penobscot Bay.

Whitten Hill [lp: 3.4 mi., 1 hr. 45 min.]. A fine woods walk over Whitten Hill, past numerous old stone walls, and along the headwaters of the Sheepscot River.

Goose Ridge Traverse [ow: 3.6 mi., 2 hr.]. This route offers a long stretch of good ridge walking, with several pretty fields en route.

Bald Rock Mtn. [rt: 3.4 mi., 2 hr. 40 min.]. A pleasant hike via Bald Rock Mtn., Multi-Use, and Frohock Mtn. trails to Bald Rock Mtn. and sweeping views of the Midcoast islands, where you can see Islesboro and Deer Isle on a clear day.

Moderate Hikes

Ragged Mtn. (ME 17 Access) [rt: 4.8 mi., 3 hr.]. Tackle this pretty section of the GHP and climb to the extensive open ledges on the ridgetop of Ragged Mtn., where there are fine coastal views.

Mt. Megunticook Loop [lp: 5.4 mi., 3 hr. 20 min.]. A pleasant loop hike combining Mt. Megunticook, Ridge, Slope, and Multi-Use trails. The highpoint of the hike is the spectacular view from Ocean Lookout.

Mt. Megunticook Traverse [ow: 5.6 mi., 3 hr. 25 min.]. Combining the Maiden Cliff, Scenic, Ridge, Tablelands, and Mt. Battie trails, this is one of finest walks in the Camden Hills, offering excellent views and plenty of good ridge walking. The trip is equally good in either direction. Spotting a car at both trailheads is necessary.

Strenuous Hike

Frye Mtn. Loop [rt: 10.2 mi., 5 hr.]. The longest trail in this section, this route travels through the scenic woods of the Frye Mtn. Wildlife Management Area. A good autumn foliage hike.

SECTION EIGHT
DOWNEAST

Moosehorn National Wildlife
   Refuge 280

Magurrewock Mtn. 280

Bald Mtn. (Baring
   Plantation) 281

Bells Mtn. and Crane Mtn. . . . 281

Cobscook Bay State Park 282

Littles Mtn. 282

Cunningham Mtn. 283

Donnell Pond Public Reserved
   Land 283

Schoodic Mtn. 284

Black Mtn. 285

Caribou Mtn. 287

Tunk Mtn. 289

Catherine Mtn. 290

Baker Hill 291

Pigeon Hill 291

Blue Hill 292

John B Mtn. 294

Great Pond Mountain
   Wildlands 295

Great Pond Mtn. 295

Oak Hill and Flag Hill. 296

Bald Mtn. (Dedham) 297

Blackcap 298

Little Peaked Mtn. 299

Peaked Mtn. 299

Bald Bluff Mtn. 300

Lead Mtn. (Humpback) 301

Peaked Mtn. (Washington
   County) 301

Passadumkeag Mtn. 302

Washington Bald Mtn. 302

Wabassus Mtn. 303

Pocomoonshine Mtn. 304

Suggested Hikes 305

The Downeast section includes all of Hancock and Washington counties in eastern Maine. The section extends from Chiputneticook Lake, St. Croix River, and Passamaquoddy Bay on the Canadian border in the east, to the Penobscot River and Penobscot Bay in the west. To the north, the county lines meet with the Aroostook and Penobscot County lines in a generally southwest-northeast direction. To the south is the rugged, rocky coastline on the Gulf of Maine and many islands large and small, including Mt. Desert Island and Deer Isle. The northern interior of the section is the lowland home to many lakes and streams, notably West Grand Lake and its neighbors Junior, Sysladobsis, and Big lakes. The Union, Narraguagus, and Machias rivers have their source in the forested interior and flow south to meet the Atlantic Ocean.

This section describes 19 mountains and 35 trails. Extending west to east across the center of the region is ME 9. Many hills and mountains, ranging in elevation from just several hundred feet to close to 1,500 ft., are scattered in relative proximity to this highway. These include the low hills in the area around Cobscook Bay, the peaks of Peaked and Lead mountains, and Bald Bluff, Peaked, and Little Peaked mountains. Moosehorn National Wildlife Refuge is the largest public reserve in the Downeast region, with nearly 25,000 acres of unique wildlife habitat, designated wilderness, and a number of hiking trails. Donnell Pond PRL is the second-largest publicly held land parcel in the section and is home to its namesake Donnell Pond and a variety of other lakes large and small, and to a cluster of mountain peaks, including Schoodic, Black, Caribou, and Tunk mountains, and many miles of foot trails. Several isolated hills along the coast afford great views with minimal effort.

Camping

Camping is available at Cobscook Bay and Lamoine state parks. Cobscook has 125 campsites, and Lamoine offers 62 campsites. Both feature hot showers, restrooms, picnic facilities, and other amenities. A selection of privately operated campgrounds is also available. Primitive backcountry camping is permitted at Donnell Pond and Cutler Coast public reserved lands only.

Moosehorn National Wildlife Refuge

The easternmost national wildlife refuge in the United States, Moosehorn provides an important stop for a wide variety of migratory birds on the Atlantic flyway. The diverse habitats found at Moosehorn are carefully managed for birdlife as well as for animals. One-third of the refuge is designated wilderness and is part of the National Wilderness Preservation System. The refuge consists of two divisions, the 17,200-acre Baring Division located southwest of Calais, and the 7,200-acre Edmunds Division situated between Dennysville and Whiting. Magurrewock, Bald, Bells and Crane mountains are within the refuge and offer short hikes and scenic coastal views.

Magurrewock Mtn. (384 ft.)

This small mountain in Calais is situated just inside the northern boundary of MNWR, Baring Division. The trailhead is on Ice House Rd. on the south side of US 1/ME 9, 3.1 mi. west of the international bridge in Calais and 2.8 mi. east of the jct. of US 1/ME 9 and ME 191. Park outside the gate on the shoulder of US 1. Follow Ice House Rd. (part of the East Coast Greenway, a 2,500-mile multi-use recreation trail from Maine to Florida) for 0.4 mi to start of trail.

Magurrewock Mtn. Trail (MNWR)

The unblazed Magurrewock Mtn. Trail leaves left and follows a snowmobile trail. At 0.7 mi., the trail forks. Bear left off the snowmobile trail to reach the summit at 1.0 mi., just southeast of a communications tower. In front of and slightly downhill from the tower is a viewpoint over Magurrewock Bog and St. Croix River.

Magurrewock Mtn. (USGS Calais quad, DeLorme map 36)

Distance from US 1 (100 ft.) to
  • Magurrewock Mtn. summit (384 ft.): 1.0 mi., 35 min.

Bald Mtn. (Baring Plantation) (448 ft.)

Bald Mountain, one of eighteen so-named in Maine, is located in the Baring Division of Moosehorn National Wildlife Refuge. From US 1/ME 9, at a point 3.5 mi. west of the international bridge in Calais and 2.4 mi. east of the jct. of US 1/ME 9 and ME 191, turn south onto Charlotte Rd. In 2.4 mi., turn right (west) onto Headquarters Rd. (gated after sunset), and proceed to the refuge headquarters and parking lot. A kiosk provides brochures and maps.

Follow Headquarters Rd. Trail 0.8 mi. west to Mullen Meadow and bear left onto the blue-blazed trail. Pass through Bertrand E. Smith Natural Area, and, at 2.1 mi., turn left onto the white-blazed Tower Trail. Descend into a wet area before climbing steadily to the heavily wooded summit at 2.8 mi. Here, the 100-ft.-tall wooden tower, erected in 1937, lies on the ground like a fallen giant. Limited views can be seen through the trees to the south and east.

Bald Mtn. (USGS Meddybemps Lake East, DeLorme map 36)

Distance from refuge headquarters (200 ft.) to
- Bald Mtn. summit (448 ft.): 2.8 mi., 1 hr. 30 min.

Bells Mtn. (213 ft.) and Crane Mtn. (269 ft.)

These small mountains in the Edmunds Division of MNWR in Edmunds Township are adjacent to each other and offer easy hiking over interesting terrain, and good views. Both are located in the Tide Mill Farm day-use multi-use public access site administered by the Maine Dept. of Inland Fisheries and Wildlife. From US 1 at a point 2.8 mi. north of Whiting and 1.5 mi. south of Cobscook Bay State Park, turn west onto Bell Mtn. Rd. and drive 0.2 mi. to a large parking area (sign).

From the register box, bear left and climb the white-blazed loop trail leading 0.3 mi. to the Bells Mtn. summit and views to the east over Tide Mill Farm on Whiting Bay. Continue on the forested trail over several ledges and along a fractured cliff face on the backside of the mountain. Reach the trailhead and the end of the loop at 0.7 mi.

From Bells Mtn. trailhead, the Crane Mtn. trailhead is reached by continuing on Bell Mtn. Rd. for an additional 0.7 mi., and then bearing right at 0.8 mi. to a parking area. A loop trail leaves from the kiosk and register box. Ascend to an outlook at 0.2 mi., with views west and north. At 0.3 mi., reach the wooded summit of Crane Mtn. and a second outlook on a ledge just below. A third viewpoint is reached at 0.6 mi. Complete the loop at the parking area at 0.7 mi.

Bells Mtn. and Crane Mtn. (USGS Whiting quad, DeLorme map 27)

Distances from first parking area (100 ft.) to
- Bells Mtn. summit (213 ft.): 0.3 mi., 15 min.
- complete loop: 0.7 mi., 25 min.

Distances from second parking area (150 ft.) to
- Crane Mtn. summit (269 ft.): 0.3 mi., 15 min.
- complete loop: 0.7 mi., 25 min.

Cobscook Bay State Park

This coastal park occupies 888 acres on Whiting Bay in Edmunds Township. Tides at Cobscook average 24 ft. and can be as much as 28 ft. when the meteorological conditions are just right. The nutrient-rich waters of the bay support a wide range of sea and birdlife, making wildlife watching here a popular activity. In addition, camping, hiking, sea kayaking, and boating are available. Several short hiking trails lead to park highpoints at Littles and Cunningham mountains.

Littles Mtn. (200 ft.)

From US 1 at a point about 4.3 mi. north of Whiting and about 5.2 mi. south of the jct. of US 1 and ME 86 in Dennysville, turn east on South Edmunds Rd. Drive 0.5 mi., then turn right to reach the park entrance and ranger station. Just beyond, on Burnt Cove Rd., are parking and restrooms on the right.

Walk 0.1 mi. back to South Edmunds Rd. and turn right. In another 0.1 mi., the trailhead is on the left. It is a short but steep 0.2-mi. climb to the 60-foot steel fire tower (closed to public) on the summit, and views.

Littles Mtn. (USGS Whiting quad, DeLorme map 27)
Distances from park entrance (100 ft.) to
  • start of trail via park road and South Edmunds Rd.: 0.2 mi., 5 min.
  • Littles Mtn. summit (200 ft.): 0.4 mi., 15 min.

Cunningham Mtn. (140 ft.)

Nature Trail begins near the park entrance and leads through forests and across several brooks to views of Burnt Cove. At a jct. at 0.6 mi., turn left, and at 0.7 mi. and a second jct., turn right again. Reach an overlook atop the peak at 0.8 mi. and views to Whiting Bay and Broad Cove.

To return, retrace your steps, or turn right at the base of the climb and hike east 0.1 mi. to Burnt Cove Rd. The parking lot is about 0.4 mi. left (north) along this road.

Cunningham Mtn. (USGS Whiting quad, DeLorme map 27)
Distances from park entrance (100 ft.) to
  • Cunningham Mtn. summit (140 ft.) via Nature Trail: 0.8 mi., 20 min.
  • complete loop via Burnt Cove Rd.: 1.4 mi., 40 min.

Donnell Pond Public Reserved Land

This 15,384-acre preserve, owned and managed by MBPL, is located in Franklin, Sullivan, T9 SD, and T10 SD. The preserve offers more than a dozen miles of hiking trails on Schoodic, Black, and Caribou mountains. The central feature of the area is the scenic Donnell Pond, which has a number of campsites on its south and east shores. These can be reached only by foot trail or by canoe or motorboat. Schoodic Beach offers picnicking, swimming, tent camping, and outhouses.

Northeast of Donnell Pond, along ME 182 (also known as Blackwoods Scenic Byway), the unit encompasses much of the north and east shoreline of pristine Tunk Lake, as well as the entirety of Spring River Lake and a number of smaller ponds. Tunk Mtn. rises to more than 1,000 ft. at the west edge of the property and offers several miles of hiking trails. West of Tunk Mtn. is the 9,000-acre Spring River Preserve owned by TNC. As of this writing in 2011, TNC and MBPL were working collaboratively on plans to develop a complementary system of trails on Tunk Mtn.

The main trailhead for Schoodic and Black mountains is located at the end of Schoodic Beach Rd., 0.5 mi. by trail from Schoodic Beach. From the jct. of US 1 and ME 3 in Ellsworth, travel 13.4 mi. east on US 1 to ME 183 in East Sullivan. Turn left (north) and drive 4.3 mi. to Donnell Pond Rd. on the left (blue and white sign), just after crossing an old railroad bed (now the Downeast Sunrise Trail). Turn here, passing by Black Mtn. Rd. on the right at 0.3 mi. (leads 2.0 mi. to Big Chief Trail on Black Mtn. South Ridge). Reach the end of the road and the Schoodic Beach parking lot and a pit toilet at 3.1 mi.

Schoodic Mtn. (1,069 ft.)

This attractive mountain in T9 SD in the southwest corner of the preserve offers fine views of Frenchman Bay and the mountains of Acadia from its bare summit. Two trails ascend the peak from the east leaving from the Schoodic Beach parking lot.

Schoodic Mtn. via Schoodic Beach (MBPL)

To ascend via Donnell Pond, take the wide trail at the far right end of the parking lot just beyond the information kiosk. Follow this 0.5 mi. to Schoodic Beach on Donnell Pond. Just before reaching the pond, pass an outhouse on the left. Turn left (west) here. Ahead, ascend steeply at first, then gradually on switchbacks, to a jct. at 1.1 mi., where the direct trail from the parking lot joins from the left. Bear right and climb ledges on the south side of the mountain before reaching the summit tower at 1.5 mi.

Schoodic Mtn. Trail (MBPL)

A more direct ascent leaves the left end of the parking lot, to the right of the pit toilet. Descend briefly, then climb steadily, passing several huge boulders with overhangs. Reach the top of a cliff and good views to Black Mtn. Beyond, the trail levels out, then climbs gradually to meet the trail from Schoodic Beach at 0.9 mi. Bear left to reach the summit at 1.3 mi.

Schoodic Mtn. (USGS Sullivan quad, DeLorme map 24)

Distances from Schoodic Beach parking lot (300 ft.) to

- Schoodic Beach (150 ft.): 0.5 mi., 15 min.
- Schoodic Mtn. summit (1,069 ft.) via Schoodic Beach: 1.5 mi., 1 hr. 15 min.
- Schoodic Mtn. summit (1,069 ft.) via Schoodic Mtn. Trail: 1.3 mi., 1 hr. 5 min.

Black Mtn. (1,094 ft.)

This mountain in T10 SD rises to the east of Donnell Pond and offers good views in all directions from its broad open summit. Black Mtn. Trail ascends the mountain from both Schoodic Beach parking lot and Schoodic Beach. A good loop hike over the Black Mtn. cliffs can be done by combining the trails from these points. Another shorter loop over the summit and around the Wizard Pond area is possible by combining Black Mtn. Trail with Big Chief Trail and its summit spur trail.

Black Mtn. from Schoodic Beach parking lot (MBPL)

Black Mtn. Trail leaves from the right end of the Schoodic Beach parking lot. Go past the kiosk, cross a small brook, and head right, uphill. Follow a mostly level woods road over many bog bridges to the base of the mountain. The trail then turns left (north) and climbs steeply on switchbacks and rock steps, weaving between ledges to reach the top of the ridge and a jct. at 1.2 mi. Here, the trail to Schoodic Beach via Black Mtn. Cliffs leaves left (it's a short distance to several viewpoints, 1.2 mi. to the beach, and 1.7 mi. back to the parking lot—a nice loop).

Bear right, proceed easily through the woods, and at 1.8 mi., reach a jct. The left fork leads 2.3 mi. to Redmans Beach on Donnell Pond or 2.4 mi. to Caribou Mtn. Continuing to the right, descend, steeply at times, to a notch at 2.0 mi. and a jct. To the right, a trail leads 1.1 mi. down to Black Mtn. Rd. (Big Chief Trail, but not signed as such. Use the upper part of this trail to make a loop over the summit if desired.) Bear left, and soon break out onto open ledges, following cairns to reach the summit at 2.3 mi. (large cairn and sign) and the east jct. of Caribou Mtn. Trail.

Black Mtn. Trail (USGS Sullivan and Tunk Lake quads, DeLorme map 24)

Distances from Schoodic Beach parking lot (300 ft.) to
- Black Mtn. base (450 ft.): 0.8 mi., 30 min.
- trail to Black Mtn. Cliffs and Schoodic Beach (900 ft.): 1.2 mi., 55 min.
- Caribou Mtn. Trail, west jct. (1,050 ft.): 1.8 mi., 1 hr. 15 min.
- trail to Black Mtn. Rd. (900 ft.): 2.0 mi., 1 hr. 25 min.
- Black Mtn. summit (1,094 ft.) and Caribou Mtn. Trail, east jct.: 2.3 mi., 1 hr. 35 min.

Black Mtn. via Schoodic Beach (MBPL)

The trail to Black Mtn. diverges right (east) from Schoodic Beach Trail just before reaching Donnell Pond (0.5 mi. from Schoodic Beach parking lot). The trail to Black Mtn. crosses a stream in a ravine on a wooden footbridge, then climbs gently to cross three small brooks in succession. The trail merges with a woods road and proceeds easily to cross another brook. Beyond, the trail begins a steady, steep ascent using switchbacks. Cross a brook on a short footbridge and continue to climb moderately to gain the ridge. Traverse to the right (southeast) along the top of the cliffs, passing a number of overlooks with views to Donnell Pond and Schoodic Mtn. Join Black Mtn. Trail (direct from Schoodic Beach parking lot) at 1.2 mi. Turn left to continue to the summit of Black Mtn. (1.1 mi. ahead).

Black Mtn. via Schoodic Beach (USGS Sullivan and Tunk Lake quads, DeLorme map 24)

Distances from Schoodic Beach parking lot (300 ft.) to
- Schoodic Beach (150 ft.) and jct. for trail to Black Mtn.: 0.5 mi., 15 min.
- cliffs on southwest side of Black Mtn. (800 ft.): est. 0.9 mi., 50 min.
- Black Mtn. Trail jct. (900 ft.): 1.2 mi., 1 hr. 5 min.
- Black Mtn. summit (1,094 ft.): 2.3 mi., 1 hr. 40 min.

Black Mtn. via Big Chief Trail on South Ridge (MBPL)

To reach the Black Mtn. South Ridge trailhead, take Black Mtn. Rd. for 2.0 mi. from its jct. with Schoodic Beach Rd. Just beyond a small parking area is a sign for Big Chief Trail. Take this well-worn path and ascend steadily to a fork at 0.6 mi. To the right, the trail dips to cross the outlet of Wizard Pond, then climbs steeply over ledges to the open summit of the east peak of Black Mtn. at 1.2 mi. To the left, the trail continues easily to reach Black Mtn. Trail at 1.1 mi. From there, it is 0.3 mi. to the summit.

Black Mtn. via Big Chief Trail on South Ridge (USGS Tunk Lake quad, DeLorme map 24)

Distances from Black Mtn. Rd. (300 ft.) to
- Black Mtn. summit (1,094 ft.) via right fork: 1.2 mi., 1 hr.
- Black Mtn. summit (1,094 ft.) via left fork and Black Mtn. Trail: 1.4 mi., 1 hr. 5 min.

Caribou Mtn. (960 ft.)

This mountain in T10 SD lies to the north of Black Mtn. in the heart of the backcountry of Donnell Pond PRL. Caribou Mtn. can be reached via a short hike from Dynamite Brook Rd. in the north or by a longer hike from the south from Schoodic Beach parking lot via Black Mtn. Crossing the remote terrain around Rainbow Pond, Caribou Mtn. Trail makes a 5.6-mi. loop over the mountain.

Caribou Mtn. Trail (MBPL)

This loop trail is described in a counterclockwise direction from the summit of Black Mtn. Leaving the summit, follow cairns, blue flagging, and blue blazes along the ridge, trending gradually downhill. At the bottom of the initial descent, an unmaintained side trail leaves right, leading to Tunk Lake. Continuing ahead on Caribou Mtn. Trail, pass beneath a cliff face on the left, cross a brook, and continue to descend easily. Make an arc around a bog area to the left (west), crossing several outlet streams en route. Descend into a drainage and cross the outlet of Rainbow Pond at 2.1 mi.

Beyond, begin the ascent of Caribou Mtn. Pass to the right of a large square-edged boulder, and above, weave between boulders, climbing steadily. Break out onto open ledges and climb a slab up to the right to reach a viewpoint looking out to Tunk Lake, Rainbow Pond, and Black Mtn. Here, the trail from the north comes in on the right (leads about 1 mi. to Dynamite Brook Rd., passing a side trail to Catherine Mtn. along the way).

Traverse the semi-open south face of the mountain on slabs and ledges, passing numerous viewpoints and ascending to a parklike meadow area at 3.2 mi., just below the true summit. Continuing on, descend gradually on the long west ridge. Near the end of the ridge at a large open slab (great views), turn sharply left and make a steep descent, switchbacking between ledges. Pass under a rock roof, go over a knob, and reach a jct. at 4.7 mi. Here, Redmans Beach Trail leads right (west) 1.4 mi. to the beach on the east shore of Donnell Pond.

Continue ahead, descend to a notch, then begin to ascend the north side of Black Mtn. Climb steadily, passing through a stand of old-growth spruce to gain the level ridge top, and soon reach the jct. with Black Mtn. Trail at 5.6 mi.

Caribou Mtn. Trail (USGS Tunk Lake quad, DeLorme map 24)

Distances from Black Mtn. summit (1,094 ft.) to
- Rainbow Pond outlet (300 ft.): 2.1 mi., 2 hr. 5 min.
- highpoint on Caribou Mtn. (900 ft.): 3.2 mi., 2 hr. 55 min.
- Redmans Beach Trail jct. (500 ft.): 4.7 mi., 3 hr. 40 min.
- Black Mtn. Trail jct. (1,050 ft.): 5.6 mi., 4 hr. 25 min.

Caribou Mtn. from the north (MBPL)

From the jct. of US 1 and ME 182 in Franklin, drive east on ME 182 for 14 mi. to T10 SD and Dynamite Brook Rd. on the right. (The trailhead for Tunk Mtn. is just ahead on the left.) Turn here and drive 0.8 mi. to a small parking area on the left. The trail starts 0.1 mi. farther ahead, turning left off the road just before a bridge.

Follow the wide trail gradually uphill, then ascend more steeply to a jct. at 0.5 mi. To the left, an unmaintained trail leads 0.7 mi. to the summit of Catherine Mtn. Continue to the right and proceed on level ground.

Ahead, climb steadily, sometimes on rough, rocky trail, to gain the east ridge of the mountain at an open slab and the jct. with Caribou Mtn. Trail at about 0.9 mi. Continue to the right to reach more lookout points with good views to Tunk Lake and Black Mtn.

Caribou Mtn. from the north (USGS Tunk Lake quad, DeLorme map 24)

Distances from Dynamite Brook Rd. (400 ft.) to
- trail to Catherine Mtn. (600 ft.): 0.5 mi., 15 min.
- Caribou Mtn. Trail jct. (800 ft.): 0.9 mi., 40 min.
- highpoint on Caribou Mtn. (900 ft.): 1.3 mi., 55 min.

Tunk Mtn. (1,157 ft.)

This mountain offers good views to the south and east from its extensive summit ledges. From the jct. of US 1 and ME 182 in Franklin, travel east on ME 182, the Blackwoods Scenic Byway. Reach the main Tunk trailhead on the left at 14 mi.

(*Note:* In 2011, MBPL built a new parking lot for the Tunk trailhead, including a vault toilet, information kiosk, and signage. Other changes at Tunk Mtn. are also in progress, including construction of rock steps, installation of water bars, removal of old ropes, trail relocations, and new signage on Tunk Mtn. Trail. A new loop trail in the Hidden Ponds area is also being built. Hikers may wish to check with MBPL on the status of these projects.)

Tunk Mtn. Trail (MBPL)

This popular and well-worn trail leaves the parking lot on ME 182 and heads north on a wide track, rising gradually to Salmon Pond. The trail skirts the west shore of the pond to reach a junction with Hidden Ponds Loop, which leads 0.5 mi. to Little Long Pond, eventually circling back to Tunk Mtn. Trail. Beyond the junction, Tunk Mtn. Trail continues on to Mud Pond, following its south and west shores.

Leaving the pond, the trail turns uphill to the left, climbing steeply on rock steps. Follow the rough trail upward, passing through a spruce forest. Eventually, the trail breaks onto the semi-open and climbs over open ledges. Use caution on the steep and often slippery rocks. Above, scramble over a rock wall and reach a plaque dedicated to Harold Pierce, who in 1994 donated the land on Tunk Mtn. to the state of Maine for preservation.

Above, climb over more ledges to gain the ridge proper. Bear left (south) along the ridge and soon reach a small communications tower and outbuilding. Just ahead is the summit survey marker at 1.5 mi. A short distance farther along the ridge are the great cliffs of the southwest face of Tunk, a worthwhile side trip.

Tunk Mtn. Trail (USGS Tunk Mtn. quad, DeLorme maps 24 and 25)

Distances from ME 182 (300 ft.) to
- Salmon Pond (310 ft.): 0.5 mi., 15 min.
- Mud Pond (470 ft.): 0.8 mi., 30 min.
- Tunk Mtn. summit (1,157 ft.): 1.5 mi., 1 hr. 15 min.

Catherine Mtn. (940 ft.)

This mountain in T10 SD lies east of Caribou Mtn. and just outside the boundary of Donnell PRL. To reach the trailhead, drive east on ME 182 from the main Tunk trailhead. At 1.1 mi., a dirt road on the right leads 100 ft. to a grassy parking area.

A woods road to the right (west) is the start of the hike. Follow the road on the level. Beyond, ascend steeply up the east ridge of the mountain. After the angle eases, pass a spur trail on the right leading 100 yd. to an overlook and views to the north and east. Just ahead, a short side trail on the left leads to views of Tunk Lake and Black Mtn. Ahead on the main trail, cross a town line (orange blazes) and pass several areas of mined rocks. Continue along the cliff edge with good views to Tunk Lake. Pass the upper jct. of the summit loop on the left. Ahead, traverse easily, passing beneath the true summit at about 0.7 mi. From here, retrace your steps, or continue to the upper end of the summit loop trail and swing back just below the face to rejoin the trail for the descent. (*Note:* Beyond this upper jct., the unmaintained trail descends to join the trail to Caribou Mtn., which can be followed to Dynamite Brook Rd. [1.2 mi. from the highpoint on Catherine Mtn.].)

Catherine Mtn. (USGS Tunk Lake quad, DeLorme maps 24 and 25)
Distance from ME 182 (500 ft.) to
  • highpoint on Catherine Mtn. (900 ft.): est. 0.7 mi., 35 min.

Baker Hill (360 ft.)

A 58-acre conservation easement managed by FBC protects the scenic
south slope of Baker Hill in Sullivan. About 1 mi. of trail loops through
the property, leading to ledges with views to the bay and beyond to the
peaks of Acadia.

From the jct. of US 1 and ME 200 in Sullivan, travel east on US 1 for
1.5 mi. Turn left (north) onto Punkinville Rd. and go 0.2 mi. to trailhead
parking on the left (sign).

The trail leaves the parking lot and proceeds west to a fork. Take the
left fork and follow Overlook Trail, which climbs easily to open ledges and
good views at about 0.3 mi. Beyond the viewpoint, continue up the ridgeline following blue markers, passing several more viewpoints. Ahead, turn
right (east) away from the cliffs, pass a jct. on the right, and reach the top
of the hill. Beyond, at a boundary line, turn sharply right, cross a wet area,
and descend gently and then more steeply to the base of the hill. Bear right
and take the mostly level trail back to the parking area.

Baker Hill (USGS Sullivan quad, DeLorme map 24)
Distances from Punkinville Rd. (200 ft.) to
  • ledges overlook (320 ft.): 0.3 mi., 15 min.
  • complete loop: est. 1.0 mi., 45 min.

Pigeon Hill (317 ft.)

Pigeon Hill in Steuben, the highest point along the coast in Washington
County, is part of the 170-acre Pigeon Hill Preserve managed by DCC.
The easy-to-moderate hike rewards hikers with good views that range west
to Blue Hill and Mt. Desert Island, south to Petit Manan Lighthouse and
the islands of the Pleasant Bay archipelago, and northwest to the peaks of
Donnell Pond PRL.

From US 1 in Steuben, 2 mi. west of Milbridge and 25 mi. east of Ellsworth, drive south on Pigeon Hill Rd. for 4.6 mi. to trailhead parking on the right (sign), opposite an old cemetery.

Follow the distinct but unblazed Historic Trail to the jct. with Summit Loop Trail at 0.3 mi. Continue straight ahead to a viewpoint atop the east ledges. Reach the partially wooded summit at 0.4 mi. Descend via Summit Loop Trail, and pass several ledges with views before reaching the jct. with Historic Trail at 0.7 mi.

Pigeon Hill (USGS Petit Manan Point quad, DeLorme map 17)

Distances from Pigeon Hill Rd. (50 ft.) to

- Pigeon Hill summit (317 ft.) via Historic Trail: 0.4 mi., 20 min.
- complete loop via Summit Loop and Historic trails: 1.1 mi., 40 min.

Blue Hill (934 ft.)

This coastal monadnock rises prominently just to the north of the village Blue Hill and affords excellent views of Blue Hill Bay and beyond to the mountains of Acadia on Mt. Desert Island. The town of Blue Hill and the Blue Hill Heritage Trust jointly manage nearly 500 acres of conservation land on the mountain.

From the jct. of ME 15 and ME 172/176 in the center of Blue Hill, drive north on ME 15 for 0.9 mi. Turn right onto Mountain Rd. and go 0.4 mi. to the trailhead for Osgood Trail (sign). Parking is along the road. The trailhead for Hayes Trail (sign, kiosk) is 0.4 mi. farther ahead, with a large parking lot on the south side of the road.

Osgood Trail (BHHT)

Follow the wide, well-used trail into the woods to an information kiosk. Bear right and switchback easily up the mountain following blue blazes. The way becomes steeper as the trail climbs rock steps to a jct. with South Face Trail on the right (contours 0.25 mi. east across the south face of the hill to connect with Hayes Trail).

Continue straight ahead, and soon after a rough section of trail (rocks and roots), the path breaks out onto open slabs with views to the south.

Ahead, the angle lessens before the final scramble to the peak, which is reached at 0.9 mi. The concrete stanchions of the old fire tower remain just below, and a communications tower is to the left.

> **Osgood Trail (USGS Blue Hill quad, DeLorme map 15)**
> Distance from Mountain Rd. (350 ft.) to
> • Blue Hill summit (934 ft.): 0.9 mi., 45 min.

Hayes Trail (BHHT)

Follow a grassy track across a large field with views ahead to Blue Hill on the summit tower. At the top of the field, reach a jct. with Tower Trail (a road originally built to service the tower, but also a good hiking route) on the right.

Climb the rock staircase to the left to reach the jct. with South Face Trail (contours 0.25 mi. west across the south face of the hill to connect with Osgood Trail). Beyond, switchback up the slope, then traverse east to cross an old trail (closed). Ascend steeply on rocky trail to a series of rock steps and staircases. Beyond, reach the jct. with Tower Trail, which enters from the right. Walk easily west, passing behind the tower (no trespassing) to reach the summit ledges at 0.7 mi.

> **Hayes Trail (USGS Blue Hill quad, DeLorme map 15)**
> Distance from Mountain Rd. (400 ft.) to
> • Blue Hill summit (934 ft.): 0.7 mi., 35 min.

Tower Trail (BHHT)

Combined with the lower and upper portions of Hayes Trail, Tower Trail makes for a longer but easier route to the summit. Tower Trail leaves Hayes Trail 0.3 mi. from the trailhead on Mountain Rd. Continue to the right on the two-wheel track, which winds gradually up the hill. Above, traverse west on the level, and then climb steeply to the summit ridge. The trail rejoins Hayes Trail at 0.7 mi., and follows it a short distance to the top.

Tower Trail (USGS Blue Hill quad, DeLorme map 15)
Distances from lower Hayes Trail jct. (500 ft.) to
- Upper Hayes Trail jct.: 0.7 mi., 30 min.
- Blue Hill summit via lower and upper Hayes Trail (934 ft.): 1.1 mi., 45 min.

South Face Trail (BHHT)

This short 0.25-mi. connector trail links Osgood Trail with Hayes Trail, allowing the opportunity for a loop hike over the summit and eliminating the need to walk along Mountain Rd. Excellent views may be had along this trail.

John B Mtn. (250 ft.)

This low mountain in Brooksville lies in the heart of 38 undeveloped acres just north of Eggemoggin Reach and East Penobscot Bay and provides good views from numerous outlooks. Hikers are urged to stay on the trail to protect the fragile mountaintop ecosystem. The preserve is managed by BHHT.

From the jct. of ME 15 and ME 172/176 in Blue Hill, drive west on ME 15/172/176 for 5.0 mi. to Grays Corner. Turn left (south) onto ME 15/175/176 and go 2.7 mi. to Black Corner. Turn right here onto ME 175/176 and drive 0.6 mi. In Brooksville, where ME 175 turns right, proceed left on ME 176 and take this 3.9 mi. to Breezemere Rd. on the left. Drive 0.8 mi. to trailhead parking on the right (sign, kiosk).

From the parking area, walk right, behind the cemetery. Switchback up the hillside at a moderate grade, passing rock ledges on the left. Soon, reach a trail jct. A short (0.1-mi.) side trail leads south over the summit and loops past several outlooks.

Returning to the main trail, quickly reach another jct. The trail to the left leads to open ledges with a wood bench and more views, and beyond, the path descends. The trail to the right drops down through pleasant woods. Where the trails merge, bear left downhill to reach a woods road. Follow this along the base of the mountain, passing a large rock face, back to the trailhead.

John B Mtn. (USGS Cape Rosier quad, DeLorme map 15)
Distances from Breezemere Rd. (50 ft.) to
  • John B Mtn. summit and viewpoint (250 ft.): est. 0.4 mi., 20 min.
  • complete loop: est. 1.5 mi., 50 min.

Great Pond Mountain Wildlands

This preserve in Orland, encompassing 4,300 acres of mountain peaks, forests, and streams, is owned and managed by GPMCT. Purchased in 2005, this is one of the largest parcels of land ever acquired by a Maine land trust. Miles of gravel roads crisscross the property, but vehicular access is limited to summer and fall weekends only. Travel on foot, bicycle, and horseback is allowed any time. Footpaths lead to Great Pond Mtn., which rises to over 1,000 ft. in the Dead River section, and to Flag and Oak hills in the Hothole Valley section.

Great Pond Mtn. (1,038 ft.)

This mountain is known for the impressive cliffs on its southeast face and for broad summit views that take in Acadia, Blue Hill, Penobscot Bay, and the Camden Hills.

On US 1/ME 3 in East Orland, 6.0 mi. east of Bucksport and 14.0 mi. west of Ellsworth, turn north onto Hatchery Rd. (sign for Craig Brook National Fish Hatchery). At 0.9 mi., the road turns to dirt. At 1.3 mi., pass through the fish hatchery complex. Just beyond, turn right uphill onto Don Fish Rd. and proceed to trailhead parking at the Dead River gate on the left at 1.8 mi.

Walk up the road. Just before a gate across the road (about 0.4 mi.), turn left at a trail sign for Stuart Gross Path and head into the woods. This well-used footpath ascends moderately, levels off, and descends to meet an old jeep road (Mountain Trail, not signed). Proceed straight ahead on this old road, which is worn down to bare rock, climbing easily up the long west ridge. Ahead, views to the south open up. At the base of the summit ledges, enjoy more-extensive views to the west and south. (More ledges to the east invite further exploration.) Continue up to the left over the bare ledges, duck into the woods beyond, and reach the wooded summit at 2.0 mi. (sign).

Great Pond Mtn. (USGS Orland quad, DeLorme map 23)

Distance from Dead River parking area (200 ft.) to
- Great Pond Mtn. summit (1,038 ft.): 2.0 mi., 1 hr. 25 min.

Oak Hill (829 ft.) and Flag Hill (946 ft.)

This pair of hills lies along the east boundary of the Wildlands, and their open summits offer fine views of the surrounding woods and mountains along this part of the coast. The trailhead for both is at the South Gate (sign, kiosk) of the preserve at Diamond Rd. (also known as Valley Rd.), 4.1 mi. east of the jct. of US 1/ME 3 and ME 15 in Orland.

Oak Hill

Pass by the South Gate (green) and walk about 100 yd. to the jct. with Esker Trail on the right. Leave the road and take this path through a cutover area. Cross a wet area on bog bridges and, beyond, follow a small glacial esker through young hardwoods. Cross a brook and then meet Drumlin Trail coming in from the left. Pass several large glacial erratic boulders on the left before reaching a viewpoint to Great Pond Mtn. Ahead, contour across the hillside to a second viewpoint and soon reach Hillside Trail, a grassy road, at 1.2 mi.

Turn right and follow this road uphill toward Oak Hill. Reach the jct. with Oak Hill Path on the right at about 1.5 mi. Turn right and climb the slope on switchbacks, reaching a grassy meadow on the semi-open summit at 1.9 mi. and the jct. with East Ridge Path. Views here take in Great Pond Mtn., Craig Pond, and Flag Hill nearby, and range north to Katahdin.

Oak Hill (USGS Orland and Branch Lake quads, DeLorme map 23)

Distance from South Gate at US1/ME 3 (350 ft.) to
- Oak Hill summit (via Esker Trail, Hillside Trail, and Oak Hill Path) (829 ft.): 1.9 mi., 1 hr. 10 min.

Flag Hill

To reach Flag Hill from Oak Hill, follow the wide East Ridge Trail north across the semi-open summit plateau. Beyond a clearing, begin a steady descent through the woods. Cross Flag Brook, then a small meadow to reach Flag Hill Trail (a dirt and gravel road) at 1.2 mi. Turn right and take this old logging road uphill. Soon after the road narrows, bear left uphill. Continue to climb the ridge, breaking out onto bare granite slabs with views south to Acadia and east to Branch Lake. Follow cairns to the open summit at about 2 mi. Beyond, a short loop trail leads to views all the way north and west to Bigelow, Sugarloaf, and Katahdin.

When South Gate is open (weekends in summer and early fall), vehicles may be driven into the preserve, making the approach to Flag Hill much shorter. Drive on Valley Rd. for 2.6 mi. Turn right onto Flag Hill Rd., go another 0.7 mi. to the jct. of Flag Hill Rd. and Mtn. View Rd., and park. Walk straight ahead on Flag Hill Trail to Flag Hill Path to reach the summit in about 1.3 mi.

Flag Hill (USGS Orland and Branch Lake quads, DeLorme map 23)
Distances from Oak Hill (via East Ridge Trail) (850 ft.) to
- Flag Hill Trail (via East Ridge Trail) jct. (540 ft.): 1.2 mi., 35 min.
- Flag Hill summit (via Flag Hill Trail and Flag Hill Path) (946 ft.): 2.0 mi., 1 hr. 10 min.

Distance from jct. Flag Hill Rd. and Mountain View Rd. (via Flag Hill Trail and Flag Hill Path) (550 ft.) to
- Flag Hill summit (946 ft.): 1.3 mi., 50 min.

Bald Mtn. (Dedham) (1,234 ft.)

This mountain in Dedham, also known as Dedham Bald Mtn., is a short hike that offers good views for the effort. From the jct. of US 1A and ME 46 in East Holden, proceed south on US 1A and, in 100 ft., turn right (south) onto Upper Dedham Rd. In 2.8 mi., take a left onto Bald Mountain Rd. (fire station on left). Then, at 6.2 mi. from US 1A, where the road bears right, continue straight ahead on Johnson Rd. for 100 ft. and park on ledges to the left.

The trail, the old fire tower service road, leads through open fields and over bare granite ledges to the top of the peak, where there are a number of communications towers. Good views are to the north and northwest. The nearby ledges on the north side of the mountain look out over Phillips Lake. The east side offers views of the mountains on Mt. Desert Island.

Bald Mtn. (USGS Green Lake quad, DeLorme map 23)

Distance from Johnson Rd. (700 ft.) to
- Bald Mtn. summit (1,234 ft.): 0.5 mi., 30 min.

Blackcap (1,022 ft.)

This mountain ridge, rising just east of Bangor and the Penobscot River in East Eddington, has a series of communications towers on its summit. Limited views may be had eastward over Fitts Pond to the hills beyond.

From the jct. of ME 9 and ME 46 in East Eddington, drive south on ME 46 for 0.6 mi. Take a left onto Blackcap Rd. (sign for Camp Roosevelt and Katahdin Scout Reservation) and follow this for 0.4 mi. Go left again on Camp Roosevelt Rd. Soon, pass under the entrance arch to the camp and reach a large open area. To the left a sign points to the scout camp base area. On the right is Fitts Pond, a boat launch and kiosk. Park off the road in the large open area.

Blue Trail leaves from the kiosk and quickly crosses a brook on a wooden bridge. It soon bears left and follows the west shore of Fitts Pond. At 0.4 mi., reach a jct. with Blue and White Trail. Turn right and follow Blue and White Trail, climbing steadily. Cross a woods road at 0.5 mi. and, beyond, climb steeply up the hillside. After a scramble up rock slabs, the angle eases, and views to the east begin to open up. Proceed easily up the ridgeline through the predominantly spruce forest. The summit towers come into sight at 0.9 mi. Ahead, at 1.1 mi., with a long rock wall to the left, climb up to the summit ridge and the towers and road at 1.1 mi.

Blackcap (USGS Chemo Pond quad, DeLorme map 23)

Distances from trailhead at Fitts Pond boat launch (300 ft.) to
- Blue and White Trail jct. (via Blue Trail) (300 ft.): 0.4 mi., 15 min.
- Blackcap summit ridge (via Blue and White Trail) (1,022 ft.): 1.1 mi., 55 min.

Little Peaked Mtn. (890 ft.)

Little Peaked Mtn. (also known as Little Chick Hill) lies just to the west of Peaked Mtn. (see below) and features airy cliffs and fine views.

From the jct. of ME 9 and ME 180 in Clifton, drive east on ME 9 for 3.5 mi. Turn left (north) onto a paved road and proceed 1.3 mi. The paved road ends at a dirt parking lot, the trailhead for Peaked and Little Peaked mountains.

Walk back to the pavement, turn left, and follow a logging road uphill. In 100 yds., look for a trail on the right marked by a piece of wood nailed to a tree (used to be a sign). Leave the road and climb the steep bank to start up the trail. At 0.1 mi., bear right onto a gullied old woods road. Bear right at a fork at 0.2 mi. Follow occasional cairns to another jct. at 0.3 mi. Turn left uphill at this point. The trail is marked with orange dots and colored flagging tape, and the climbing is moderate to steep. Cross a slab at 0.4 mi. with a view to the right. Just ahead, break out of the trees and climb steep slabs. Follow the cliff edge to the summit with excellent views to the south. Pass a natural rock bench at 0.5 mi. and, just beyond, enter the trees and reach the wooded summit. A short spur trail leads right to more views. To the left, a trail leads steeply down the mountain, but the lower part of it has been obliterated by logging and is not recommended.

Little Peaked Mtn. (890 ft.) (USGS Hopkins Pond quad, DeLorme map 24)
Distance from trailhead parking lot (300 ft.) to
• Little Peaked Mtn. summit (890 ft.): 0.5 mi., 30 min.

Peaked Mtn. (1,160 ft.)

Peaked Mtn., commonly called Chick Hill, straddles the Clifton–Amherst line about 18 mi. east of Bangor. The sweeping granite cliffs on the south face of the mountain can be seen from miles around and offer long views that include the peaks of Acadia to the south and Katahdin to the north.

From the jct. of the logging road and the trail to Little Peaked Mtn., continue ahead on the logging road. At a height-of-land, the road turns right (a two-wheel track continues straight ahead). Continue on the road. At 0.8 mi., bear right off the road onto a foot trail at utility pole 18. The trail climbs steeply through the woods on rock slabs. Emerge into the open with the summit communications tower visible ahead. Climb steeply on bare rock. At the top of the pitch, traverse to the right. Pass through a semi-open patch of woods to reach the cliff edge at 1.1 mi. Turn left here and follow the cliff edge to the summit and the site of a former fire tower.

Peaked Mtn. (1,160 ft.) (USGS Hopkins Pond quad, DeLorme map 24)

Distance from trailhead parking lot (300 ft.) to
• Peaked Mtn. summit (1,160 ft.): 1.1 mi., 1 hr.

Bald Bluff Mtn. (1,011 ft.)

Located in the Amherst Mountains Community Forest in Amherst east of Bangor, Bald Bluff Mtn. offers fine views of the lower Penobscot River watershed from its summit ledges. The preserve, owned by MBPL and managed jointly with the town of Amherst, encompasses nearly 5,000 acres of scenic ledges, forest and wetland, and five remote ponds.

From the jct. of ME 9 and ME 180 in Clifton, travel west on ME 9 for 8.9 mi. to a snowplow turnout on the right. Just ahead on the left is a blue-and-white MBPL sign that reads "Amherst." Turn left (north) off ME 9 at the sign and follow the old road, which soon turns to gravel. At 3.0 mi. from ME 9, bear left (gated road on right). At a jct. at 4.8 mi., turn left. Reach the trailhead and parking on the right at 6.1 mi., at the end of the improved gravel road.

Bald Bluff Mtn. Trail (MPBL)

Follow the rocky bed of an eroded old woods road, alternating over rock slabs. The trail climbs moderately and then levels off before arriving at a jct. at 0.4 mi. Here a spur trail leads right 0.1 mi. to ledges and several outlooks.

Continuing ahead on the main trail, the woods road becomes a footpath and the going is easy. At 0.8 mi., begin to climb moderately, passing through a large stand of old-growth spruce. Reach a semi-open area at 0.9 mi. and follow occasional cairns to the flat summit (large open area surrounded by woods) at 1.0 mi. Reenter the woods and descend 100 ft. to a ledge (views) where the trail terminates.

Bald Bluff Mtn. (1,011 ft.) (USGS The Horseback quad, DeLorme map 24)
Distance from trailhead parking area (600 ft.) to
 • Bald Bluff Mtn. summit (1,011 ft.): 1.2 mi., 1 hr.

Lead Mtn. (Humpback) (1,475 ft.)

Lead Mtn. is located in T28 MD in Hancock County, just west of the Washington county line. From the jct. of ME 9 and ME 193 in T22 MD, drive 1.1 mi. east. Turn left (north) at the sign for the MFS Forest Protection Division, Beddington Range Station. This point is 0.1 mi. west of the bridge over the Narraguagus River on ME 9. Proceed on CC Rd. (also called 30-00-00 Rd.), passing a snowmobile trail on the left at the MFS station, and, just beyond, turn left onto a gravel road leading 1.8 mi. to a parking area at a gate (Bear Pond is passed at 1.5 mi.; a side trail leads 200 yd. to the pond).

Beyond the gate, walk 0.4 mi. along the road. Just before the University of Maine acid rain project structures, turn right onto a much-eroded trail. At 0.7 mi., reach the old fire warden's cabin. (No blazes mark the trail. An ATV trail parallels the route.) Continue past the cabin and then bear left (west) uphill with limited views of Pleasant Mtn. (highest point in Washington County, but trailless) to the east. At 1.2 mi., reach the former fire tower site, a fenced-in communications tower, and the broad summit plateau. There are no views from the top of the mountain.

Lead (Humpback) Mtn. (1,475 ft.) (USGS Lead Mtn. quad, DeLorme maps 24, 25)
Distance from gate and parking area (700 ft.) to
 • Lead Mtn. summit (1,475 ft.): 1.2 mi., 1 hr.

Peaked Mtn. (Washington County) (938 ft.)

Peaked Mtn., in T30 MD BPP in Washington County, rises just north of ME 9, less than 30 mi. east of the mountain of the same name in Clifton.

On the north side of ME 9 at a point 9.8 mi. east of the Narraguagus River and 14.8 mi. west of Wesley, a gravel road (marked by two yellow posts) leaves the north side of the highway. Pass a private camp at 0.2 mi., take a right fork at 0.3 mi., and park at 0.6 mi.

Follow the tote road a short distance to the former fire warden's cabin (now private). Behind the main building, the trail starts at a large fallen tree trunk and is occasionally marked with white, handmade signs bearing a hiker stick figure in black. The trail rises to an open ledge at 0.5 mi., and reaches the site of the former fire tower, with limited views, at 1.0 mi.

Peaked Mtn. (Wash. Co.) (USGS Peaked Mtn. quad, DeLorme map 25)
Distance from parking area on tote road (550 ft.) to
• Peaked Mtn. summit (938 ft.): 1.0 mi., 45 min.

Passadumkeag Mtn. (1,463 ft.)

Passadumkeag Mtn., in Grand Falls Township southeast of Enfield, rises well above the relatively level countryside and extends in a gradual east–west arc for about 5 mi. The approach is from the west. From the jct. of US 2 and Greenfield Rd. in Costigan, proceed east on Greenfield Rd. for about 18 mi. Most of the road is paved, but the last several miles are dirt, and the conditions may vary. Drive as far as is comfortable and then park alongside the road.

Follow the road on foot, climbing gradually. Beyond a power line, bear left. Continue to climb, passing the site of the old fire warden's camp en route to the summit. The old fire tower site has limited views.

Passadumkeag Mtn. (USGS Brandy Pond and Saponac quads, DeLorme map 34)
Distance from Greenfield Rd. (450 ft.) to
• Passadumkeag Mtn. summit (1,463 ft.): est. 2.0 mi., 1 hr. 30 min.

Washington Bald Mtn. (983 ft.)

This mountain in T42 MD BPP rises above Third Machias Lake, just west of Farm Cove Community Forest and Machias River PRL. From ME 9, 14.0 mi. east of the Narraguagus River in Beddington and 10.5 mi. west of Wesley, turn north onto a wide gravel road. (*Note:* This road is labeled on DeLorme maps from south to north as CCC Rd., Machias River Rd., and Little River Rd., although no signage is in place en route.) Pass a sign board at 0.1 mi. At 3.8 mi., pass a campsite and cross the West Branch of the Machias River. At 8.9 mi., bear right onto Stud Mill Rd. and cross the Machias River. Just ahead, turn left onto Little River Rd. Pass a campsite on the left at Second Machias Lake at 10.8 mi. At 13.3 mi., a gravel road leads left (west) to the trailhead, but the road washed out in 2011 and is no longer recommended. At 14.5 mi., turn sharply left back toward the south end of Third Machias Lake. The washed-out road comes in from the left at 15.5 mi. Bear right here, pass a road entering from the right, and park at the boat launch and campsite on the right.

Walk the wide gravel road across the outlet of the lake, and reach a locked gate at 0.1 mi. Continue past the gate and, at 0.5 mi., turn right onto another wide gravel road. Follow this to the first gravel road entering from the left at 1.5 mi. Descend to cross Thompson Brook at 1.7 mi. Beyond, ascend steadily. Pass a grassy tote road on the right at 2.6 mi. and continue until the road ends in a large clearing (former log yard) at 2.9 mi., with the mountain visible ahead. The trail at the other end of the clearing has been obscured by timber harvesting, but can be located with care. Pass through the clearing and climb moderately, reaching the summit at 3.5. mi. (Numerous trails leave the south and west side of the peak, but are not recommended.) The site of the former fire warden's cabin and fire tower (removed in 2007 and 2008, respectively) are ahead on semi-open ledges, offering views of the lakes and mountains to the north and east.

Washington Bald Mtn. (USGS Fletcher Peak and Monroe Lake quads, DeLorme map 35)

Distance from boat launch on Third Machias Lake (300 ft.) to
  • Washington Bald Mtn. summit (983 ft.): 3.5 mi., 2 hr. 5 min.

Wabassus Mtn. (844 ft.)

This mountain in T43 MD BPP in Washington County is situated in the Farm Cove Community Forest on land conserved by the Downeast Lakes Land Trust. Access from the south is similar to that of Washington Bald

Mtn. From ME 9, follow CCC Rd./Machias River Rd/Little River Rd. for 15.9 mi. Turn left onto a road signed "60-00-0" and drive 1.5 mi. to Wabassus Mtn. Rd. Turn right (at a sign marked Wabassus Mtn. Trail), and drive 0.7 mi. to the trailhead.

At the trailhead, the road crosses a small stream. Next to the stream is a sign for Reggie's Way. Just to the left, the yellow-blazed trail starts uphill. The trail follows and then crosses the stream. At 0.3 mi., the trail bears away from the stream and ascends gradually through a hardwood forest. At 0.7 mi., the summit loop trail enters from the right, and in 200 ft., the broad, wooded summit is reached. Along the 0.2-mi. summit loop, limited views are possible through the trees.

Wabassus Mtn. (USGS Grand Lake Stream quad, DeLorme map 35)

Distance from Wabassus Mtn. Rd. (600 ft.) to
• Wabassus Mtn. summit (844 ft.): 0.7 mi., 30 min.

Pocomoonshine Mtn. (610 ft.)

Located in Princeton, this mountain rises nearly 500 ft. above Pocomoonshine Lake. MFS built a road on the back side of the mountain to the tower, but abandoned it in 1970. This is now the trail route.

From US 1, 2.3 mi. south of Princeton, turn southwest onto South Princeton Rd. At 0.9 mi., turn right onto gravel Pokey Rd. Travel 3.8 mi. to a fork, and turn right onto the old MFS road. (*Note:* If Pokey Rd. is impassable because of mud or washouts, an alternate approach can be made from Princeton using West St. This intersects Pokey Rd. at a point 7.2 mi. from US 1. From here, continue 2.2 mi. to the old MFS road on the left.) In 0.3 mi., the road forks. The right fork leads to a parking area with a view of Pocomoonshine Lake.

The old MFS road ascends to the summit and tower foundation in 0.4 mi. A trail (faint blue blazes) loops north from the summit to a rock outcrop and views to the north.

Pocomoonshine Mtn. (USGS Princeton quad, DeLorme map 36)

Distance from parking area (430 ft.) to
• Pocomoonshine Mtn. summit (610 ft.): 0.4 mi., 30 min.

SUGGESTED HIKES

Easy Hikes

Bells Mtn. [lp: 0.7 mi., 25 min.]. A short but highly rewarding hike with views to the east over Tide Mill Farm on Whiting Bay.

Schoodic Beach [rt: 1.0 mi., 30 min.]. An easy walk to a sandy beach on the scenic south end of Donnell Pond, where there is swimming and picnicking.

Pigeon Hill [lp: 1.1 mi., 40 min.]. A short but rewarding hike with good views ranging from Blue Hill and Mt. Desert Island, to Petit Manan Lighthouse and the islands of the Pleasant Bay archipelago, to the peaks of Donnell Pond PRL.

Baker Hill [lp: 1.0 mi., 45 min]. A short loop hike leading to ledges with views to Frenchman Bay and beyond to the peaks of Acadia.

Bald Mtn. (Dedham) [rt. 1.0 mi., 50 min.]. This climb leads to several ledge outlooks with views over beautiful Phillips Lake and to the mountains of Acadia.

Blue Hill [lp: 1.9 mi., 1 hr. 30 min.]. An easy loop hike to the summit of Blue Hill via Osgood, Hayes, and South Face trails, featuring extensive views of the Mt. Desert Island mountains and Blue Hill Bay.

Schoodic Mtn. Loop [rt: 2.8 mi., 1 hr. 50 min.]. The top of this popular mountain, reached via Schoodic Mtn. Trail, provides good views of Mt. Desert Island and Frenchman's Bay. Descend to Schoodic Beach on Donnell Pond for a picnic and swim before circling back to the car.

Tunk Mtn. [rt: 3 mi., 2 hr.]. Tunk Mtn. Trail leads past several hidden ponds to the cliffs on the southwestern ridgeline of Tunk Mtn. and nice views over Spring River and Tunk lakes.

Moderate Hikes

Black Mtn. via Black Mtn. Cliffs [lp: 4.6 mi., 3 hr.]. A steep climb to the open summit of Black Mtn. via cliffs overlooking Donnell Pond and Schoodic Mtn.

Oak Hill and Flag Hill Loop [lp: 8.6 mi., 4 hr. 45 min.]. A good hike on interesting trails (Esker and Hillside trails; Oak Hill, East Ridge, and Flag Hills paths) in Great Pond Mtn. Wildlands to views taking in Great Pond Mtn., Craig Pond, and Flag Hill, and ranging north to Bigelow, Sugarloaf, and Katahdin. Return via the gravel Flag Hill and Valley roads (closed to vehicles most of the time).

Strenuous Hike

Caribou Mtn. Loop [lp: 8.0 mi., 6 hr. 20 min.]. Enjoy a hike through the remote backcountry of Donnell Pond PRL, taking in the summits of Caribou and Black mountains on the Black and Caribou mountain trails.

SECTION NINE
ACADIA

Champlain Mtn. 312

The Beehive 316

Gorham Mtn. 316

Dorr Mtn. 318

Kebo Mtn. 322

Cadillac Mtn. 324

Jordan Pond. 326

North Bubble and
  South Bubble. 328

Pemetic Mtn. 330

The Triad 332

Day Mtn. 333

Sargent Mtn. and Penobscot
  Mtn. 334

Gilmore Peak and
  Parkman Mtn. 339

Norumbega Mtn. 341

Acadia Mtn. 343

St. Sauveur Mtn. 344

Flying Mtn. 345

Beech Mtn. 346

Bernard Mtn. and Mansell
  Mtn. 350

AMC map 5: Eastern Mt. Desert Island

AMC Western Mtn. map (p. 352)

AMC Isle au Haut map (p. 356)

Isle au Haut 357

Suggested Hikes 362

Acadia National Park is located on Mt. Desert Island about 10 mi. south of Ellsworth. The island is connected to the mainland by a short bridge and causeways. The island is about 15 mi. long and 13 mi. wide, roughly heart-shaped, and is divided into distinct east and west sides by Somes Sound. The park encompasses much of Mt. Desert Island, and includes portions of Schoodic Point to the east across Frenchman Bay and Isle au Haut offshore to the southwest at the lower east end of Penobscot Bay.

A chain of pink granite mountain peaks rises from near sea level to more than 1,500 ft. and extends across the island from the northeast to the southwest. A variety of sparkling lakes, ponds, streams, wetlands, forests, and meadows are nestled in the deep valleys between the long mountain ridges, and bold ocean cliffs and sand-and-cobble beaches define the coastline of this diverse and unique landscape, which supports a wide range of bird and animal life.

The park was established as Sieur de Monts National Monument in 1916. It became the first national park east of the Mississippi River in 1919, named Lafayette National Park in honor of the Marquis de Lafayette, a key French supporter of the American Revolution. The park was renamed Acadia National Park in 1929.

The park encompasses an area of nearly 45,000 acres and features a network of more than 120 mi. of well-maintained and marked trails for a wide range of interests and abilities, from easy hikes to challenging "ladder trails" with iron rungs and ladders secured to the rock to aid ascent and descent. This section describes 95 trails and 22 mountains.

Many of the mountain summits, especially on the east side of the island, are relatively treeless and open and provide far-reaching ocean and mountain views. Rock cairns mark the trail routes along these open stretches and care should be taken to locate the next cairn before moving ahead.

Although the trails in Acadia are mostly within a short distance of roads and villages, the terrain is often sharp and precipitous, and hikers who stray off the marked paths may encounter rough going and dead ends at cliff edges and ravines. Hikers should be prepared for the changeable weather of the Maine coast, which can, for example, turn quickly from bright sun to thick fog and rain.

A 50-mi. system of fine-graveled carriage paths (closed to vehicular traffic) offers additional opportunities for pleasant walking, bicycling, horseback riding, and, in winter, cross-country skiing and snowshoeing. The trail descriptions in this section are limited primarily to mountain trails, and as such don't cover some of the easier walks or the carriage paths. These paths are, however, delineated on the map. (For a full listing of trails, see AMC's *Discover Acadia National Park*, 3rd edition, available at outdoors.org.)

Trail Ratings

The trails listed in this section are well-marked, officially recognized, maintained paths that provide access to all of the preferred summits on Mt. Desert Island. For the most part, the individual summits can be reached in comfortable half-day walks. To simplify reference and to conform to Acadia National Park nomenclature, the hikes have been divided into an eastern district and a western district. NPS maintains all of the trails described here. Trail markings include signs, cairns, and blue-painted blazes.

NPS rates each trail based on the following criteria:

- Easy: Fairly level ground.
- Moderate: Uneven ground with some steep grades and/or gradual climbing. Footing may be difficult in places.
- Strenuous: Steep and/or long grades; steady climbing or descending; sometimes-difficult footing; difficult maneuvering.
- Ladder: Iron-rung ladders and handrails placed on steep grades or difficult terrain. These trails are considered very difficult.

Camping

The park service operates two campgrounds, and a range of accommodations is available elsewhere on the island, from campgrounds to B&Bs, motels, and hotels. (*Note:* Bar Harbor offers a wide range of other visitor amenities, including restaurants and grocery stores.) No backcountry camping is allowed in Acadia on Mt. Desert Island, although there is primitive camping at Duck Harbor Campground on Isle au Haut. Campers may not transport firewood from home into the park because of the risk of insect infestation. Firewood is available for purchase at both Blackwoods and Seawall campgrounds.

Blackwoods Campground is located on ME 3, about 5 mi. south of Bar Harbor. The campground is open all year and features 306 campsites that accommodate tents, campers, and RVs (up to 35 ft.). No hook-ups are available. Amenities include restrooms with cold running water, a dump station, picnic tables, fire rings, and water faucets. Showers and a small store are available during summer a short distance from the campground on ME 3 in Otter Creek. A fee is charged from May 1 through October 31; reservations are recommended during this period. Campground facilities are limited in winter and the entrance road is not plowed. Winter campers should check with park officials in advance of arrival.

Seawall Campground, located on ME 102A about 4 mi. south of Southwest Harbor, is open from late May through September 30, and features 214 campsites. Reservations are recommended, although about half the sites are made available on a first-come, first-served basis. Amenities are similar to those at Blackwoods. A privately operated shower facility is available a short distance from the campground on ME 102A.

Fees and Seasons

The park is open all year. An entrance fee is charged from May 1 through October 31 regardless of how or where visitors enter the park. Entrance fees may be paid at the entrance station (north of Sand Beach on the Park Loop Rd.), Hulls Cove Visitor Center, Park Headquarters, Blackwoods and Seawall campgrounds, Thompson Island Information Center, and the Bar Harbor Village Green.

Thompson Island Information Center on ME 3 at the northern tip of the island is open from mid-May to mid-October. Hulls Cove Visitor Center at the start of Park Loop Rd. is open from April 15 through October 31. Outside of that period, information is available at Park Headquarters on ME 233 west of Bar Harbor. Operating hours of these facilities vary by season.

Visitor amenities are limited in winter months, when most park buildings are closed. Park Loop Rd., including the road to the summit of Cadillac Mtn., is closed from December 1 through April 14, and at other times when conditions warrant.

Getting Around

The 20-mi. Park Loop Rd. and the 3.5-mi. spur road to the summit of Cadillac Mtn. are open from April 15 through November 30 (weather dependent). Park roads can be very congested during the busy summer months, so visitors are encouraged to take advantage of the Island Explorer bus, a free shuttle that operates from late June through Columbus Day.

Island Explorer buses offer service on eight routes that link park destinations, the local towns and villages, and the regional airport in Trenton. Regularly scheduled buses stop at points throughout the park, including campgrounds, carriage road entrances, and many trailheads. Hikers can also flag down buses along their route. The bus is an easy and efficient way to get around and see the park while helping reduce traffic congestion, alleviate parking problems, and reduce air pollution on the island.

Hikers may also consider leaving their cars parked in Bar Harbor and hiking on the "village connector trails" that link the town to park trails. These easy trails include Schooner Head Path, Great Meadow Loop, and Jesup Path. The ball field on Main St. in Bar Harbor has ample parking and is near these trails.

East of Somes Sound
Trailheads

For ease of traveling to the trailheads on the east side of Mt. Desert Island, the following mileages are provided, to be used in conjunction with Map 4:

From Hulls Cove Visitor Center via Park Loop Rd. to
- jct. ME 233: 2.6 mi.
- start of one-way section of Park Loop Rd.: 3.1 mi.

Start of one-way Park Loop Rd. to
- Cadillac North Ridge Trail: 0.3 mi.
- Gorge Path: 0.9 mi.
- Kebo Mtn. Trail: 1.5 mi.
- Stratheden Path: 1.7 mi.
- Sieur de Monts Spring access road: 2.7 mi.
- Champlain North Ridge Trail: 3.5 mi.
- Orange & Black Trail crossing: 4.1 mi.
- Precipice Trail: 4.6 mi.
- Park Entrance Station: 5.4 mi.
- Sand Beach: 6.0 mi.
- Gorham Mtn.: 7.1 mi.
- end of one-way: 13.4 mi.

From Hulls Cove Visitor Center via Park Loop Rd. (two-way section) to
- jct. start of one-way section of Park Loop Rd.: 3.1 mi.
- jct. Cadillac Summit Rd.: 3.6 mi.
- Bubble Pond: 5.1 mi.
- Bubble Rock: 6.2 mi.
- Jordan Pond: 7.7 mi.
- Jordan Pond House: 7.8 mi.

Champlain Mtn. (1,058 ft.)

The Champlain Mtn. area consists of Champlain Mtn. and the subsidiary peaks of Huguenot Head (714 ft.), The Beehive (520 ft.), and Gorham Mtn. (522 ft.), all of which provide excellent views. Champlain and The Beehive are very popular because of their exciting ladder trails that climb steep cliff faces overlooking the open ocean, but access to both peaks can be had by easier trails that are better options for children or those with a fear of heights.

Precipice Trail

This trail starts from Precipice Trail parking area, located 1.9 mi. beyond Sieur de Monts Spring entrance on Park Loop Rd. at the foot of Champlain Mtn. The trailhead is on Park Loop Rd., 0.8 mi. before the park entrance station. Following a rugged talus of large boulders, the trail ascends northwest for 0.6 mi. to a jct. with Orange & Black Path (leads right to Champlain North Ridge Trail at a point 0.6 mi. from the summit on the north ridge). From this jct., Precipice Trail climbs southwest, rising steeply to a point directly west of the parking area. The direction is now west-northwest. Along this section of the trail, ladders and iron rungs help hikers negotiate precipitous vertical dropoffs. The final climb to the summit follows gentle slopes and ledges.

Caution: According to the NPS, Precipice Trail is maintained as a nontechnical climbing route, not a hiking trail. Hikers should attempt this route only if they are in good physical condition, are wearing proper footwear, and have experience climbing near exposed cliffs and heights. This route is to be avoided in inclement weather or darkness. Please stay on the trail and do not throw or dislodge rocks onto hikers below.

Note: Precipice Trail can be closed for an undetermined amount of time each spring and summer because of the reintroduction of peregrine falcons to the park. Violators of the closure are subject to a $10,000 fine. Those wishing the experience of a ladder trail should consider the Beehive, Ladder (Dorr Mtn.), Jordan Cliffs, Beech Cliffs, or Perpendicular trails.

Precipice Trail (AMC map 5: D8, E8) (NPS rating: ladder)

Distances from Park Loop Rd. (150 ft.) to
- Orange & Black Path (400 ft.): 0.6 mi., 15 min.
- Champlain Mtn. summit (1,058 ft.): 1.3 mi., 1 hr.

Orange & Black Path

Damaged by an earthquake in 2006, this trail was closed to the public until 2011. It begins from Schooner Head Rd. at a point 1.3 mi. south of the jct. with ME 3 in Bar Harbor. Parking is along the road.

Start out on Schooner Head Trail, and in 50 ft., Orange & Black Path diverges right. Follow this easily uphill to Park Loop Rd. at 0.2 mi. Cross the road and proceed into the woods. Ahead, scramble over rocks and climb via stone steps to a fork. The right fork leads 0.1 mi. to a jct. with Champlain North Ridge Trail. Continuing on the left fork, traverse the face of the mountain with minor ups and downs and numerous viewpoints en route. Descend a crevice in the rocks on stone steps, then continue to traverse to the south. Cross a steep section of the slope using a wooden steps and an iron ladder to reach a jct. with Precipice Trail at 0.9 mi. To the right, it is 0.7 mi. to the summit of Champlain Mt. To the left, it is 0.6 mi. to the Park Loop Rd. and The Precipice parking area.

Orange & Black Path (AMC map 5: D8, E8) (NPS rating: ladder)

Distances from Schooner Head Rd. (50 ft.) to
- Park Loop Rd (200 ft.): 0.2 mi., 10 min.
- Champlain North Ridge Trail jct. (550 ft.): 0.4 mi., 30 min.
- Precipice Trail jct. (400 ft.): 0.9 mi., 50 min.

Champlain North Ridge Trail

Beginning on Park Loop Rd., 0.2 mi. east of the entrance to Bear Brook picnic area, this trail ends at the summit of Champlain Mtn., where Champlain South Ridge Trail continues on to meet Bowl Trail at the south end of The Bowl, a pretty mountain tarn.

This trail climbs gradually from the parking area through a mixed forest of birch, pine, and spruce to a jct. on the north slope of Champlain Mtn., with Orange & Black Path entering left at 0.5 mi. Continuing right (southwest), Champlain North Ridge Trail steadily emerges from the forest canopy, giving outstanding views of Frenchman Bay and Schoodic Peninsula on the mainland to the east. At 1.1 mi., the trail reaches the open, rocky summit of Champlain Mtn.

Champlain North Ridge Trail (AMC map 5: D8) (NPS rating: moderate)
Distances from Park Loop Rd. (150 ft.) to
- Orange & Black Path jct. (550 ft.): 0.5 mi., 30 min.
- Champlain Mtn. summit (1,058 ft.): 1.1 mi., 1 hr.

Champlain South Ridge Trail

This trail provides a route from The Bowl to the summit of Champlain Mtn. The trail begins at a jct. with Bowl Trail, 0.7 mi. from Park Loop Rd. and Sand Beach parking area. Champlain South Ridge Trail skirts the southern edge of The Bowl, a small glacial tarn, before ascending to the southern ridgeline of the mountain. Ahead, the trail climbs moderately and soon enters a semi-open forest of pitch pines. Climbing over pink granite, the trail reaches open views and the summit of Champlain Mtn. at 1.5 mi.

Champlain South Ridge Trail (AMC map 5: D8, E8) (NPS rating: moderate)
Distances from Park Loop Rd. (50 ft.) to
- start of trail (450 ft.) (via Bowl Trail): 0.7 mi., 30 min.
- Champlain Mtn. summit (1,058 ft.) and Champlain North Ridge and Precipice trails jct.: 1.5 mi., 1 hr. 20 min.

Beachcroft Path

This path offers a convenient route from the Sieur de Monts Spring area to the summit of Champlain Mtn. via Huguenot Head. The trail officially starts at the jct. of Jesup Path, Kurt Diederich's Climb, and Kane Path, 0.1 mi. west of ME 3 and the parking area at the north end of The Tarn. After crossing ME 3, Beachcroft Path starts up a flight of granite steps and then runs southeast, often on carefully placed stonework. Following switchbacks and stone steps, the trail rises across the west face of Huguenot Head. The trail passes just below the summit of Huguenot Head at about 0.7 mi. A brief, gradual descent into the notch between Huguenot Head and Champlain Mtn. is followed by a sharp, difficult ascent over rocks up the northwest slope of the mountain to the summit at 1.4 mi.

Beachcroft Path (AMC map 5: D7–D8) (NPS rating: moderate)
Distances from north end of The Tarn (50 ft.) to
- ME 3 parking area (100 ft.): 0.1 mi., 2 min.
- shoulder of Huguenot Head (650 ft.): 0.7 mi., 30 min.
- Champlain Mtn. summit (1,058 ft.): 1.4 mi., 1 hr. 5 min.

Bowl Trail

This trail leaves from opposite Sand Beach parking area, 0.6 mi. south of the park entrance station on Park Loop Rd. Bowl Trail is a gently sloping path that offers access to Beehive and Gorham Mtn. trails. Bowl Trail connects Sand Beach to The Bowl, a pretty mountain tarn. At The Bowl, Beehive Trail bears right and climbs over The Beehive, and Champlain South Ridge Trail bears left to Champlain Mtn.

Bowl Trail (AMC map 5: E8) (NPS rating: moderate)
Distances from Sand Beach parking area (50 ft.) to
- Beehive Trail jct. (150 ft.): 0.2 mi., 5 min.
- Gorham Mtn. Trail jct. (250 ft.): 0.5 mi., 15 min.
- The Bowl and jct. Beehive and Champlain South Ridge trails (450 ft.): 0.7 mi., 25 min.

The Beehive (520 ft.)

Rising dramatically above Sand Beach and Park Loop Rd., The Beehive is one of the most popular mountains in Acadia. The trail to the summit is challenging and not for people who are uneasy on precipitous heights, but the views of Frenchman Bay, Sand Beach, and Otter Cliff are spectacular.

Beehive Trail

This trail begins 0.2 mi. up Bowl Trail from Sand Beach parking area. Take a sharp right at the sign marked "Beehive." For 0.3 mi., the trail rises abruptly via switchbacks and iron ladders over steep ledges to the summit of The Beehive. The trail continues down the northwest slope of The Beehive and dips steeply to the south for 0.2 mi. to a jct. with The Bowl and Champlain South Ridge trails. Take the left fork for 0.7 mi. to return to Park Loop Rd. and Sand Beach.

> **Beehive Trail (AMC map 5: E8) (NPS rating: ladder)**
> Distances from Sand Beach parking area (50 ft.) to
> - start of trail (150 ft.): 0.2 mi., 5 min.
> - The Beehive (520 ft.): 0.5 mi., 30 min.
> - complete loop back to Sand Beach (via Bowl Trail): 1.4 mi., 55 min.

Gorham Mtn. (522 ft.)

Located south of Champlain Mtn. and The Beehive, the long, low ridge of Gorham Mtn. offers fine walking and outstanding ocean views.

Gorham Mtn. Trail

Starting at Gorham Mtn. parking area (also known as Monument Cove parking area) on Park Loop Rd., 1.1 mi. past Sand Beach, this trail rises gently over open ledges 0.3 mi. to a jct. with a side trail to Cadillac Cliffs (NPS rating: strenuous) that leads right and rejoins Gorham Mtn. Trail at 0.8 mi., after passing under ancient sea cliffs and by an ancient sea cave.

The trail continues over easy, open granite ledges to where the Cadillac Cliffs loop rejoins the main trail, then climbs north to the bare summit of Gorham Mtn. at 1.1 mi. and some of the finest panoramas in Acadia. Descending, at 1.4 mi. the trail reaches a connector trail that leaves left and offers a more direct route to The Bowl. Ahead, the trail reaches a jct. with Bowl Trail at 1.7 mi. For The Bowl, go left 0.2 mi. To reach The Beehive, turn right, then left at the next jct., about 0.1 mi. farther. (Continuing straight ahead at this jct. will bring you to Park Loop Rd. at Sand Beach.)

Gorham Mtn. Trail (AMC map 5: E8) (NPS rating: moderate)

Distances from Gorham Mtn. parking area (50 ft.) to
- Gorham Mtn. summit (522 ft.): 1.1 mi., 45 min.
- Bowl Trail jct. (250 ft.): 1.7 mi., 1 hr. 5 min.

Great Head Trail

This scenic, short walk passes largely along cliffs directly above the sea. From Sand Beach parking area on Park Loop Rd., cross Sand Beach to its east end. Near the seaward end of the interior lagoon, look for a trailhead post and a series of granite steps with a handrail ascending a high bank. The trail quickly reaches a huge millstone, where the trail turns sharply right (south), switchbacking up the cliff. The path continues to the extremity of the peninsula, then turns northeast along the cliff to the highpoint at Great Head, where there are ruins of a stone teahouse. The trail descends northwest to a jct. and a shortcut trail back to Sand Beach. Continuing on Great Head Trail, the path leads north and soon reaches an abandoned road in about 0.3 mi. Turn left on the road, and follow it south for about 0.3 mi. to close the loop at the east end of Sand Beach. Walk along the beach back to the parking area.

Great Head Trail (AMC map 5: E8) (NPS rating: moderate)

Distances from east end of Sand Beach (sea level) to
- south end of peninsula (via millstone): 0.5 mi., 15 min.
- Great Head (145 ft.) and teahouse ruins: 0.8 mi., 20 min.
- jct., abandoned road: 1.3 mi., 35 min.
- to start at east end of Sand Beach (via abandoned road): 1.6 mi., 55 min.

Dorr Mtn. (1,265 ft.)

This mountain lies immediately west of Sieur de Monts Spring, where two routes up the mountain originate. Trails also ascend from the north and south over long ridges. The east and west slopes are steep. A parking area is located at the north end of The Tarn on ME 3. Hikers are encouraged to take the Island Explorer bus rather than park at the very congested Sieur de Monts Spring parking area. Hikers can also gain access to the Sieur de Monts Spring on foot via Beachcroft Trail and either Wild Garden Path or Jesup Path, a distance of 0.4 mi.

Emery Path

Follow the paved path from the Nature Center parking area at Sieur de Monts Spring toward the Springhouse. At the rock inscribed "Sweet Waters of Acadia," turn right onto Emery Path, which is paved for a few feet. The path continues, following a series of switchbacks up the northeast shoulder of Dorr Mtn. The first half has many stone steps. At 0.3 mi, Homans Path enters from the right. At 0.5 mi., Emery Path ends at its jct. with Kurt Diederich's Climb (descends left [east] to the north end of The Tarn), and Schiff Path, which continues to the summit.

> **Emery Path (AMC map 5: D7) (NPS rating: strenuous)**
> Distances from Sieur de Monts Spring (50 ft.) to
> - Homans Path jct. (400 ft.): 0.3 mi., 20 min.
> - Kurt Diederich's Climb and Schiff Path jct. (550 ft.): 0.5 mi., 30 min.
> - Dorr Mtn. summit (1,265 ft.) (via Schiff Path and Dorr North Ridge Trail): 1.6 mi., 1 hr. 30 min.

Schiff Path

This trail begins at the jct. of Emery Path and Kurt Diederich's Climb, 0.5 mi. above Sieur de Monts Spring and 0.6 mi. above The Tarn. Traverse the east face of the mountain, ascending moderately, to reach a jct. with Ladder Trail at 0.6 mi. Here, Schiff Path makes a sharp right and climbs steeply to meet Dorr North Ridge Trail at 1.2 mi. Follow Dorr North Ridge Trail south for 0.1 mi. to the summit of Dorr Mtn.

Schiff Path (AMC map 5: D7) (NPS rating: strenuous)
Distances from jct. of Emery Path and Kurt Diederich's Climb (550 ft.) to
- Ladder Trail (800 ft.): 0.6 mi., 20 min.
- Dorr North Ridge Trail (1,250 ft.): 1.2 mi., 1 hr. 5 min.
- Dorr Mtn. summit (1,265 ft.) (via Dorr North Ridge Trail): 1.3 mi., 1 hr. 10 min.

Homans Path

An alternative approach to Dorr Mtn. from Sieur de Monts Spring, Homans Path begins from Hemlock Rd., a few yards west of Jesup Path, 0.1 mi. from Sieur de Monts Spring. Homans Path rises steeply over switchbacks and stone steps to views of Great Meadow and Frenchman Bay, ending at its jct. with Emery Path at 0.4 mi.

Homans Path (AMC map 5: D7) (NPS rating: strenuous)
Distance from Hemlock Rd. (50 ft.) to
- Emery Path (400 ft.): 0.4 mi., 20 min.

Kurt Diederich's Climb

This trail takes a direct route from the north end of The Tarn to the jct. of Schiff and Emery paths. The trail starts at a jct. with Kane and Jesup paths 0.1 mi. west of The Tarn parking area on ME 3 via Beachcroft Trail. Look for an inscription in the stone stairs that reads "Kurt Diederich's Climb." The trail climbs steeply via stone steps to good views and the Emery and Schiff paths at 0.6 mi.

Kurt Diederich's Climb (AMC map 5: D7) (NPS rating: strenuous)
Distance from The Tarn (50 ft.) via Beachcroft Trail to
- Emery and Schiff paths jct. (550 ft.): 0.6 mi., 45 min.

Kane Path

This path starts at the north end of The Tarn, 0.1 mi. west of the parking area on ME 3 via Beachcroft Trail. Kane Path leads south to Canon Brook Trail and links the Sieur de Monts Spring area to the southern trails of Dorr and Cadillac mountains. At its start, Kane Path runs south over a talus slope directly along the west side of The Tarn. After reaching the south end of the pond, the path continues past Ladder Trail at 0.5 mi. to end at Canon Brook Trail at 0.8 mi.

Kane Path (AMC map 5: D7, E7) (NPS rating: moderate)

Distances from north end of The Tarn (50 ft.) to
- Ladder Trail (150 ft.): 0.5 mi., 20 min.
- Canon Brook Trail (150 ft.): 0.8 mi., 25 min.

Ladder Trail

This trail leaves from ME 3 just south of The Tarn and climbs the east side of Dorr Mtn. Parking is at the roadside. From the parking area, the trail soon crosses Kane Path before making its steep ascent to reach Schiff Path at 0.6 mi. (The trail is steep, climbing many stone steps and over iron rungs.)

Ladder Trail (AMC map 5: D7) (NPS rating: ladder)

Distances from ME 3 (150 ft.) to
- Schiff Path (800 ft.): 0.6 mi., 40 min.
- Dorr Mtn. summit (1,265 ft.) (via Schiff Path and Dorr North Ridge Trail): 1.3 mi., 1 hr. 15 min.

Canon Brook Trail

From a pullout on ME 3 about 0.5 mi. south of the south end of The Tarn, Canon Brook Trail swings west around the south ridge of Dorr Mtn. and climbs over the South Ridge of Cadillac Mtn. to join Bubble and Jordan Ponds Path in the valley south of Bubble Pond. The trail provides access (via Bubble and Jordan Ponds Path) to the Jordan Pond area, as well as to the trails leading north to Dorr and Cadillac mountains.

From the road, the trail descends west to cross a beaver flowage, intersecting with Kane Path at 0.2 mi. Turn left (south) at the jct. and follow the beaver flowage down through the valley. After a brief, sharp rise, the trail reaches a jct. with Dorr South Ridge Trail, which diverges right at 0.9 mi. Canon Brook Trail then descends to a jct. with A. Murray Young Path, which goes right at 1.1 mi. The trail crosses Otter Creek and climbs gently along the north side of Canon Brook before crossing and then climbing steeply past the cascades on the upper part of Canon Brook. The trail then swings away from the brook, passes a beaver pond, and ascends to a small pond known as The Featherbed, where the trail crosses Cadillac South Ridge Trail at 2.0 mi. Descending the west face of Cadillac Mtn., the trail ends in the valley between Cadillac and Pemetic mountains at its jct. with Bubble and Jordan Ponds Path at 2.7 mi.

Canon Brook Trail (AMC map 5: D7, E7) (NPS rating: strenuous)

Distances from ME 3 (150 ft.) to
- Kane Path jct. (150 ft.): 0.2 mi., 10 min.
- Dorr South Ridge Trail jct. (250 ft.): 0.9 mi., 25 min.
- A. Murray Young Path jct. (250 ft.): 1.1 mi., 30 min.
- Cadillac South Ridge Trail jct. (1,000 ft.): 2.0 mi., 1 hr. 25 min.
- Bubble and Jordan Ponds Path jct. (300 ft.): 2.7 mi., 1 hr. 45 min.

Dorr North Ridge Trail

Dorr North and South Ridge trails offer more gradual alternatives to the summit of Dorr Mtn. than do those trails that climb the steeper east face of the mountain. Dorr North Ridge Trail begins as an extension of Kebo Mtn. Trail at 0.9 mi. from Park Loop Rd., and climbs the north ridge at a moderate grade, reaching a jct. with Schiff Path and Cadillac-Dorr Connector at 1.0 mi. The summit is just ahead at 1.1 mi.

Dorr North Ridge Trail (AMC map 5: D7) (NPS rating: moderate)

Distances from Kebo Mtn. Trail (300 ft.) to
- Schiff Path, Cadillac-Dorr Connector, Dorr South Ridge Trail jct. (1,250 ft.): 1.0 mi., 1 hr.
- Dorr Mtn. summit (1,265 ft.): 1.1 mi., 1 hr. 5 min.

Dorr South Ridge Trail

This trail diverges right from Canon Brook Trail 0.9 mi. from ME 3 at the southern end of Dorr Mtn. Dorr South Ridge Trail rises at a moderate grade over rocky ledges and through semi-open softwood forest. Views of Champlain and Cadillac mountains and the ocean are frequent during the ascent of the ridge to the summit, which is reached at 2.2 mi.

Dorr South Ridge Trail (AMC map 5: D7, E7) (NPS rating: moderate)

Distances from ME 3 (150 ft.) to
- start of trail (250 ft.) (via Canon Brook Trail): 0.9 mi., 25 min.
- Dorr Mtn. summit (1,265 ft.): 2.2 mi. 1 hr. 35 min.

Cadillac-Dorr Connector

This short trail (only 0.2 mi.) starts just north of the summit of Dorr Mtn. and runs east to west, connecting Dorr North Ridge Trail with Gorge Path at its jct. with A. Murray Young Path.

A. Murray Young Path

Ascending the narrow valley between Dorr and Cadillac mountains from the south, this trail leaves Canon Brook Trail 1.1 mi. west of ME 3. A. Murray Young Path climbs gradually through the gorge separating Cadillac and Dorr mountains to meet Gorge Path at its jct. with Cadillac-Dorr Connector. To the right (east), it is 0.3 mi. to the summit of Dorr Mtn. via Cadillac-Dorr Connector and Dorr North Ridge Trail. To the left (west), it is 0.4 mi. to the summit of Cadillac Mtn. via Gorge Path.

A. Murray Young Path (AMC map 5: D7, E7) (NPS rating: moderate)

Distances from ME 3 (150 ft.) to
- start of trail (250 ft.) (via Canon Brook Trail): 1.1 mi., 30 min.
- Cadillac-Dorr Connector (1,050 ft.): 2.4 mi., 1 hr. 35 min.
- Dorr Mtn. summit (1,265 ft.) (via Cadillac-Dorr Connector and Dorr North Ridge Trail): 2.7 mi., 1 hr. 55 min.
- Cadillac Mtn. summit (1,528 ft.) (via Gorge Path): 2.8 mi., 2 hr. 5 min.

Kebo Mtn. (407 ft.)

This low peak lies just off Park Loop Rd. at the end of the long north ridge of Dorr Mtn.

Kebo Mtn. Trail

This trail leaves the south side of Park Loop Rd. 1.5 mi. after the road becomes one-way. (*Note:* No parking is available at the start of the trail. Parking is available 0.2 mi. east at the gravel pullout for Stratheden Path.) Kebo Mtn. Trail climbs south to the summit of Kebo Mtn. at 0.3 mi., then traverses a second hump, and reaches its end at a jct. with Hemlock and Dorr North Ridge trails 0.9 mi. from Park Loop Rd.

Kebo Mtn. Trail (AMC map 5: D7) (NPS rating: easy)
Distances from Park Loop Rd. (200 ft.) to
- Kebo Mtn. summit (407 ft.): 0.3 mi., 15 min.
- Hemlock and Dorr North Ridge trails (300 ft.): 0.9 mi., 30 min.
- Dorr Mtn. summit (1,265 ft.) (via Dorr North Ridge Trail): 1.8 mi., 1 hr. 25 min.

Stratheden Path

Running from Park Loop Rd. to Hemlock Trail, this easy walk bypasses the summit of Kebo Mtn. Stratheden Path begins on Park Loop Rd., 0.2 mi. east of Kebo Mtn. Trail. The path takes a fairly level route through hemlocks on its way to Hemlock Trail, where the path ends at 0.7 mi.

Stratheden Path (AMC map 5: D7) (NPS rating: easy)
Distances from Park Loop Rd. (200 ft.) to
- Hemlock Trail jct. (50 ft.): 0.7 mi., 20 min.
- Sieur de Monts Spring (50 ft.) (via Hemlock Trail and Hemlock Rd.): 1.2 mi., 35 min.

Hemlock Trail

This trail on the lower end of the north ridge of Dorr Mtn. connects Gorge Path to Dorr North Ridge Trail and Sieur de Monts Spring. Hemlock Trail begins on Gorge Path, 1.0 mi. below the Cadillac-Dorr notch and 0.4 mi. above Park Loop Rd., and heads east, rising slightly to meet Dorr North Ridge Trail in 0.2 mi. Hemlock Trail then descends moderately to end at a jct. with Stratheden Path and Hemlock Rd. (no cars allowed on this road) at 0.4 mi. Sieur de Monts Spring is 0.5 mi. south via Hemlock Rd.

> **Hemlock Trail (AMC map 5: D7) (NPS rating: easy)**
> Distances from Gorge Path (250 ft.) to
> - Dorr North Ridge Trail (250 ft.): 0.2 mi., 5 min.
> - Stratheden Path and Hemlock Rd. (50 ft.): 0.4 mi., 10 min.

Cadillac Mtn. (1,528 ft.)

The highest point on the island, this mountain is also the highest on the Atlantic Coast north of Brazil. An automobile road, the Cadillac Summit Rd., leads to the summit, where there is a parking area, a paved summit walking trail with interpretive signs, a small gift shop, and restrooms. Accessibility by car makes this summit the busiest in the park. The open terrain of the rocky summit offers commanding views in all directions.

Cadillac South Ridge Trail

A relatively long hike for Acadia, this trail starts on the north side of ME 3 about 50 yd. west of the entrance to Blackwoods Campground. (A level 0.7-mi. connector trail links the campground to the road and trailhead.) The trail climbs generally north. At 0.9 mi., a short loop trail on the right leads to Eagles Crag, with good views to the east and southeast. The loop trail rejoins the main trail in 0.3 mi.

After leaving the woods, South Ridge Trail rises gently over open ledges to meet Canon Brook Trail at The Featherbed at 2.0 mi. Continuing in the open, South Ridge Trail reaches a jct. with Cadillac West Face Trail on the left at 2.7 mi. Ahead, the trail passes close to a switchback in the Cadillac Summit Rd. and ends at the Cadillac Mtn. summit parking area at 3.2 mi.

> **Cadillac South Ridge Trail (AMC map 5: D7, E7, F7) (NPS rating: moderate)**
> Distances from ME 3 (150 ft.) to
> - Eagles Crag spur trail, south jct. (600 ft.): 0.9 mi., 40 min.
> - Canon Brook Trail jct. (1,000 ft.): 2.0 mi., 1 hr. 25 min.
> - Cadillac Mtn. summit (1,528 ft.): 3.2 mi., 2 hrs. 20 min.

Cadillac West Face Trail

This steep trail is the shortest route to the summit of Cadillac Mtn. It is a difficult trail at any time, but especially in wet weather, when the rock slabs can be extremely slippery. The trail begins where Park Loop Rd. passes north of Bubble Pond, using the short spur road off Park Loop Rd. to reach the pond, parking area, and trailhead. Cadillac West Face Trail rises steeply through woods and over open ledges to a jct. with Cadillac South Ridge Trail at 1.1 mi. Turn left (north) and climb steep slabs to reach the summit at 1.6 mi.

Cadillac West Face Trail (AMC map 5: E6–E7) (NPS rating: strenuous)
Distances from north end of Bubble Pond (350 ft.) to
- Cadillac South Ridge Trail jct. (1,400 ft.): 1.1 mi., 1 hr. 10 min.
- Cadillac Mtn. summit (1,528 ft.): 1.6 mi, 1 hr. 30 min.

Cadillac North Ridge Trail

Following the north ridge of Cadillac, this trail quickly rises through stunted softwoods onto open ledges. The trailhead is on Park Loop Rd., 0.3 mi. east of where it becomes one-way. A pullout on the north side of the road provides very limited parking.

The trail starts on the south side of the road and climbs steadily, always keeping to the east of Cadillac Summit Rd., although the trail closely approaches road switchbacks on two occasions. For much of the distance, both sides of the ridge are visible. The views of Bar Harbor, Eagle Lake, Egg Rock, and Dorr Mtn. are excellent.

Cadillac North Ridge Trail (AMC map 5: D7) (NPS rating: moderate)
Distance from Park Loop Rd. (400 ft.) to
- Cadillac Mtn. summit (1,528 ft.): 2.2 mi., 1 hr. 30 min.

Gorge Path

This trail ascends the scenic gorge between Cadillac and Dorr mountains and provides good access to both peaks. The trailhead is on Park Loop Rd., 0.9 mi. east of where it becomes one-way.

The trail rises moderately up the gorge, passing Hemlock Trail at 0.4 mi. Gorge Path reaches a jct. with Cadillac-Dorr Connector and A. Murray Young Path in a deep notch between the two mountains at 1.4 mi. At this point, Gorge Path turns right (west) and climbs steeply to the summit of Cadillac Mtn., reaching it at 1.8 mi.

Gorge Path (AMC map 5: D7) (NPS rating: moderate)
Distances from Park Loop Rd. (200 ft.) to
- Dorr-Cadillac notch (1,050 ft.): 1.4 mi., 1 hr. 5 min.
- Cadillac Mtn. summit (1,528 ft.): 1.8 mi., 1 hr. 35 min.

Jordan Pond

Jordan Pond is a central trailhead to the eastern side of Acadia. Here also is the popular Jordan Pond House. Known for its fine dining and scenic view of The Bubbles and Penobscot Mtn., Jordan Pond House has been serving park visitors since 1871. Gain access via Park Loop Rd. from the north or south. Parking is also available 0.1 mi. north of Jordan Pond House.

Jordan Pond Path

This circuit around Jordan Pond is level most of the way, but crosses a rocky slope with occasional loose boulders at the pond's northeastern shore. Directions here are for traveling the east shore first. From Jordan Pond parking area, follow the boat-launch road to the south shore of the pond. At the pond, turn right to start the circuit. Follow the south shore, and in 0.4 mi. reach a jct. with Bubble and Jordan Ponds Path. At 1.3 mi., Jordan Pond Carry and Bubbles Trail diverge to the right. Farther along the northeast shore, at 1.7 mi., Bubbles Divide Trail heads right and climbs to Bubbles Gap. Beyond, reach the jct. with Deer Brook Trail, which leads up Penobscot Mtn. Finally, turn south along the west shore of the pond, where the trail runs under the precipitous Jordan Cliffs. There are numerous wet areas en route, which are crossed via bog bridges. The circuit is completed at the south end of Jordan Pond at 3.4 mi.

Jordan Pond Path (AMC map 5: E6) (NPS rating: moderate)

Distances counterclockwise from Jordan Pond parking area (300 ft.) to
- Bubble and Jordan Ponds Path (to Canon Brook Trail): 0.4 mi., 10 min.
- Jordan Pond Carry (to Eagle Lake): 1.3 mi., 35 min.
- Bubbles Trail (to South Bubble summit): 1.3 mi., 35 min.
- Bubbles Divide Trail (leads to Bubble Gap): 1.7 mi., 50 min.
- Deer Brook Trail (to Penobscot Mtn.): 1.9 mi., 55 min.
- Jordan Pond parking area: 3.4 mi., 1 hr. 45 min.

Asticou & Jordan Pond Path

This trail is reached by a short connecting path from the west side of Jordan Pond House. Asticou & Jordan Pond Path follows a level course for most of its distance, yet gains some elevation to reach Asticou Ridge Trail. The path provides an important link to Eliot Mtn., as well as to a potential leg of a loop over Sargent and Penobscot mountains.

Leaving the trailhead, Asticou & Jordan Pond Path proceeds through a mixed forest. At 0.9 mi., the path crosses a carriage road. At 1.0 mi., the path crosses another carriage road, and at 1.1 mi., Penobscot Mtn. Trail leaves right. Harbor Brook Trail enters from the left soon after crossing the brook. Asticou & Jordan Pond Path then begins to climb up Asticou Ridge. At 1.5 mi., Asticou Ridge Trail leaves left. Asticou & Jordan Pond Path levels once again, and continues straight ahead to a jct. with Sargent South Ridge Trail at 1.8 mi. Beyond this point, Asticou & Jordan Pond Path continues to its end at a private drive and is not recommended.

Asticou & Jordan Pond Path (AMC map 5: E6, F5–F6) (NPS rating: easy)

Distances from Jordan Pond House (300 ft.) to
- start of trail: 0.1 mi., 5 min.
- Penobscot Mtn. Trail jct. (150 ft.): 1.1 mi., 30 min.
- Asticou Ridge Trail jct. (350 ft.): 1.5 mi., 50 min.
- Sargent South Ridge Trail jct. (250 ft.): 1.8 mi., 1 hr.

Asticou Ridge Trail

To reach this trail, follow Asticou & Jordan Pond Path for 1.5 mi. from Jordan Pond House. Traversing a rocky ridge, Asticou Ridge Trail climbs over Eliot Mtn. (456 ft.), offering views to the south and east of the ocean, Day

Mtn., and The Triad. Beyond, the trail reaches a monument to Charles William Eliot, one of the founders of the park, at 0.9 mi. Descending into the woods, the trail comes to a jct. with a side trail leading 0.6 mi. to ME 3. Keeping right, the trail descends into beautiful Thuya Gardens, where it ends (very limited parking).

Asticou Ridge Trail (AMC map 5: F5) (NPS rating: moderate)
Distances from jct. Asticou and Jordan Pond Path (350 ft.) to
- Eliot Mtn. summit (456 ft.): 0.8 mi., 25 min.
- Eliot monument: 0.9 mi., 30 min.
- jct. side trail to ME 3: 1.1 mi., 35 min.
- Thuya Gardens: 1.4 mi., 45 min.

Amphitheater Trail

This trail connects Hadlock Brook Trail to Sargent South Ridge Trail and the carriage roads southwest of of Jordan Pond. Amphitheater Trail begins on a carriage road between posts 20 and 22, about 1.5 mi. from Jordan Pond via Asticou & Jordan Pond Path and a carriage road. Amphitheater Trail parallels Harbor Brook, crossing it numerous times before and after passing under Amphitheater Bridge (the largest carriage road bridge in the park) at 0.8 mi. Beyond the bridge, the trail climbs more steeply to Birch Spring and a jct. with Sargent South Ridge Trail at 1.4 mi. Amphitheater Trail then descends to meet Hadlock Brook Trail at 1.7 mi.

Amphitheater Trail (AMC map 5: E5, F5) (NPS rating: moderate)
Distances from carriage road crossing between posts 20 and 22 (150 ft.) to
- Amphitheater Bridge (350 ft.): 0.8 mi., 25 min.
- Sargent South Ridge Trail jct. (850 ft.): 1.4 mi., 1 hr. 15 min.
- Hadlock Brook Trail jct. (700 ft.): 1.7 mi., 1 hr. 30 min.

North Bubble (872 ft.) and South Bubble (766 ft.)

The finely shaped, almost symmetrical North Bubble and South Bubble rise above the north end of Jordan Pond. Formerly covered with heavy tree growth, they were swept by fire in 1947, leaving many open views. The best access is from Bubble Rock parking area about 1.1 mi. south of Bubble Pond on the west side of Park Loop Rd.

Bubbles Trail

This trail connects the north shore of Jordan Pond with Eagle Lake, taking the high route and climbing over The Bubbles and Conners Nubble in the process. The trail leaves from Jordan Pond Path at a point 0.9 mi. from Jordan Pond parking area.

Bubbles Trail rises very steeply almost immediately, climbing over boulders and scrambling over ledges before leveling off just before reaching the summit of South Bubble at 0.4 mi. The views of Jordan Pond and beyond from the ledges below the summit are spectacular. At the summit, a spur trail leaves right for a short walk to Bubble Rock, a large glacial erratic perched on the edge of the mountain.

From the summit of South Bubble, the trail descends moderately for 0.3 mi., then turns right, coinciding with Bubbles Divide Trail for a short distance before turning left and making a steep climb to the summit of North Bubble at 1.0 mi. Bubbles Trail continues north past the summit, descending at an easy pace over open ridgeline for several hundred yards. At 1.7 mi., the trail crosses a carriage road before making a short climb to the summit of Conners Nubble and its excellent views of Eagle Lake and Cadillac Mtn. at 1.8 mi. The trail continues north over the summit, and descends into the woods, reaching Eagle Lake Trail near the shore of Eagle Lake at 2.3 mi.

Bubbles Trail (AMC map 5: D6, E6) (NPS rating: strenuous)
Distances from Jordan Pond Path (275 ft.) to
- South Bubble summit (766 ft.): 0.4 mi., 25 min.
- North Bubble summit (872 ft.): 1.0 mi., 1 hr.
- Conners Nubble (550 ft.): 1.8 mi., 1 hr. 30 min.
- Eagle Lake Trail (250 ft.): 2.3 mi., 1 hr. 45 min.

Bubbles Divide Trail

Leaving Bubble Rock parking area 1.1 mi. south of Bubble Pond on the west side of Park Loop Rd., this trail heads east over the small notch between the Bubbles and down to the north shore of Jordan Pond. By providing quick access to Bubbles Trail, this is the quickest route to the summit of either mountain.

Bubbles Divide Trail (AMC map 5: E6) (NPS rating: moderate)

Distances from the Bubble Rock parking area (450 ft.) to
- Jordan Pond Carry jct.: 0.1 mi., 5 min.
- North Bubble summit (872 ft.) (via Bubbles Trail): 0.5 mi., 25 min.
- South Bubbles summit (766 ft.) (via Bubbles Trail): 0.5 mi., 25 min.
- Jordan Pond Path jct. (275 ft.): 0.6 mi., 30 min.

Pemetic Mtn. (1,247 ft.)

This mountain is located roughly in the center of the eastern half of the island and offers some of the best views in Acadia. Trails up the west side are short and relatively steep, whereas routes from the north and south are more gradual and wooded. If you do not take the shuttle bus: For the trails from the south, park at Jordan Pond parking area. From the north, park at Bubble Pond. From the west, parking is located at Bubble Rock. Gain access to all parking areas via Park Loop Rd.

Pemetic North Ridge Trail

This trail ascends the mountain from the north and offers outstanding views of Jordan Pond, The Bubbles, Sargent Mtn., and Eagle Lake. The trail leaves from Bubble Pond parking area at the north end of Bubble Pond. The trail crosses a carriage road, then quickly climbs through the forest to a jct. with Pemetic Northwest Trail at 1.0 mi. Pemetic North Ridge Trail reaches the summit of Pemetic Mtn. at 1.1 mi., where there are excellent views of The Triad, Cadillac Mtn., and Jordan Pond. The trail continues down the south ridge as Pemetic South Ridge Trail (described next).

Pemetic North Ridge Trail (AMC map 5: E6) (NPS rating: strenuous)

Distances from Bubble Pond parking area (350 ft.) to
- Pemetic Northwest Trail jct. (1,150 ft.): 1.0 mi., 55 min.
- Pemetic Mtn. summit (1,247 ft.): 1.1 mi., 1 hr.

Pemetic South Ridge Trail

This trail climbs to the summit of Pemetic Mtn. via the south ridge. The trail begins at Bubble & Jordan Ponds Path, 0.7 mi. east of Jordan Pond parking area, and climbs steadily to a jct. at 0.6 mi. with Pemetic East Cliff Trail, which leads to the right. Continuing straight ahead, climb over open ledges with spectacular views and reach the summit and Pemetic North Ridge Trail at 1.3 mi.

Pemetic South Ridge Trail (AMC map 5: E6) (NPS rating: strenuous)
Distances from Bubble & Jordan Ponds Path (450 ft.) to
- Pemetic East Cliff Trail (950 ft.): 0.6 mi., 25 min.
- Pemetic summit (1,247 ft.): 1.3 mi., 1 hr.

Pemetic East Cliff Trail

This short, but steep trail (NPS rating: strenuous) climbs from the intersection of Bubble and Jordan Ponds Path and Triad Trail to Pemetic South Ridge Trail in 0.3 mi. and approximately 10 min.

Pemetic Northwest Trail

This trail begins at Bubble Rock parking area, on the west side of Park Loop Rd. 1.1 mi. south of Bubble Pond. The path enters the woods east of the road and climbs in almost constant cover. Sometimes following a rocky stream bed, the trail ends at a jct. with Pemetic North Ridge Trail about 0.1 mi. north of the summit.

Pemetic Northwest Trail (AMC map 5: E6) (NPS rating: strenuous)
Distances from Bubble Rock parking area (450 ft.) to
- Pemetic North Ridge Trail jct. (1,150 ft.): 0.6 mi., 35 min.
- Pemetic Mtn. summit (1,247 ft.) (via Pemetic North Ridge Trail): 0.7 mi., 40 min.

Bubble & Jordan Ponds Path

This slightly graded path leads from the southeast shore of Jordan Pond to the valley south of Bubble Pond, where the path meets the west end of Canon Brook Trail. Bubble & Jordan Ponds Path leaves the pond and proceeds east, crossing Park Loop Rd. at 0.1 mi., where there is a small parking area. Continuing through heavy woods and by easy grades, the path swings into the valley between The Triad and Pemetic Mtn. The path crosses Pemetic South Ridge Trail at 0.5 mi., and then turns left at a jct. with Triad Pass. Bubble & Jordan Ponds Path continues northeast to a jct. with Pemetic East Cliff Trail (goes left) and Triad Trail (goes right) at 0.8 mi. Beyond, Bubble and Jordan Ponds Path joins a carriage road at 1.1 mi. and, after a short distance, leaves the road and continues 0.4 mi. to merge with Canon Brook Trail (climbs to the south ridge of Cadillac Mtn., 1.2 mi. south of the summit).

Bubble & Jordan Ponds Path (AMC map 5: E6–E7) (NPS rating: moderate)
Distances from Jordan Pond (275 ft.) to
- Pemetic South Ridge Trail (450 ft.): 0.5 mi., 20 min.
- carriage road (400 ft.): 1.1 mi., 40 min.
- Canon Brook Trail (400 ft.): 1.5 mi., 1 hr. 5 min.

Triad Pass

This short trail (NPS rating: easy) begins on Bubble & Jordan Ponds Path, 0.5 mi. east of Jordan Pond parking area and heads southeast for 0.2 mi., ending at Hunters Brook Trail. This link provides trail access from Jordan Pond to The Triad and Day Mtn.

The Triad (698 ft.)
Triad Trail

This trail provides a route from Pemetic Mtn. to Day Mtn. via The Triad. The trail heads southeast from Bubble & Jordan Ponds Path (0.8 mi. from Jordan Pond parking area), where Pemetic East Cliff Trail heads northwest. Triad Trail rises moderately for 0.4 mi. to cross Hunters Brook Trail before reaching the top of The Triad, then descends for 0.6 mi. to end at a carriage road and the start of Day Mtn. Trail.

Triad Trail (AMC map 5: E6, F6) (NPS rating: moderate)
Distances from Bubble & Jordan Ponds Path (550 ft.) to
- Hunters Brook Trail (650 ft.): 0.4 mi., 15 min.
- Day Mtn. Trail (250 ft.): 1.0 mi., 30 min.

Day Mtn. (583 ft.)
Day Mtn. Trail

This trail starts on the north side of ME 3 about 1.5 mi. south of the entrance to Blackwoods Campground. A parking area is located on the south side of the road. The trail climbs moderately through the forest for its entire length. Periodically crossing carriage roads, the trail offers good views of Hunters Beach and Seal Harbor from ledges at 0.7 mi. At 0.9 mi., the summit is reached. (A carriage road also rises to the summit of Day Mtn.) Beyond, the trail descends into the forest and ends at another carriage road at 1.4 mi., Here, Triad Trail continues north toward The Triad and Pemetic Mtn.

Day Mtn. Trail (AMC map 5: F6–F7) (NPS rating: moderate)
Distances from ME 3 (250 ft.) to
- Day Mtn. summit (583 ft.): 0.9 mi., 35 min.
- carriage road (250 ft.): 1.4 mi., 50 min.
- Pemetic Mtn. summit (1,247 ft.) (via Triad, Pemetic East Cliff, and Pemetic South Ridge trails): 3.4 mi., 2 hrs. 10 min.

Hunters Brook Trail

Beginning on Park Loop Rd. 0.1 mi. north of the ME 3 bridge over Park Loop Rd. and at a point 1.2 mi. southwest of the entrance to Blackwoods Campground, this trail follows along pretty Hunters Brook. At 1.25 mi., the trail bears west away from the brook and climbs to a carriage road at 1.4 mi. Crossing it, the trail climbs to a jct. with Triad Trail just north of The Triad at 1.9 mi. Turning right (north) on Triad Trail leads to the summit of Pemetic Mtn. in 1.4 mi., while turning left (south) leads 0.1 mi. to the summit of The Triad. Continuing straight ahead, Hunters Brook Trail descends for 0.3 mi., passes Triad Pass on the right, takes a left, and heads south, ending at a carriage road (0.2 mi. west of post 17) at 2.7 mi.

Hunters Brook Trail (AMC map 5: F6–F7, E6–E7) (NPS rating: moderate)

Distances from Park Loop Rd. (50 ft.) to
- carriage path (350 ft.): 1.4 mi., 45 min.
- Triad Trail jct. (650 ft.): 1.9 mi., 1 hr. 15 min.
- Triad Pass jct. (550 ft.): 2.2 mi., 1 hr. 25 min.
- carriage road (350 ft.): 2.7 mi., 1 hr. 45 min.

Sargent Mtn. (1,379 ft.) and Penobscot Mtn. (1,196 ft.)

These two open summits rise to the west of Jordan Pond. Sargent Mtn. Pond is a pretty little pond that lies between the two peaks. From the south, the preferred starting point is Jordan Pond parking area. The outlying territory to the west contains an interesting maze of trails and carriage roads around Gilmore Peak (1,030 ft.), Parkman Mtn. (950 ft.), and Cedar Swamp Mtn. (950 ft.). Ample parking is available at two areas. One is on the west side of ME 3/198, about 0.3 mi. north of Upper Hadlock Pond (reservoir, no swimming). The other parking area is on the east side of ME 3/198, about 0.5 mi. north of Upper Hadlock Pond. Upper Hadlock Pond is approximately 2.5 mi. south of where ME 3/198 splits from ME 233.

Penobscot Mtn. Trail

The trail leaves from from Asticou & Jordan Pond Path at a point 1.1 mi. west of Jordan Pond House. Penobscot Mtn. Trail heads north, climbing at an easy pace and crossing three carriage roads in its first 0.3 mi. The trail then climbs more steeply, occasionally breaking out into the open with excellent views to the south. The trail attains the south ridge of the mountain and the jct. with Spring Trail at 1.2 mi. Penobscot Mtn. Trail then climbs gradually over open granite ledges to the summit at 2.1 mi. Beyond, the trail continues north, descending to a jct. with Deer Brook Trail at 2.2 mi. Penobscot Mtn. Trail turns left here and soon reaches Sargent Mtn. Pond. From the pond, the trail makes a short climb to the Sargent South Ridge Trail at 2.4 mi.

Penobscot Mtn. Trail (AMC map 5: E5–E6) (NPS rating: strenuous)

Distances from Asticou and Jordan Pond Path (150 ft.) to
- Spring Trail jct. (650 ft.): 1.2 mi., 1 hr.

- Penobscot Mtn. summit (1,196 ft.): 2.1 mi., 1 hr. 30 min.
- Sargent South Ridge Trail jct. (1,150 ft.): 2.4 mi., 1 hr. 40 min.

Spring Trail

This trail provides the quickest access to Penobscot Mtn. from Jordan Pond House. Short, but very steep in places, this trail should be avoided for descents, especially in wet conditions. The trail starts from the west side of Jordan Stream, about 100 yd. west of Jordan Pond House at a jct. with a carriage road and Asticou & Jordan Pond Path. The trail runs west and passes Jordan Cliffs Trail at 0.3 mi., shortly before crossing a carriage road. The trail then climbs steeply with the assistance of iron rungs and wooden handrails to the join Penobscot Mtn. Trail at 0.5 mi.

Spring Trail (AMC map 5: E6) (NPS rating: strenuous)
Distances from Jordan Pond House (300 ft.) to
- Jordan Cliffs Trail jct. (400 ft.): 0.3 mi., 15 min.
- Penobscot Mtn. Trail jct. (650 ft.): 0.5 mi., 30 min.

Jordan Cliffs Trail

This challenging and scenic trail leaves Spring Trail at a point 0.3 mi. west of Jordan Pond House, just northeast of the jct. of Spring Trail and a carriage road. Soon after leaving the carriage road, Jordan Cliffs Trail heads north and rises up the east shoulder of Penobscot Mtn. in gradual pitches to reach the cliffs. The trail traverses Jordan Cliffs, via ladders and handrails, to a jct. with East Trail at 1.6 mi. (leads left [west] 0.4 mi. to the summit of Penobscot Mtn.). Although very rugged, this section of Jordan Cliffs Trail is spectacular, with views of The Bubbles, Pemetic Mtn., and Jordan Pond. Straight ahead, Jordan Cliffs Trail continues the traverse, reaching its end at a jct. with Deer Brook Trail and Sargent East Cliffs Trail at 1.9 mi.

Jordan Cliffs Trail (AMC map 5: E6) (NPS rating: ladder)
Distances from Jordan Pond House (300 ft.) to
- start of Jordan Cliffs Trail (400 ft.) (via Spring Trail): 0.3 mi., 15 min.
- East Trail jct. (900 ft.): 1.6 mi., 1 hr. 10 min.
- jct., Deer Brook and Sargent East Cliffs trails (650 ft.): 1.9 mi., 1 hr. 20 min.

Sargent East Cliffs Trail

This short but steep trail connects Jordan Cliffs Trail to the summit of Sargent Mtn. Sargent East Cliffs Trail is recommended more for ascent than descent, especially in wet weather, when the steep climb down wet rocks and ledges can be hazardous. The trail starts at Deer Brook and the jct. of Jordan Cliffs and Deer Brook trails. Sargent East Cliff Trail climbs quickly up the southeast face of Sargent Mtn. and has excellent views for much of its 0.7-mi. length.

Sargent East Cliff Trail (AMC map 5: E5–E6) (NPS rating: strenuous)
Distance from Deer Brook Trail (650 ft.) to
* Sargent Mtn. summit (1,379 ft.): 0.7 mi., 35 min.

Deer Brook Trail

Deer Brook Trail makes a steep, quick ascent to Sargent Mtn. Pond from Jordan Pond Path at the north end of Jordan Pond. The route is entirely wooded and follows the course of Deer Brook, crossing a carriage road at 0.2 mi. and reaching a jct. with Jordan Cliffs and Sargent East Cliff trails at 0.3 mi. Deer Brook Trail ends at Penobscot Mtn. Trail in the col between Sargent and Penobscot, 0.8 mi. from the shore of Jordan Pond. Turn right for Sargent Mtn. Pond, a 10-minute walk.

Deer Brook Trail (AMC map 5: E5–E6) (NPS rating: strenuous)
Distance from Jordan Pond Path (275 ft.) to
* Penobscot Mtn. Trail jct. (1,050 ft.): 0.8 mi., 45 min.

Sargent South Ridge Trail

From Brown Mtn. Gatehouse parking lot (about 1 mi. north of Upper Hadlock Pond), follow carriage roads toward Jordan Pond for 0.7 mi., bearing right at intersections 18 and 19. From there, the trail heads north to the summit of Sargent Mtn., or south 0.1 mi. to Asticou & Jordan Pond Path.

Sargent South Ridge Trail rises over a wooded shoulder and passes just southeast of the summit of Cedar Swamp Mtn. at 1.3 mi. (a spur trail bears left to the summit). Beyond, the trail drops to cross Amphitheater Trail at 1.4 mi. Sargent South Ridge Trail then leaves the woods and rises sharply to another jct. at 1.9 mi. Here, Penobscot Mtn. Trail enters from the right. Sargent South Ridge Trail continues north over open ledges, past junctions to the left with Hadlock Brook Trail at 2.1 mi. and the Maple Spring Trail at 2.3 mi. The summit is reached at 2.6 mi.

Sargent South Ridge Trail (AMC map 5: E5) (NPS rating: moderate)

Distances from carriage road (350 ft.) to
- Cedar Swamp Mtn. spur trail (900 ft.): 1.3 mi., 1 hr.
- Penobscot Mtn. Trail jct. (1,150 ft.): 1.9 mi., 1 hr. 20 min.
- Hadlock Brook Trail jct. (1,200 ft.): 2.1 mi., 1 hr. 30 min.
- Maple Spring Trail jct. (1,250 ft.): 2.3 mi., 1 hr. 35 min.
- Sargent Mtn. summit (1,379 ft.): 2.6 mi., 1 hr. 50 min.

Giant Slide Trail

The trail leaves the east side of ME 3/198, 1.0 mi. south of ME 233 (limited parking is available on the west side of the road). The trail climbs up a gradual slope to a carriage road at 0.7 mi. The trail turns sharply right (south) and, following Sargent Brook, rises steeply over the tumbled boulders of Giant Slide. At 1.2 mi., Parkman Mtn. Trail diverges to the right and Sargent Northwest Trail leaves left. Giant Slide Trail continues uphill, crosses another carriage road, and proceeds through the notch between Parkman Mtn. and Gilmore Peak to a jct. with Grandgent Trail at 1.9 mi. Beyond, Giant Slide Trail descends to end at a jct. with Maple Spring Trail at 2.4 mi.

Giant Slide Trail (AMC map 5: D4–D5, E5) (NPS rating: ladder)

Distances from ME 198 (50 ft.) to
- carriage road crossing (250 ft.): 0.7 mi., 25 min.
- Parkman Mtn. and Sargent Northwest trails jct. (550 ft.): 1.2 mi., 50 min.
- notch between Parkman Mtn. and Gilmore Peak (750 ft.): 1.9 mi., 1 hr. 10 min.
- Maple Spring Trail jct. (550 ft.): 2.4 mi., 1 hr. 30 min.

Sargent Northwest Trail

Leaving Giant Slide Trail at a point 1.2 mi. from ME 3/198, Sargent Northwest Trail ascends east and crosses a carriage road at 0.3 mi. Ahead, the trail rises over slanting pitches for 0.3 mi. before making a sharp right (south) turn. The final stretch to the summit is over open ledges offering spectacular views.

Sargent Northwest Trail (AMC map 5: E5) (NPS rating: moderate)
Distance from Giant Slide Trail (550 ft.) to
  • Sargent Mtn. summit (1,379 ft.): 1.1 mi., 1 hr. 10 min.

Hadlock Brook Trail

This trail provides access to Sargent Mtn. from the southwest, as well as leading to several other trails lacking roadside access. From the east side of ME 3/198 just north of Upper Hadlock Pond and opposite Norumbega Mtn. parking area, Hadlock Brook Trail heads east, passing Bald Peak and Parkman Mtn. trails, a carriage road, and Hadlock Ponds and Maple Spring Trail, all in the first 0.4 mi. From here, Hadlock Brook Trail follows the east branch of Hadlock Brook through mature forest for 0.4 mi. before crossing a carriage road at Waterfall Bridge and an excellent view of a 40-ft. waterfall. The trail then gets steeper, continuing to parallel the brook over rough footing to a jct. with Amphitheater Trail at 1.1 mi. Hadlock Brook Trail climbs steeply before reaching the open terrain of the south ridge and Sargent South Ridge Trail at 1.6 mi.

Hadlock Brook Trail (AMC map 5: E5) (NPS rating: strenuous)
Distances from ME 3/198 (300 ft.) to
  • Maple Spring Trail jct. (350 ft.): 0.4 mi., 10 min.
  • Amphitheater Trail jct. (700 ft.): 1.1 mi., 50 min.
  • Sargent South Ridge Trail jct. (1,200 ft.): 1.6 mi., 1 hr. 15 min.

Maple Spring Trail

This trail climbs to the south ridge of Sargent Mtn. from the southwest, following the west branch of Hadlock Brook for much of its length. It also provides access to Gilmore Peak via Grandgent Trail.

The start of the trail is reached by following Hadlock Brook Trail from Norumbega Mtn. parking area on ME 3/198 for 0.4 mi., where Maple Spring Trail leads left. It closely follows Hadlock Brook, crossing it several times. In high water, there are some nice cascades and small waterfalls before and after crossing under Hemlock Bridge 0.3 mi. from Hadlock Brook Trail. Beyond, Maple Spring Trail climbs through a small gorge before reaching Giant Slide Trail at 0.4 mi. Grandgent Trail is reached at 0.9 mi. (Gilmore Peak is 0.1 mi. to the left via the Grandgent Trail.) Here, Maple Spring Trail makes a sharp right and climbs steeply, reaching the open south ridge and Sargent South Ridge Trail at 1.4 mi. The summit of Sargent is 0.3 mi. to the left (north) via this trail.

Maple Spring Trail (AMC map 5: E5) (NPS rating: strenuous)
Distances from Hadlock Brook Trail (350 ft.) to
- Giant Slide Trail jct. (550 ft.): 0.4 mi., 15 min.
- Grandgent Trail jct. (750 ft.): 0.9 mi., 40 min.
- Sargent South Ridge Trail jct. (1,250 ft.): 1.4 mi., 1 hr. 10 min.
- Sargent Mtn. summit (1,379 ft.) (via Sargent South Ridge Trail): 1.7 mi., 1 hr. 20 min.

Gilmore Peak (1,030 ft.) and Parkman Mtn. (950 ft.)
Grandgent Trail

Grandgent Trail connects the summits of Sargent Mtn., Gilmore Peak, and Parkman Mtn. From the summit of Sargent Mtn., the trail leaves west and steeply descends to a saddle and a jct. with Maple Spring Trail at 0.5 mi. After a right turn and a climb of 0.1 mi., Grandgent Trail reaches Gilmore Peak. Then the trail gradually descends for 0.3 mi., crossing Giant Slide Trail before climbing another 0.2 mi. to the summit of Parkman Mtn.

Grandgent Trail (AMC map 5: E5) (NPS rating: strenuous)
Distances from Sargent Mtn. summit (1,379 ft.) to
- Maple Spring Trail jct. (950 ft.): 0.5 mi., 20 min.
- Gilmore Peak summit (1,030 ft.): 0.6 mi., 25 min.
- Giant Slide Trail jct.: 0.9 mi., 35 min.
- Parkman Mtn. summit (950 ft.): 1.1 mi., 45 min.

Parkman Mtn. Trail

Diverging left (north) from Hadlock Brook Trail a short distance from ME 3/198, Parkman Mtn. Trail then leads 1.5 mi. through woods and over a series of knobs to the summit of Parkman Mtn. The trail crosses a carriage road three times on the way to the summit. Bald Peak Trail joins from the right at 1.4 mi. At the summit, Grandgent Trail leaves right (east) toward Gilmore Peak. Parkman Mtn. Trail continues north over open ledges, then through the woods, crossing a carriage road 0.5 mi. beyond the summit. The trail ends 0.3 mi. farther at the jct. of Giant Slide and Sargent Northwest trails.

Parkman Mtn. Trail (AMC map 5: E5) (NPS rating: moderate)
Distances from ME 3/198 (300 ft.) to
- Parkman Mtn. summit (950 ft.): 1.5 mi., 1 hr. 20 min.
- Giant Slide and Sargent North Ridge trails jct. (550 ft.): 2.3 mi., 1 hr. 45 min.

Bald Peak Trail

This is the most direct route up Bald Peak, one of several small and rocky, open summits to the west of Sargent Mtn. The trail is reached by following Hadlock Brook Trail for 0.2 mi. from Norumbega Mtn. parking area on ME 3/198. At this point, Bald Peak Trail leaves left and climbs gradually, reaching the summit of Bald Peak at 0.9 mi. Ahead, the trail joins Parkman Mtn. Trail at 1.1 mi. The summit of Parkman Mtn. is 0.1 mi. north.

Bald Peak Trail (AMC map 5: E5) (NPS rating: moderate)
Distances from ME 3/198 (300 ft.) via Hadlock Brook Trail to
- start of trail: 0.2 mi., 10 min.
- Bald Peak summit (950 ft.): 0.9 mi., 55 min.
- Parkman Mtn. Trail (850 ft.): 1.1 mi., 1 hr. 5 min.

Norumbega Mtn. (852 ft.)

Although the summit of this mountain is wooded, its trails offer good views of Somes Sound and the mountains west of the sound en route. (*Note*: This area is honeycombed with abandoned and unofficial paths. Pay careful attention to trail markers and maps.)

Goat Trail

Goat Trail leaves the Norumbega Mtn. parking lot on the west side of ME 3/198 about 0.3 mi. north of Upper Hadlock Pond. The trail ascends quickly and very steeply for the first 0.3 mi. through woods to granite ledges, then swings south to the summit at 0.6 mi. Occasional views can be seen from the ledges before reaching the wooded summit, and excellent views can be seen from Norumbega Mtn. Trail about 150 yd. beyond.

Goat Trail (AMC map 5: E5) (NPS rating: strenuous)
Distance from ME 3/198 (300 ft.) to
• Norumbega Mtn. summit (852 ft.): 0.6 mi., 45 min.

Norumbega Mtn. Trail

This trail connects the summit of Norumbega Mtn. with Lower Hancock Pond Trail via Hadlock Ponds Trail. Beginning from the end of Goat Trail on the summit of Norumbega, Norumbega Mtn. Trail follows the south ridge over semi-open ledges with occasional views, descending moderately before entering the forest and reaching the jct. with Golf Course Trail at 0.7 mi. Veering left at this jct., Norumbega Mtn. Trail continues its moderate descent, reaching Lower Hadlock Pond and Hadlock Ponds Trail at 1.3 mi. A nice loop hike is possible via Norumbega Mtn. Trail and Lower Norumbega Trail.

Norumbega Mtn. Trail (AMC map 5: E5, F5) (NPS rating: moderate)
Distances from Norumbega summit (852 ft.) to
• Golf Course Trail jct. (550 ft.): 0.7 mi., 15 min.
• Hadlock Ponds Trail jct. (200 ft.): 1.3 mi., 40 min.

Hadlock Ponds Trail

This relatively flat trail leaves Hadlock Brook Trail at a point 0.3 mi. from Norumbega Mtn. parking area on ME 3/198. Hadlock Ponds Trail follows the eastern shoreline of Upper Hadlock Pond, crosses ME 3/198, and continues to Lower Hadlock Pond and Lower Norumbega and Norumbega Mtn. trails. The views of the ponds from the trail are excellent.

Hadlock Ponds Trail (AMC map 5: E5, F5) (NPS rating: moderate)

Distances from Hadlock Brook Trail (300 ft.) to
- ME 3/198 at south end of Upper Hadlock Pond (250 ft.): 0.7 mi., 20 min.
- Lower Norumbega Trail (250 ft.): 1.0 mi., 30 min.
- Norumbega Mtn. Trail (200 ft.): 1.6 mi., 45 min.

Lower Norumbega Trail

This trail connects Goat Trail, just west of the Norumbega Mtn. parking area, to Hadlock Ponds Trail near the north shore of Lower Hadlock Pond. Lower Norumbega Trail is 0.9 mi. long, often quite wet, and follows uneven terrain in a spruce forest while paralleling ME 3/198.

Lower Norumbega Trail (AMC map 5: E5, F5) (NPS rating: moderate)

Distance from Goat Trail (300 ft.) to
- Hadlock Ponds Trail (250 ft.): 0.9 mi., 30 min.

Lower Hadlock Trail

This short trail follows the east side of Lower Hadlock Pond. The trail starts at the inlet to Lower Hadlock Pond, where the trail leaves Hadlock Ponds Trail, crosses the stream, and follows the shore through a pleasant softwood forest, reaching Hadlock Pond Rd. in 0.7 mi.

Lower Hadlock Trail (AMC map 5: F5) (NPS rating: easy)

Distance from Hadlock Ponds Trail (200 ft.) to
- Hadlock Pond Rd. (200 ft.): 0.7 mi., 20 min.

West of Somes Sound

Acadia Mtn. (681 ft.)

This mountain provides dramatic views of Somes Sound and the Cranberry Isles from open ledges interspersed with pitch pines and scrub oaks. A loop over the summit can be made using Acadia Mtn. Trail and Man o' War Brook fire road.

Acadia Mtn. Trail

Parking for this trail is located at Acadia Mtn. parking area on the west side of ME 102, 3.0 mi. south of Somesville and 3.0 mi. north of Southwest Harbor. (Please do not block the fire road gates on the east side of ME 102.)

The trail begins on the east side of the road, across from the parking area. Reach a fork at 0.1 mi., and turn left and climb the west slope, soon leaving the woods for open rocks and frequent views. The trail passes over the true summit and reaches the east summit, with views of the sound, at about 1 mi. The trail then descends southeast and south very steeply to cross Man o' War Brook fire road. A jct. about 50 yd. beyond the brook marks the end of the trail. To return to ME 102 via the fire road, go right (west) at the jct. and proceed past trails to St. Sauveur and Valley Cove, which diverge left about 100 yd. south of the brook. The east end of the Man o' War Brook fire road is another 200 yd. ahead. Follow the fire road west over gradual grades for 0.8 mi. to intersect Acadia Mtn. Trail. Turn left here, and at the next jct., turn right to return to the parking area.

Acadia Mtn. Trail (USGS SW Harbor quad) (NPS rating: strenuous)
Distances from ME 102 (150 ft.) to
- Acadia Mtn. summit (681 ft.): 0.8 mi., 40 min.
- Man o' War Brook fire road (100 ft.): 1.5 mi., 1 hr.
- ME 102 (100 ft.) (via Man o' War Brook fire road and Acadia Mtn. Trail): 2.4 mi., 1 hr. 25 min.

St. Sauveur Mtn. (690 ft.)

This mountain overlooking Valley Cove on Somes Sound can be climbed from ME 102 in the west or from Fernald Cove Rd. in the south.

St. Sauveur Trail

This trail is an easy route to the summit of St. Sauveur Mtn. from the north. Parking for this trail is located at Acadia Mtn. parking area on the west side of ME 102, 3.0 mi. south of Somesville and 3.0 mi. north of Southwest Harbor. (Please do not block the fire road gates on the east side of ME 102.)

Start 0.1 mi. up Acadia Mtn. Trail, and go right at the fork. St. Sauveur Trail runs south through a softwood forest and over open slopes, rising continually to a jct. at 0.9 mi., where Ledge Trail enters on the right. The summit of St. Sauveur Mtn. is reached at 1.2 mi. St. Sauveur Trail continues past the summit to a jct. Here, Valley Peak Trail leaves left, while St. Sauveur Trail continues right, descending the south ridge of the mountain. At 1.6 mi., the trail ends at its jct. with the lower end of Valley Peak Trail. Ahead, it is 0.5 mi. to Fernald Point Rd. via Valley Peak Trail.

St. Sauveur Trail (USGS SW Harbor quad) (NPS rating: moderate)
Distances from ME 102 (200 ft.) to
- start of trail (250 ft.): 0.1 mi., 5 min.
- Ledge Trail jct. (650 ft.): 0.9 mi., 40 min.
- St. Sauveur Mtn. summit (690 ft.): 1.2 mi., 50 min.
- Valley Peak Trail, upper jct. (650 ft.): 1.3 mi., 55 min.
- Valley Peak Trail, lower jct. (500 ft.): 1.6 mi., 1 hr. 5 min.
- Fernald Point Rd. (50 ft.) (via Valley Peak Trail): 2.1 mi., 1 hr. 20 min.

Ledge Trail

This trail begins at St. Sauveur parking area on the east side of ME 102 about 0.2 mi. north of the NPS entrance road leading to the south end of Echo Lake. The parking area is also about 0.2 mi. south of the access road to AMC's Echo Lake Camp (facilities include platform tents, bathhouse, and a full-service dining hall; reservations required). The trail enters the woods and rises over ledges to its end. The trail meets St. Sauveur Trail

0.6 mi. from the road at a point 0.2 mi. northwest of the summit of St. Sauveur Mtn.

Ledge Trail (USGS SW Harbor quad) (NPS rating: moderate)

Distances from ME 102 (200 ft.) to
- St. Sauveur Trail jct. (650 ft.): 0.6 mi., 30 min.
- St. Sauveur Mtn. summit (690 ft.): 0.8 mi., 40 min.

Valley Peak Trail

Leaving from the west side of the Valley Cove fire road (no vehicle access) a few yards north of the parking area at Fernald Cove, this trail rises steeply northwest through shady woods over Valley Peak (the south shoulder of St. Sauveur Mtn.). At 0.4 mi., St. Sauveur Trail leads left. Staying right, Valley Peak Trail then skirts the top of Eagle Cliff, with outstanding views of Valley Cove below and the mountains east of Somes Sound. At 0.8 mi., a spur path leads to the summit of St. Sauveur Mtn., and Valley Peak Trail continues straight, steeply descending the northeast shoulder of the mountain to end at a jct. with Acadia Mtn. Trail and Valley Cove Trail near Man o' War Brook and the east end of the Man o' War fire road at 1.5 mi.

Valley Peak Trail (USGS SW Harbor quad) (NPS rating: strenuous)

Distances from the Valley Cove fire road (50 ft.) to
- St. Sauveur Trail jct. (500 ft.): 0.4 mi., 25 min.
- St. Sauveur Mtn. summit (690 ft.) (via spur trail): 0.8 mi., 45 min.
- Acadia Mtn. and Valley Cove trails jct. (100 ft.): 1.5 mi., 1 hr. 10 min.

Flying Mtn. (284 ft.)

A short climb to the open top of Flying Mtn. offers a fine panorama of Somes Sound, Southwest Harbor, Northeast Harbor, and the islands to the south, including the Cranberries, Greening, Sutton, Baker, and Bear.

Flying Mtn. Trail

This scenic trail leaves the east side of the parking area at the Fernald Cove end of Valley Cove fire road, just off Fernald Point Rd. The trail rises quickly and steeply through spruce woods, reaching the summit of Flying Mtn. in 0.3 mi. The trail then descends to the shore of Valley Cove and follows the cove to the left, reaching Valley Cove Trail and Valley Cove fire road at 0.9 mi. For an easy return to Fernald Cove parking area, follow the fire road south for about 0.5 mi.

Flying Mtn. Trail (USGS SW Harbor quad) (NPS rating: moderate)
Distances from Fernald Cove parking area (50 ft.) to
- Flying Mtn. summit (284 ft.): 0.3 mi., 15 min.
- Valley Cove Trail and fire road (sea level): 0.9 mi., 25 min.
- Fernald Cove parking area (50 ft.) (via Valley Cove fire road): 1.4 mi., 45 min.

Valley Cove Trail

This trail connects Fernald Cove parking area to Acadia Mtn. Trail. Valley Cove Trail starts on the shoreline of Valley Cove at the end of Valley Cove fire road, 0.5 mi. from the parking area on Fernald Point Rd.

From the fire road, Valley Cove Trail goes left, and Flying Mtn. Trail goes right. Valley Cove Trail follows the shoreline under the ledges of Eagle Cliff high above and ends at the jct. of Acadia Mtn. and Valley Peak trails in 1.1 mi.

Valley Cove Trail (USGS SW Harbor quad) (NPS rating: easy)
Distances from Fernald Cove parking area (50 ft.) to
- start of Valley Cove Trail (sea level) (via Valley Cove fire road): 0.5 mi., 15 min.
- Acadia Mtn. and Valley Peak trails jct. (100 ft.): 1.6 mi., 50 min.

Beech Mtn. (841 ft.)

This mountain lies between Echo Lake and Long Pond. Its summit can be reached from either the Beech Mtn. parking area, located at the end of Beech Hill Rd. in the notch between Beech Cliff and Beech Mtn., or from the pumping station area at the south end of Long Pond.

Beech and Canada Cliffs on the east side of the mountain overlooking Echo Lake can be can be reached by short trails from Beech Mtn. parking area, or from Echo Lake parking area (reached by a short access road from ME 102 north of Southwest Harbor).

To reach the pumping station, follow Seal Cove Rd. west from the jct. with ME 198 in Southwest Harbor. At 0.6 mi., turn right onto Long Pond Rd., and follow this until it ends at the pumping station at 1.8 mi.

Beech Cliff Trail

This trail offers quick but extremely steep access to Beech Cliff from the Echo Lake parking area at the south end of Echo Lake. After about 0.1 mi. of moderate hiking through the woods, the trail climbs very steeply for the rest of the way, via a series of stone staircases and iron ladders. The trail levels off atop Beech Cliff at 0.5 mi., where Canada Cliff Trail leads left. Beech Cliff Trail continues right for about 100 yd., where it ends at Beech Cliff Loop Trail. Views of Echo Lake and the mountains to the east are excellent.

Beech Cliff Trail (USGS SW Harbor quad) (NPS rating: ladder)
Distance from Echo Lake parking area (100 ft.) to
  • Canada Cliff and Beech Cliff Loop trails (550 ft.): 0.5 mi., 30 min.

Canada Cliff Trail

This trail starts from south end of the Echo Lake parking area at a set of wooden stairs. The trail runs on the level through the woods parallel to the road for 0.2 mi., then climbs steeply via switchbacks and rock steps to a ravine at 0.4 mi. The trail climbs the left side, then crosses to the right side before reaching a fork at 0.6 mi. The left fork leads 0.4 mi. to Beech Mtn. parking area via Canada Cliffs and Valley trails.

Continuing to the right, Canada Cliff Trail contours across the east face of the mountain with occasional viewpoints. At 0.7 mi., reach open ledges and views to Southwest Harbor. Continue to traverse north along the ridge with minor ups. After a short scramble, gain the top of the ridge and break into the open with views to Beech Mtn. fire tower to the west. Come to a big ledge overlooking Echo Lake at 1.0 mi. and a jct. with Beech Cliff Trail. Here the views of Somes Sound and Sargent, Acadia, and St. Sauveur mountains are spectacular. Continue ahead on Beech Loop Trail or turn left (west) to reach Beech Mtn. parking area in 0.1 mi.

Canada Cliff Trail (USGS SW Harbor quad) (NPS rating: moderate)
Distances from Echo Lake parking area (100 ft.) to
- fork in trail (400 ft.): 0.6 mi.
- Beech Cliff and Beech Cliff Loop trails (via right fork) (550 ft.): 1.0 mi., 45 min.
- Beech Cliff parking area via Valley Trail (via left fork) (500 ft.): 1.1 mi., 50 min.

Beech Cliff Loop Trail

The trail climbs moderately and sometimes steeply up the western, wooded slope of Beech Cliff from Beech Mtn. parking area at the end of Beech Hill Rd. To reach this trailhead, follow ME 102 south through Somesville and take Pretty Marsh Rd. (the first right after the fire station). Follow Pretty Marsh Rd. west for about 0.5 mi., where Beech Hill Rd. intersects from the left. Follow Beech Hill Rd. south until it ends at the trailhead, 3.2 mi. from Pretty Marsh Rd.

In 0.2 mi., Beech Cliff Loop Trail reaches a jct. where Beech Cliff Trail leads right toward Echo Lake and Beech Cliff Loop Trail leads straight or left, depending on which direction this 0.4-mi. section of the loop is walked. The loop follows the edge of the cliff for about half of its length. The views are spectacular to the east.

Beech Cliff Loop Trail (USGS SW Harbor quad) (NPS rating: moderate)
Distances from Beech Cliff parking area (500 ft.) to
- loop jct. and Beech Cliff Trail (550 ft.): 0.2 mi., 10 min.
- return to parking area via loop: 0.8 mi., 30 min.

Beech Mtn. Loop Trail

Leaving the northwest side of Beech Mtn. parking area, the trail forks in 100 yd. The trail to the right (northwest) is 0.7 mi. long and provides a beautiful vista of Long Pond before climbing to the summit. The trail to the left (south) is 0.4 mi. long and climbs more steeply to the summit of Beech Mtn. and its fire tower. The two trails can be combined to form a short, scenic loop hike. From the summit, Beech West Ridge and Beech South Ridge trails depart to the southwest and south, respectively, providing access to the parking area at the south end of Long Pond.

Beech Mtn. Loop Trail (USGS SW Harbor quad) (NPS rating: moderate)
Distances from Beech Cliff parking area (500 ft.) to
- Beech Mtn. summit (841 ft.) (via north fork): 0.4 mi., 20 min.
- Beech Cliff parking area (via north fork, then south fork): 1.1 mi., 45 min.

Valley Trail

This graded path is a convenient link between the Long Pond area and Beech Cliff parking area, located in the notch between Beech Cliff and Beech Mtn. This also permits a circuit or one-way trip over Beech Mtn. because the trail provides direct access to Beech South Ridge Trail.

Valley Trail starts at the parking area next to the pumping station at the south end of Long Pond and heads south to cross a service road in 0.3 mi. By easy grades over wooded slopes, the trail runs east before climbing via a series of switchbacks on the south slopes of Beech Mtn. At 0.7 mi., Beech South Ridge Trail leaves left. Continuing east, Valley Trail soon swings north to maintain altitude as it runs up the valley separating Beech Mtn. and Canada Cliff. At 1.3 mi., Canada Cliff Trail comes in from the right. Continue directly ahead to reach Beech Cliff parking area at 1.5 mi.

Valley Trail (USGS SW Harbor quad) (NPS rating: moderate)
Distances from parking area at Long Pond (50 ft.) to
- Beech South Ridge Trail jct. (400 ft.): 0.7 mi., 30 min.
- Canada Cliff Trail jct. (450 ft.): 1.3 mi., 50 min.
- Beech Cliff parking area (500 ft.): 1.5 mi., 55 min.

Beech South Ridge Trail

This well-marked trail diverges left from Valley Trail about 0.7 mi. east of the pumping station parking area at the south end of Long Pond. Beech South Ridge Trail steadily ascends the south ridge to the summit along open ledges, offering views to the south.

Beech South Ridge Trail (USGS SW Harbor quad) (NPS rating: moderate)
Distances from Long Pond parking area (50 ft.) to
- start of trail (400 ft.) (via Valley Trail): 0.7 mi., 30 min.
- Beech Mtn. summit (841 ft.): 1.5 mi., 1 hr. 10 min.

Beech West Ridge Trail

Leaving from the east side of the Long Pond pumping station, this trail skirts the edge of Long Pond for 0.3 mi. Here, the trail begins to climb, rising steeply at times. Ledges offer good views of the pond and Mansell Mtn. The trail reaches Beech Mtn. Loop Trail at 0.9 mi., which leads 0.1 to the Beech Mtn. summit.

Beech West Ridge Trail (USGS SW Harbor quad) (NPS rating: moderate)

Distances from Long Pond parking area (50 ft.) to
- Beech Mtn. Loop Trail jct. (750 ft.): 0.9 mi., 50 min.
- Beech Mtn. summit (841 ft.) (via Beech Mtn. Loop Trail): 1.0 mi., 55 min.

Bernard Mtn. (1,010 ft.) and Mansell Mtn. (938 ft.)

Western Mtn. comprises two main summits: Bernard Mtn. to the west and Mansell Mtn. to the east. Both summits are wooded, and extensive views are rare. Trails in this area have three primary trailheads, at the pumping station at the south end of Long Pond, at Gilley Field, and at Mill Field.

- To reach the pumping station, follow Seal Cove Rd. west from ME 102 in Southwest Harbor. At 0.6 mi., take the first right (toward the landfill) onto Long Pond Rd. and follow this until it ends at the pumping station at 1.8 mi.
- To reach Gilley Field, follow Seal Cove Rd. west from ME 102 in Southwest Harbor. The pavement ends at the ANP boundary at 3.9 mi. Take a right off the dirt road at 4.6 mi. (no sign), bear right at the first fork at 5.0 mi., and right again at the second fork at 6.2 mi. The road ends at Gilley Field at 6.3 mi.
- To reach Mill Field, follow Seal Cove Rd. west from ME 102 in Southwest Harbor. The pavement ends at the ANP boundary at 3.9 mi. Take a right off the dirt road at 4.6 mi. (no sign), bear right at the first fork at 5.0 mi., and left at the second fork at 6.2 mi. The road ends at Mill Field at 6.4 mi.

Long Pond Trail

This excellent footpath starts from the pumping station parking area at the south end of Long Pond. The trail follows the west shore of the pond for 1.5 mi., then bears west away from it. Turning south, the trail passes through a beautiful birch forest and follows Great Brook for a short distance. The trail then continues to a jct. with Great Notch Trail.

Long Pond Trail (AMC Western Mtn. map) (NPS rating: easy)
Distances from pumping station parking area (50 ft.) to
- Perpendicular Trail jct. (100 ft.): 0.2 mi., 5 min.
- Great Notch Trail jct. (500 ft.): 2.9 mi., 1 hr. 40 min.

Perpendicular Trail

This trail ascends Mansell Mtn., leaving left from Long Pond Trail on the west shore of Long Pond, 0.2 mi. north of the pumping station parking area. Perpendicular Trail follows a steep course up the east slope of Mansell, crossing a rock slide. Stone steps, a few iron rungs, and one iron ladder appear along the trail. The upper portion has an excellent view southeast. At an open ledge near the top, watch for a trail sign where an abrupt left turn left leads sharply down into woods and marsh before the trail goes up to the actual summit. The summit is wooded. A loop hike is possible by taking Mansell Mtn. Trail south from the summit to Cold Brook Trail (at Gilley Field), which can then be followed back to the parking area.

Perpendicular Trail (AMC Western Mtn. map) (NPS rating: strenuous)
Distances from pumping station parking area (50 ft.) to
- start (via Long Pond Trail): 0.2 mi., 5 min.
- Mansell Mtn. summit (938 ft.): 1.2 mi., 1 hr. 10 min.

Cold Brook Trail

An important link between the pumping station parking area at the south end of Long Pond and the trails leaving from Gilley Field, this trail is a natural beginning or finish to a loop hike over both Mansell and Bernard mountains. This trail is a pretty woodlands walk.

Cold Brook Trail (AMC Western Mtn. map) (NPS rating: easy)
Distance from pumping station parking area (150 ft.) to
- Gilley Field (150 ft.): 0.4 mi., 15 min.

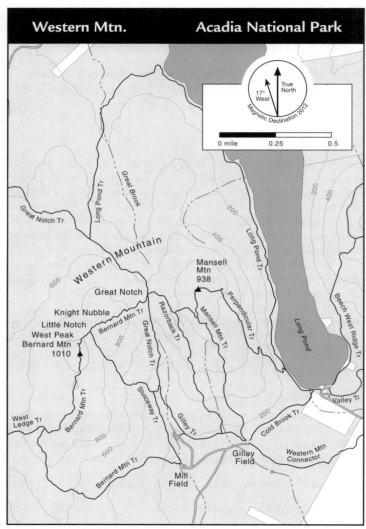

Western Mtn.   Acadia National Park

True
North
17°
West
Magnetic Declination 2012

0 mile   0.25   0.5

Long Pond Tr
Great Brook
Great Notch Tr
Western Mountain
600
Great Notch
Knight Nubble
Little Notch
West Peak
Bernard Mtn
1010
Bernard Mtn Tr
800
Great Notch Tr
Razorback Tr
Mansell Mtn Tr
Mansell
Mtn
938
Perpendicular Tr
200
400
Long Pond Tr
200
400
Long Pond
Beech West Ridge Tr
Sluiceway Tr
Gilley Tr
Cold Brook Tr
200
Valley Tr
West
Ledge Tr
Bernard Mtn Tr
800
600
Bernard Mtn Tr
Mill
Field
Gilley
Field
Western Mtn
Connector

© Appalachian Mountain Club

Gilley Trail

This trail starts at Gilley Field parking area at the eastern end of the Western Mtn. Rd. The trail provides access to Mansell and Bernard mountains via Razorback, Great Notch, and Sluiceway trails. The trail starts next to Mansell Mtn. Trail, but instead of climbing the peak, Gilley Trail follows easy grades to the west, passing Razorback Trail in 0.1 mi., then turning north and climbing moderately to its end at the jct. of Great Notch and Sluiceway trails at 0.6 mi.

Gilley Trail (AMC Western Mtn. map) (NPS rating: easy)
Distances from Gilley Field parking area (150 ft.) to
  • Razorback Trail jct. (150 ft.): 0.1 mi., 5 min.
  • Great Notch and Sluiceway trails jct. (350 ft.): 0.6 mi., 20 min.

Mansell Mtn. Trail

This trail leaves from Gilley Field and offers a nice hike up Mansell Mtn. The trail climbs gradually from the trailhead to ledges, where there are views of Southwest Harbor, Beech Mtn., Long Pond, and Northeast Harbor. At 0.8 mi., Razorback Trail enters from the left. It is then a short walk the summit of Mansell Mtn. on Mansell Mtn. Trail.

Mansell Mtn. Trail (AMC Western Mtn. map) (NPS rating: moderate)
Distances from Gilley Field (150 ft.) to
  • Razorback Trail jct. (850 ft.): 0.8 mi., 45 min.
  • Mansell Mtn. summit (938 ft.): 1.0 mi., 55 min.

Razorback Trail

Razorback Trail diverges right from Gilley Trail at a point 0.2 mi. from Gilley Field parking area at the east end of Western Mtn. Rd. This hike climbs moderately up the west side of Mansell Mtn., offering views of Great Notch and Bernard Mtn. Razorback Trail climbs over ledges and through softwood forest to reach a fork between the summit of Mansell and Great Notch at 0.7 mi. The left fork leads to Great Notch in 0.2 mi. The right fork leads 0.2 mi. to Mansell Mtn. Trail, 0.2 mi. below the summit of Mansell.

Razorback Trail (AMC Western Mtn. map) (NPS rating: strenuous)

Distances from Gilley Field (150 ft.) to
- start of Razorback Trail (150 ft.) (via Gilley Trail): 0.2 mi., 5 min.
- Mansell Mtn. (938 ft.) (via right fork and Mansell Mtn. Trail): 1.3 mi., 1 hr. 10 min.
- Great Notch (650 ft.) (via right fork): 1.1 mi., 55 min.

Sluiceway Trail

Starting from Mill Field, this trail runs north 0.4 mi. to a jct. with a connector trail that leads a short distance east to Great Notch and Gilley trails. At this jct., Sluiceway Trail swings northwest and climbs rather steeply to a jct. with Bernard Mtn. Trail at 0.9 mi. To reach the summit of Bernard Mtn., follow Bernard Mtn. Trail left (south) for 0.2 mi.

Sluiceway Trail (AMC Western Mtn. map) (NPS rating: strenuous)

Distances from Mill Field parking area (150 ft.) to
- Great Notch Trail jct. (350 ft.): 0.4 mi., 25 min.
- Bernard Mtn. Trail jct. (850 ft.): 0.9 mi., 50 min.
- Bernard Mtn. summit (1,010 ft.) (via Bernard Mtn. Trail): 1.1 mi., 1 hr.

Bernard Mtn. Trail

This trail also starts at Mill Field on Western Mtn. Rd. The trail leads west for 1.0 mi., where West Ledge Trail enters from the left. Here, Bernard Mtn. Trail turns right, rising north to the summit of Bernard Mtn. at 1.5 mi. The trail reaches a jct. with Sluiceway Trail in Little Notch at 1.7 mi. Beyond the jct., Bernard Mtn. Trail continues straight, passing over Knight Nubble before descending to Great Notch at 2.2 mi.

Bernard Mtn. Trail (AMC Western Mtn. map) (NPS rating: strenuous)

Distances from Mill Field parking area (150 ft.) to
- West Ledge Trail jct. (900 ft.): 1.0 mi., 55 min.
- Bernard Mtn. summit (1,010 ft.): 1.5 mi., 1 hr. 10 min.
- Great Notch (650 ft.): 2.2 mi., 1 hr. 30 min.

West Ledge Trail

This trail connects the west end of Western Mtn. Rd. to the system of trails on Bernard and Mansell mountains. The views to the west of Blue Hill Bay, the Atlantic Ocean, and the islands south and west of Mt. Desert Island are spectacular. The trail starts from Western Mtn. Rd. about 0.3 mi. east of Seal Cove Pond. The trail begins by climbing, reaching open ledges very quickly. It briefly reenters the woods twice before beginning a very steep climb over open granite ledges. From here, the views stretch from Bass Harbor to the Camden Hills. After entering the woods, at 1.1 mi., the trail ends at its jct. with Bernard Mtn. Trail.

West Ledge Trail (USGS Bartlett Island and SW Harbor quads) (NPS rating: strenuous)
Distance from Western Mtn. Rd. (150 ft.) to
  • Bernard Mtn. Trail (800 ft.): 1.1 mi., 50 min.

Great Notch Trail

This is the only trail providing access to Western Mtn. from the north. No open vistas can be had. The trailhead is located on Long Pond Fire Rd., about 0.1 mi. beyond the Pine Hill turnaround and parking area, at a point 1.0 mi. east of its jct. with ME 102 (this jct. is about 1.1 mi. south of the jct. with the road to Pretty Marsh picnic area).

The trail trends southeast and rises by easy grades to a jct. with Long Pond Trail (entering left) at 1.1 mi. Great Notch Trail reaches Great Notch at 1.5 mi., where Bernard Mtn. Trail leads right toward Bernard Mtn. and Razorback Trail leads left toward Mansell Mtn. Great Notch Trail continues through the notch and down to Gilley Trail at 1.9 mi., where Great Notch Trail ends. Follow Gilley Trail for another 0.6 mi. to Gilley Field parking area.

Great Notch Trail (AMC Western Mtn. map) (NPS rating: moderate)
Distances from Long Pond Fire Rd. (150 ft.) to
  • Long Pond Trail jct. (500 ft.): 1.1 mi., 45 min.
  • Great Notch (650 ft.): 1.5 mi., 1 hr.
  • Gilley Trail (350 ft.): 1.9 mi., 1 hr. 15 min.
  • Gilley Field parking area (150 ft.) (via Gilley Trail): 2.5 mi., 1 hr. 30 min.

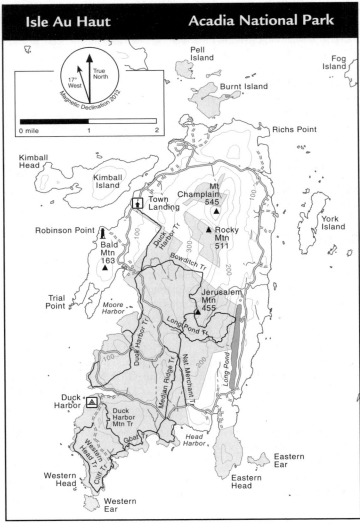

Isle Au Haut

Acadia National Park

True North

17° West

Magnetic Declination 2012

0 mile   1   2

Pell Island

Fog Island

Burnt Island

Richs Point

Kimball Head

Kimball Island

Mt Champlain 545

York Island

Town Landing

Robinson Point

Rocky Mtn 511

Bald Mtn 163

Duck Harbor Tr

Bowditch Tr

Trial Point

Moore Harbor

Jerusalem Mtn 455

100

100

200

200

Long Pond Tr

Long Pond

Duck Harbor Tr

Median Ridge Tr

Nat Merchant Tr

Duck Harbor

Duck Harbor Mtn Tr

Goat Tr

Head Harbor

Eastern Ear

Western Head Tr

Cliff Tr

Western Head

Eastern Head

Western Ear

© Appalachian Mountain Club

Isle au Haut

A range of low mountains extends the length of this 6-mi. island. Mt. Champlain, near the north end, is its highest summit. Farther south along the ridge are Rocky Mtn., Sawyer Mtn., and Jerusalem Mtn. Continuing, there are Bowditch Mtn. and Wentworth Mtn., and near the southwest tip, Duck Harbor Mtn. About half of the island is within ANP. NPS maintains a primitive campground at Duck Harbor, on the southwest side of the island and about 4 mi. from Isle au Haut village. Eighteen mi. of trails lead along spectacular rocky shorelines and through scenic forests, marshes, and bogs. The 12-mi. road around the island is partially paved. Some sections of the road, however, are very rough and not recommended for bike riding. The road passes the foot of Long Pond, which offers swimming. A small store is located near the town landing. No private campgrounds are available on the island.

Isle au Haut is reached by a passenger ferry from Stonington on the mainland. The trip takes about 45 min. one way. The ferry, operated on a first-come, first-served basis, runs year-round to the town landing, and from mid-June to mid-September, the ferry also continues on to Duck Harbor. Contact Isle au Haut Boat Services at 207-367-5193 or visit isleauhaut. com for schedule and rate information.

During the summer season, a park ranger may board the ferry at the town landing to answer visitor questions en route to Duck Harbor. The number of visitors to the island is limited by the park, and on rare occasions, visitors may be denied access.

Five lean-tos offer primitive camping at Duck Harbor Campground. These sites are available by advanced reservation only. Each lean-to is equipped with a fire ring, picnic table, and storage locker for food and toiletries. A hand pump for water is located nearby, as are several composting toilets. No trash containers are available, so campers must carry out all trash.

Hikers may obtain a camping reservation request form at nps.gov/acad or by calling 207-288-3338. Requests must be postmarked on or after April 1 (no phone reservations) and must include a $25 special-use permit fee, in addition to the per-night camping fees. Mail requests to

Acadia National Park
Attn: Isle au Haut Reservations
P.O. Box 177
Bar Harbor, ME 04609

The trails on Isle au Haut are mostly at or near sea level with only minor ups and downs, and as such, trail elevations are not indicated in the summary boxes following each trail description.

Duck Harbor Trail

As a major connector, this trail offers hiking access to Duck Harbor, Moore Harbor, Eli Creek, Bowditch, and Nat Merchant trails, and the park campground. Duck Harbor Trail begins at the park ranger station on the northwest side of the island.

Following the marshy lowlands, this trail passes through mature stands of softwoods. At 0.9 mi., a small pond appears on the left. At 1.5 mi., Bowditch Trail leaves to the left. Just ahead, Duck Harbor Trail crosses a road. At 1.9 mi., the trail crosses a sandy beach, and at 2.2 mi., an NPS cabin comes into view. A short side trail to views of Deep Cove leads to the right at 2.7 mi. After crossing the road, Duck Harbor Trail offers outstanding views of the ocean and harbor as the trail descends to the road yet again, where the trail finally ends on the north side of Duck Harbor. Follow the road left and then shortly bear right on Western Head Rd. to reach the ferry and campground.

> **Duck Harbor Trail (AMC Isle au Haut map) (NPS rating: moderate)**
> Distances from park ranger station to
> - Bowditch Trail jct.: 1.5 mi., 45 min.
> - road crossing: 1.5 mi., 45 min.
> - NPS cabin: 2.2 mi., 1 hr. 10 min.
> - side trail to Deep Cove: 2.7 mi., 1 hr. 20 min.
> - second jct. with road: 3.0 mi., 1 hr. 30 min.
> - views of harbor and ocean: 3.7 mi., 1 hr. 50 min.
> - Duck Harbor and road: 3.9 mi., 2 hrs.

Bowditch Trail

This trail connects Duck Harbor and Long Pond trails and offers spectacular views from Bowditch Mtn. Starting from Duck Harbor Trail, Bowditch Trail follows marshlands for its first 0.8 mi., then crosses a stream and turns onto an old firebreak. After following the firebreak, the trail begins to climb gradually, offering good views to the west. The trail continues to climb through a softwood forest over ledges to reach the summit of Bowditch Mtn. At this point, the trail ends at its jct. with Median Ridge Trail at 2.0 mi.

Bowditch Trail (AMC Isle au Haut map) (NPS rating: moderate)
Distance from jct. with Duck Harbor Trail to
- Bowditch Mtn. summit and jct. with Median Ridge Trail: 2.0 mi., 1 hr. 30 min.

Long Pond Trail

Although this trail is relatively level at its start, the change of elevation is more pronounced on the loop. Despite the strenuous climb, this trail offers wonderful views of the largest pond on Isle au Haut, as well as access to the summit of Bowditch Mtn. and to Bowditch and Median Ridge trails. The trail makes a nice loop hike.

The Long Pond trailhead is located on the main road on the western side of the island. Starting at the road, the trail follows a low, wet area for 0.4 mi. to meet Median Ridge Trail, which enters from the right, and the other end of the Long Pond Trail loop coming in from the left. Continue straight ahead and follow along an old streambed for quite a while. At 1.1 mi., Long Pond Trail passes over an old building foundation, follows along a stone wall, and gradually climbs onto a ridge. At 1.7 mi., Long Pond comes into view. The trail follows the pond north for a short time, then bears west and climbs gradually through softwoods to the summit of Bowditch Mtn. At the summit, Bowditch Trail enters from the right. Long Pond Trail continues straight ahead and returns to the loop jct. and Median Ridge Trail.

Long Pond Trail (AMC Isle au Haut map) (NPS rating: strenuous)
Distances from main road to
- Median Ridge and Long Pond Trail loop jct.: 0.4 mi., 15 min.
- old building foundation: 1.1 mi., 35 min.
- Long Pond: 1.7 mi., 55 min.
- Bowditch Mtn. summit and jct. with Bowditch Trail: 2.4 mi., 1 hr. 30 min.
- complete Long Pond Trail loop: 3.2 mi., 2 hr.

Median Ridge Trail

The trailhead is located on the main road in the southern part of the island. To the south, a spur trail follows marshlands to connect with Goat Trail in 0.3 mi. To the north, Median Ridge Trail quickly ascends to a ridge. Ahead, the trail follows the ridge into a Japanese garden, with views to the east. At 0.7 mi., excellent views can be had from a ledge area surrounded by small conifers. The trail then descends into a bog, and at 1.0 mi., intersects with Nat Merchant Trail. Median Ridge Trail continues ahead through marsh, softwoods, and a cedar bog to its end at a jct. with Long Pond Trail.

Median Ridge Trail (AMC Isle au Haut map) (NPS rating: moderate)

Distances from main road to
- Goat Trail (via spur trail to south): 0.3 mi., 25 min.
- Nat Merchant Trail jct.: 1 mi., 45 min.
- to jct. of north spur with the Long Pond Trail: 1.6 mi, 1 hr. 30 min.

Nat Merchant Trail

The trailhead is located on the main road on the western side of the island. This trail begins by entering marshlands with an overstory of cedar and pine. The trail crosses several intermittent streams until it intersects Median Ridge Trail at 0.8 mi. Beyond, Nat Merchant Trail climbs gradually and passes over a boulder field to crest at the top of a field with fine views. Ahead, the trail passes through a softwood forest and then ends at the main road on the southeast side of the island.

Nat Merchant Trail (AMC Isle au Haut map) (NPS rating: moderate)

Distances from main road to
- Median Ridge Trail jct.: 0.8 mi., 25 min.
- jct. with main road: 1.2 mi., 45 min.

Goat Trail

This trail runs from the southern portion of the main road and ends at the end of the Western Head Rd. (closed to vehicles). The trail parallels the shoreline and offers spectacular views of Eastern Head, Head Harbor, Merchant Cove, Barred Harbor, Squeaker Cove, and Deep Cove.

The trail begins in a marshy lowland and gradually rises to a ridge. Passing through a softwood forest, the trail emerges onto a rocky beach at 0.6 mi. Shortly thereafter, the trail climbs again and passes the southern end of

Median Ridge Trail at 0.9 mi. Once again, Goat Trail passes alternately over both beaches and highlands, offering a variety of perspectives on the southern coast of Isle au Haut. Goat Trail passes Duck Harbor Mtn. Trail on the right at 1.8 mi., then reaches Western Head Rd. at 2.2 mi.

Goat Trail (AMC Isle au Haut map) (NPS rating: moderate)

Distances from main road to
- Median Ridge Trail jct.: 0.9 mi., 30 min.
- Duck Harbor Mtn. Trail jct.: 1.8 mi., 1 hr.
- Western Head Rd.: 2.2 mi., 1 hr. 15 min.

Duck Harbor Mtn. Trail

This trail begins on Western Head Rd. and is one of the most challenging on Isle au Haut. The trail climbs over Duck Harbor Mtn., with great views of the harbor as well as the southern end of the island. The trail begins steeply, ascends ledges, and at 0.2 mi., levels out for a short stretch. At 0.3 mi., after a short descent, the trail again ascends steeply, passing through a mixture of softwood forest and open ledges to the summit of Duck Harbor Mtn. Beyond, the trail continues along the ridge. The trail goes over the Puddings before descending through softwood forest and ledges down to a jct. with Goat Trail.

Duck Harbor Mtn. Trail (AMC Isle au Haut map) (NPS rating: strenuous)

Distances from Western Head Rd. to
- Duck Harbor Mtn. summit: 0.4 mi., 35 min.
- Goat Trail jct.: 1.2 mi., 1 hr. 30 min.

Cliff Trail

This trail leaves from the end of Western Head Rd. and heads south, climbing steeply (50 ft.) to reach a ridge, and then passing through a softwood forest. At 0.6 mi., the trail crosses a cobble beach, offering views of Deep Cove and the coast. Western Head Trail is reached at 0.7 mi.

Cliff Trail (AMC Isle au Haut map) (NPS rating: moderate)

Distance from Western Head Rd. to
- Western Head Trail jct.: 0.7 mi., 40 min.

Western Head Trail

This trail follows the western shore of Western Head and offers spectacular cliff-top views of the ocean. Combined with Cliff Trail, this trail makes a nice loop around Western Head. The trailheads are a short walk apart on Western Head Rd.

Western Head Trail climbs gradually to a ridge, and shortly thereafter, crosses a stream. Beyond, the trail continues to ascend through a softwood forest on a ledge, where there are views to the west. At 0.4 mi., the trail descends onto a cobble beach. It then continues to follow along the coast, ascending and descending between headlands and beach, reaching a jct. with Cliff Trail at 1.6 mi.

Western Head Trail (AMC Isle au Haut map) (NPS rating: moderate)
Distance from Western Head Rd. to
  • Cliff Trail jct.: 1.6 mi., 1 hr. 15 min.

SUGGESTED HIKES

Note: The hikes suggested here are rated according to NPS standards. See "Trail Ratings" at the start of this section. A variety of easy walks and hikes may be had in Acadia. Consult AMC map 4 (or AMC's *Discover Acadia National Park* book or waterproof *Acadia National Park Discovery Map*) or ask a park ranger for suggestions.

Moderate Hikes

Flying Mtn. [lp: 1.2 mi., 45 min.]. A short hike via Flying Mtn. Trail to good views of Valley Cove and The Narrows at the entrance to Somes Sound. Return via Valley Cove Trail and the Valley Cove fire road.

The Bubbles [rt: 1.6 mi., 1.5 hr.]. This hike visits the distinctive summits of North Bubble and South Bubble at the north end of Jordan Pond, as well as Bubble Rock.

Great Head [lp: 1.8 mi., 1.0 hr.]. A walk along Sand Beach is followed by a semi-wooded climb to the top of 145-ft. cliffs at Great Head overlooking the ocean. This hike uses Great Head Trail and an abandoned service road.

Huguenot Head and Champlain Mtn. [lp: 3.3 mi., 2.5 hr.]. Climb up over pink granite to spectacular views via Beachcroft Trail. Return via Champlain North Ridge Trail and Park Loop Rd.

Gorham Mtn. [lp: 3.5 mi., 2.0 hr.]. A fun hike up to panoramic ocean views on Gorham Mtn. Trail. A descent via Bowl Trail is followed by a walk along the rugged coastline on Ocean Path.

Cadillac Mtn. [rt: 7.0 mi., 4.0 hr.]. Enjoy a relatively long ridge hike via Cadillac South Ridge Trail over open ledges to the summit of the highest mountain on Mt. Desert Island, with views along most of the route.

Strenuous Hikes

The Beehive and The Bowl [lp: 1.3 mi., 1.0 hr.]. A challenging climb up iron rungs to spectacular ocean vistas followed by a visit to a beautiful mountain pond via Bowl and Beehive trails.

Acadia and St. Sauveur mountains [lp: 3.7 mi., 3.0 hr.]. Get a bird's-eye view of Somes Sound from two open summits via this hike on the Acadia Mtn., Valley Cove, and St. Sauveur Mtn. trails.

Pemetic Mtn. and Bubble Pond [lp: 4.1 mi., 2.5 hr.]. This hike via Pemetic North and South Ridge trails, Bubble & Jordan Ponds Path, and a carriage road takes some effort at first but leads to some of the most spectacular views on Mt. Desert Island.

Mansell and Bernard mountains [lp: 4.2 mi., 3.5 hr.]. The views may be limited, but the hiking over the highest peaks on the western side of Mt. Desert Island is still very rewarding.

Eastern Side Traverse [ow: 11.0 mi., 6.5 hr.]. This long traverse of the eastern side of Mt. Desert Island takes in some of the best-known features and quietest trails in Acadia. Uses Bowl, Beehive, Champlain South Ridge, and Beachcroft trails, Kane Path, Canon Brook Trail, Bubble & Jordan Ponds, and Asticou & Jordan Pond paths.

SECTION TEN
AROOSTOOK COUNTY

Number Nine Mtn. 366

Mars Hill 366

Quaggy Jo Mtn. 367

Haystack Mtn. 368

Hedgehog Mtn. 369

Deboullie Public Reserved
   Land 370

Deboullie Mtn. 371

Black Mtn. 371

Round Pond Mtn. 373

Priestly Mtn. 374

Allagash Mtn. 375

Round Mtn. 376

Horseshoe Mtn. 377

Oak Hill 378

Suggested Hikes 379

The Aroostook County section includes the entirety of this sprawling, 6,830-acre county (Maine's largest), an area larger than Connecticut and Rhode Island combined. Often called the "Crown of Maine" because of its geographic expanse across the northern part of the state, the county stretches 120 mi. from north to south and 104 mi. from east to west. The county is bounded to the west, north, and east by Canada. The St. Francis and St. John rivers form part of its northern boundary. To the south are the counties of Somerset, Piscataquis, Penobscot, and Washington.

Aroostook is known for its wealth of forestlands, lakes, ponds, rivers, hills, and mountains. It is nearly 90 percent forested, and much of this is commercial timberlands. Extensive farmlands are located along the US 1 corridor in the east near the U.S.–Canada border and upward into the St. John River valley. The Fish, Allagash, and St. John rivers flow northward through Aroostook, and the northern portion of the famous 92-mile-long Allagash Wilderness Waterway is found here. Long, Square, Cross, Eagle;

and Scopan lakes are in the northeast. Just to the south, the Aroostook River flows east into Canada.

This section describes 13 mountains and 16 trails. The mountains of Aroostook County are widely scattered and very often remote, some requiring considerable driving over gravel woods roads to reach. They generally range in elevation from 1,500 to 2,000 ft., but several are around 1,000 ft. There are no ranges or compact mountain areas except for the clusters of peaks in the 22,000-acre Deboullie PRL, where Deboullie and Black mountains are prominent, and the hills west of Bridgewater and around Number Nine Lake. Solitary Mars Hill, which rises from almost level country just west of the Canadian border in the town of the same name, is probably the best-known mountain, and the twin-peaked Quaggy Jo Mtn. in Aroostook State Park may be the most-climbed. Peaked Mtn., a trailless summit in the wild country west of Ashland, is the county's highest at 2,260 ft.

Many of the Aroostook mountains lie within the boundaries of North Maine Woods, a large block of forestland, most of which is privately owned and cooperatively managed for renewable forest resources while providing outdoor recreational opportunities for the public. Visitors must register at a checkpoint and pay camping and day-use fees to enter the area. See p. xvii for information on access to the lands managed by North Maine Woods.

The International Appalachian Trail (IAT) threads its way across Aroostook County en route from BSP through New Brunswick, Quebec, Nova Scotia, and Prince Edward Island to its northern terminus at Crow Head in Newfoundland, a total distance of 1,900 miles. The IAT enters Aroostook north of Patten and leaves the United States northeast of Mars Hill. The section of trail leading to the summit of Mars Hill is described.

Camping

Aroostook State Park features 30 drive-in campsites, hot showers, restrooms, trailhead parking, and other amenities, including swimming and picnicking at Echo Lake. The park also administers two backcountry campsites on Quaggy Jo Mtn. Backcountry camping is also found at Deboullie PRL, where numerous roadside primitive campsites are also available. Primitive water-access campsites are at Scopan PRL. A number of privately operated campgrounds may also be found throughout Aroostook.

Number Nine Mtn. (1,638 ft.)

This peak is west of Bridgewater in a small group of mountains clustered around Number Nine Lake. Entering Bridgewater from the south, turn left (west) off US 1 onto Bootfoot Rd. (paved) and continue for 3.1 mi. to a T intersection. Turn right onto the unmarked gravel road (Number Nine Lake Rd.). Pass Whitney Brook Rd. on the right at 4.5 mi. At 11.4 mi., bear left at the fork and go uphill to reach the Number Nine Lake parking lot and boat launch site at 12.1 mi. (*Note:* Number Nine Lake Rd. follows a power line for about the first 10 mi. Where the power line leaves the road on the left at 11.4 mi., proceed directly to Number Nine Lake.) No camping is allowed in the area of the boat launch (posted).

From the boat launch and parking area, the trail follows the camp road across a bridge over the outlet stream and south along the east side of the lake. At 0.4 mi., pass a gravel road on the left. At 0.5 mi., the route departs on a left fork through a yellow gate and starts climbing on what appears to be a gravel road at the start, but is paved. At 1.1 mi, pass through a second yellow gate. The pavement extends to a communications tower and small building owned by the Fraser Company. The actual summit is beyond the tower and has some open ledges. Even though no access is available to the tower, there are views.

Number Nine Mtn. (USGS Number Nine Lake quad, DeLorme map 59)
Distance from parking area and boat launch (1,100 ft.) to
• Number Nine Mtn. summit (1,638 ft.): 1.5 mi., 1 hr.

Mars Hill (1,748 ft.)

This monadnock rises abruptly from an almost-level area of farms and woodland in the eastern section of the town of the same name. The mountain extends in a north–south direction for about 3 mi. and parallels the Canadian border just to the east. The mountain is the site of the first large-scale wind-power project in New England, with 28 turbines lining the long ridge top.

To reach the trailhead from the jct. of US 1A and US 1 in Mars Hill, take US 1A north for 0.3 mi. Turn right (east) onto Boynton Rd., and go 1.3 mi. to a T intersection. Turn right onto Country Club Rd., and take the first left (Graves Rd.) to Big Rock Ski Area. Park in the large lot in front of the ski area base lodge.

The trail to Mars Hill, part of the IAT, is marked with light-blue blazes and International Appalachian Trail/Sentiers International des Appalaches (IAT/SIA) markers as far as the summit. The trail to Mars Hill starts the right of the Bigrock Ski Area base lodge at the South Star Triple Chairlift. Begin climbing up the ski trail (Outer Orbit) to the right (south) of the lift, past the ski area maintenance building. Follow this trail to the top terminal of the chairlift, then proceed to another ski trail (Ho Chi Minh) that merges in 150 ft. to the left (north) of the ski lift terminal. Follow this trail to a large clearing, just below a noticeably steeper section of the ski trail. At this point, look to the left (northeast) for a trail marker and an opening in the woods for the first in a series of four switchbacks. Hikers will use the ski trail for short segments while progressing to each subsequent switchback. After the final switchback, proceed on the ski trail to a footpath on the right (east) side of the ski trail. This trail intersects with a gravel road on the ridgeline at about 0.8 mi.

Turn right (south) and walk beneath several towers to reach a lean-to (sleeps 6, privy, no water) and a large grassy area. The south summit is just ahead at about 1.2 mi. Views extend across the forest and farmland in all directions, ranging as far as Katahdin to the southwest and across the St. John River Valley into New Brunswick to the east.

An alternative route for ascent or descent uses the access road.

Mars Hill (USGS Mars Hill quad, DeLorme map 59)

Distance from Big Rock ski area parking lot (650 ft.) to
- Mars Hill south summit (1,748 ft.): 1.2 mi., 1hr. 10 min.

Quaggy Jo Mtn. (1,213 ft.)

Quaggy Jo is located in Aroostook State Park, an 800-acre park just south of Presque Isle that offers hiking and camping, as well as swimming, boating, and picnicking at Echo Lake. The park holds the honor of being Maine's first state park, established in 1939.

From Presque Isle, drive south on US 1 for 4.0 mi. and turn right (west) onto Spragueville Rd. (sign for state park). At 1.0 mi. from US 1, turn left onto State Park Rd. and proceed to the park entrance. The day-use parking area is a short distance beyond. The park is open all year, and an entry fee is charged.

Quaggy Jo Trails (MBPL)

Park officials recommend hiking the 3.0-mi. loop over Quaggy Jo Mtn. in a clockwise direction, starting with South Peak. South Peak Trail starts from the campground, between sites 18 and 19, and climbs steeply to the ridge in 0.75 mi., where rock outcroppings provide good views to the east. South Peak itself is wooded and access is not available to the tower, but 100 ft. northwest of the top is an outlook with views to the west and north. From South Peak, North–South Ridge Trail leads 1.0 mi. to North Peak. Midway along the ridge between South and North peaks is a viewpoint to the east overlooking Echo Lake. North Peak has open ledges, which afford views to the west and north. Beyond, North Peak Trail descends to the day-use parking lot in 1.25 mi.

Two backcountry campsites are located on the top of the ridgeline. A large tent pad is situated on South Peak, on an exposed ledge looking out to the west. A large Adirondack shelter is located at the overlook between North and South peaks. These primitive sites have no water or toilets, and campfires are not allowed. Sites are available on a first-come, first-served basis, and a fee is charged.

Quaggy Jo Mtn. (USGS Echo Lake quad, DeLorme map 65)

Distances from campground (550 ft.) to
- Quaggy Jo, South Peak (1,213 ft.): 0.75 mi., 45 min.
- Quaggy Jo, North Peak (1,150 ft.): 1.75 mi., 1 hr. 15 min.
- complete loop: 3.0 mi., 1 hr. 45 min.

Haystack Mtn. (1,142 ft.)

Haystack Mtn. is located on the north side of ME 163 in Castle Hill, east of Ashland and west of Presque Isle. The 215-acre property encompassing the mountain is owned and managed by MBPL. In 2011, the summit trail was named in honor of Marine Cpl. Dustin J. Libby of Castle Hill, who was killed in action in Iraq in 2006. The trail is maintained by the town of Castle Hill.

The trailhead, a well-marked parking lot and picnic area at a height-of-land on the north side of ME 163, is 10.0 mi. east of Ashland, or 4.0 mi. west of Mapleton. No water and no toilets are available. No camping or overnight parking is allowed.

Cpl. Dustin J. Libby Summit Trail (MPBL)

The yellow-blazed trail starts to the left of the information kiosk at the north end of the parking lot and rises very steeply. At the base of the open ledges, the trail forks. To the left, an easier, but still rugged, trail loops around to the summit. To the right, the trail continues straight up, climbing across the exposed ledge face. (*Note:* MBPL recommends tackling this ledge face on the ascent only.) The grassy, rocky summit offers a panoramic view that includes Katahdin to the southwest, the Mapleton farmlands to the east and south, Quaggy Jo Mtn. and Mars Hill to the south-southeast, and Round Mtn. in the heart of the North Maine Woods to the west and north.

Cpl. Dustin J. Libby Summit Trail (USGS Mapleton quad, DeLorme map 64)
Distance from ME 163 parking area (950 ft.) to
• Haystack Mtn. summit (1,142 ft.): 0.25 mi., 30 min.

Hedgehog Mtn. (1,594 ft.)

Hedgehog Mountain in TR15 R6 rises just west of St. Froid Lake. The trailhead is on the west side of ME 11, 3.5 mi. south of Winterville and 12.7 mi. north of Portage. Parking is at a well-marked rest area where there is picnicking and a spring, but no camping or overnight parking.

The trail leaves from the southwest corner of the picnic area to the right of the spring and soon passes between the old warden's cabin and a white building. The trail climbs steadily to the summit, where there was once a fire tower. From the open ledge are fine views south to Portage Lake and west to Deboullie Mtn.

Hedgehog Mtn. (USGS Winterville quad, DeLorme map 63)

Distance from the picnic area (1,000 ft.) to
  • Hedgehog Mtn. summit (1,594 ft.): 0.6 mi., 35 min.

Deboullie Public Reserved Land

Deboullie is one of the most remote properties in the Maine PRL system. Its 22,000 acres in T15 R9 WELS include a cluster of low, rugged mountains and more than a dozen scenic ponds. Deboullie and Black mountains are the highest of the group in this wild region south of St. Francis and northwest of Portage. Frontcountry campsites are available at Pushineer, Deboullie, Togue, Crater, Denny, and Perch ponds. Remote backcountry campsites are found at the west end of Deboullie Pond, and the east end of Gardner Pond.

MBPL has designated the road from the north at St. Francis Checkpoint (North Maine Woods access and camping fee) as the primary access route into Deboullie. This road (designated as St. Francis Rd. on DeLorme map 63) turns left off ME 161 about 6.5 mi. southwest of St. Francis. The road heads south for about 8.5 mi. Here, turn left onto an unnamed gravel road and follow this south into Deboullie PRL and then east, passing Togue, Perth, and Upper ponds before reaching another gravel road on the left in about 10 mi. Turn left here, and drive past Pushineer Pond to reach the end of the road at Deboullie Pond at about 1 mi. The total distance from ME 161 to the trailhead is about 20 mi. The trailhead and parking for Deboullie and Black mountains and Deboullie Loop are located here. A number of campsites and outhouses are also in the immediate area.

Alternative access is from the east in Portage: Take West Rd. for 1.0 mi., turn left on Fish Lake Rd., and continue to the Fish River Checkpoint (fee). Beyond, continue on Fish Lake Rd. Turn right onto Hewes Brook Rd. at about 7 mi. At about 10.5 mi., cross a bridge over Fish River. At about 12.5 mi., pass a road on the left leading to Fish River Lake. Continue on Hewes Brook Rd. and cross Red River on a bridge at about 19.5 mi. Just beyond, turn left and follow signs for Red River Camps. At about 26 mi., turn right at a T intersection, and shortly thereafter, enter Deboullie PRL at about 27 mi. Reach Pushineer Pond at about 27.7 mi., and the end of the road at Deboullie Pond at about 28 mi.

Deboullie Mtn. (1,981 ft.)

This peak rises steeply above the west end of Deboullie Pond. The peak is reached via Deboullie Loop and Deboullie Mtn. trails. The 48-ft. fire tower on the summit affords 360-degree views that extend south to Katahdin, southeast to Haystack Mtn., and southwest to Horseshoe Mtn.

Deboullie Mtn. Trail (MBPL)

Leave the northwest corner of the parking lot on an old tote road. In about 200 yd., the road forks (sign). The right fork is Black Mtn. Loop Trail. The left fork is Deboullie Loop Trail, which leaves the tote road and heads to the shore of the pond.

Follow Deboullie Loop Trail along the north shore of the pond, crossing a large rock slide en route, and passing several ice caves (marked). Beyond, the trail enters a clearing with a picnic table at 1.3 mi. This is a designated campsite and can be reached by boat. At this point, turn right (north) on Deboullie Mtn. Trail, which proceeds up a long set of stone steps. Beyond, continue to climb steeply to the summit of Deboullie Mtn. and its fire tower at 1.9 mi.

Deboullie Mtn. (1,981 ft.) (USGS Gardner Pond and Deboullie Pond quads, DeLorme map 63)

Distances from Deboullie Pond trailhead (1,150 ft.) to
- Deboullie Mtn. Trail jct. and campsite (1,200 ft.) (via Deboullie Loop Trail): 1.3 mi., 45 min.
- Deboullie Mtn. summit (1,981 ft.) (via Deboullie Mtn. Trail): 1.9 mi., 1 hr. 30 min.

Black Mtn. (1,980 ft.)

This mountain is just northeast of Deboullie Mtn. The approach to the peak passes by Little Black Ponds and Black Pond and features numerous outlooks with good views. A fine loop hike may be had by continuing over Deboullie Mtn. and returning to the trailhead via the north shore of Deboullie Pond.

Leave the northwest corner of the parking lot on an old tote road. In about 200 yd., the road forks (sign). The left fork is Deboullie Loop Trail, which circles the pond. Deboullie Mtn. Trail leading to the summit of Deboullie is 1.3 mi. down this trail. Black Mtn. Loop Trail continues straight ahead on the old tote road to a height-of-land above Black Pond at 0.6 mi. Here, the tote road forks. The left fork is a short side trail leading to Little Black Ponds. Bear right here and descend to Black Pond. Near the pond, the trail bears northwest to swing around the west end of Black Pond. The trail then rises up the mountainside to Black Mtn. Outlook at 1.3 mi. Not far ahead, near the crest of the ridge, is Four Ponds Outlook. From here, the trail crosses over the ridge to an unnamed outlook, then turns southwest on the north side of Black Mtn. to reach Fifth Pelletier Lake Outlook. The next outlook (unnamed) is just under the wooded summit of Black Mtn., which is reached at 2.1 mi.

Ahead, the trail drops into a saddle before swinging back around and climbing to reach the summit of Deboullie from the west at 3.6 mi. Just below the summit is Gardner Outlook. Most of the trail on the ridge between the peaks of Black and Deboullie mountains travels through beautiful hardwoods. No water is available beyond Black Pond. From the summit of Deboullie, descend Deboullie Mtn. Trail to Deboullie Loop Trail. Turn left (east) on Deboullie Loop Trail to complete the loop hike.

Black Mtn. (1980 ft.) (USGS Gardner Pond and Deboullie Pond quads, DeLorme map 63)

Distances from Deboullie Pond trailhead (1,150 ft.) to
- Black Mtn. summit (1,980 ft.) (via Black Mtn. Loop Trail): est. 2.1 mi., 1 hr. 30 min.
- Deboullie Mtn. summit (1,981 ft.): 3.6 mi., 2 hr. 30 min.
- complete loop: 5.5 mi., 3 hr. 30 min.

Deboullie Loop Trail (MBPL)

Leave the northwest corner of the parking lot on an old tote road. In about 200 yd., the road forks (sign). The right fork is Black Mtn. Loop Trail. The left fork is Deboullie Loop Trail, which leaves the tote road and heads to the shore of the pond. Follow Deboullie Loop Trail along the north shore of the pond, crossing a large rock slide en route, and passing several ice caves (marked). Beyond, the trail enters a clearing with a picnic table at 1.3 mi. This is a designated campsite and can be reached by boat. At this point, Deboullie Mtn. Trail diverges right and leads 0.6 mi. to the Deboullie summit. Deboullie Loop Trail continues ahead along the shore, reaching the west end of the pond at 2.1 mi. Here, the trail intersects a trail linking Deboullie Pond with Gardner Pond to the west. Camping is available at both ends of this short connecting trail. Ahead, the trail forks at 2.3 mi. The right fork is Denny Pond Trail, which leads 1.4 mi. south to Denny Pond and its campsite and trailhead. Deboullie Loop Trail continues to the left (east) to the road at Pushineer Pond at 5.0 mi., where the trail ends. It is a 1.0 mi. walk north on the road to the trailhead parking area.

Deboullie Loop Trail (USGS Gardner Pond and Deboullie Pond quads, DeLorme map 63)

Distances from Deboullie Pond trailhead (1,150 ft.) to

- Deboullie Mtn. Trail jct. and campsite (1,200 ft.): 1.3 mi., 45 min.
- Denny Pond Trail jct. (1,150 ft.): 2.3 mi., 1 hr. 15 min.
- complete loop: 6.0 mi., 3 hr.

Round Pond Mtn.

The trailhead for Round Pond Mtn. is located on the east shore of Round Pond in Round Pond PRL in the heart of the 92-mile Allagash Wilderness Waterway. The trailhead is accessible only by canoe, kayak, or motorboat. The mountain is most often climbed by persons paddling the Allagash River trip, but day hikers can make the hike as well. The nearest boat launch site is located at Henderson Brook Bridge, about 2.5 mi. west of the trailhead. Vehicle access from the east in Portage is via Blanchet-Maibec and Rocky Brook roads. A fee is charged to pass through the North Maine Woods Fish River Checkpoint. Access from the town of Allagash in the north is via Michaud Farm Rd. A fee is charged to pass through the North Maine Woods Allagash Checkpoint. Travel distances are considerable either way, and camping is recommended for hikers wishing to climb Allagash Mtn.

From the boat launch site, paddle or motor downriver and across the pond to Tower Trail campsite (sign), located on the east shore of Round Pond. Round Pond Mtn. Trail leaves the campsite and climbs more than 700 ft. in 2.5 mi. to reach the summit of Round Pond Mtn. Although the trail is steep in several places, and rocks and roots make for rough footing, the pleasant forest and the solitude of the location make the effort worthwhile. (*Note:* As of 2011, the tower was in poor condition and closed to the public.)

Round Pond Mtn. Trail (USGS Round Pond and Five Finger Brook quads, DeLorme map 62)

Distance from Tower Trail campsite and trailhead on Round Pond (781 ft.) to
• Round Pond Mtn. summit (1,490 ft.): 2.5 mi., 1 hr. 40 min.

Priestly Mtn. (2,084 ft.)

This mountain rises above Priestly Lake, a few miles west of the Allagash River and Allagash Wilderness Waterway in northern Piscataquis County, and just south of the Aroostook County line. It is about 60 mi. south and west of ME 11 in Ashland.

The trailhead is reached from Ashland by traveling west on American Realty Rd. for about 60 mi. to Churchill Dam Rd. A fee is charged to pass through the North Maine Woods Six Mile Checkpoint just beyond mile marker 6. It is then 49 mi. to Umsaskis Thoroughfare (between Umsaskis and Long lakes), and an additional 6 mi. to Churchill Dam Rd. At this jct., turn south (left) and drive another 7.5 mi.

The trailhead, which has no sign or flagging, is at a jct. with a logging road heading south-southwest. The road north of the trailhead is flat. At the trailhead, Churchill Dam Rd. heads 0.2 mi. up a hill. A town boundary marker sign is 150 yd. farther up the hill on the east side. Camping is available just beyond the top of the hill in a large gravel pit on the west side. No water is available.

The trail follows the logging road until it ends at a log yard. At the southeast corner of the yard, turn south-southeast and proceed 200 ft. into the woods to intersect the old fire warden's trail and find flagging. Follow the tread and flagging south-southwest. The trail crosses Drake Brook, which flows between the north end of Priestly Lake and a small pond. As of 2011, beavers had dammed the area, which flooded the trail and made it impassable. An alternate route follows the edge of the beaver flowage north, crosses at the head of the beaver flowage, and turns south along the water to get back to the original trail at the north end of Priestly Lake at 1.6 mi. Here, the old fire warden's trail follows the west shore of the lake to the old fire warden's cabin at 2.1 mi. Beyond, the trail turns and climbs to the top of the mountain at 2.8 mi.

The fire tower was removed in 2009, which eliminated the opportunity for any views. The state of Maine maintains a communications tower on the summit.

Priestly Mtn. (USGS Umsaskis Lake West quad, DeLorme map 55)
Distances from Churchill Dam Rd. (1,050 ft.) to
- fire warden's cabin (1,135 ft.): 2.1 mi., 1 hr.
- Priestly Mtn. summit (2,084 ft.): 2.8 mi., 2 hr.

Allagash Mtn. (1,750 ft.)

Allagash Mtn. rises above the southwest end of 4,210-acre Allagash Lake, part of the Allagash Wilderness Waterway system and headwaters for the Allagash River, in T7 R14 WELS. There is no direct vehicle access to Allagash Lake. Access by canoe or kayak is possible from either Allagash Stream or Johnson Pond west of the lake. Access by foot is possible from the south via Carry Trail, an old road that leads 1.0 mi. from a gate to Carry Trail campsite and the ranger station at the southwest corner of the lake, where the trailhead is located. A number of driving routes are possible to reach the Allagash Lake area; all involve considerable driving time over gravel roads. Camping is recommended. See DeLorme's *Maine Atlas & Gazetteer* for more information on road travel to Allagash Mtn.

The trail to Allagash Mtn. leaves to the right of the ranger station and at 0.1 mi. starts to ascend through mixed forest. The climbing is moderate over a series of stepped rises. At 0.3 mi., the trail begins a steady ascent, reaching the summit of Allagash Mtn. at 0.7 mi. The renovated fire tower provides outstanding views of the remote Allagash River region, including Chamberlain, Eagle, and Churchill lakes in the east, and the forestlands of the St. John River watershed to the west.

Allagash Mtn. (USGS Allagash Lake quad, DeLorme map 55)
Distance from ranger station on Allagash Lake (1,038 ft.) to
  • Allagash Mtn. summit (1,750 ft.): 0.7 mi., 45 min.

Round Mtn. (2,147 ft.)

Round Mtn. is west of Ashland, south of American Realty Rd., and just north of Jack Mtn. Rd. Round Mtn. is the northernmost of three adjacent peaks (Round, Middle, and Peaked) that extend northeast to southwest. Peaked Mtn. (2,260 ft.) is the highest mountain in Aroostook County, but there is no trail to the summit.

Round Mtn. is reached from Ashland by traveling west on American Realty Rd. A fee is charged to pass through the North Maine Woods Six Mile Checkpoint. Just beyond the checkpoint, bear left on Pinkham Rd. and continue southwest, crossing the Machias River at 8.7 mi. Turn right onto Jack Mtn. Rd. at 8.8 mi. This road passes Weeks Brook Campsite at 12.2 mi. At 16.4 mi., turn right turn onto a logging road with a sign for Week's Pond. Follow this road to where the forest canopy covers the roadway just before the descent to Round Mtn. Pond. Ample parking is located at 20.2 mi.

The unmarked trail follows the canopied road down toward the pond and stays above but in view of the pond on the west side. Midway along the west shore is an angler's carry and boat access to the pond. About 200 yd. beyond, take the old roadway to the left (southwest), climbing gently uphill. The road soon passes a camp driveway on the right (the green-roofed camp is partially visible through the trees). Continue southwest and gently uphill on the old road.

The next landmark is a camp with a sign, Round Mountain Lodge. This is the site of the old warden's cabin that is incorporated into one of the two buildings. The old warden's trail leaves the camp lot near the covered spring. Look for yellow, orange, and pink flagging tape on trees along the trail, which leads generally straight up the steep mountainside (no switchbacks) in typical fire-warden-trail style. The trail is overgrown, but shows some evidence of the old tread on the ground, and the tape is easily followed. The trail ends at the old fire tower, which is still standing but has no cab. The fire tower offers excellent 360-degree views, with Katahdin to the south-southwest, Mt. Chase to the south-southeast, Horseshoe Mtn. to the west, Haystack Mtn. to the east, and Deboullie Mtn. to the north.

Round Mtn. (USGS Round Mtn. quad, DeLorme map 63)

Distance from parking area (1,100 ft.) to
  • Round Mtn. summit (2,147 ft.): 1.5 mi., 1 hr. 15 min.

Horseshoe Mtn. (2,084 ft.)

This mountain is part of the Rocky Brook Mtns., which rise just to the north of the Aroostook County-Piscataquis County line west of the Allagash River. (*Note:* Horseshoe Mtn. is shown as Rocky Brook Mtn. on DeLorme map 62.)

The trailhead is reached from Ashland by traveling west on American Realty Rd. A fee is charged to pass through the North Maine Woods Six Mile Checkpoint. The trailhead is 26.6 miles west of the checkpoint, or 2.4 miles east of McNally Pond Campsite (the closest campsite). The trailhead is located on the south side of American Realty Rd., on the east side of the Rocky Brook Mtn. Range. Ample parking is located just off the road. There are no signs for the trail.

The trail (a woods road) enters the woods going westerly, and almost immediately takes a left (south). (Continuing straight ahead leads quickly back to American Realty Rd.) At 1.0 mi., continue south through a jct. with a road running east, and soon pass an old overgrown road on the right (goes up through a cut in the bank and ends at an old camp). The trail (still a woods road) goes down and up twice, and as it begins to go down a third time, Horseshoe Mtn. and the tower become visible.

Continue to the base of the steep-sided mountain and a fork. Bear left at the fork and proceed downhill for about 100 yd. to a low point and an intermittent stream. Just before the stream are pruned trees with colored tape and the flagged trail. The path has been kept open and the tread is visible, particularly on its upper portions. The colored tape generally follows the watercourse for a few hundred yards, then moves left to go straight and steeply to a sag just below the summit. Beyond, the trail climbs the last few hundred yards to the fire tower.

Climb the steel fire tower (which is in excellent condition, but has no cab) for 360-degree views. Katahdin and Traveler Mtn. are visible to the south-southwest, Chase Mtn. to the southeast, Round Mtn. to the east, Priestly Mtn. to the west, and Deboullie Mtn. to the north.

Horseshoe Mtn. (USGS Mooseleuk Lake and Fifth Musquacook Lake quads, DeLorme map 62)

Distance from American Realty Rd. (1,050 ft.) to
* Horseshoe Mtn. summit (2,084 ft.): 1.3 mi., 1 hr. 10 min.

Oak Hill (1,099 ft.)

Oak Hill and its accessible fire tower are located north of Knowles Corner and to the west of ME 11 in the township of T8 R5 WELS.

The trailhead is reached by turning west (left) off ME 11 about 11 mi. north of Knowles Corner in Moro Plantation and proceeding due west for 1.2 mi. (shown as Unnamed 3 Rd. on DeLorme map 58). At this point, take a right turn (north) and continue for about 0.5 mi. before the road turns left (west) and rises to a highpoint (2.2 miles from ME 11). Here is a cairn on the south (left) side of the road. The roadbed is wide enough for parking.

The path is flagged and has a worn tread. The tower is about 200 yd. up the hillside to the south. The summit is wooded with large oak trees. The tower offers a 360-degree view.

Oak Hill (USGS Umcolcus Lake quad, DeLorme map 58)

Distance from parking area (950 ft.) to
* Oak Hill summit (1,099 ft.): 0.2 mi., 15 min.

SUGGESTED HIKES

Easy Hikes

Oak Hill [rt: 0.4 mi., 25 min.]. A quick hike to a fire tower with panoramic views.

Haystack Mtn. [lp: 0.5 mi., 45 min.]. A short but steep hike to an open grassy summit with broad views of Katahdin and the North Maine Woods.

Hedgehog Mtn. [rt: 1.2 mi., 50 min.]. A nice hike to the former site of a fire tower and open ledges where there are fine views south to Portage Lake and west to Deboullie and Black mountains.

Allagash Mtn. [rt: 1.4 mi., 1 hr. 30 min.]. Outstanding views of the remote Allagash Wilderness Waterway are possible from the summit fire tower. Trailhead access is by foot trail or canoe or kayak.

Mars Hill [rt: 2.4 mi., 1 hr. 50 min.]. The trail to Mars Hill is part of the IAT, a long-distance hiking path extending from Maine to Newfoundland. Atop the mountain are the turbines of Maine's first windpower project and extensive views.

Quaggy Jo Mtn. [lp: 3.0 mi., 1 hr. 45 min.]. A loop hike over the south and north peaks of Quaggy Jo with good views to the northwest and east across the Aroostook countryside.

Moderate Hikes

Round Pond Mtn. [rt: 5.0 mi., 3 hr. 30 min.]. Paddle a canoe or kayak to the water-access-only trailhead on Round Pond in the Allagash Wilderness Waterway, then hike to the old fire tower on the summit.

Deboullie and Black mountains [lp: 5.5 mi., 3 hr. 30 min.]. A great loop hike that takes in a number of ponds and has extensive views of the vast remote country in the northern reaches of Aroostook County.

Appendix A

HELPFUL INFORMATION AND CONTACTS

Organization	Office	Phone Number or Email
Appalachian Mountain Club (AMC)	Main Office	617-523-0636 (membership, headquarters) 603-466-2727 (reservations)
AMC Echo Lake Camp		echoreg@aol.com (registration information)
AMC Maine Wilderness Lodges		603-466-2727 information@outdoors.org
AMC Maine Chapter		
AMC Four Thousand Footer Club		207-695-3085
Acadia National Park	Headquarters	207-288-3338 TTY 207-288-8000
Allagash Wilderness Waterway		207-287-3821
Appalachian Trail Conservancy (ATC)	Main Office	304-535-6331 info@appalachiantrail.org
ATC New England Regional Office		413-528-8002 atc-nero@appalachiantrail.org
Baxter State Park	Headquarters	207-723-5140 TTY 207-723-9905
Belgrade Region Conservation Alliance		207-495-6039 brca@gwi.net
Blue Hill Heritage Trust		207-374-5114 info@bluehillheritagetrust.org
Chatham Trails Association		zlogar@chathamtrails.org
Coastal Mountains Land Trust		207-236-7091 info@coastalmountains.org
DeLorme		800-561-5105
Downeast Coastal Conservancy		207-255-4500 info@downeastcoastal conservancy.org

Address or Location	*Website*
5 Joy St., Boston, MA 02108	outdoors.org
P.O. Box 219, Mt. Desert, ME 04660	amcecholakecamp.org
P.O. Box 310, Greenville, ME 04441	outdoors.org/lodging/mainelodges
	amcmaine.org
P.O. Box 444, Exeter, NH 03833	amc4000footer.org
P.O. Box 177, ME 233 McFarland Hill, Bar Harbor, ME 04609	nps.gov/acad
	parksandlands.com
P.O. Box 807, Harpers Ferry, WV 25425	appalachiantrail.org
P.O. Box 264, South Egremont, MA 01258	
64 Balsam Dr., Millinocket, ME 04462	baxterstateparkauthority.com
P.O. Box 250, Belgrade Lakes, ME 04918	belgradelakes.org
P.O. Box 222, Blue Hill, ME 04614	bluehillheritagetrust.org
22 Grove Pl., Unit 29, Winchester, MA 01890	chathamtrails.org
101 Mt. Battie St., Camden, ME 04843	coastalmountains.org
2 DeLorme Dr., Yarmouth, ME 04096	delorme.com
P.O. Box 760, Machias, ME 04654	downeastcoastalconservancy.org

Organization	Office	Phone Number or Email
Frances Small Heritage Trust		207-637-3510 mail@fsht.org
Frenchman Bay Conservancy		207-422-2328 info@frenchmanbay.org
Georges River Land Trust		207-594-5166
Great Pond Mountain Conservation Trust		207-469-7190 info@greatpondtrust.org
Great Works Regional Land Trust		207-646-3604 info@gwrlt.org
Greater Lovell Land Trust		207-925-1056 info@gllt.org
International Appalachian Trail (IAT)	Maine Chapter	
Kennebec Land Trust		207-377-2848 tkerchner@tklt.org
Leave No Trace	Main Office	800-332-4100 info@lnt.org
Loon Echo Land Trust		207-647-4352
Mahoosuc Land Trust		207-824-3806 info@mahoosuc.org
Maine Appalachian Trail Club (MATC)		
Maine Audubon	Headquarters	207-781-2330 info@maineaudubon.org
Maine Bureau of Parks and Lands (MBPL)	Headquarters	207-287-3821
Maine Campground Owners Association		207-782-5874
Maine Dept. of Inland Fisheries and Wildlife	Headquarters	207-287-8000
Maine Forest Service (MFS)	Headquarters	207-287-2091 TTY 207-287-2213
Fire permits	Ashland office Augusta office Greenville office Old Town	207-435-7963 207-624-3700 207-695-3721 207-827-1800

Address or Location	*Website*
P.O. Box 414, Limerick, ME 04048	fsht.org
P.O. Box 150, Hancock, ME 04640	frenchmanbay.org
8 N. Main St., Ste. 200, Rockland, ME 04841	grlt.org
P.O. Box 266, Orland, ME 04472	greatpondtrust.org
P.O. Box 151, South Berwick, ME 03908	gwrlt.org
208 Main St., Lovell, ME 04051	gllt.org
P.O. Box 916, Gardiner, ME 04345	internationalatmaine.org
124 Main St., Room 2B, Winthrop, ME 04364	tklt.org
P.O. Box 997, Boulder, CO 80306	lnt.org
1 Chase St., Bridgton, ME 04009	loonecholandtrust.org
P.O. Box 981, Bethel, ME 04217	mahoosuc.org
P.O. Box 283, Augusta, ME 04332	matc.org
20 Gilsland Farm Rd., Falmouth, ME 04105	maineaudubon.org
22 State House Station, Augusta, ME 04333	parksandlands.com
10 Falcon Rd., Suite 1, Lewiston, ME 04240	campmaine.com
41 State House Station, Augusta, ME 04333	maine.gov/ifw
22 State House Station, Augusta, ME 04333	maine.gov/doc/mfs

Organization	Office	Phone Number or Email
Maine Huts & Trails		207-265-2400
Maine Land Trust Network c/o Maine Coast Heritage Trust		207-729-7366
Maine Outdoor Adventure Club		207-775-6622 info@moac.org
Maine State Park Campground Reservations		800-332-1501 (in Maine) 207-624-9950 (outside of Maine) TTY 888-537-7294 campground.reservations@ maine.gov
Maine State Police		911 (emergency) 207-624-7200
Moosehorn National Wildlife Refuge		207-454-7161
Mt. Agamenticus Conservation Region		207-361-1102 robin@agamenticus.org
National Park Service (NPS)	Acadia Nat'l Park	207-288-3338 TTY 207-288-8800
National Recreation Reservation Service		877-44-6777 TTY 877-833-6777
North Maine Woods, Inc.	Main Office	207-435-6213 info@NorthMaineWoods.org
Sheepscot Wellspring Land Alliance		207-589-3230
The Nature Conservancy	Maine Field Office	207-729-5181 naturemaine@tnc.org
U.S. Geological Survey (USGS)	Headquarters	888-ASK-USGS
White Mountain National Forest (WMNF)	Headquarters	603-536-6100 TTY 603-536-3665
	Androscoggin Ranger District	603-466-2713 TTY 603-466-2856
	Saco Ranger District	603-447-5448 TTY 603-447-3121

Address or Location	Website
375 N. Main St., Kingfield, ME 04947	mainehuts.org
1 Bowdoin Mill Island, Topsham, ME 04086	mltn.org
P.O. Box 11251, Portland, ME 04104	moac.org
	campwithme.com
	maine.gov/dps/msp
103 Headquarters Rd., Baring, ME 04694	fws.gov/northeast/moosehorn
186 York St., York, ME 03909	agamenticus.org
P.O. Box 177, Bar Harbor, ME 04609	nps.gov/acad
	recreation.gov
P.O. Box 425, Ashland, ME 04732	northmainewoods.org
P.O. Box 371, Liberty, ME 04949	swlamaine.org
14 Maine St., Suite 401, Brunswick, ME 04011	nature.org
12201 Sunrise Valley Dr., Reston, VA 20192	usgs.gov
71 White Mountain Dr., Campton, NH 03223	fs.fed.us/r9/forests/white_mountain/
300 Glen Rd., Gorham, NH 03581	
33 Kancamagus Highway, Conway, NH 03818	

Appendix B

FOUR THOUSAND FOOTERS

The Four Thousand Footer Club was established in 1957 to encourage hikers to explore the less-frequented areas of the White Mountains. The committee developed a list of the 4,000-footers in the White Mountains, using the criteria that for a peak to be included, it must be 4,000 feet or higher and must rise 200 feet above the low point on the ridge connecting it to a higher neighbor. These criteria are still used to determine those peaks that belong on the lists.

The Four Thousand Footer Committee recognizes three official lists: the White Mountain Four Thousand Footers, the New England Four Thousand Footers, and the New England Hundred Highest. Additionally, awards are given for climbing all of the peaks on a given list in the winter. To qualify as a winter ascent, the hike must not begin before the hour and minute of the beginning of winter (winter solstice) or end after the hour and minute of the end of winter (spring equinox).

All of the peaks on the New England Four Thousand Footer list have well-defined trails, with the exception of Mt. Redington in Maine, which may be reached by a series of logging roads and herd paths or by bushwhacking, and Owl's Head in the White Mountains of New Hampshire, on which there is an unofficial and un-maintained trail to the summit. Many of the peaks on the New England Hundred Highest list don't have trails, and to summit them requires significant skill in the use of map and compass at a minimum. Hand-held GPS units and altimeter watches are very helpful and increasingly popular for off-trail travel.

Persons interested in becoming a member of one or more of the clubs may obtain information and an application by visiting amc4000footer.org, or by sending a printed application and self-addressed stamped envelope to the Four Thousand Footer Committee, Appalachian Mountain Club, P.O. Box 444, Exeter, NH 03833. If you wish to receive the list of the New England Four Thousand Footers or the New England Hundred Highest, you need to specifically ask for them (otherwise only the White Mountain Four Thousand Footers are included in the information packet). Applicants for any of the clubs do not need to be members of the Appalachian Mountain Club, although the committee strongly encourages any hiker using the trails to contribute to their maintenance in some manner.

On the lists developed by the committee, the elevations have been obtained from the latest USGS maps. Where no exact elevation is on the map, the elevation has been estimated by adding half of the contour interval to the highest contour shown on the map. Elevations so obtained are marked on the list with an asterisk.

Maine Four Thousand Footers

	Mountain	Elevation	Date Climbed
1.	Katahdin, Baxter Peak	5,268	
2.	Katahdin, Hamlin Peak	4,756	
3.	Sugarloaf	4,250*	
4.	Crocker Mtn., North Peak	4,228	
5.	Old Speck	4,170*	
6.	North Brother	4,151	
7.	Bigelow, West Peak	4,145	
8.	Saddleback	4,120	
9.	Bigelow, Avery Peak	4,090*	
10.	Abraham	4,050*	
11.	Crocker Mtn., South Peak	4,050*	
12.	Saddleback, The Horn	4,041	
13.	Redington	4,010*	
14.	Spaulding	4,010*	

New Hampshire Four Thousand Footers

	Mountain	Elevation	Date Climbed
1.	Washington	6,288	
2.	Adams	5,774	
3.	Jefferson	5,712	
4.	Monroe	5,384*	
5.	Madison	5,367	
6.	Lafayette	5,260*	
7.	Lincoln	5,089	
8.	South Twin	4,902	
9.	Carter Dome	4,832	
10.	Moosilauke	4,802	
11.	Eisenhower	4,780*	
12.	North Twin	4,761	
13.	Carrigain	4,700*	
14.	Bond	4,698	
15.	Middle Carter	4,610*	
16.	West Bond	4,540*	
17.	Garfield	4,500*	
18.	Liberty	4,459	
19.	South Carter	4,430*	

	Mountain	Elevation	Date Climbed
20.	Wildcat	4,422	
21.	Hancock	4,420*	
22.	South Kinsman	4,358	
23.	Field	4,340*	
24.	Osceola	4,340*	
25.	Flume	4,328	
26.	South Hancock	4,319	
27.	Pierce (Clinton)	4,310	
28.	North Kinsman	4,293	
29.	Willey	4,285	
30.	Bondcliff	4,265	
31.	Zealand	4,260*	
32.	North Tripyramid	4,180*	
33.	Cabot	4,170*	
34.	East Osceola	4,156	
35.	Middle Tripyramid	4,140*	
36.	Cannon	4,100*	
37.	Hale	4,054	
38.	Jackson	4,052	
39.	Tom	4,051	
40.	Wildcat D	4,050*	
41.	Moriah	4,049	
42.	Passaconaway	4,043	
43.	Owl's Head	4,025	
44.	Galehead	4,024	
45.	Whiteface	4,020*	
46.	Waumbek	4,006	
47.	Isolation	4,004	
48.	Tecumseh	4,003	

Vermont Four Thousand Footers

	Mountain	Elevation	Date Climbed
1.	Mansfield	4,393	
2.	Killington	4,235	
3.	Camel's Hump	4,083	
4.	Ellen	4,083	
5.	Abraham	4,006	

Appendix C

NEW ENGLAND HUNDRED HIGHEST

The following list excludes the previously listed New England Four Thousand Footers. Those peaks must also be climbed to achieve the goal of climbing the New England Hundred Highest peaks. Where no exact elevation is on the map, the elevation has been estimated by adding half of the contour interval to the highest contour shown on the map. Elevations so obtained are marked on the list with an asterisk.

Maine

	Mountain	Elevation	Date Climbed
1.	South Brother	3,970	
2.	Snow (Chain of Ponds quad)	3,960*	
3.	Goose Eye	3,870*	
4.	Fort	3,867	
5.	White Cap	3,856	
6.	Unnamed (Boundary Peak)	3,855	
7.	Bigelow, South Horn	3,805	
8.	Coe	3,795	
9.	East Kennebago	3,791	
10.	Baldpate	3,790*	
11.	Snow (Little Kennebago Lake quad)	3,784	
12.	Kennebago Divide (N. Peak)	3,775	
13.	Elephant	3,772	

New Hampshire

	Mountain	Elevation	Date Climbed
1.	Sandwich	3,980*	
2.	The Bulge	3,950*	
3.	Nancy	3,926	

4. The Horn	3,905	_____
5. North Weeks	3,901	_____
6. South Weeks	3,885	_____
7. Vose Spur	3,862	_____
8. East Sleeper	3,860*	_____
9. Peak Above the Nubble	3,813	_____
10. Scar Ridge, West Peak	3,774	_____
11. NE Cannonball	3,769	_____

Vermont

Mountain	Elevation	Date Climbed
1. Pico Peak	3,957	_____
2. Stratton	3,940	_____
3. Jay Peak	3,858	_____
4. Equinox	3,850*	_____
5. Mendon Peak	3,840	_____
6. Breadloaf	3,835	_____
7. Wilson	3,790*	_____
8. Big Jay	3,786	_____
9. Dorset Peak	3,770*	_____

INDEX

Trail names written in **bold type** indicate that a detailed description can be found in the text.
Where multiple page references appear, **bold numbering** indicates the main entry or entries for
the trail or feature.
[Bracketed information] indicates which of the seven maps displays the feature and where, by
section letter and number.

A

Abol Campground, 10–12
Abol Pond, 51–53
Abol Pond Trail (Baxter SP) [1: E3], **52**, 60
Abol Slide, 8
Abol Stream Trail (Baxter SP) [1: E3], **52**
Abol Trail (Katahdin) [1: E3], **11**, 61
Abraham, Mount, 108, **151–152,** 166
Acadia Mountain, 343, 363
Acadia National Park, xvi, 308–362, 380–381
            camping in, 309–310
            entrance fees, 310
            Isle au Haut, 357–362
            maps, 352, 356
            suggested hikes, 362–363
            trail descriptions, 311–362
            trail ratings, 309
            transportation in, 310–311
Adam's Lookout Trail (Mt. Megunticook)
            [4: B2], **261–262**
Agamenticus, Mount, 252–254, 255
Albany Brook Trail (WMNF) [7: F15],
            202–203
Albany Mountain [7: F14–F15], **200–202,**
            211
Allagash Mountain, 375–376, 379
Allagash Wilderness Waterway, xvii, 364–365,
            373–376, 380–381
Amherst Mountains Community Forest, 300
Amphitheater Trail (Acadia NP) [5: E5,
            F5], **328**
A. Murray Young Path (Dorr Mtn.) [5: D7,
            E7], **322**
Appalachian Mountain Club (AMC), xvi,
            380–381
            conservation and, 65
AMC Maine Woods Trails, 76–80
Appalachian Trail (AT), xv, xvi, xviii–xxix
            in 100-Mile Wilderness, 63–64, 66–68,

            70–75, **72–73, 85–88,** 90, 103–104
            in Baxter State Park, 7–9, **9–10,** 28, **30**
            in Kennebec River region, 214, **221–223**
            in western Maine mountains, 108, 109–
            110, **111, 118–123, 133–135, 149–150,**
            152–155, 157–158, 161–162
Appalachian Trail Conservancy, 380–381
Appalachian Trail shelters, xxix–xxx, 53, 111,
            118
Aroostook State Park, 365
Asticou & Jordan Pond Path (Acadia NP)
            [5: E6, F5–F6], **327**
Asticou Ridge Trail (Acadia NP) [5: F5],
            327–328
Avery Peak (Bigelow Mtn.) [3: B2–B3], 108,
            157–158, 166
Aziscohos Mountain, 108, **145–146,** 165

B

backcountry hazards, xxxii–xl
Baker Hill, 291, 305
Baker Pond Trail (AMC Maine Woods Trails)
            [2: E2], **78**
Bald Bluff Mountain, 300–301
Bald Cap, 107
Bald Mountain (Baring Plantation), **281**
Bald Mountain (Camden), **267,** 277
Bald Mountain (Dedham), **297–298,** 305
Bald Mountain (Oquossoc), 108, **146,** 164
Bald Mountain (Oxford Hills), 168, **174–175,**
            211
Bald Mountain (Weld), 107, **144,** 165
Bald Pate Mountain (South Bridgton),
            241–242
            from the north, 241–242
            from the south, 242
Baldpate Mountain (North Oxford) [6: B13–
            B14], 107, **121–124**

via Appalachian Trail from the north, 123–124
via Appalachian Trail from the south, 122
Bald Peak Trail (Acadia NP) [5: E5], **340**
Bald Peak Trail (Pleasant Mtn.), **237–238**
Bald Rock Mountain [4: A2, B2], **265**, 277
Barnes Trail (Mt. Cutler), **247**, 255
Barren-Chairback Range, 63, 85–89
Barren Mountain [2: G1–G2, F1–F2], **87–89**
approach from Greenville, 88
approach from Monson, 87–88
Battie, Mount [4: C1], **257–259**, 276, 277
Bauneg Beg Mountain, 251–252
Baxter, Percival P., 2
Baxter Peak (Katahdin), 7, 10, 16, 17, 61
Baxter Peak Cutoff (Katahdin) [1: E3], **17**
Baxter State Park, xvi, 1–61, 380–381
camping in, 4–5
park access, 2–4
regulations, 6–7
reservations, 5
suggested hikes, 59–61
trail descriptions, 9–59
Beachcroft Path (Champlain Mtn.) [5: D7-D8], **315**
Bear Mountain, 168, **173**
Beech Cliff Loop Trail (Acadia NP), **348**
Beech Cliff Trail (Acadia NP), **347**
Beech Hill, 270–271, 276
Beech Mountain, 346–347
Beech Mountain Loop Trail, 348–349
Beech South Ridge Trail (Acadia NP), **349**
Beech West Ridge Trail (Acadia NP), **350**
The Beehive [5: E8], **316**, 363
Bells Mountain, 281–282, 305
Bemis Mountain, 107, **133–135**
via Appalachian Trail, 134
via Bemis Stream trail, 135
Bemis Stream Trail, 135
Bernard Mountain, 350–351, **354**, 363
Bickford Brook Trail (Speckled Mtn.) [7: F12–F13], **188–189**
Big Chief Trail (Black Mtn.), **287**
Bigelow Mountain, 108, 156–162, 166
via Appalachain Trail from the south, 157–158
Bigelow Preserve, 107, 156–162, 166
Bigelow Range Trail [3: B1–B2], **160**
Big Moose Mountain, 63, **93–95**, 104

Big Spencer Mountain, 63, **100,** 104
Blackcap, 298
Black Cat Mountain, 38
Black Mountain (Aroostook County), **371–372,** 379
Black Mountain (Downeast), **285–287,** 306
from Schoodic Beach parking lot, 285–286
via Schoodic Beach, 286
Black Mountain (Peru), 168, **173–174**
Blackwoods Campground, 309
Blue, Mount, 143, 165
Blueberry Ledges Trail (Baxter SP) [1: E3], **52–53**
Blueberry Mountain (Evans Notch), 191–194, 211
Blueberry Mountain (Weld), 107, **142,** 165
Blueberry Ridge Trail (Blueberry Mtn., Weld) [7: F13], **191–192**
Blue Hill, 292–294, 305
Bob Chase Scenic Loop, 241–242
Borestone Mountain, 63, **89–90,** 104
Boundary Bald Mountain, 228, 230
Bowditch Trail (Isle au Haut), **358–359**
Bowl Trail (Champlain Mtn.) [5: E8], **315**
Bradbury Mountain, 232–233, 255
break-ins, xxxix
Bridle Trail (Kineo Mtn.), **98**
Bri-Mar Trail, 234
Brook Trail (Tumbledown Mtn.), **137**
Bubble & Jordan Ponds Path (Acadia NP) [5: E6–E7], **331–332**
The Bubbles [5: D6, E6], **328–330,** 362
Bubbles Divide Trail (Acadia NP) [5: E6], **329–330**
Bucks Ledge, 168, **177–178,** 211
Burnt Jacket Mountain, 227, 230
Burnt Meadow Mountain, 244–246, 255
Burnt Meadow Trail, 245
Burnt Mill Brook Trail (Royce Mtn.) [7: F12], **196–197**
Burnt Mountain (Carrabassett Valley), **155–156,** 165
Burnt Mountain Trail (Baxter SP) [1: B2], **35,** 60
Butters Mountain, 197–200

C

Cadillac-Dorr Connector, 322

Cadillac Mountain, 324–326, 363
Cadillac North Ridge Trail [5: D7], **325**
Cadillac South Ridge Trail [5: D7, E7, F7], **324**
Cadillac West Face Trail, [5: E6–E7], **325**
Camden Hills State Park, 256, 257
Cameron Mountain [4: A2, B1–B2], **265–266**
campfires, xxix–xxx
camping, xxix
    in Acadia National Park, 309–310
    in Aroostook County, 365–366
    in Baxter State Park, 4–6
    in Downeast Maine, 279–280
    in Hundred-Mile Wilderness, 64
    in Kennebec Valley region, 214
    on Maine Woods Initiative land, 65
    in midcoast region, 257
    reservations, 384
    in southwestern Maine, 232
    in western Maine mountains, 108, 143
    in White Mountain National Forest, 169
Canada Cliff Trail (Acadia NP), **347–348**
Canon Brook Trail (Dorr Mtn.) [5: D7, E7], **320–321**
Caribou Mountain (Downeast), **287–289,** 306
    from the north, 288–289
Caribou Mountain (Evans Notch) [7: E13–E14], **184–185,** 211
Caribou-Speckled Mtn. Wilderness, 170
Carlo, Mount, 107, 116–117
Carlo Col Trail [6: C12, D12–D13], **117**
Carriage Road Trail (Mt. Battie) [4: C1], **258**
Carriage Trail (Mt. Battie) [4: C1], **258–259**
Cathedral Trail (Katahdin) [1: E3–E4], **16**
Catherine Mountain, 290–291
Caverly Lookout Trail (Baxter SP) [1: C4, D4], **24–25,** 60
Celia and Jackson Ponds Trail (Baxter SP), **32**
Center Hill Nature Trail, 143–144, 164
Center Ridge, 39
Center Ridge Trail (Baxter SP) [1: B4, C4], **40**
Chairback Mountain [2: F3], **85–86**
Champlain Mountain, 312–315, 363
Champlain North Ridge Trail [5: D8], **314**
Champlain South Ridge Trail [5: D8, E8], **314**
Chase, Mount, 56–57
Chick Hill, 299–300

children, hiking with, xxiv
Chimney Peak (Katahdin), 7
Chimney Pond, 8
Chimney Pond Campground, 14–19
Chimney Pond Trail (Katahdin) [1: D4–E4], **13**
Christopher, Mount, 168, 179–180
Cliff Trail (Isle au Haut), **361**
climate, xxii
Coastal Mountains Land Trust, 380–381
Cobscook Bay State Park, 279, 282–283
Coburn Mountain, 225–226, 230
Mount Coe Trail [1: D2–D3], **27–28,** 61
Cold Brook Trail (Acadia NP), **351**
Cold Brook Trail (Speckled Mtn) [7: F–13-F14], **189–190**
Cold River Campground, 183–184
Conant Trail [7: G13], **205–207**
conservation, xl–xli, 65
    organizations, 380–385
Cpl. Dustin J. Libby Summit Trail (Haystack Mtn.), **369**
Cranberry Peak (Bigelow Preserve) [3: B2–B3], 108, **157–158**
Cranberry Pond Trail (Baxter SP) [1: E4, F4], **51**
Crane Mountain, 281–282
Crocker Hill, 168, **172,** 210
Crocker Mountain, 108, **152–154**
    from Caribou Valley Rd., 153–154
    from ME 27, 153
Crocker Pond Campground, 169, 201–203
Cunningham Mountain, 283
Cupsuptic Lake, 107
Cutler, Mount, 246–250, 255
Cutler Coast Public Reserved Land, 279

D
Daicey Pond Campground, 28–31
Day Mountain [5: F6–F7], **333**
Deasey Mountain [1: C6, D5–D6, E5], **54–55**
Deboullie Loop Trail, 372–373
Deboullie Mountain, 371, 379
Deboullie Public Reserved Land, 365, 370–373
Debsconeag Backcountry Trail (Nahmakanta PRL), [2: B5], **68–69**
Debsconeag Lakes Wilderness Area, 64
Deer Brook Trail (Sargent Mtn.) [5: E5–E6], **336**

Deer Hills [7: G12–G13], **207–209,** 211
Deer Hills Bypass [7: G13], **209**
Donnell Pond Public Reserved Land, 279,
283–289, 306
Dorr Mountain, 318–322
Dorr North Ridge Trail [5: D7], **321**
Dorr South Ridge Trail [5: D7, E7], **321–322**
Doubletop Mountain [1: D2, E2], **33–34,** 61
Douglas Mountain, 239–241, 255
drinking water, xxxviii–xxxix
Duck Harbor Campground, 309
Duck Harbor Mountain Trail (Isle au Haut),
361
Duck Harbor Trail (Isle au Haut), **358**
Dudley Trail (Katahdin) [1: E4], **14–15**
Durgin Mountain, 197–200
Dwelley Pond Trail (Baxter SP) [1: B2, C2], **35**

E

Eagle Rock, 95–96
Eagle Scout Trail (Douglas Mtn.), **240,** 255
Eastern Side Traverse (Acadia NP), 363
East Royce Trail (Royce Mtn.) [7: F12–F13],
194–195
ecology, xxiii
Elephant Mountain, 63, **96,** 103
Emery Path (Dorr Mtn.) [5: D7], **318**
Evans Notch, 168–169
hikes accessible from, 182–197
Evergreen Link Trail (Speckled Mtn.)
[7: F13], **190–191**
Eyebrow Trail (Old Speck Mtn.) [6: B13],
111–112

F

Fire Warden's Trail (Mt. Abraham), **151–152**
Fire Warden's Trail (Mt. Bigelow) [3: B2–B3],
158–159
Firewarden's Trail (Pleasant Mtn.), **236**
fishing, 6, 32, 65, 91, 169
Five Ponds Trail (Baxter SP) [1: B4–B5],
46, 60
Flag Hill, 297, 306
Flagstaff Lake, 107–108
Flying Mountain, 345–346, 362
Foss and Knowlton Pond Trail (Daicey Pond
Campground) [1: E2–E3], **31–32**
Four Thousand Footer Club, 387–389

Fowler Brook Trail (Baxter SP) [1: B4], **44–45**
Fowler Ponds, 44–46
Freezeout Trail (Baxter SP) [1: A2–A4, B2],
42–43
French Mountain, 220, 229
Frohok Mountain Trail (Mt. Megunticook)
[4: A2–A3], **264**
Frost Pond Trail (Baxter SP) [1: A3–A4,
B3–B4], **43**
Frye Mountain, 271–272, 277

G

gear, xxvii–xxviii
geography, xxix–xxxi
geology, xxi–xxii
Georges Highland Path (Ragged Mtn.),
268–270
Barnestown Rd. access, 269–270
ME 17 access, 269
Thorndike Brook Access, 268
getting lost, xvii
Giant Slide Trail (Acadia NP) [5: D4–D5,
E5], **337**
giardia, xxxviii–xxxix
Gilley Trail (Acadia NP), **353**
Goat Trail (Isle au Haut), **360–361**
Goat Trail (Norumbega Mtn.) [5: E5], **341**
Goose Eye Mountain, 107, 113–116, 166
Goose Ridge, 274–275, 277
Gorge Path (Cadillac Mtn.) [5: D7], **325–326**
Gorham Mountain [5: E8], **316–317,** 363
Gorman Chairback Lodge and Cabins, 65
Grafton Loop Trail [6: B13–B15, C13–C15],
124–130, 166
eastern section, 124–127
western section, 127–130
Grafton Notch State Park, 107, 108–109, 124
Grand Falls Trail (Baxter SP) [1: C4, D4], **24**
Grandgent Trail (Acadia NP) [5: E5], **339**
Grassy Pond Trail (AMC Maine Woods
Trails) [2: E2], **79**
Grassy Pond Trail (Daicey Pond Camp-
ground), **31**
Great Basin (Katahdin), 8
Great Brook Trail (Caribou-Speckled Mtn.
Wilderness) [7: F13–F14], **199–200**
Great Head Trail (Acadia NP) [5: E8], **317,**
362
Great Notch Trail (Acadia NP), **355**

Great Pond Loop (The Mountain), **219**
Great Pond Mountain, 295–296
Green Mountain, 63, **101–102**
Gulf Hagas, 73–76, 104

H

Hadlock Brook Trail (Sargent Mtn) [5: E5], **338**
Hadlock Ponds Trail (Acadia NP) [5: E5, F5], **342**
Hamlin Peak (Katahdin), 7, 19, 61
Hamlin Ridge Trail (Baxter SP) [1: D3–D4], **19**
Harndon Hill, 205–207
Hayes Trail (Blue Hill), **293**
Haystack Mountain, 368–369, 379
Haystack Notch Trail (Evans Notch) [7: E14, F13–F14], **186–187**
Head of the Gulf Trail (Gulf Hagas) [2: E2–E3, F3], **75–76**
heat exhaustion, xxxiv
Hedgehog Mountain, 369–370, 379
Helon Taylor Trail (Baxter SP) [1: D4–E4], **12–13**
Hemlock Trail (Dorr Mtn.) [5: D7], **322–323**
Henderson Brook Trail (AMC Maine Woods Trails) [2: F2], **85,** 103
Hiker Responsibility Code, xxv
Hogback Mountain, 272–273
Homans Path (Dorr Mtn.) [5: D7], **319**
The Horn (Saddleback Mtn.), 108, **149–150**
The Horns (Bigelow Preserve) [3: B2–B3], 108, **157–158**
Horns Pond Trail (Bigelow Preserve) [3: B2–B3], **159–160**
Horse Mountain [1: B5], **47**
Horseshoe Mountain, 377–378
Horseshoe Pond Trail (AMC Maine Woods Trails) [2: E2], **79–80**
Horseshoe Pond Trail (Stoneham) [7: G13], **205**
Howe Brook Trail (Baxter SP) [1: B4], **39–40,** 60
Howe Peak (Katahdin), 7
Huguenot Head, 312, 315, 363
Hundred-Mile Wilderness, 62–90
  camping in, 64
  trails in, 66–90
Hunters Brook Trail (Day Mtn.) [5: F6–F7,

E6-E7], **333–334**
hunting, xxxviii, 6, 42, 65, 169
Hunt Trail (Baxter SP) [1: E2–E3], **9–10,** 61
hypothermia, xxxiii–xxxiv

I

Indian Mountain area, 81–85
Indian Mountain circuit [2: E2], **81**
Indian Trail (Kineo Mtn.), **98**
injuries, xxxii–xxxiii
insects, xxxv–xxxvi
International Appalachian Trail (IAT), xxix, 53, **54–56,** 365, 367, 379, 382–383
Isle au Haut, 356–362
  map, 356

J

Jackson Mountain, 107, **141–142**
Jack Williams Trail (Mt. Megunticook) [4: B1–B2], **261**
Jockey Cap, 243–244, 255
John B. Mountain, 294–295
Jordan Cliffs Trail (Acadia NP) [5: E6], **335**
Jordan Pond Path (Acadia NP) [5: E6], **326–327**

K

Kane Path (Dorr Mtn.) [5: D7, E7], **319–320**
Katahdin, 1–2, 7–9
  trails on, 9–22
  views from, 8–9
Katahdin Lake, 48–50, 61
Katahdin Lake Trail (Baxter SP) [1: E4–E5], **49,** 54
Katahdin Stream Campground, 9–10, 25, 52–53
Katahdin Stream Falls, 9, 59
Kebo Mountain [5: D7], **323**
Kelly Mountain, 224–225
Kennebec Highlands, 216–218
Kennebec River Valley, 213–214
Kettle Pond Trail (Baxter SP) [1: E3–E4], **51**
Kibby Mountain, 108, **148–149,** 165
Kidney Pond Campground, 29–30, 32–33
Kidney Pond Outlet Trail (Baxter SP), **33**
KI-Jo Mary Multiple Use Forest, xxvii, xxix, 64, 71
Kineo, Mount, 63, **97–99,** 104

Klondike Pond, 8
Knife Edge (Katahdin) [1: E3–E4], 7, **15**, 61
Kurt Diederich's Climb (Dorr Mtn.)
[5: D7], **319**

L

Ladder Trail (Dorr Mtn.), [5: D7], **320**
Lamoine State Park, 279
Lapham Ledge, 168, **177–178**
Larry's Loop Trail (Maine Huts & Trails)
[3: B4], **163–164**, 206
Laughing Lion Trail (Royce Mtn.) [7: F12–
F13], **195**
Laurie's Ledge Trail (Indian Mtn.) [2: E2],
81–82, 103
Leach Link Trail [7: G12], **210**
Lead Mountain, 279, **301**
Leave No Trace principles, xli
Ledges Trail (Baxter SP) [1: B4], **36**, 59
Ledges Trail (Deer Hills) [7: G12], **209**
Ledges Trail (Douglas Mtn.), **240**
Ledges Trail (Pleasant Mtn.), **237**
Ledge Trail (St. Sauveur Mtn.), **344–345**
lightning, xxxiv
Lily Pad Pond Trail (Baxter SP), **33**
Little Abol Falls Trail (Baxter SP) [1: E3],
12, 59
Little Bigelow Mountain [3: B3–B4], 108,
161–162
Little Jackson Connector (Tumbledown
Mtn.), **139**
Little Jackson Mountain, 107, **140–141**
Little Kineo Mountain, 63, **99**
Little Lyford Lodge and Cabins, 65
Little Moose Mountain, 63, **91–93**
approach from the east, 91–92
approach from the north, 92
approach from the west, 93
Little Moose Public Reserved Land, 64,
91–95, 104
map of, 94
Little Mountain, 63
Little Peaked Mountain, 279, **299**
Little Russell Mountain, 102–103
Littles Mountain, 282–283
Little Spencer Mountain, 63, **100–101,** 104
Little Wilson Falls, 90, 103
lodges, 64–65, 76–77, 380
Long Pond Loop (The Mountain), **219**

Long Pond Trail (Acadia NP), **350–351**
Long Pond Trail (Isle au Haut), **359**
Loop Trail (Tumbledown Mtn.), **136–137**
Lord Hill, 205–207
Lost Pond Trail (Daicey Pond Campground), **31**
Lower Fowler Pond Trail (Baxter SP), **45**
Lower Hadlock Trail [5: F5], **342**
Lower Norumbega Trail [5: E5, F5], **342**
Lunksoos Mountain [1: C6, D5–D6, E5],
54–55

M

Machias River Public Reserved Land, 302
Maggie's Park, 178–179
Magurrewock Mountain, 280
Mahoosuc Arm, 107
Mahoosuc Notch, xviii, 109, 113, 118
Mahoosuc Public Reserved Land [6: C12–
D12], 107, 109–110
trail access from the west, 110
Mahoosuc Trail [6: E10–E11, D11–D12,
D13, C13, B13], **118–121**
Maiden Cliff Trail (Mt. Megunticook),
[4: B1], **262,** 277
Maine Appalachian Trail Club (MATC),
xviii, xli
Maine Dept. of Conservation, xvi
Maine Huts & Trails system, 162–164
Maine Hut Trail [3: A4–A5, B4–B5, C4],
162–163
Maine Wilderness Lodges, 65
Maine Woods Initiative, 65
Mansell Mountain, 350–351, **354,** 363
Maple Spring Trail (Sargent Mtn.) [5: E5],
338–339
Mars Hill, 365, **366–367,** 379
Marston Trail (Baxter SP) [1: D2–D3], **26–27**
Martin Ponds Trail (Baxter SP) [1: D5, E5],
49–50
Medawisla Lodge and Cabins, 65
Median Ridge Trail (Isle au Haut), **359–360**
Megunticook, Mount [4: B2, C2], 257,
259–260, 259–264, 277
Middle Fowler Pond Trail (Baxter SP)
[1: B4], **45–46**
Miles Notch Trail (Caribou-Speckled Mtn.
Wilderness), [7: E14–F14], **197–198**
Monument Hill, 215–216, 229
Moosehead Lake, 63

hikes in Moosehead Lake region, 91–103
Moosehorn National Wildlife Refuge, xvi, 279, 280–282
Mooselookmeguntic Lake, 107
Moose Ponds (Little Moose PRL), 64, 92–93, 104
Mosquito Mountain, 223–224, 230
The Mountain (Rome), **219–220,** 229
Mountain Brook Pond Trail (AMC Maine Woods Trails), [2: E2], **77–78**
Mount Blue State Park, 107, 143–144
Moxie Bald Mountain, 220–222, 230
    via Appalachian Trail from the west, 221–222
Mud Brook Trail (Evans Notch) [7: E13–F13], **185–186**
Multi-Use Trail (Mt. Megunticook) [4: A2, B2, C2], **260, 263–264,** 277

N
Nahmakanta Public Reserved Land, 64, 66–70
Nation's Nature Trail (AMC Maine Woods Trails) [2: E2], **84,** 103
Nat Merchant Trail (Isle au Haut), **360**
The Nature Conservancy (TMC), xvi–xvii
Nature Trail (Daicey Pond Campground), **31**
Nature Trail (Mt. Battie) [4: C2], **259**
Nesowadnehunk Field Campground, 33–35
Nesuntabunk Mountain [2: B4–B5], **70,** 103
Niagara Falls (Little and Big), 28, 30, 59
North Basin (Baxter SP), 8, 18
North Basin Cutoff (Baxter SP) [1: D4], **18**
North Basin Trail (Baxter SP) [1: D4], **18**
North Brother, 26–27
Northern Headwaters Loop Trail (Whitten Hill), **273–274**
North Katahdin Lake Trail (Baxter SP) [1: D4–D5], **49–50**
North Maine Woods (NMW), xvii, 64, 365, 384–385
North Ridge Trail (Pleasant Mtn.), **239**
North Trail (Kineo Mtn.), **98**
North Trail (Mt. Cutler), **249–250**
North Traveler Mountain, 39, 61
North Traveler Trail [1: B4], **39**
Northwest Basin Trail (Baxter SP) [1: D3–D4], **19–20**
Norumbega Mountain [5: E5, F5], **341**
Norway Bluff, 58–59

Notch Trail [6: C12–C13], **113–114**
Number Four Mountain, 63, **96–97**
Number Nine Mountain, 366

O
Oak Hill (Aroostook County), **378,** 379
Oak Hill (Orland), **296,** 306
Odyssey Trail (Mt. Christopher), **180**
OJI, Mount [1: D2, E2], 25–26, **26**
Old Blue Mountain, 107, **133,** 166
Old South Ridge Trail (Mt. Cutler), **249**
Old Speck Mountain [6: B13–C13], 107, **110–111,** 166
Orange & Black Path (Champlain Mtn.) [5: D8, E8], **313**
Orange/Red Trail (Rumford Whitecap), **132**
Osgood Trail (Blue Hill), **292–293**
The Owl [1: E3], 25, **25**
Owl's Head Trail, 56, 60
Oxford Hills, 167–168

P
Pamola Peak (Katahdin), 7, 12
Parker Ridge Trail (Tumbledown Mtn.), **139–140**
parking fees, 170
Parkman Mountain Trail [5: E5], **340**
Passadumkeag Mountain, **302**
Peaked Mountain (Aroostook County), 365
Peaked Mountain (Clifton), 279, **299–300**
Peaked Mountain (Oxford Hills), 168, **179**
Peaked Mountain (Washington County), **301–302**
Pearl Ponds Trail (AMC Maine Woods Trails) [2: E2], **80**
Peary Mountain, 244
Pemetic East Cliff Trail, 331
Pemetic Mountain, 330–332, **344,** 363
Pemetic North Ridge Trail [5: E6], **330**
Pemetic Northwest Trail [5: E6], **331**
Pemetic South Ridge Trail [5: E6], **331**
Penobscot Mountain [5: E5–E6], **334–335**
Perpendicular Trail (Acadia NP), **351**
Phillip, Mount, 218, 229
Pigeon Hill, 291–292, 305
Pine Hill, 205–207
Pisgah, Mount, 214–215, 229
Pleasant Mountain, 232, 234–239, 255
    map of, 235

Pleasant Pond Mountain, 222–223, 229
    via Appalachain Trail from the east, 222
    via Appalachain Trail from the west,
    222–223
Pocomoonshine Mountain, 304
Pogy Notch Trail (Baxter SP) [1: B4, C4,
    D4], **36–37**
poison ivy, xxxvi–xxxvii
Pond Link Trail (Tumbledown Mtn.), **140**
Pond Loop Trail (AMC Maine Woods Trails)
    [2: E2], **83–84**
Precipice Trail (Champlain Mtn.) [5: D8,
    E8], **312–313**
Priestly Mountain, 374–375
Puzzle Mountain, 107, 125–127, 166

Q

Quaggy Jo Mountain, 365, **367–368,** 379

R

Ragged Mountain, 267–270, 277
Rangeley Lake, 107
Rattlesnake Mountain, 233–234
Razorback Trail (Acadia NP), **353–354**
Red Rock Trail (Caribou-Speckled Mtn.
    Wilderness) [7: F13–F14], **198–199,** 211
Richardson Lakes, 107
Ridge Trail (Mt. Megunticook) [4: B1–B2],
    263, 277
Rim Trail (Gulf Hagas) [2: F2–F3], **74–75**
Ring Hill, 168, **178–179,** 210
Ring Trail Loop (Mt. Agamenticus), **253–254**
River Trail (AMC Maine Woods Trails)
    [2: E2–F2], **82–83,** 103
Roaring Brook Campground, 4–5, 12–14,
    21–22, 48–49
Rocky Pond Trail (Baxter SP), **32**
The Roost [7: E13], **182–183,** 210
Round Mountain (Aroostook County),
    376–377
Round Pond (WMNF), 202–203, 211
Round Pond Mountain (Allagash Wilder-
    ness), **373–374,** 379
Round Pond Public Reserved Land, 373
Round Top Mountain, 216–217, 229
Royce Mountain (East and West), 194–197,
    211
Royce Trail [7: F12], **195–196**

Rumford Whitecap, 107, **131–132,** 165
Rum Pond Trail (Baxter SP) [1: E4], **51–52**
Russell Pond Campground, 19–20, 22–24,
    36–37
Russell Pond Trail (Baxter SP) [1: D4],
    20–21

S

Sabbatus Mountain, 181–182, 211
Saco Ridge Trail (Mt. Cutler), **248**
The Saddle (Baxter SP), 8
Saddleback Mountain, 108, **149–150**
Saddle Slide (Katahdin), 8, 16
Saddle Trail (Katahdin) [1: E3–E4], **16–17**
safety considerations, xxiii–xxv
Safford Brook Trail (Bigelow Preserve)
    [3: A4, B3–B4], **160–161**
Sally Mountain, 226–227, 230
Sandbank Stream (Deasey/Lunksoos Mtn.),
    55
Sanders Hill, 217–218, 229
sanitation, xxxix
Sargent East Cliffs Trail [5: E5–E6], **336**
Sargent Mountain, 334, 336–339
Sargent Northwest Trail [5: E5], **338**
Sargent South Ridge Trail [5: E5], **336–337**
Sawyer Mountain, 250–251
Scenic Trail (Mt. Megunticook) [4: B1],
    262, 277
Schiff Path (Dorr Mtn.) [5: D7], **318–319**
Schoodic Beach, 283–286, 305
Schoodic Mountain, 279, **284–285,** 305
    via Schoodic Beach, 284
Scientific Forest Management Area (Baxter
    SP), 42–44
Scopan Public Reserved Land, 365
search and rescue, xxxix–xl
Seawall Campground, 310
Sentinel Link Trail, 30
Sentinel Mountain [1: E2], **29,** 60
Shell House Trail (Albany Mtn.) [7: G13],
    203–204
Shell Pond Loop (Albany Mtn.) [7: F13–
    G13], **204**
Singepole Ridge, 168, **171–172**
Sky Blue Trail (Cameron Mtn.) [4: B1–B2],
    266
Slide Mountain, 107
Slope Trail (Mt. Megunticook) [4, B1–B2],

260–261, 277
Sluiceway Trail (Acadia NP), **354**
Smith Trail (Sawyer Mtn.), **251**
Snowmobile Trail (Mt. Cutler), **248**
Snow Mountain, 108, **147–148**
snowshoeing, xxx–xxxii
South Basin (Katahdin), 8
South Branch Mountain [1: B4, C3–C4], **38**
South Branch Pond Campground, 35–41, 45
South Brother, 26–27, 61
South Face Trail (Blue Hill), **294**
South Peak (Katahdin), 7
South Turner Mountain [1: D4], 2, 48, **48**, 60
Southwest Ridge Trail (Pleasant Mtn.),
    236–237, 255
Spaulding Mountain, 108, **155**
Speckled Mountain (Evans Notch), 187–191,
    198, 211
Speckled Mountain (Peru), 168, **175–176**
    route from Bald. Mtn., 175
Speckled Mountain Pasture Trail, **176**
Speck Pond, 107
Speck Pond Trail [6: C12–C13], **112–113**
Spring Trail (Penobscot Mtn.) [5: E6], **335**
Spruce Hill Trail (Speckled Mtn.) [7: F13],
    188
Starr Trail (Rumford Whitecap), **132**
Stone House Trail (Blueberry Mtn.) [7: F13],
    192–193
Stone Mountain, 246
Stratheden Path (Kebo Mtn.) [5: D7], **322**
Streaked Mountain, 168, **171**
stream crossings, xxxvii
St. Sauveur Mountain, **344**, 363
Success, Mount, 107
Sue's Way (Pleasant Mtn.), **238–239**
Sugarloaf Mountain (Carrabassett Valley),
    108, **154–155**
Sugarloaf Mountain (Dixfield), **144–145**
Sugarloaf Mountain (T5 R7 WELS), **57–58**
Summit Road Trail (Beech Hill), **270–271**
Sunday River Whitecap, 107, 127–130

T

Tableland Trail (Mt. Battie) [4: B2, C1–C2],
    261, 277
Table Rock Trail [6: B13], **121–122**, 206
Third Mountain [2: F3], **86**, 104
Thoreau Spring, 7

Tire'm, Mount, **180–181**
Togue Pond, 51–53
Tom, Mount, **242–243**, 255
Tower Trail (Blue Hill), **293–294**
Tower Trail (Mt. Pisgah), **215**
Tracy and Elbow Ponds Trail (Daicey Pond
    Campground), **31**
trail courtesy, xvii–xviii
trail maintenance, xl–xli
The Traveler, 39
Traveler Mountain Trail [1: B4, C4], **40–41**,
    61
Triad Pass (Acadia NP), **332**
Triad Trail [5: E6, F6], **332–333**
trip planning, xxiii–xxiv, xxvii–xxviii
Trout Brook Campground, 41–44, 47
Trout Brook Mountain [1: B4], 46–47, **47**, 60
Tumbledown Dick Trail (Nahmakanta PRL)
    [2: C5–C6], **67–68**
Tumbledown Mountain, 107, 136–140, 165
Tumbledown Public Reserved Land, 107,
    135–142
    map of, 138
Tumbledown Ridge Trail, **139**
Tunk Mountain, **289–290**, 305
Turner, Charles Jr., 8
Turtle Ridge Loop Trail (Nahmakanta PRL)
    [2: C5], **66–67**
Twin Brook Trail (Burnt Meadow Mtn.),
    245–246

V

Valley Cove Trail (Acadia NP), **346**
Valley Peak Trail (St. Sauveur Mtn.), **345**
Valley Trail (Acadia NP), **349**

W

Wabassus Mountain, **303–304**
Wadleigh Brook Trail (Baxter SP) [1: A2–A3,
    B2–B3], **43–44**
Waldo, Mount, **275–276**, 276
Washington Bald Mountain, **302–303**
Wassataquoik Lake Trail (Baxter SP) [1: C2–
    C4, D2, D4], **23**
Wassataquoik Public Reserved Land, xxxix, 55
Wassataquoik Stream Trail (Baxter SP)
    [1: D4], **22**
waterfall hikes

in Acadia National Park, 338–339
in Baxter State Park, 9, 12, 19, 22–24, 39–40, 59–60
in Evans Notch region, 184–185
in Hundred Mile Wilderness, 73, 85, 90, 103–104
in western Maine mountains, 123, 126, 163–164
Western Head Trail (Isle au Haut), **362**
Western Mountain (Acadia NP), 350–355
West Kennabago Mountain, 108, **147**
West Ledge Trail (Acadia NP), **355**
West Peak (Bigelow Mtn.) [3: B2–B3], 108, **157–158,** 166
Wheeler Brook Trail (Evans Notch) [7: E13], **183–184**
White Brook Trail (White Cap Mtn.) [2: F3, E3-E4], **70–71**
White Cairn Trail (Blueberry Mtn.) [7: F13], **193–194**
White Cap Mountain [2: F3, E3–E4], **72–73,** 104
via Appalachian Trail from the north, 72–73
via Appalachian Trail from the south, 72
White Cap Range, 63, 70–73
White Flag Trail (Mt. Cutler), **250**
White Mountain National Forest (WMNF), xvi, 168–170, 384–385
trails in, 183–190, 196–203
Whitten Hill, 273–274, 277
wildlife, xxxv
recommended spots for viewing, 22, 51, 59, 83, 91, 279, 324
Will, Mount, 107, **131,** 206
winter hiking, xxx–xxxii
of 4,000-foot peaks, 387
Woods Loop Trail (Beech Hill), **271**
Woods Trail (Douglas Mtn.), **241**
Woodsum Spur Trail (Grafton Notch) [6: C15], **127**
Wright Trail [6: C13], **115–116**

Z

Zeke's Trail (Cameron Mtn.) [4: B1–B2], **266**
Zircon, Mount, 168, **176–177,** 211